THE FIRST CAUSE

THE FIRST CAUSE

The Secrets of the Universe,
The Brain,
&
Our Ancient Past

Finally ANSWERED!

Written and Edited by
Rosemary Klem

Zodbooks

First Edition Published in 2011 by

Zodbooks

PO Box 117 Riverstone NSW 2765 Australia
Website: www.zodbooks.com.au
Email: info@zodbooks.com

Paperback Edition published in 2014
Copyright © 2011 by Rosemary Klem
www.zodbooks.com.au
Photographs Copyright © Dream Shots
www.dreamshots.com.au

All rights reserved. No part of this book may be reproduced in whole or in part, copied, stored in a retrieval system, or transmitted in any form or by any means – electronic, mechanical, photocopying, recording, or otherwise – without the prior written permission of the publisher or the author.

Disclaimer
The information that is found in this book has been solely written, and intended to be, for educational purposes only. This book provides general education and information. It is not to be used for diagnosis, prescription, or treatment of any kind regarding any type of medical disorder of any nature whatsoever. For advice that is fitting to your circumstances or condition, at all times a qualified medical health-care practitioner should be consulted. The publisher and author are in no way liable for any misuse of the material contained within this book.

Photographs by Jack Lord and Rosemary Klem
Cover design and artwork: Rosemary Klem
Interior design: Rosemary Klem
Typeset by Typeskill

Cataloging in Publication details are available from the National Library of Australia
ISBN: 9780987116734

*To all those forgotten people
Who have no parents, no family,
Or, have parents who raised them but
Never wanted them; never bonded with them:*

*There is a reason for everything,
Even though there will be no window to this truth in your lifetime.
You must look upon this negative as merely a challenge
That you were presented in your journey.
Handle the challenge well,
So that it never presents itself again,
For because, this is only one of many journeys you will have,
And only one of many challenges you will face.*

*The memory of your present life
Will one day be just another tome,
That you will look back upon as an ancient reference
In that vast collection you will have spent lifetimes writing.*

Upcoming Books
Time Travel. No date given

Contents

∙⁀

The First Word   9
Introduction   13
  1 ∙⁀ **The First Cause**   25
      The Era of the Antimatter Void
      The Era of the Neutron Void
      The Era of the Solid Void
      The Era of Consciousness
      The Era of the Unification of the Elders
      The Era of the Amoeba
      The Era of the Vision
      The First Creation
      A Snapshot of the Universe
      A Teasing Peak at CTC – Time Travel
      The Large Hadron Collider
      The "Expanding" Universe
      This chapter will trace the evolution of the universe and the creation of consciousness. It is a revealing look at the workings of our cosmos and intelligent design.
  2 ∙⁀ **The Era of the Metaphysical World**   83
      Where does instinct come from? Here we will uncover how it is that every living thing with consciousness acquires instinct.
  3 ∙⁀ **The Phase-1 Human**   91
      This first model of human being created was "perfect." How could it then have become a dismal failure?
  4 ∙⁀ **The Phase-2 Human**   109
      Post-Analysis of Phase-2 Humans
      A new concept was invented. The next model of human being was intentionally "corrupted" by it.

5 ⇝ **The Phase-3 Human**   **127**

Our Human Race on Earth

This model of human being was given all the ingredients in its "software" and "hardware" to become the right human product.

6 ⇝ **The Architects of Life**   **143**

Intelligent designers need a purpose and a challenge. How we (and all life) became their challenge is the answer to the profound questions: What is our connection to them? Why are we here? Where does our ultimate destination lie?

7 ⇝ **Transmigration of Consciousness**   **155**

Reincarnation became a valuable method of shaping an intellect in a toughened, versatile way. It enabled an intellect to become a superior mold of intelligence not otherwise proven to be attainable.

8 ⇝ **The Human Brain and Consciousness**   **163**

How does consciousness team up with the human brain? How is knowledge acquired and processed?

9 ⇝ **The Sweetest Breath of Life**   **177**

The Journey into the Moongate

The Feather of Truth

The Great Darkness

The Bottle

After the physical body dies, the intellect goes through a series of processes before it is sent back to a new arena of life. Take a breathtaking tour of this cycle, from the moment that precedes death, to the moment that precedes rebirth. The question of euthanasia is discussed.

10 ⇝ **The Unconventional Wisdom of Challenge**   **197**

What is life? Life is a challenge and a test. One life is just a chapter of one course in a curriculum of subjects designed to advance the intellect.

11 ⇝ **The Science of Good and Evil**   **209**

Good and Evil in a Nutshell

Meditation

Within us, we possess the competing forces of good and evil. This chapter examines in what way the negative force within us influences us.

12 ⇝ **The Final Cause**   **231**

The Meat-in-the-Sandwich Principle

Trapped in the "Labyrinth of the Minotaur"

Overcoming the "Labyrinth": Conquering the "Minotaur"

Reason

How can we control this negative force? How is an evil mind forged? What drives those who turn to evil?

13 — The Loophole in Man — 273
The Root of all Compulsions, Obsessions, and Addictions
Dangerous Mind Control

How is it humans can so readily give up their will to the control of another? Why do humans succumb to unscrupulous users and vices? This chapter answers these questions by looking at what the loophole is within each one of us that makes us vulnerable.

14 — Understanding Happiness — 297
The desire of every human is to attain happiness. But where do we go wrong in our quest for it? How do we find it? It is not necessarily where we think it is!

15 — What Makes a Success? — 309
Success does not correlate to assets or status in the corporate world or even society; the true value of success lies in one's state of mind.

16 — To "Read" from the "Closed Book" — 319
Positive Affirmation and its "Rewards"
As Above: So Below – The Compendium of All Knowledge
When what is "As Above" is not "So Below"
Guilt, Conscience, Karma

A beguiling chapter that reveals how we can access the vaulted knowledge of our past lives, and attain the power of genius.

17 — Journeying into the Unknown — 341
The Conscious and Subconscious Minds
The Meadow of Dreaming
Inspiration and Talent
Telepathy and Prophetic Dreams
The Art and Science of Astral Travel
Wanderers in the Halfway Meadow
Humble Minds of the Past

This chapter solves the mystery of one of the greatest uncharted conquests: the human brain.

Conclusion — 387
Humbleism and Abstractism

Well-nigh the Last Word — 395

The Last Word — 397

The First Word

Man[i] (male and female humans) will only truly know of god
When he is able to believe in himself.
For it is in believing in himself
That he can come to realize the existence of god.
The world and its people must come together
– Irrespective of color, creed, or philosophical system –
And accept the fact: to live together man
Must have a new beginning and a new belief
– That is, he must believe in himself!
When he can do this,
Then will he come to know of god.

-A wise man

Once upon a time, as a little girl, I heard the voice of fate in my mind telling me that my father knew the answers to the secrets of the universe and the mysteries of our ancient past. That the whisperings of fate should persist throughout my childhood was bewildering to me, since I knew of no such father so rich in wisdom and knowledge. What I could not know, however, was that after an unfruitful passage of time those words would become real.

While it may seem impossible to consider, destiny played the part that had been foretold. This book, as a result, is dedicated to a humble and unrecognized man: the wise man often quoted in this book: the "father" my childhood voice was referring to. It is to him that credit is due for the knowledge I possess, which has come to me by one means or another … "Jack Lord" – my "adopted" father and teacher.

When I was twenty-two years of age, I met an unusual elderly man, and was in a way introduced to a real-life version of Dr Who. The difference was that there was no Tardis (time machine / spaceship). I quickly learned the mind was the Tardis! At the start of my journey, when I saw what this man could do with his mind, I wanted nothing more out of life than to do the same things with my mind and live the esoteric life he lived. From that moment on, my priorities in life were completely overhauled, and I ceased to live like everyone else. I dedicated my life to an intellectual quest for truth and knowledge. My twenty-seven years of living a haywire – and impossible to believe – style of life, where I was able to research into the unknown and fulfill a childhood fantasy of learning the secrets of the universe, has culminated in this book.

What you are about to read in this book is not like anything you have ever read or ever will read, and it will challenge everything you ever thought you understood about yourself and the world around you. For humanity, it will be like rediscovering the wheel: like rediscovering fire: like rediscovering time. We will be rediscovering ourselves. For this reason, this book has an incredible power to help those of us who are lost; those of us who feel despair; those of us who do not understand why our lives are the way they are; those of us who want to change but do not know how to change; those of us who want something but simply do not know what that something is; and those of us searching for meaning and a sense of "place" and understanding. Believe it or not, this book has the power to make you what you don't even know you want to be!

·—

The passage of this book into your hands has been a difficult one, wrought with hardship and challenge. A book of this kind had to find a way into the mainstream of this civilization. A lot of this world has been built on vested interests, and truth is not always able to find its way as it should. Sometimes that which is logical — truth — appears to be ridiculous when set against accepted norms, which, in themselves, are truly illogical, but are not seen in such a sense from a standpoint of ignorance. Mostly, this happens when security is built upon falsehoods, which have no basis or solid foundation upon which to structure security. This is why such foundations crumble under the scrutiny of logical reasoning, when a mind truly allows logical and unbiased reasoning.

That this book was rejected by the publishing world is not surprising, and certainly not a bad thing, by any means; it has only seeded a "flower" in my "blossoming garden." For, in life, we face challenges of all kinds; these are what we behold in life; these are what blind us to the "flip" side of life. For because, with each challenge that challenges, a flower has the potential to blossom in your garden, of which you are unlikely to be aware.

I have taken on the challenge of publishing this book myself, and have named my publishing company *Zodbooks*, after my German Shepherd, Zod, whose gentle but persistent persuasion kept me from being totally immersed in my work and losing all sense of inner balance.

Reading this book and the forthcoming books I have to publish will take you on a trek into the "magical" domain of the truly wise and knowing.

Introduction

How can humans even begin to understand what lies beyond the egg,
When they are still cocooned inside of it?
The human species is not meant to abide within the shell of an egg;
The ideal is for humans to break free of the eggshell and venture beyond it,
Where they can explore their place in that vast unknown,
Where they rightfully belong.

For in the eyes of the universe,
Humans on Earth have not even hatched,
Let alone exist!

Imagine a fictitious scenario where you subsist as fungus below the crust of the Earth. Your grasp of the tangible world around you would be limited to the environment you perceive and the annals passed down to you by your forbears (often around the campfire) – whether real or embellished over time is another matter! In this cocooned sphere you could not imagine the mystery of the realm above the surface of the crust: A domain where the heavenly bodies appear to conflate by day to present one great illumination in the sky, only to appear to scatter into countless imposing illuminations by night. A domain where ambrosial fragrances and sensations as a consequence of the "poetry" of the seasons overwhelm the senses. How can you then begin to postulate the existence of such a world you have never seen and cannot possibly imagine? Indeed, wouldn't it be like the blind trying to imagine sight, or the deaf trying to imagine sound?

Conceptualize the notion that, begotten from these fungi, a mushroom thrusts out of the ground to experience that elusive domain above the surface for the first time. How can the mushroom then unveil the answers to the greatest mysteries its species has pursued since time immemorial? How can the mushroom possibly open the minds of its species to see the true nature of the domain above the surface, and in the process challenge and set straight many of the current theories that have a stranglehold on its civilization?

As incredulous as it may seem, this book presents knowledge to us from the perspective of the "mushroom." It will, in simple terms, solve the challenging questions to which mankind has been seeking answers: How did our universe originate? What existed prior to the formation of the universe? What is consciousness and how did it emanate? It is only because of our inquiring nature that we have endeavored to unravel these questions. Once upon a time, in the past, physics and philosophy were a unitary discipline that explored and attempted to answer these questions, with the main means of interpretation being mathematical analysis and postulation. Today, despite physicists attempting to probe into the elementary nature of matter with technology as a means of interpretation, no inquiry by science or philosophy has been able to begin to attempt to address or elucidate the nature of consciousness.

In attempting to deal with these questions, a growing number of people has drawn away from mainstream religious beliefs and scientific vagaries (that is, wild ideas). Two celebrated scientific vagaries include the accepted theories for the origin of the universe and the origin of life on Earth.

In the case of the latter, the steady advancement in technology has continually heightened our awareness and appreciation of the intricate biological complexity and subtle intelligence found in all life that exists. Consequently, many have come to conclude that to have such engineering marvels and intelligence originate from disorder – as per the theory of natural selection – is beyond the bounds of mathematical probability. Not only is it deemed absurd; it requires the acceptance of impossible odds. Even Darwinists admit that natural selection alone cannot provide an explanation for a First Cause of biology, let alone consciousness, and there is no explanation for a First Cause of physics in the universe.

It is easy to see why many are not satisfied with and have drawn away from not merely the scientific, but the creationist, view of our origins. Instead, they have treaded parallel waters to the creationist proponents in terms of respecting the universal theme of creationists: that the order and design of our universe had to have an intelligent agent of some kind at work. Some have even termed such intelligence an "intelligent designer." Others still think of it as a god without giving regard to any of the frameworks that have been founded upon it.

Once we establish that there is such a thing as a designer, the ensuing questions beg an answer: What is he? Where is he? Why have we been left alone, so to speak? One could ask many questions along these lines. None of our philosophies can begin to satisfy judicious humans in addressing these questions, which we have all asked ourselves during our lifetime. This does not suggest that the answers are not there. Someone wise once said that for every why there is a because. Perhaps we need to look closer at ourselves and there within us may lie an indication of the answers.

For example, in the cycle of life, as a creator of your children, your overwhelming desire is to see those children travel down the right path in life. Intentionally you guide them, educate them, and shape their lives so that one day they become adults that both you and society can be proud of. This moral instinct in us, to shape the destiny of our offspring, has been with us since the very beginning of man's reign on Earth. Now, if we were created in the likeness of a creator – and we would believe this to be so according to all historical sources and relevant ancient texts known to us – wouldn't it be feasible to assume that such a creator would possess a "maternal" desire toward shaping the destiny of his children, and be guiding them? Logically, then, we must assume that a creator could not possibly allow his creations to develop without some form of intervention or guidance.

As a plausible continuation of this, if a creator were to keep a "tab" on his creations and guide them, wouldn't this be on a subconscious level? Wouldn't this then explain our instinctive desire to look up to the sky in search of spiritual answers? Aren't we subconsciously seeking out that which we emulate and have a subconscious tie with?

If we go back to our primitive fathers, who lived in the "cradle" of civilization, we find that even then the kindle of "fire" flared in their souls for an understanding of the unknown. These humans held a belief in the passage of the soul into the afterworld, as well as a belief in supreme beings presiding over worldly affairs. Civilizations that followed produced philosophical greats that rival humans today, and whether they were the primitive humans or the philosophical greats, we find that humans have unfailingly looked up to the sky in search of answers to an inner spiritual desire. Tantamount to human existence was this belief in a god or gods. The root of this spiritual need must, therefore, be traced back to some subconscious connection between humans and their creator.

It appears that we have every right to reach a rational conclusion that there exists a subconscious connection between a creator and his creation. First, we know that the principal vein of guidance toward one's offspring pulses through almost every living creation on this planet. We have deduced that this must be in accord with the concept that the principles of a creation concur with the principles of its creator. Secondly, no evidence in the present suggests direct guidance or intervention, even though we could reason that long, long ago there were precedents to suggest direct guidance, based on wisdom handed down from this time, and withstanding time there stand unexplained testaments to that direct intervention.

Now things become stimulating and provocative, because, in conceding to a subconscious connection, aren't we surrendering to the idea that this subconscious connection has created a loophole within us? If there were not a loophole, then why are there so many competing philosophical structures and proponents of scientific vagaries trying to edify (teach) humans with their own brand of so-called verity (lasting truth)?

Alas, in having noted this loophole we come to the purpose of this book: to merge science with intelligent design, as well as "plug" that spiritual loophole in humans for the last time! This spiritual loophole can only be plugged when we satisfy our spiritual desire, which can only be accomplished by ridding the vagaries, "realigning" some of the existing details, and "filling in" the missing details, which have become as lost to us as has the lost tribe of Israel to the Israelites.

The question then arises: How is this possible? How is this book able to present us with knowledge from the perspective of the proverbial mushroom? If we look back into ancient times, we can see that there were seers who were able to acquire or were handed down philosophical knowledge on which we have structured all our philosophical systems. If we scrutinize their legacy, we can see fundamental commonalities in their methods of tackling the great mysteries of life and the way of the universe. They believed that all the answers we have been seeking could be found in the depths of the mind and the soul. It is in the spirit of this tradition that this book has been written. Lost knowledge and ancient wisdom have been rediscovered by the technique of astral projection, and by tapping into a source of knowledge with the mind by way of savant-like skills.

That this book will take us to a revolutionary new level of understanding, with such knowledge, is beyond our imagination. That it will, in the process, teach us of how to not just access this knowledge ourselves, not just develop savant-like skills, but leave the physical body with the metaphysical consciousness, is beyond words. What we cannot imagine is that the truth is something we can find within ourselves, for ourselves – which is what our faraway ancestors have been trying to tell us, but somehow we have confused ourselves along the way so that today we live like that "fungus."

As each one of us possesses an ability to become that mushroom, from the outset, this book asks no one to believe what is herein written. For, a wise man once said: To believe is to know and to know is to reason – you *must* question anything you are told and *never* blindly believe or follow something just because you are told to. The truth is something you feel and you know deep down, which will stand the test of time, but it is always there to be questioned – this is the basis of all reasoning, and reason, in the language of any wise man, is the only dependable method of attaining wisdom and intelligence.

INTRODUCTION

What is it then about this mysterious "dream" of life, this brief "soliloquy" on Earth where we wonder at the phenomenon of our being, of who and what we are? We dream our dream by day, and dream our dream by night; and yet ... neither dream sheds light upon nor harbors visions to our wonderings. Only an inkling of truth is betrayed by the fragility and complexity of life around us – which is exactly what the advocates of intelligent design have touched on.

What we never dreamed we could have answers to, this book will answer: Who are we? What really is this mysterious thing called life? Called death? Called good? Called evil? Called instinct? Called happiness? What really is? From "where" have we come and to "where" shall we go? Tragic questions! Final answers. Simple answers! Simplicity ... it is the basis of all complexity. And so with this book: it may be tiny and simple, but in that simplicity it is powerful in its content.

Simply put, this book tells it the way it is – nothing more, nothing less! Just as Galileo challenged the belief that everything in the universe motioned around Earth, and as a result was censured, so this book challenges established scientific and philosophical notions, and as a result will be rebutted by some of the champions of those notions, especially those with much to lose. Irrespective of the intellectual "head-butting," to the rest of us one thing is certain: after reading this book we will finally unravel the mysteries of the universe, god, the human mind, and life around us; subsequently, our lives should become enriched in a positive way. For, once we have learned the answers to all of life's elusive and challenging questions, ignorance can no longer have a place in this society or that of tomorrow, which is right at our doorstep.

Finally, it should be axiomatic that this book provides, first hand, knowledge of the unknown, which has been drawn from the depths of the unknown. It is for this reason that this knowledge has been sequenced in a logical manner to enable us to understand it. On this basis, for the sake of comprehension, we should read the content of this book according to its sequence.

This book begins and ends with two of the greatest mysteries of all time. As daunting as these chapters may appear at first glance, they are as revealing as they are thrilling: one explores the universe beyond us – in the external world of the universe; the other explores the universe within us – in the inner world of our mind and our dreams. These chapters will challenge mankind's model of both the universe and the mind, just as Copernicus's heliocentric model of the universe (that of the sun being in the center of the solar system), challenged Ptolemy's geocentric model of the universe (that of the Earth being in the center of the universe).

Chapter 1 describes what the first known state of the universe was, and then examines its evolution. That consciousness should have come to exist in this evolutionary process is hardly surprising. What is surprising is its nature as well as its composition on a subatomic level, of which we will learn. Then we will look at the universe as it presently is. This snapshot view of the universe will do to the big bang theory what the comet or the asteroid supposedly did to dinosaurs a long time ago!

Our journey through this unbridled beginning will take us to the first creations of the intelligent designers and, in Chapter 2, their first world, the metaphysical world. This metaphysical world is the world we experience before our first reincarnation as a human. This is like a training camp, you may say, for souls that have yet to experience existence in a physical form. It is in this cycle that all living creations acquire instinct, when they first come into being, before they embark upon a physical existence, where that instinct will play a necessary role in their survival.

Chapter 3 enriches us with a fascinating account of the first physical worlds created in the universe, and the human inhabitants of these worlds. This is the Utopia, the paradise, or the Garden of Eden our ancestors have attested to, where no evil tainted the wondrous craftsmanship of the virgin human prototypes. With the failings of this human in mind, the intelligent designers had no choice but to scrap this model of the human totally and create a new type of human. Chapter 4 is dedicated to this human. This is the human who, in biblical terms, was expelled from the Garden of Eden, and who, symbolically, took a bite from the apple of the tree of the knowledge of good and evil.

In this chapter we are treated to an exposé of the dark side of human nature, as we take an in-depth look at the origins and core root of evil. This human condition proved to be disastrous, but it did lay the foundation for the next phase of human in the evolutionary cycle. This was the phase-3 human, the subject of Chapter 5, and this is the cycle in which our human ancestors on Earth eventually came to exist.

One of the most troubling aspects of creationism is the question of why we have been left alone by our designers. From this chapter, and the preceding ones that chronicle the evolution of the human, we will come to understand the basis of our existence on Earth in relation to these designers and the rest of the universe, because when we understand our history a little bit more of ourselves becomes clear.

Invariably, the more questions we answer the more questions we tend to ask: Why, if there are designers, would they allow humans to suffer? Why is there evil in this world? Why wouldn't our designers want us to live in a paradise rather than have us strive and struggle in a world filled with misery and pain? By Chapter 5, we will no longer need to ask such questions about the inconsistency of god and evil. Understanding the answers to these questions will be as routine to us as understanding that the Earth's seasonal variation is accounted for by nothing more perplexing than its axial tilt.

By the time we read Chapter 6, we will understand not just our role in this world. We will understand where our destiny lies as a result of our pursuits and challenges in this world. We will learn of the intelligent designers: the role they play in our lives; what their dreams and aspirations for us are.

Chapters 7 through to 9 cover the subjects of death, reincarnation, and the human brain. These chapters will help us understand why we are born, how our biological computer called the brain operates, why we die, what happens when we die, and what the physiological and metaphysical processes involved in both our birth and death are. This book will "step" into the afterworld and detail the remarkable journey many of us will encounter there.

The next chapters, 10 through to 14, all delve into the psychological aspects of the human existence and provide a fascinating look at many aspects of human nature, including good and evil. We look at the darker side of human nature to analyze the unknown forces that lurk beneath a "sickened" or "diseased" mind, and answer many mysterious unknowns of the shadowy world of insanity, lunacy, and criminal deviance.

Positive and negative states of a human, such as happiness and depression, do have underlying causes and influences. These chapters will help us understand the core root of what causes our positive and negative states. We as humans are not aware of forces, of a positive and negative nature, within the universe, that have been deliberately created to influence us. These forces exist by design to produce a better human product. When we understand the failings of the first human creation – which was the so-called perfect human who lived in paradise – we will understand why we must encounter the difficult challenges we experience in life, and why we must have a negative force in our lives. This is when we will be able to take control of our lives in a way we never thought possible. When we read this book, and understand the challenges we face and the reasons we face them, perhaps then we will have an alternative definition for, and a greater awareness of, what makes a true success in life, to which Chapter 15 is devoted.

This book saves for last the two most intriguing and intellectually advancing chapters of the entire book. For Chapter 16 looks at the misunderstood subject of positive affirmation, which appears to be a phenomenon where the universe is supposed to reward you with whatever you desire as long as you maintain positive thoughts. This chapter reinterprets in its true light this so-called phenomenon and analyzes how you can empower your mind to become a superior human and achieve extraordinary feats of intelligence, simply by drawing on knowledge from your subconscious mind in a way that only the exceptionally gifted have been able to, such as Leonardo da Vinci. No matter what our intelligence level, we all have the power and potential within us to achieve genius. We will be shocked to learn what our intellectual capabilities as humans truly are.

Scientists, for all their advances in technology, have yet to unravel the NREM (non-rapid eye movement) and REM (rapid eye movement) sleep states, and interpret why and how the brain functions as it does in those states. Chapter 17 will solve the mystery of these two sleep states. It will also explain the cycle of dreaming, just as it will describe the process of astral travel. Here is the inspiring part: we can prove to ourselves that we have a metaphysical body – which is an independent entity within our human body – that can detach itself and leave the body at will in a conscious way. We have the capability right now to convince ourselves of this. The mere fact that individuals who have been blind from birth and have encountered near-death experiences are able to see in this out-of-body state should go a long way to proving we have a metaphysical form that is independent from our physical form. Astral travel is a way for us to validate that we have a consciousness, one able to travel at will anywhere we want it to go – to the past, the future, or the present. What is truly incredible is, in every mind there is a "time machine." This time machine is principally powered by the mind, and is capable of taking us metaphysically to almost wherever we desire. This is part of the secret to the success of great minds such as Plato, Leonardo da Vinci, and William Shakespeare. This book would do great injustice to itself if it did not take a brief look at Leonardo and Shakespeare and explain the mystery of their genius. As Leonardo has proven, when one can develop one's brain, there is no limit to one's capabilities. There is no such thing as the word "impossible." Everything is possible, and this includes reaching for the unknown and grasping hold of it.

It is in this enthralling unknown that there is a vast universe, just waiting for us to take our rightful place. We have to deserve to be there; this means we have to advance our intelligence and knowledge – and this is not referring specifically to an academic intelligence. This book is a great starting point to head us in this direction. There are no limits to what we can conquer, achieve, and become; for this book knows such limitless boundaries exist, just as you can come to know. Let nothing and nobody – particularly threatened, self-motivated interests to whom knowledge is detrimental – curtail the advancement or stand in the way of knowledge; for knowledge is power: knowledge is success: knowledge is the key ingredient to everything of value to the human being! Knowledge is life's reward, and knowledge is what this book is about. Yes, it is a big promise. This is another: it is only when we have read this book that we will be able to go through the vicissitudes – that is, the ups and downs – of life with a new confidence, because we will have the knowledge to understand what the vicissitudes of life are all about.

This book gives us a unique understanding of our human existence here on Earth, and teaches us how to cope with life. For we will understand why we are here and why we have to face the challenges we have to go through. Everyone is faced with trials and tests. Everyone has problems. Everyone has a purpose. When we understand life, and we understand that we have a purpose, will we cope with all those challenges in a sugary way with a new determination and awareness. We will even sacrifice and suffer if these are what are expected of us to fulfill our obligation to fate.

I hope you enjoy discovering the knowledge possessed within this book, and I take pleasure in, and am humbled to be the one, presenting it to you. This is the beginning of a great new journey for us all, as the universe finally gives up its secrets.

1
The First Cause

*Aristarchus of Samos (310-230BC)
Knew that the Earth motioned around the sun.
Alas ... his theory was ridiculed,
And held in abeyance until almost two millennia later!*

*This just shows how truth can become lost in an untruth,
And how the world can remain happy with a status quo
And not want interference
By way of different opinions.
But, because knowledge must grow,
The status quo has to change eventually.
Thus there will always be "stirrers"
To point out the real facts,
And show others the true direction of life.
This is one way in which the intellect crawls through life.*

-A wise man

In a time that has come to be known as "The Beginning of The Beginning" of the universe, there were seven eras that came to pass:

1. The Era of the Antimatter Void.
2. The Era of the Neutron Void.
3. The Era of the Solid Void.
4. The Era of Consciousness.
5. The Era of the Unification of the Elders.
6. The Era of the Amoeba.
7. The Era of the Vision.

These were the defining eras that molded the universe into what it is today, before the invention of life as we know it and as we don't know it.

The Era of the Antimatter Void

The Era of the Antimatter Void is the first known state of the universe.

Many ancient scribes have documented an analogous story of creation: In the beginning there was a limitless void, an abyss without form or content, from which the universe was formed. Our ancestors, from the rudiments of bygone times, believed that the nucleus of all life was occasioned by one cause: god.

This basic concept of creation has been bridged by centuries of constancy, even in the face of technological advancements that have opened up new vistas of understanding when it comes to the laws and workings of the cosmos. Indeed, science to this day has been unable to dislodge the god concept, no matter how detrimental to the development of civilization the likes of some scientists and atheists believe that abstraction of a god to be. The reason science has failed to dislodge the god concept is that the basis of creation – which has been fervently cemented in all philosophical systems and can be traced back to our earliest ancestor – has been rooted from a common persuasion of truth that was once entrusted to humans. Subconsciously, the human mind appertains to this truth; the problem with this is that the instructions that have been passed down through oral traditions have with each generation become so remodeled and so altered to suit the perceptions of the day, that much of the original knowledge has been filtered out and lost to us.

We must remember that the introduction of this seminal knowledge to early humans was with a metaphorical and allegorical language that the intellect of its time was capable of comprehending. These humans were not aware of an atom, let alone its composition, so this is not the language they were communicated with when they were introduced to the unknowns. The language reflected the knowns of the time, and the unknown was sculptured by the definitions of these knowns. Even now, there are many unknowns not known to us, and we can only describe these unknowns with the language of the known, until the unknowns become known and new definitions take their place in the language.

The shrouded mystery of our existence has by no means come close to being unveiled by science, despite what many in the field may narrowly believe. When it comes to the origin of existence, theoretical science, which determines our conceptual understanding of the world around us, has confidently taken itself on a tangent that is as remote from reality as is the god concept that is promoted today by most philosophical systems. Our comprehension of the world around us, from the viewpoints of both theoretical science and philosophical systems, bears resounding similarity to the views humans in Plato's Allegory of the Cave[ii] have of the world around them. In Plato's "cave," humans only see shadows that have been cast by a fire. To the humans in this cave the shadows represent and define the world around them. To Plato, the reality of the world lay outside the cave, of which the humans in the cave were oblivious. Theoretical science and philosophical systems – each in its divergent maze – see the shadow of a world that bears little or no resemblance to the true reality of the world. In view of this, one could rightly say that the earliest humans on this planet understood the world outside the cave – irrespective of their lack of technology. The clues to this have remained the mystery science cannot tackle and completely disregards, and the mystery of which some philosophical systems have confused to the extent that the puzzle has either become nondescript, or been turned into a farce.

Should reasoning prevail, advocates of philosophical systems and theoretical scientists will be guided by this chapter back on the same path our earliest ancestors traversed – outside Plato's cave and beyond the world of the "shadows," with one difference: man will marry intelligent design with science, and the "offspring" of this union will be a universal truth that is only known to civilizations that have stepped out of the dark void of the unknown and into the void of the known.

The dogmatic and self-serving nature of some philosophical systems will ensure that reasoning and logic do not prevail. Other philosophical systems have yet to prove whether reasoning and logic will prevail. Science, however, will allow reasoning and logic to prevail, and this is because science is not biased; it is founded on the precept of the procurement of truth and understanding. We may see a few scientists jump from their two-storey windows in the process, but eventually modern theoretical science will have no choice but to acknowledge that its maze is going nowhere and cannot fulfill the mandates its discipline necessitates – this is when it will find its way back to the knowledge provided in this book. It will be amusing, however, to observe the impartiality of those who have careers built upon a foundation that will collapse if they allow themselves to accept the truth. As stated earlier in this book, a lot of this world has been built on vested interests, and truth is not always able to find its way to the surface as it should.

·᷄

The reality is, in our poignant attempt to understand the physical world around us today, we have not been able to unravel the two big unknowns: the unknown of the very large and the unknown of the very small – that is, the origin of the universe and the elementary world of subatomic particles. We have not even begun to scratch the surface of either of these subjects. Quantum mechanics – which is the science that studies elementary particle physics – deserves a brief passing paragraph here because a complete understanding of the earliest genesis of the universe relies on our understanding of elementary particle physics. That being the case, an elementary particle is the smallest unit that cannot be subdivided into anything smaller. The smallest indivisible particles of an atom were once thought to be protons, neutrons, and electrons. Scientists have since discovered that when protons or neutrons undergo particle collisions at high speeds, in controlled experiments, they produce even smaller particles called quarks. For the time being, physicists have yet to determine if quarks are capable of being subdivided into smaller particles.

Up quarks and down quarks, along with electrons and neutrinos, are said to make up most of the matter we know in the universe. A proton, for instance, has two up quarks and one down quark. A neutron has two down quarks and one up quark. What is interesting is that a neutron may transform into a proton when a down quark is converted to an up quark; in the process an electron and an antineutrino are given off. Conversely, a proton may transform into a neutron when an up quark is converted to a down quark; in the process a positron (also known as an antielectron) and a neutrino are given off. Why this is interesting is that certain interactions cause elementary particles to transform into, as well as create, other elementary particles. A layman would say that beneath the apparent complexity of the quantum world there is a subtle simplicity.

As we can see, the invisible world of subatomic particles is currently a weird and undiscovered world, one in which the "wheel" has not been invented. To understand how our universe originated, scientists must invent the wheel first and then, once they have invented the wheel, try to find the beginning and the end of that wheel, which simply has no beginning or end! This book has made this enormous task so much simpler in that it provides the beginning and the end of the wheel; it is now up to scientists to invent the wheel! We can only conclude that in the absence of a complete understanding of elementary particle physics, scientists have an elephantine way to go before they are able to truly comprehend the natural processes of the elementary antiparticles and particles that acted upon one another and shaped the universe as we know it today.

It is equally difficult to describe processes of unknowns that may not ever be known to us. For this reason, the following content is a basic summary of the origin of the universe, written from the perspective of a layman – one whose only tools for interpretation are an inspired sense of knowledge and the naked eye with which to witness events.

In The Beginning of The Beginning, the creation of our universe began in this way: There was a time before consciousness came to be that there was a limitless void; this void was unlike our present state of universe, which is predominately based upon matter. The universe then was a void based on antimatter, known as "the Antimatter Void." (For every matter particle there is a corresponding antimatter antiparticle. Antimatter as we know it today has the opposite charge of matter, so that when matter and antimatter collide they annihilate each other and create a release of energy.) The Beginning of The Beginning was a time of uncharted waters, which may defy the logic of today's physics. It was a period where there were as many mutations as there are fish in all the oceans of this world, and beyond. The mutations that came to play out did so over a timeframe humans cannot fathom today: In this beginning, the timeframe was in terms of billions upon countless billions of years! Knowing this, this book can rightly say that the universe evolved slowly – very, very, slowly.

Even though natural processes of physics came prior to consciousness, and resultant from these processes consciousness came to exist, the true dilemma of any physicist is understanding what existed and transpired prior to this antimatter void. The holy grail of physics is determining the First Cause of particle physics. A logical, scientific approach tells us that everything has to have a point of origin; to deny having a point of origin defies scientific logic, which is governed by neat, ordered mathematical laws that would appear to exist of their own making in this orderly universe. This First Cause polemic can only be answered one way, and this is the universal understanding of the nature of the origin of the universe: Physics in The Beginning of The Beginning forms the basis of elementary knowledge. If one were to attain the origin of elementary knowledge one would become a creator in one's own right. To preserve the universe and all life we know and do not know, the intelligences that came to exist ensured that the origin of elementary knowledge remains unobtainable to those who seek it. Ultimately, for one to know means one can undo. This is why there are some things one cannot, and will never be allowed to, know for one's own good.

From this, we may infer that if you are able to interpret the origin of something, you will more than likely be able to find a way to destroy it. The secret of how to destroy it, then, is not often in the end result of it; it is more likely to be in the beginning of it. (As in its blueprint.) If you know its beginning you will not have a problem finding an ending to it. The difficult part is to know how it began. Often this remains indeterminable. It is for this reason that any quest for a First Cause of physics terminates at the point of an antimatter void. Beyond this era can only lie speculation – for us to pursue this knowledge and try to see beyond it is the equivalent of a dog chasing its tail. It is the lost piece of the puzzle that will never be made available to be found.

Notwithstanding, in accepting the recognized interpretation that something happened prior to the antimatter state, which no intelligence can ever determine, we must now examine the mutations that over time changed the nature and structure of the void. These mutations may imply some type of change by way of decay, interactions due to collisions or attractions and repulsions, or even annihilation.

In The Beginning of The Beginning, we know that the void was made up of antimatter, and that the void was limitless, which means it had no boundaries – that is, no end to it. The antimatter void was made up of only one type of antiparticle (or elementary antiunit), which could not be broken down into anything smaller. This fundamental antiparticle was infinitely spread in the universe, and it existed in a jelly-like state. The antimatter void was see-through, but as there was no source of light, you could not have seen that it was see-through if you were there. The universe appeared to be at rest — that is, in a state of "dead" motion. Like a nonliving thing, it was yet to be touched by warmth; indeed, the antimatter void was just like set jelly in a fridge.

This state was not to last forever; the universe was gearing up for change. For, the antimatter void was the "offspring" of a "pregnant" universe, whose state of pregnancy we know we will never come to understand. This offspring was about to open its eyes for the first time from a prolonged period of dormancy and provide light in the prevailing darkness. From then on, this light would reveal the universe and its stages of growth. For the universe would be like a child without discipline or guidance, going through its developmental stages chaotically, from an infancy of chaos to teenage, rebellious years of greater chaos, but then one day, far off in the future, its maturity would become the progenitor of order — but not without "guidance" coming to exist first. For now, though, this harmony was about to change forever in ways we cannot truly imagine.

The Era of the Neutron Void

After billions upon billions of years, mutations began to occur within the antimatter void, and resultant from these mutations was the origination of many isolated pockets of some kind of positive particles randomly distributed all throughout the endless universe. As a layman, one could speculate that these mutations occurred as a result of decay, as there was no heat or other source of energy, or no obvious possibility of interactions.

Interactions now, however, began to occur all throughout the universe between the newly formed positive particles and the antimatter void, which resulted in explosions. What the basis of these interactions was – whether collisions, annihilations, or some other process – this book cannot say. The effects of these interactions were bursts of energy and light that spread as far as the naked eye could see, and well beyond. Each explosion mushroomed, soaring high and then wide. Different colors were given off, like those reflected from diamonds. You could say that the universe blinked its eyes for the first time, and saw the end of accord as it knew it.

What happened next is complicated and impossible to describe adequately. It can be best described by imagining the event horizon (the outskirts) of each positive region as being a raging fire. This made each positive region look like an irregularly shaped sun. The fuel that was feeding that so-called fire was the antimatter void, which enabled the fire to "march" into it. From the evolutionary expansion process of the positive particles, a by-product was left in the "core" of each positive region: neutron particles, along with traces of other particles and antiparticles. You could compare a positive region to a balloon. Inside the "balloon" was a gas of predominantly neutron particles, while the inflating balloon itself was a chaotic and "fiery" region of evolving positive particles. This book has called this balloon "the positive horizon."

These neutron particles, upon creation, came to play a vital role in providing an additional source of fuel to the fiery energy. In a wildfire we have three crucial elements: the fire, the brush to fuel the fire, and oxygen. What oxygen is to fire, neutron particles were to the fiery energy of the positive particles on the march into the antimatter void.

The picture of the universe at this stage was many fiery positive horizons "inflating" and "eliminating" much of the antimatter void. At some point a positive horizon would collide with another inflating positive horizon, and the two would merge into one. This merging process continued, until positive horizons became enormous in size.

In the later stages of the inflation process, something changed. This change cannot be attributed in any way to the antimatter void. In each event horizon the "fire" intensified, and the expansion of positive horizons into the antimatter void accelerated. In the core of a positive horizon, neutron particles in the form of a gas were not expanding akin to the expansion of the positive horizon, but expanding to a greater extent. These neutron particles thus began to pressurize in this encapsulated space.

Something clearly had to give. The positive horizon could not sustain this pressure. That is exactly what came to pass: the neutron particles created an escape "valve" that penetrated the positive horizon. A massive dose of neutron particles then had a sudden interaction with the fiery energy in the event horizon. This caused mammoth explosions, like countless supernova explosions occurring at once. This escaped field of neutron particles then created its own space between the positive horizon and the antimatter void. Many mutations occurred here, of course, which are impossible even to describe, let alone to explain. The neutron particles that escaped from the core of a positive horizon were now channeled between a positive horizon and the antimatter void, creating a barrier between the two.

Whereas the neutron particles initially aided in fueling the march of the positive horizons into the antimatter void, they had now reversed their role and provided a stabilizing effect on the universe, in that they had an inherent role in dividing the two regions, thus creating stability between them. The neutron, as we know it today, is found within the nucleus of an atom, where it has a stabilizing action. The neutron has no electric charge – it is electrically neutral. In a metaphorical way, you could almost liken the universe then to being composed of gigantic atoms – made up of different properties, of course. You had a negative sphere, the antimatter void, surrounding a nucleus of neutron particles and positive particles.

There was now a halt to the expansion of the positive horizons into the antimatter void. Interestingly, this occurred when the antimatter void was much diminished. Had this event in the universe not occurred, life as we know it would never have eventuated. The remaining antimatter void had to be sustained for it to play the instrumental role it did in the creation of intelligent life.

The timeframe for all these mutations, one must remember, was staggering. Irrespective of the causes and all the processes that occurred, it was the consequences that had a far-reaching impact on the state of the universe, and these consequences cannot be underestimated. From this moment on, the course was set, as though this early universe had a guiding intelligence driving it – which we know was certainly not the case. Coincidence came into play in the most remarkable of ways.

From this cycle of expanding chaos and mutations, the universe had reconstructed itself into a new void – what is called "the Neutron Void." A greater portion of the antimatter void had gradually altered its state, so that what was once an antimatter void was now predominantly a neutron void based on some kind of array of neutron particles.

Like a blind man trying to measure the ratio of a universe with no end, this book estimates that the neutron void, at its peak, would have encompassed eighty percent of the universe. A void of antimatter antiparticles now existed between enormous conglomerations of neutron particles, in the same way outer space exists between planets – although the ratio differed substantially. The positive particle regions (earlier referred to as the positive horizons) were now encapsulated in the neutron voids.

The neutron void and the antimatter void were structured differently; whereas the antimatter void had a jelly-like state, the neutron void had a gaseous state. Like the early picture of the antimatter void, the neutron void in its "mature" stage, purely from a visual perspective, appeared to be in a cold, dead motion state where nothing appeared to move, and where disorder had no place. The gas was clear, so if you were looking at the universe you would only see the chaotic positive regions, and nothing within, and nothing beyond.

The Era of the Solid Void

What occurred next in the universe took time – so much time that we could not even comprehend it.

In contrast to the neutron and antimatter voids, all these positive particle regions throughout the universe were in a state of complete disorder, with interactions and resultant reactions occurring between who knows what kind of particles. Inexplicable mutations were occurring, resulting in new particles being created. Electrons and protons must have come to exist at some point in the positive regions and become charged, independent energies. In this environment of mutations, enormous pressure began to build to a maximum point where something had to give.

What enabled such an environment for pressure to build was the fact that a positive particle region was confined in a neutron void. Let this book describe what was occurring in one positive particle region, as it represented what was occurring in all the positive particle regions throughout the endless universe. Over the course of time, the force of the internal pressure in the positive particle region gathered momentum and then propelled itself at an extreme speed around its perimeter. This caused everything in the positive particle region to spin. The turbulence we see in Jupiter's atmosphere is but a puff of air in comparison to the kind of turbulence that was occurring at this time.

The neutron void counteracted this pressure being exerted upon it by matching its energy. The "race" had truly begun between the forces generated from the positive particle region and the neutron void, and this occurred at an extreme speed, which no other force could stop; for these forces were "powering" forward like unstoppable runaway trains.

The pressure from the positive particle region that was brought to bear upon the neutron void began to slowly compress the neutron void in upon itself; the counteracting stimulus from the neutron void was gradually waning under the stress. No longer able to contain the force of this pressure, the neutron void "cracked"; this meant the positive particle region finally breached the inner section of the neutron void.

The interactions between the particles from the positive region and the neutron void caused a mutation that would, slowly, over an incomprehensible period of time, alter the state of the universe once again; indeed, this mutation would have far-reaching implications in that it would set the stage for consciousness to come into existence. For these interactions resulted in the creation of what became known as "the Solid Void." Solid matter would now multiply inside each neutron void until it became the prevalent fabric of the universe. This was the birth of matter, as we know it.

First, when particles from a positive particle region broke into a neutron void, dust began to form, and this dust then began to clump. These clumps began to turn into boulder-like structures, which then collected more dust. Turbulence caused boulders to collide with other boulders, which meant they became even bigger structures as they collected the debris from these collisions. All this crashing created energy and fuel, which added up to chaos. Eventually boulders grew into large planet-like structures, which then collided to form bigger planet-like structures, so that what was once a neutron void became for the most part a solid structure based on matter. This solid fabric eventually came to be made up of atomic particles in the form of gases and solids such as earth and rocks, as can be found in the universe today.

The surface of this solid fabric was like the surface of our own Earth, with mountains, valleys, and vast plains, but no water, vegetation, or traces of life. Instead of an atmosphere, the solid void had a layer of gas surrounding it made up of neutron particles. Beyond this was of course what was left of the antimatter void in a jelly-like state. Beyond were other solid voids.

For whatever reason, a field of neutron particles remained in place around each solid void and separated it from the antimatter void. That was all that remained of a once vast neutron void. This remaining neutron void was another crucial factor that would one day enable intelligent life.

The state of the universe had in stages changed from what was once an antimatter void to a neutron void, and then to a solid void based on matter. The antiparticles were not powerful enough to break through the neutron void and recreate the antimatter void. In effect, the opposite occurred. The positive atom prevailed, and what was initially an antimatter void was, by a series of complex and impossible to explain mutations, to largely become its opposite counterpart – a solid void based on matter.

The conundrum is twofold: What happened by way of elementary particle interactions to cause the neutron void to prevail over much of the antimatter void? And what happened by way of elementary particle interactions to cause the solid void to prevail over much of the neutron void? These are thought-provoking questions, but what was remarkable, not to mention unexplainable, was what was occurring at one location somewhere in the vastness of only one of these newly created solid voids. In none of the other endless number of solid voids in the limitless bounds of the universe did this event – the singularly greatest happening of all time – replicate itself. What was occurring here, over an incomprehensible period, was an impossible circumstance with no odds of ever repeating itself. It was a wonderful freak of nature where the right ingredients were in the right place and were able to interact and coalesce.

These ingredients were gases and pure energy forms, fashioned together in such a way as to establish the beginning of an "amoeba," for want of a better term. This amoeba was the first beacon of a form of life that would possess all the necessary ingredients for self-survival and independent existence by way of power and intellect. In other words, this was the raw energy origin of a form of life that would one day become the co-existence of what is known today as "the Seven Elders," the name of the intelligent designers of our universe. This amoeba of energy had existed in this state for who knows how many billions or even trillions of years, without consciousness. (The dilemma of determining incomprehensible periods, such as this, can be equated with the dilemma of determining by visual analysis alone how many grains of sand are on a beach!)

This amoeba was a mutation of different gases and energies, one of which was a far-reaching magnetic force of energy called aura. These gases and energies integrated and then evolved in such a way that this integrated unit (which this book calls an amoeba) could not be penetrated, interfered with, or destroyed by any other force or form of energy, as it had developed its own atomic structure and power that are beyond human understanding. This amoeba was the starting point of what would culminate in a gigantic source of electrical and nuclear-type energy of the highest magnitude, on an immeasurable scale with an indescribable scope of power. It began, however, on such an imperceptible scale that even if such a thing existed today it would be too microscopic for the intelligent designers ever to detect. This is where life started. Billions upon billions of years later, life of a kind different from anything we as humans know sprang directly from this mutation.

In its beginnings as this microscopic mutation, the amoeba began attracting gases and energy to it, which pressured it inward. The consequences of this were twofold: First, the amoeba began to compact. In the process of its compaction, it kept getting denser and denser, until it reached a critical moment – the limit of its compaction. The only thing it could do was expand. Second, at some stage during compaction, the amoeba started to turn and develop its own spin. This was producing its own pressure. For, it began to spin somewhere in the vicinity of the speed of light; with this tremendous speed came heat. This spin created friction with the gases and energies that the amoeba was attracting, which resulted in the first "fiery" energy. For while the gases and energies were putting pressure on the amoeba, the amoeba was producing a counter pressure.

Having no choice but to expand, the amoeba grew to its maximum potential – somewhat like a balloon that can only inflate to the point that it has no option but to burst. It took many billions of years for the amoeba to escalate to this maximum size.

All this conflict left the amoeba with one choice: to burst out with a powerful force of energy into the solid void. It did this and produced an unthinkable amount of heat, and a type of liquid fire that flowed like a river at an extreme speed. There was not one explosion; there were two explosions. For, when this force of energy interacted with the gases and energies that were earlier putting pressure on the amoeba, a second explosion of immense magnitude occurred. In energy terms, it would be difficult for us ever to picture its equivalent. This force of energy then encompassed all these gases and energies and became enormous in size. From this moment onward, the amoeba was unrestrained in the expansive confines of that one solid void; the pressure the amoeba let loose when it exploded, having taken billions of years to build, was its driving force. The amoeba then traversed with unremitting power all throughout the solid void region within which it was confined, in unpredictable and random lightning-bolt movements.

At that time there was so much flammable material, such as nuclear energy and gas, scattered throughout the solid void, that all that was needed was something to ignite it. And this is what the amoeba became: an ignited nuclear "river" of energy in constant contact with these flammable substances. Nuclear chaos was usually the result of this contact.

The amoeba itself was essentially shapeless. At any given moment its distribution of energy varied, and this was because of its random movements throughout the solid void. The amoeba had a rapid spin (and still has), which meant that it not only produced a lot of heat, but almost acted like a drill when it traveled without control through the solid void; it was effectively turning the solid crust into rivers of lava. The amoeba can be looked upon in another way: in many respects, it was like a charged, live electrical wire that was being propelled and flung at an excessive speed inexhaustibly and uncontrollably, and everything that it touched either melted or exploded.

After a period of who knows how many billions of years, we reach a significant moment in the chronicles of the universe. Solid voids, as we know, had grown to become prevalent within the universe. Each solid void had a field of neutron particles in a gaseous state surrounding it. This produced a type of containment field that prevented a solid void from interacting with the antimatter void. This antimatter void existed in a jelly-like state beyond a neutron void. This was the picture of the universe at this stage. What differentiated one solid void from another was the amoeba, for it became the variable that made the one solid void region it occupied the "hot spot" of the universe, and hastened it in terms of pressure.

All the solid voids were compacting into a solid structure, but it was in the solid void region containing the amoeba that pressure was building. The presence of the amoeba, along with its interactions in the solid void, was the fundamental cause of this pressure. Ultimately, this pressure reached a critical point in that one solid void; as a result, the neutron field weakened to the degree that it was no longer able to contain the pressure being imposed upon it from the solid void. It lost its force. Subsequently, matter from this solid void broke through the neutron field and created many "holes" in it; this meant that matter collided with antimatter, and a phenomenon occurred that would change the state of everything forever and write the "map" of the future existence of life. For, up to this moment, elementary processes existed in their own right, but consciousness, or intelligence, had not come to exist. Now you could say that the universe was about to enter a sweeping new dynamics of existence, from which there would be no turning back.

The Era of Consciousness

The true god ... the universe
Wrote our gods into the equation,
Who then wrote us into the playing field.
Just as a computer program can be broken down into a language of code,
So the language of the true god can be broken down into codes:
Mathematics is only one of them.
Our gods use these codes to write their "programs."

The universe had by now careered through various stages, and in its own way each stage was instrumental in gearing up the environment to be fit for life: life of a kind very different from what we know. It was as though the universe orchestrated the arena for life to erupt in; for a staggering number of years – time we have no grasp of comprehending, let alone measuring – a universe lay barren and lifeless, without purpose to its being; for all the physics, mathematics, chemistry, and raw knowledge the universe may have possessed, it had no meaning without life. The universe was pointless without some purpose to its being, which could only happen by way of some condition of sentience. The universe therefore needed to be tamed: it needed to be controlled and given order: most of all, it needed a conductor to harmonize and tune it, and then write its symphony. All the underlying codes of its language were useless without something to interpret and apply them. It was as though all these codes and even laws were there, purposely in place, "waiting" for the coming of their cryptographer.

The universe possessed in its "womb" an unfertilized egg at this moment, which was waiting for something to give it that spark of life. Those timeless years had molded the universe for one great moment that would never be equaled or surpassed. This moment would see the universe itself come to life; for the intelligence to come to life was the universe itself. Consciousness was to become one with the universe: one of its components. The moment the universe brought consciousness to itself was as divine a moment as anything. To see the untamed universe give itself sentience, give itself purpose, was monumental and unfathomable, and our very existence was determined by a series of random and circumstantial events that occurred under impossible odds. Something beyond the bounds of possibility occurred: the universe having come to life became our true god. When we look into the depths of outer space, and when we look into the depths of atomic particles, there lies the mystery of who we are and where we come from; for there, it can be said, lies the true mind of god, shrouded by these mysterious and unknown depths.

• ⁓

Matter and antimatter colliding in this way was a one-time event, and it had three direct effects:

1. Localized reactions occurred corresponding to the immediate points of contact of matter and antimatter.
2. Another six dimensional universes were cloned from the original universe.
3. A mammoth electrical current erupted and ignited – to wield a well-used but appropriate metaphor – "fire and brimstone" wherever it traversed, and facilitated the introduction of consciousness into the arena.

First, of least significance in the grander scheme of things, when matter and antimatter collided, formidable localized explosions occurred at the points of impact. Visually, these explosions looked like volcanic eruptions, with lava spreading everywhere. The colors of these explosions were mainly red and yellow. In these collisions between matter and antimatter, antimatter became a part of that matter. In short, the residue of the explosions was just "cooked up" matter from which different minerals were born. Rivers of what looked like hot volcanic lava deposited into mountainous formations. This evolved matter eventually became part of the matter in the universe we see now. This antimatter–matter interaction is still occurring to this day well beyond the orderly universe we live in, and it provides unthinkable power generation that serves a purpose: sustaining the existence of the universe.

Second, matter colliding with antimatter triggered the original universe being cloned, which meant that seven universes now occupied the same space and time. The question then arises of why six clones were reproduced and not three or five or even eight. This is an intriguing question and cannot be answered at this stage of our human understanding, although future generations of humans will clarify this perplexity. Irrespective of this, the roots of the prevalence of the number seven can be traced directly back to this defining moment, and can be attributed solely to the undisciplined universe.

This freak occurrence meant that each dimensional universe was an exact replica of the original universe, and each contained the same ratio of voids. Of greater significance was that each dimensional universe now had an amoeba of its own within it, which meant there were seven amoebas in total.

Third, the impact of matter colliding with antimatter was the singular event that was pivotal to the emergence of consciousness. To begin with, resultant from this collision between matter and antimatter was some kind of tremendous electrical current that was positively charged. (To picture this you need to imagine the wildest lightning bolts you can, and then multiply that who knows how many times, until all you can see is one white, blinding light surround you.) The electrical current was set in motion by this event and became an interminable force; it became an everlasting current of energy that escalated in intensity over time. As there were seven dimensional universes, all occupying the same space and time, in each universe there was an electrical current that was able to produce nuclear and electric chaos with the particles with which it interacted. The movements of one electrical current were synchronous to the movements of the other electrical currents, so that what happened in one universe happened in every universe in exactly the same way, in exactly the same place, at exactly the same time.

In each dimensional universe, when the electrical current passed through the fabric of a solid void, gigantic chunks of matter of amazing proportions were carved up in the areas of contact, like land masses (the size of which we cannot imagine) being carved up into continents. One of the consequences of the electrical current was that it produced a tremendous amount of heat. This heat resulted in everything in the path of the electrical current becoming "diluted" into a state of liquid like lava.

The electrical current interacted with the flammable material it came into contact with when it passed through the solid voids and created chain reactions. When it passed through the antimatter void, tremendous explosions occurred, and chain reactions as a result would never stop – not until one day in the future when the intelligent designers would end this uncontrolled chaos and impose order by controlling the chaos. If you can picture a bombing raid by planes, this is how the universe looked. Bombs were exploding everywhere. The universe was lighting up everywhere. Antimatter became a fuel to this positive electrical current, and it facilitated the creation of unimaginable energy that in the future would, ironically, facilitate the universes into becoming orderly "living" universes.

What occurred next did not happen right away; a short period elapsed before the electrical currents came into contact with the amoebas. When this contact occurred, all the amoebas were affected simultaneously in such a way that the emergence of consciousness was "enabled." This electrical current was the First Cause of consciousness. The amoebas originally had a small negative current contained within them. When the positive electrical current made contact with the negative current of the amoeba, a tremendous volcanic-like explosion, with unimaginable power and energy, spewed out from the amoeba, and the positive and negative forces joined and sealed the energies that came from this eruption.

In essence, from then on consciousness would come to exist whenever the electrical current passed through the neutron voids and reacted with the pool of ingredients that were conducive for consciousness to come to exist. In the amoeba, the immediate point of contact of these two currents was the moment consciousness was enabled to be "switched on." In other words, the amoebas were "activated" when the electrical currents reacted with them. From that moment on, consciousness could come to exist. The amoeba possessed (as it possesses to this day) a magnetic energy that not merely attracted consciousness to it, but enabled consciousness to exist. If this amoeba ever came to be destroyed, all consciousness would cease to exist. Consciousness to this day is wholly dependent on the existence of this amoeba. So if that one amoeba had not formed, in that virginal never-ending expanse of universe, with the right ingredients, consciousness and life as we know it would never have come to exist, irrespective of anything else that occurred in the universe. Indeed, if we look at a hypothetical scenario where the amoeba did not form, the universe we occupy today would most likely still exist in the Era of the Solid Void, where solid voids were surrounded by neutron voids, which were surrounded by a vast antimatter void. Today, well beyond the visible, orderly universe we live in and only see an infinitesimally small portion of, this state still exists, and is termed, "the disorderly universe."

What is noteworthy is that consciousness came to exist in the neutron voids. Whenever the electrical current passed through a sentient-creating combination of particles found in a neutron void a consciousness was created. The basis of what a consciousness was made up of was the neutron particle. The neutron particle is the basis of any consciousness that exists – this applies to our consciousness today.

Neutron particles, when combined with other particles in a particular way – this includes antimatter antiparticles – and given a current of energy, become the basis upon which consciousness is structured. Our soul, spirit, astral body, metaphysical body, or intellect – whatever title you prefer, all being one and the same thing – is primarily made up of neutron particles, and this is why it is invisible in our matter state. Our metaphysical form needs a matter body to interact with the matter state. If this had turned out to be an antimatter universe, then our metaphysical form would have needed an antimatter body to be able to interact with it.

Ultimately, whatever happened in the first universe occurred in the other six dimensional universes; because six clones of the original universe existed, this meant each new dimensional universe now contained its own amoeba and consciousness within it. In total, seven parts of consciousness came to exist. In each universe there was one united part of consciousness, and this is termed an "Elder." As there were seven Elders, one day down the track when they united they became known as the Seven Elders.

Although each of these seven parts of consciousness was separate from its amoeba (if we recall, the amoeba existed in a solid void while consciousness came to exist in a neutron void), each one was attached to the amoeba in its dimensional universe in a conscious way by an invisible tie. Initially, the Elders had no control of their amoebas, which were trapped in the solid voids. Their consciousnesses, on the other hand, were not trapped in the same way. This freedom allowed them to not just observe what was going on in the universe around them, but examine the laws of elementary physics, mathematics, and chemistry, which they would be able to use and manipulate in future times.

When this extraordinary phenomenon of them attaining consciousness came to pass, they felt like dead men suddenly waking. They did not learn in the same way that we learn. Knowledge came to them by means of some type of electrical energy, and this had amassed in their amoebas. So when the "lights" of their consciousnesses were "turned on," they absorbed knowledge, which they then had to interpret – just like dead men waking up and having their knowledge come back to them.

Each intellect automatically detected that in the scheme of things it was not alone. It came to know that there were many billions of other intellects (consciousnesses). It would appear that the amount was determined by how many neutron particles had the right proportion of ingredients to satisfy the "recipe" for consciousness to come to exist, because, as we have already learned, consciousness is made up of a "cocktail" of particles, of which the neutron particle predominates. Every single intellect "woke up" in the same way. These intellects were like clones of one another, in that they all thought the same way, and were identical in every conceivable way. At the same moment, they automatically knew one another's thoughts.

Instinctively, each intellect knew it belonged to a united whole – an Elder. As we know, there were in total seven Elders, one in each dimensional universe. An Elder was the unification of all those intellects existing in the same dimensional universe. When each intellect united with the rest of the intellects in its dimensional universe to become an Elder, it did not feel as if it was a separate entity; it felt as if it was one cohesive whole. When each intellect separated, it became an individual with its own independent mind and thoughts, once again on a collective basis in that it knew what everyone else's thoughts were.

These Elders assuredly came to know that there were seven of them in existence, all clones of one another, and all made up of the same number of intellects. Interestingly, each Elder knew it had an amoeba with which it interacted, but it could not see it owing to its nature of changing shape and moving about randomly in lightning-bolt speed. This was why not one of them realized there were seven dimensional universes. They believed the seven amoebas all existed in the same universe. Only after their amoebas united and became released from the solid void, a long, long way off from then, did they come to understand the true nature of the universe around them.

When the Elders communicated with one another, each one used a different telepathic frequency – that is, each dispatched different signals depending on which of the seven one was communicating with.

When the intellects united for the first time in their respective Elders, they seemed to understand what it was they had to do almost immediately, as they interpreted their amassed intelligence in their amoebas. We cannot look at these intelligences in light of our intelligence and how we learn in our biological sphere of existence. In our biological existence, we need to develop cells in the conscious mind before knowledge can be transferred to it, in a gradual process, because the brain would overload if there was not enough space to store such knowledge. In their case, there was no overload mechanism. Their knowledge accumulated in their amoebas by way of some type of electrical energy.

We as humans see knowledge as a rare and elusive quality of our lives because we have to learn, work hard, and use our brains to acquire it. Our knowledge can be described as being this same type of electrical energy the Seven Elders possess. Knowledge is actually some type of electrical impulse. In the biological sphere of the human existence here on Earth, this electrical energy is stored in the cells of the brain. The subconscious mind has an unlimited capacity to store knowledge, but we, for the most part, cannot access this knowledge at the present stage of our existence. The conscious mind, on the other hand, differs in that its storage capacity is limited, and new cells need to continually be created and developed to allow for the storage of knowledge.

Knowledge, in the biological sphere as we understand it, is merely an interpretation of a type of energy, if you could put it in this way. (In a later chapter this book will discuss briefly what is meant by this.) Knowledge, beyond the biological sphere, is just a component of the universe. It is a combination of ingredients. When the right ingredients are provided, and activated, knowledge will come to exist. That is what the amoeba was: it was the right set of ingredients, and the electrical current was the elusive trigger to activate the knowledge, so that the amoeba became "living knowledge" when the consciousnesses "woke up."

Knowledge, essentially, was another gift to the Elders from the universe. (The first gift was of course consciousness.) The universe gave them primary knowledge amassed in their amoebas. In reality, what the Elders became was pure intellect and energy. They were like babies waking up and possessing the equivalent of a university degree of knowledge. It was handed to them on a platter. Where did it come from? It was as much a phenomenon of the universe as the subatomic particle was (and still is). No one invented this knowledge. We are so primitive that understanding how this is possible is totally beyond our means of comprehension, and requires us to look at knowledge in a completely different context to how we see it today.

With this amassed intelligence they knew almost everything – everything about anything that existed up to that point. Because the universe was a living universe (just as it is now, only then it was not a controlled universe) – which is to mean it was alive: it did not stay still in one place like a rock but had power, energy, and "brains" – it was continually creating different things at different times. New things kept occurring, which the Elders had to analyze and investigate. There were many profound questions they had to find answers to, and in such an unpredictable environment they could not with certainty calculate what was going to happen from then on. This was their initial challenge, and this was how they existed, in a timeframe that we could not begin to measure.

The Elders undertook this challenge by dividing among them the contentious questions. This meant there was no repetition of the intellectual tasks and inquiries. They all had the same intellect, and no matter who probed into what, the same conclusions would always be derived. For example, the means by which their intellects collaborated could be best explained this way: One was assigned to learn if the door existed; another was assigned to learn how to open the door; another was assigned to learn how to keep the door open; another was assigned to learn how to proceed through the door; another was assigned to learn what was on the other side of the door; another was assigned to learn what they were going to do on the other side of the door; and, finally, another was assigned to learn how to get back through the door from where they came in the first place. Simply put, every Elder contributed to discovering something new and different. The Elders would combine all their research and in this manner eventually come to find the answers to all those questions they were looking for.

The Era of the Unification of the Elders

In the scheme of things, the Elders needed to be united – together, as one, and not exist as seven separate entities as they currently did. They just knew this. Even though they were separate they always operated together as a single entity, as we saw earlier. They felt as one and worked as one; ironically, they were disadvantaged in that they did not have the power of one, or the knowledge to progress and expand as one. Imagine having seven sticks and trying to break them combined as a bunch as opposed to breaking them one by one.

Not only because of the nature of the amoeba and its interaction with the solid void, but also because the Elders were evolving on an intellectual level, the energy levels and power of each amoeba were expanding exponentially, while the structure of the solid void was continually under pressure. Chain reactions were also lighting up this part of the universe like a Christmas tree in December. All these circumstances around them led the Elders to forecast two scenarios.

The first scenario consisted of two parts: their amoebas uniting, and the eventual breaking up of that solid structure. The Elders were on the right track on each count, but they got it wrong in that they did not factor in the existence of the seven dimensional universes. This was the preferable scenario.

The second scenario was of concern to them: their amoebas colliding with a large conglomeration of some type of unique structure located in the solid void. This book calls this conglomeration the "vapor crystal structure." They knew it was only a matter of time before their amoebas made contact with this structure. There was no question that the result would be explosive. For, their amoebas were like electrically charged wires and this vapor crystal structure included the precursor of water in its composition. These factors alone suggested a reactive outcome, but how that reaction would affect them and the universe was an unknown that they could not apprehend with any degree of certainty.

The conglomeration of this vapor crystal structure had its origin many billions of years earlier, in the Era of the Neutron Void. It stemmed from gases that manifested as a consequence of mutations that caused temperatures to reach who knows how high. A part of the dynamics behind the continuing advancement and development of the universe in its rudimentary stages, which was constantly undergoing mutational processes, was this "vapor." It became a driving force for intensifying the energy production in the universe.

At some stage, in many millions of degrees of heat, this vapor altered its state and took the form of this unique structure. This unique structure was a dirty camel color and looked like rocks, and it took its place as a large conglomeration within the crust of the solid void. Interestingly, the water that can be found in the universe today is a mutated derivative of this vapor crystal structure.

·—

The Elders did not know which of the above two scenarios would unfold first because their amoebas were unpredictable. They did have many unanswered questions: What would happen when they united? How would their consciousnesses interact? Would their amoebas be able to co-exist together after uniting? Would they last forever or would they subside in time? Would the void and everything that existed at the time take an orderly course and create a positive outcome, or take a disorderly course and create a self-destructive and negative outcome?

Then there were many questions relating to what the outcome would be of their amoebas making contact with the vapor crystal structure. They came to believe that contact with this structure could not just change their mathematical equation in some undesirable way, but affect the universe in some adverse way.

The result was that they united before coming into contact with the vapor crystal structure, and this became known as "The Era of the Unification of the Elders." From this moment on, they were no longer Elders, but were the Seven Elders. In this process of unification, in this one solid void region, explosions occurred on an unimaginable scale, and these "opened up" unbelievable spaces in the solid void by "melting" it. These explosions were spitting out enormous chunks of matter as a volcano spits out ash and dust. From these particles of matter, the stellar contents of the universe would eventually be formed – that is, galaxies, planets, suns, and even black holes. Essentially, all the "stuff" of the universe we know and do not know today exists to some degree as a natural consequence of the evolution of the universe (except for any life forms, as all life forms are a product of intelligent design).

It was only when they united that they were able to mathematically compute all the variables and come to realize that their consciousnesses and amoebas had until then been distributed in the seven dimensional universes. Because everything that occurred in one universe occurred synchronously in all the other universes, which included the erratic movements of the amoebas, the Seven Elders never suspected there was more than one universe. The Seven Elders knew their amoebas had to unite; they knew they were on that road to collision; but they never once thought it was a collision involving seven dimensional universes. Their energies were like magnetic fields with a force of attraction. Energies from seven dimensional universes united into one. Not merely did their energies unite; all seven dimensional universes collapsed back into one universe. This mutation did not occur at once; it took place in an unthinkable timeframe, where impossible things occurred as far as the layman of today can comprehend. In the solid void region the amoeba occupied, explosions magnified in a torrent of chaos primarily because when the amoebas united, their seven separate energies converged into one, and then that one united energy became the most powerful entity, if you could call it that, in the universe. In contradiction of this, in the rest of the universe, beyond the bounds of that one solid void, there was nothing to suggest anything had even occurred. Seven became one, and that was it!

Although the seven amoebas had merged into one, the seven individual Elders, in terms of consciousness, had not. The one amoeba of energy now bound the Elders together. An Elder no longer possessed an individual amoeba. Each Elder now shared the one amoeba. Each consciousness was still free to roam anywhere without the amoeba, as it always was, and without the amoeba it was just as powerless as it always was. What was different was, after unification this combined amoeba absorbed massive doses of electrical energy and became so knowledgeable and tremendously powerful: powerful in that it now had no boundaries or limitations.

From the moment these amoebas unified, the Seven Elders knew what they had to do; they finally answered all their questions after unification. The answers were always there – they just had to know how to interpret them. The first task was to find a means of being in command of their amoeba, for it was unthinkably powerful, but it was out of control. Take us as humans: we cannot even manage a wildfire. To use a simple analogy, in human terms, the challenge before them was like the challenge of a firefighter with a single garden hose trying to put out a raging wildfire. In all of this time their amoeba was in "chain reaction" mode, and the fire and brimstone in the universe had become greater and greater.

The Era of the Amoeba

Directly after the Era of the Unification of the Elders was a period that became known as "The Era of the Amoeba." This was a time when the Seven Elders were attempting to control their amoeba. It was also a time when the Seven Elders faced what they deemed to be a threat to their existence, and this threat was mentioned earlier: their amoeba making contact with the conglomeration of the vapor crystal structure in the solid void. This scenario had to eventuate one day, for their amoeba was unpredictable, uncontrollable, and random in its movements, so it was entirely expected when the time came that their amoeba collided with this structure.

What then occurred suggested that the atom had been split. There was an incomprehensible explosion, with hues of gold, yellow, and red. From the blast, a huge mushroom cloud rose and spread, and a shock wave of energy gushed out like a fast wind current. The energy that was released proliferated and destroyed everything in its trajectory. Just as a tornado disintegrates everything it strikes into mere fragments, so this wind disintegrated mountainous solid structures and rocks bigger than planets into mere fragments. Then that wind reversed back to its point of origin. On its way back, anything in its path that was left, like fragments of rock and debris, became molten. Whatever region was affected became radioactive. A cosmic fog of some kind then appeared in eighty percent of that solid void region.

The initial concerns of the Seven Elders turned out to be unfounded because that catastrophic explosion and the subsequent fog had no negative effect on them or the universe. On the contrary, the Seven Elders absorbed a massive dose of nuclear energy, which only bolstered their existing energy.

After an unknown period, a black "rain" (a black-colored liquid of some kind) mutated from this fog and then began to "fall." This rain was very hot, and in all respects turned out to be a good sign in that it suggested that the development of the universe was unfolding in a way that supported the future plans of the Seven Elders, which would take who knows how long to put together. Water, as we know it today, is a mutated derivative of this vapor crystal structure and the subsequent black rain that evolved from it. This black rain enabled the "sea of life" to one day be formed on those planets such as ours – which most emphatically means our planet is not special or unique within the universe.

Furthermore, some diamonds are a mutated by-product of this vapor crystal structure. They occurred after countless years of mutations and temperature variations, including extreme cooling, because at one time the universe went through a severe "ice age" that lasted millions of years. This period came to exist after the Seven Elders took control of their amoeba. It took them millions upon millions of years to control their amoeba; this was only possible when the universe naturally cooled down. After taming their amoeba, the Seven Elders were able to manipulate the temperature of the universe as they desired from hot to cold and from cold to hot, the same as we would an air-conditioner.

After gaining control of their amoeba, the Seven Elders truly understood the potential of their power, for they could literally point a "finger" and cause a chain reaction. They answered their own question of what to do with the power they possessed. They understood its value. With time, they would exploit that power. They were a part of the universe – they always were – but now they became masters of that universe, and they were in a position to expand their intellect and energy immeasurably, as they desired, by feeding off the electrical energy that came out of the explosions in the universe. This has been "food" for them, as well as for the three Creators who were soon to be created by them.

The initial electrical current that gave the Seven Elders consciousness still traverses throughout the disorderly universe. The Seven Elders guide the electrical current in its interaction with the voids, and the end result is what we see when we observe the universe around us: order originating from chaos.

Interestingly enough, as this current continues to traverse throughout the disorderly universe, it not only grows in intensity and power, but continues to interact with the neutron voids; subsequently, consciousness is created in every neutron void it encounters where the particles are conducive for consciousness to come to exist. As we know, the very thing that turns on the light bulb of consciousness is the electrical current. When these consciousnesses come into being for the first time, they are automatically drawn to the amoeba of the Seven Elders, just as fish are drawn to a fisherman's hook. The Seven Elders therefore continually multiply their parts of consciousness by this means.

It could be said that these countless neutron voids, in the limitless expanse of the universe, are the incubators and nurseries of consciousness: in the wombs of the neutron voids these insentient consciousnesses exist, incognizant that the seminal giver of life – which is of course the electrical current – may one day unleash its powerful "murmurs" upon them.

Once united, and in control of their amoeba, the Seven Elders deliberated over whether they could separate their amoeba and become individual entities, as they were before unification, but now with a great deal more energy. The mathematical formula suggested they could not. One of the reasons their amoebas were trapped in the solid void for so long was that they were disunited; it was only when their amoebas united that they possessed enough energy to control it. There was also a concern that if they tried to divide their amoeba into seven again, they would be helpless to control what happened in the universe during such an attempt. While they are the only constant or force in the universe to maintain order, in this situation they would have put themselves in a position of helplessness and uncertainty.

The Era of the Vision

My actuality, I have made to be seen;
For I have presented to you many clues
To identify the presence of me.
Perhaps the more you know and then understand,
The more of me you will have no choice but to see.
For it is my way of telling you I am
That for instance the moon and sun
From your frame of reference align,
So that moon and sun loom the same size.

Is this one, of many, "chance" signs,
Not enough to tell you there is a me?
How many coincidences do you need
Before random luck you desist to concede?

Now the ingredients were all in place for the Seven Elders to open the door to an orderly development of the universe. For them, designing the order of the universe was like arranging chess pieces on a chessboard. Such was their power and command over the universe. The mysterious elementary forces of the universe spawned the "chess pieces" and the "chessboard" for them. They were a part of all this; for, in creating them the universe created the "players"; for, without the players the chessboard and chess pieces were of no consequence. It was up to the Seven Elders to use the resources available to them – the chessboard and the chess pieces – and invent the game of "chess." They did this by providing equilibrium and balance to that universe so that it remained orderly. This order allowed, from that moment forward, the universe to become a self-developing entity in its own right, using the pre-existing laws of physics. Then they put the equation of life into that game of chess, and that is how we can look upon ourselves today: we are the product of a designer, who came to exist in a universe that itself came about by evolutionary means.

It should be noted that the order to emerge from this initial disorder has only been by the "hand" of the Seven Elders. Order did not come about as a natural process from disorder, as many scientists of today believe regarding the so-called big bang. Chaos can only result in greater chaos, just as disorder can only result in greater disorder. Neither chaos nor disorder can eventuate in the established order we envisage now not merely within ourselves and other life forms, but in our universe and upon our world, each of which is, coincidently, remarkably fit for life. Everything around us appears to have been designed exactly right for life like us to evolve, with just the right mix of chaos and order to give us balance. This should have most atheists and scientists, who are able to look at the bigger picture, at their wits' end when it comes to interpreting the world around them without accounting for an intelligent designer. It is absurd, and a touch arrogant, for them to think otherwise. Tomorrow's humans will look back with amusement at the ignorance of today's humans in light of some of today's theories (particularly Darwin's theory of evolution and the big bang theory) in the same way we look back with amusement at yesterday's theories – such as the debate over whether the Earth was flat, even though the likes of Aristotle argued that Earth was not flat after he made simplistic observations of the shadow of the Earth on the moon, and it was always observed to be round!

One can put aside all seriousness at this point and say, that after reading this book, if atheists and the like still propose a Darwinian explanation for the origin of all species, and the big bang theory as an explanation for the origin of the universe, then they will be the last of their kind, and their fate is as determined as the fate of the last die-hard flat Earth believers!

While evolution is a natural process that occurs *after* creation, evolution cannot give rise to creation as we see it. To believe that the finer details and symmetrical order of all living beings – from the operation of the eye down to the "factories" and "workshops" in each single biological cell – came about by processes of natural selection is outright absurd and crosses the border into fantasy, no matter how glossy the picture painted by Darwinists. Even more farcical is to believe that the brain itself – the most complex and perplexing thing we know of in the universe – could have evolved by some Darwinian process of natural selection! Upon deep investigation of the complexities and amazing processes of the brain, with its trillions of neural connections, no sane person could conclude its design, let alone its sense of being (consciousness), could have occurred by random acts of nature. It is as basic as that and there is no argument to the contrary among persons of sound mind, irrespective of the well-polished protestations!

Furthermore, some scientists believe that as a natural consequence of the big bang, one day the universe could reverse and collapse back upon its origin in what is called the "big crunch." Another theory suggests the universe will keep expanding until it "chills out" in what is called the "big chill." These theories scientists have postulated will all collapse in on themselves one day in a big crunch of their own, because the foundation of all these theories has been built not of solid bricks but of sand, and just as castles of sand wash away will this unstable foundation one day totally crumble. The foundation is weak owing to a missing factor in all of their equations, without which their formulations cannot correlate to any accurate interpretation of the origin of the universe, even of life itself. This missing factor equates to the intelligent designers, whose place in the universe, and whose contribution to the order of the universe, must be conceded.

Without these intelligent designers in the equation of the orderly universe we see, scientists may as well be trying to interpret the existence of a spider's web without accounting for the fact that a spider was the determining factor in its creation.

One thing is for sure – as sure as the study of celestial bodies was instrumental to the development of the calendar – humans think small, which really is appropriate for them to do, as humans are negligible in the scheme of a universe they know comparatively nothing of. To this tiny little planet – which cannot even be seen as an infinitesimal speck in the wider scope of the cosmos – humans have tried to apply evolution as an answer to their very being. It is a noble but hopeless attempt to indulge in their desire to understand themselves. Let us not be mistaken; in the wider gamut of understanding, The Beginning of The Beginning saw the seeds of evolution, and intelligence was the final cause of this evolution: an intelligence based on pure intellect and energy. The basis of our existence is a direct consequence of this intelligence.

Creation in the universe is therefore not unique to Earth, but as abundant as there are stars we see and cannot see in the universe – many of which have their own planetary orbital systems. For, the design of our solar system is based on a standard template used by the Creators throughout the universe to facilitate the evolution of life forms, as we know and do not know them. Upon Earth, and upon all the other planets in the universes teeming with life, first came creation, and then came evolution. In terms of the universe, however, first came evolution, and then came creation. This evolution of the universe gave rise to the Seven Elders. The Seven Elders then became the causal factor in the development of life forms in the universes, to which they provided order.

The First Creation

An old, sacred work, the "Rig Veda,"[iii] documents
A one-wheeled chariot with seven names;
Its single wheel has three naves
— That is, three central parts to it —
And all life rests in the hands of these three naves.

Knowing they had to remain united as one, the Seven Elders came to conclude that down the track they would have to create individual forms of themselves to perform those singular tasks they were unable as one entity to perform. Although the Seven Elders existed as one entity after the unification of their amoebas, their consciousnesses did not unite in the same way; there was no change to their consciousnesses. Imagine your hand but with seven fingers. This is what they were: seven separate consciousnesses, or, Elders, with each Elder made up of who knows how many billions of intellects, which to this day increases in number, and will never cease to increase in number as long as there are neutron voids in the endlessness of the disorderly universe. Each Elder was powerless without an amoeba, and was now joined to this one amoeba like the fingers joined on a hand — the one-wheeled chariot with seven names. Each finger could operate independently only to the degree that the hand would allow. This meant that the Elders were unable to perform individual tasks, mainly because there was the hurdle where, for instance, if one wanted to make something, instead of one, seven would be created. There was only one solution to rectify this dilemma: they had to create less powerful, but nonetheless powerful, Creators who could exist as separate and individual entities in a way they could not. These Creators would be an "extension" of them in a conscious way, in that they would "exist" through these three Creators — the wheel with three naves.

First, the Seven Elders had to "seal" the exterior of the solid void region in which their amoeba came to exist to prevent further chaos in the universe. This was accomplished by "turning off" the "lights" in this exterior region by stopping any collisions (or the like) that were occurring. The lights went out in this exterior region for millions of years, while chaos continued to reign in its interior. Consequently, this external part of the universe went through a period of extreme cooling, and it was in this milieu that the Seven Elders proceeded to create three individual forms of themselves. They would come to be known as the Creators. This number was deemed sufficient, and each would possess tremendous power and intellect. How each Creator would come to possess such power and intellect was through the Seven Elders sacrificing a quantity of both.

When the Seven Elders decided on the number three, it was not an arbitrary choice. Just as the number seven is symbolic to the universe, so the number three is symbolic. This is intriguing, and remains to be understood. Could it be based on the fact that the seed of consciousness can be found in the number three, for, based on our current understanding of the neutron particle, consciousness primarily consists of three quarks? Could one even go further in saying that the quark's twin opposite, the antiquark, is likely to be the original seed from which the universe was formed?

Each Creator was created one by one. How the Seven Elders executed this was by "cutting off" a piece of their "hand," which was their amoeba, and then giving consciousness to this amoeba by having an equal portion of their parts unite with it. This same process was used to create each of the other two Creators. Between creation cycles, however, a long time elapsed. Once they gave up energy for a Creator, the Seven Elders had to restore their energy levels. The first Creator was significantly more powerful than the second Creator, while the second was more powerful than the third Creator.

The Seven Elders modeled the Creators on themselves by giving each an amoeba and many parts of consciousness. The parts of a Creator could unite as one whole part, and could separate into countless individual parts. The paradox is that the three Creators share the same name: Odo. The logic of this demonstrates their oneness, for all their separateness; for, when the Seven Elders summon one, all are expected to report to them. Essentially, the Seven Elders and Creators are fragmented parts of a conscious whole. Thus, to a degree, the Creators and the Seven Elders can be defined as one – after all, the three Creators act out the wishes of the Seven Elders by performing those tasks the Seven Elders are unable to perform in their state. Each of the

Creators can operate independently, and be left alone to create more or less as the Seven Elders can without their "handicap." The duties of the Creators are always provided by the Seven Elders.

Considering that the Seven Elders and the Creators are one at a fundamental level, this book liberally substitutes the name, the Creators, for the Seven Elders and the three Creators, and at times the name, Odo, for the three Creators. The first Creator that was created is the superior of the three, and often a reference to Odo is a reference to this Creator. In *this* book, it is not relevant to distinguish the differences between the Creators.

A Snapshot of the Universe

In the Era of the Vision, the Seven Elders had a plan that they were ready to turn into reality. A part of that plan was to create life as we do not know it and as we know it now. Long before the three Creators came to exist, the Seven Elders calculated all the logistics of life and the possible divergent outcomes — that is, everything was planned to the finest detail, from the paths that would be implemented to the alternatives in case a path differed from their expectations.

The first step for the Seven Elders was to create another means of interacting with the universe, hence the creation of the three Creators. Then, using the blueprint envisaged by the Seven Elders, the three Creators brought order to the area encompassing the solid void region that contained the amoeba and the regions just beyond it, which included several of the surrounding solid void regions. This region became known as "the orderly universe."

The Seven Elders then cloned the infinite universe to produce an additional 48 universes. In total, 49 infinite universes came to exist, and this number exists to this day. The universe we see around us is the original universe from which the other 48 were cloned. Why this number? The Seven Elders applied the formula that governed the creation of six additional universes in the Era of Consciousness. The equation had to be multiplied by seven, to account for the variable of the Seven Elders.

If we are to turn to the popular picture of the universe that scientists have put together in an attempt to satisfy their inherent curiosity for the origin of the universe, we will see a universe originating from a hot and dense state smaller than the size of an atom. How this initial state came to exist, they do not know. Scientists believe that it was from this point of singularity that space and time came to exist. The universe then began to inflate and expand, and in all probability, this expansion is supposed to continue until the universe runs out of energy — the big chill. Until yesterday, another probability was that the universe could slow down and then collapse in on itself — the big crunch. A newer hypothesis seems to suggest that the universe is heading for a "big rip." This is based on data that appear to support the notion that the universe is not slowing down. Because the universe appears to be accelerating, it is said that one day everything in it will be ripped apart into its elemental atomic components.

But wait ... that isn't the end of the story yet! It appears that another theory has "bounced" onto the scene: the "big bounce." According to this theory, the universe collapses in on itself (the big crunch), and then bounces outward once again, creating a new universe. This cycle of collapsing and bouncing is thought to go on and on and on. Therefore, according to these theorists, this may not be the first universe to have existed. As plausible as all this may seem to these theorists, the big bounce still fails to address the First Cause of the universe.

This all reminds one of the days when theologians branded it preposterous and absurd to suppose that the Earth moved at all. Of course, the word of the scriptures was clear in stating that Earth is stationary and does not move, so theologians had to vehemently champion and sustain the word of the scriptures. This meant they had to not just sidestep but quash any exposure to advancements in science. With the big bang theory, scientists have a similar problem to that of the theologians and their scriptures. As knowledge of the universe magnifies, scientists have to ask whether they should keep trying to make an unworkable theory fit, even if it means changing the laws of physics as they go along. The whole point is that if you don't have the blueprint right, then the physics just won't work!

The whole premise of the big bang seems to have come about because of the notion that the galaxies of the universe are moving away from us. This discovery has been hailed as one of the greatest intellectual finds of the past century. (Someone may think that other galaxies are so scared of our getting close to them that they are running away from us as fast as possible! If scientists based the big bang theory on this premise alone, then it would be a logical conclusion deserving of commendation of some sort. It would also then give credence to the evolution theory, in that we did evolve from the fish – perhaps even the one with the "mustache." All that would have been needed then was for scientists to come up with a new fish to incorporate the beard. They assuredly wouldn't be looking for a missing link today if they had followed this hypothesis!) From this motion of galaxies, scientists supposed that the universe was expanding, and here came the answer to the question of the origin of the universe: If the universe were expanding, it must have come from a source of smaller origin. The next thing you know, the big bang theory was born. How simple was that?

Scientists have built their entire theory on a foundation that has a lot in common with more than just a castle built out of sand on the seashore. Just as moths fly blindly in the dark when they have no lights in the sky or magnetic compass to guide them, so scientists have only been able to theorize blindly in the dark, without any point of reference to be guided by in terms of knowledge. In putting their theories together, scientists could even be compared to a blind chicken pecking for food on the ground with its beak and hoping to find a grain of seed amongst endless dirt – in the scientists' case, hoping to find a viable theory!

We know that the universe around us is a picture of order; we also know that beyond our orderly universe lies a disorderly one that the "hand" of order has not yet touched. The question then arises of how we can picture this established orderly universe, which is so remarkably fit for life that we have been able to call it home. This is easy to do. The orderly universe can be looked upon as being in the shape of an orb. Our Milky Way galaxy, like all galaxies, is located within this orb. This means the universe as we see it is finite. If we picture the orb as being invisible, so that everything in it becomes visible, and then we picture this orb as turning slowly, the contents of our universe would appear to be in motion. This means the galaxies, black holes, and all the stellar matter of the universe are moving in the same rotational way, as though the invisible orb itself were turning. We should note that motion by revolution, from the very small to the very large, is a central recurring theme of the universe.

This orderly movement occurs by a natural process of the universe: pressure is the cause of this rotation. This is why the universe requires energy. The energy to facilitate this rotation is derived from natural sources, such as exploding suns, collisions between planets or between galaxies, and the many other energy-creating sources that naturally occur in the universe on a daily basis. The energy derived creates pressure, and this pressure is what makes the orderly universe turn, under the watchful eyes and with the helping hand of the Creators.

Now we can understand how black holes play a vital role in the universe. Their function is to maintain as well as provide balance in all the 49 universes by distributing the pressure that makes the universes turn. Black holes, then, were turned into a vital component for maintaining order, which allows for the presence of life, in the universes. How they maintain order is simple. We already know that there is a lot of destructive energy that comes from many powerful forces in the universe. This destructive energy has the potential to create chaos and disorder in ways that are detrimental to life. This is when the black hole comes into play. There are many black holes in the universe in a deactivated state, available to harness such destructive energy. Even in our galaxy, there are at least a million black holes in a deactivated state. One of the Creators usually activates the nearest one, and the destructive energy is collected and stored within it where it is saved for use for something good in a future time.

A black hole is a space, nuclear-energy collector. It is the "vacuum cleaner" of the universe. It is a place to store energy. The Creators distribute this stored energy among the other universes when it is needed. This process maintains order and equilibrium, and keeps a balance of power among universes, which is necessary considering that all 49 universes to this day support life forms of one kind or another, just as this universe does. In every universe, there are countless black holes swallowing up an unimaginable amount of energy and matter. Anything that disappears into the depths of a black hole becomes recycled into something new, in a new cycle, in another universe or elsewhere in this universe.

Initially, the Seven Elders had a huge problem with black holes in that they were capable of swallowing up everything that was in their gravitational pull. The Seven Elders had few concerns for their existence, but they were always cautious. The only two major concerns in their past involved their unification, and their contact with the conglomeration of the vapor crystal structure. These were about as far as their concerns went. Black holes never gave the Seven Elders an ounce of disquiet for their continued existence, even though black holes were a great threat to the universe itself. At one stage there were so many of them that a lot of the solid void fell into their clutches, which left a lot of space in the universe. This was to the advantage of the Seven Elders in arranging the universe. Indeed, the Seven Elders let this happen purposely. They allowed much of the solid void region to be swallowed into the deep depths of these black holes. Matter became compressed in a black hole, like a large planet into the size of a golf ball. This compressed matter would serve its purpose one day in that it would be converted into energy for distribution elsewhere in the other universes. This helps answer the perplexing question of what happened to all the matter of the solid void, when our orderly universe appears to have so little matter in proportion to the vast expanse of outer space. Had the Seven Elders not found a means to deactivate these black holes, which were a natural product of the universe, the whole of the solid void could have been swallowed up and then eventually blown up!

Before the Seven Elders gave black holes an outlet, a black hole indiscriminately drew all the surrounding energy into its gravitational pull. Some black holes ultimately compacted to a critical point of density where they had no choice but to self-destruct. What the Seven Elders had to do was find a way of harnessing the energy from the black hole and utilizing it in such a way that benefits could be derived. This is precisely what they did: they "deactivated" each one and then gave it an outlet, which it initially did not possess. Since then, the Seven Elders and three Creators have been able to command where the energy from a black hole is to be directed, based on where it is needed. To distribute its energy they must first activate a black hole; then its energy can be sent to any of the 49 universes. The black hole is, then, a dimensional portal, able to open up to any of the dimensional universes, under the guidance of the Creators.

A Teasing Peak at CTC – Time Travel

Layman: What is CTC?
Physicist: Closed Timelike Curve, or CTC for short.
We physicists are too embarrassed
To use the term time travel!
So we came up with this code name.
This way no one cringes, no one giggles,
And, more important, we CAN take ourselves seriously.

As unorthodox as it may seem, humans on Earth will one day be capable of traveling to all of the dimensional universes. To understand how this is possible, we must understand the grand picture of the complete universe. As we exist, we can only see one universe – the one visible to our eyes. All of the universes occupy the same space and time; they are just not visible to us. What then differentiates one universe from the other is the enigma. The answer to this is not as daunting as it may appear at first glance.

Each universe exists in the same space, but in a different cycle of speed. From this, we may infer that the atomic particles in each universe travel at a different speed. How to understand this is by imagining a ruler that is 49 inches long. The first inch represents a certain speed, and each inch thereafter represents a different cycle of speed. If we are to go by Einstein's theory, how fast matter or information can move is set by an absolute speed limit – he determined it to be the speed of light. For example, the light of the sun takes approximately eight minutes to reach us. The light of the moon takes approximately one and a quarter seconds to reach us. The maximum speed light can travel in our universe is set at approximately 300,000 kilometers per second, or 186,000 miles per second. Nothing can thus exceed the speed of light, according to Einstein's theory.

The following is how we can define the 49 dimensional universes on our imaginary ruler:

1. Up to 1 inch is Universe 1 (which is where we exist), with 1 inch being the speed of light. This means this first dimensional universe has its own unique cycle of how fast matter or information can move.
2. Just over 1 up to 2 inches is Universe 2, with 2 inches being the speed of light in this universe. This means this second dimensional universe has its own unique cycle of how fast matter or information can move.
3. Just over 48 up to 49 inches is Universe 49, with 49 inches being the speed of light. This means this forty-ninth dimensional universe has its own unique cycle of how fast matter or information can move.

Of course, the universes do not look like a ruler! As stated earlier, they occupy the same space. Where you are right now, there could be a crocodile-infested river in another dimensional universe. You could be in the center of a sun in another dimensional universe. You could be in the center of a black hole in another dimensional universe. The space you see around you that you occupy, in every direction, is occupied by all 49 dimensional universes. You just cannot see them. The cycle of speed in which everything travels and exists is the differentiating factor that enables you to see and exist in the universe you are in. All the other universes have their own set cycle of speed, with each cycle of speed being relatively normal to its cycle, the same as ours is to our cycle.

Ultimately, this means, if you found a method of traveling over the speed set by Universe 1, you would disappear from that universe and find yourself in one of the other dimensional universes – which universe would depend upon the speed at which you were traveling. If, in that dimensional universe, you were to exceed the speed of light of that universe, you would enter into the next dimensional universe, and so on.

Einstein's Theory of Relativity states that no object can travel at or above the speed of light. The speed of light is said to be the absolute speed limit of this universe. Sound laws of physics appear to govern this, based on the relationship between energy and mass as per his famous equation. This means that the closer an object travels to the speed of light, the more mass it has and the more energy it requires to accelerate, until it requires an infinite amount of energy. The problem with this is that the concept of travel in the universe *is* based on traveling at speeds well in excess of the speed of light of this universe.

As stated above, there is no question that future humans will most certainly one day break the dimensional barrier and travel at speeds well in excess of the speed of light, and be able to travel to all the dimensional universes and not be subject to the time-dilation paradox. (Einstein said that time slows down for the space traveler in relation to the observer, which makes our ideas for travel simply not practical. With the vast distances that exist in the universe, we need to travel fast; yet there remains a dilemma: if time slows down the faster you travel, then when you for instance return to Earth from an interstellar or even intergalactic journey that may have only taken you a few months, many thousands of years may have passed on Earth. There is a lot that is wrong with this, and this will be addressed in another book dedicated to that exciting subject: space and time travel.)

Despite sounding far-fetched – as far-fetched as it would have been if someone told primitive, early man that one day he would leave his footprints on the moon – one day we will even travel at speeds of up to one million times the speed of light. There are quite a few ways for space travel to occur. The concept of space travel, as opposed to time travel, is not complicated at all; it will certainly not happen in the way we envisage it today with our present comic-book theories. (Sorry!) Our technology and limited understanding of the universe, time, and ourselves, for that matter, make it impossible for us to see the direction we will take, just as a caterpillar, in its form, has no way of grasping how it will one day fly. Just as the caterpillar has to transform from one form to another to comprehend how it will fly, so we have to transform our concept of ourselves to understand how we will "fly." Only then can we postulate on the real concept of space travel and even time travel.

For any of this to happen, there are many other things we have to discover first. One of the faraway "high-end" discoveries includes particles that are unknown to us. When we discover these particles, traveling through space will not be measured by the speed of light; it will be measured by the "speed of kenyons." Kenyons are particles that travel at speeds faster than the speed of light. How does one explain something that is beyond one's capacity to truly understand it? The following is a layman's interpretation. Kenyons are particles to which you can "attach" matter. Matter particles can be manipulated so that when you attach them to kenyons they do not have weight.

We know that Einstein said that as you approach the speed of light an object becomes heavier and heavier, which is why it makes perfect sense that matter can never reach the speed of light. As opposed to matter, light (photons) can travel at the speed of light. Photons do not have mass, just as kenyons do not have mass.

Kenyon particles build into "blocks," the same as matter does. Kenyons, though, do not have the same properties as matter; they have similar properties to photons, which enable them to travel in a similar way light does. The difference between light and kenyons is that light has its own limitation, and we know its speed limit in this universe. The kenyon does not have such a limitation; this enables it to travel through all the 49 universes, at speeds of up to one million times the speed of light.

When matter is "converted" into blocks of kenyons to build a spaceship, this spaceship does not need an attached energy source – that is, it does not carry energy such as fuel. Kenyons harness their energy from natural sources in the universe, but have a different energy base. "Universal energy" is "loose" energy that exists in the universe, and it comes from naturally occurring, energy-creating sources like explosions and collisions. Exactly what particles kenyons convert to energy to give them their properties is something we are going to figure out, believe it or not, but a long way off from now! How to "catch" one of these speedy particles is interesting, and it will challenge physicists for some time to come. One clue is that these particles are passing through us all the time.

The faster these spaceships travel, the lighter they become. Sometimes they hit places that are "heavy" and difficult to pass through, or are dangerous. Then they have to go faster, in which case they become even lighter. How does something already light become lighter? When a kenyon spaceship travels through mass it has a tendency to attract mass, which means the spaceship becomes heavy. This weight then slows the spaceship down. This spaceship has a capability to get rid of this mass and thus become lighter. Apart from a capability to "shed" mass, really, the only thing needed on a spaceship of this kind is a brake.

Of this we should have no doubt: as sure as the bending of light has a practical application to astronomy, some civilizations that *do* exist "out there" in the universe manipulate the speed of these particles so as to allow them to travel to all these 49 dimensional universes. Knowledge of this kind is reserved for those civilizations that have reached the ultimate end of technology. This is our future. The weirdness of "spooky action at a distance" (Einstein) is only a small clue to the weirdness of speed and travel and its so-called limitations.

While few would argue that this subject – time travel, or, to use the academic code name, CTC – has captured the imagination and interest of both the novice and the professional, few would suspect that time travel does exist and is possible right now. In our acceptance of its possibility, we must come to terms with knowing that it will not be possible in the way it has been theorized or envisaged to date, so some of its paradoxes and ideas like backward causation – the present negating or causing a past event – are simply not relevant. Of this, this book is certain: some will be reluctant to accept that time travel is outside the current realm of physics and delves into the ostracized branch of metaphysics. Heaven forbid – if physicists want to pursue *this*, they may now have to put their thinking caps on and find a new academically convincing code name to fool us ordinary laymen into thinking they have disassociated themselves from something heretical that ranks high in their culture in the giggle factor!

The Large Hadron Collider

Without pontificating in a disparaging way about all those enthusiastically employed in this venture of uncovering the mysterious forces of the unknown by means of high-energy particle colliders, this book has a direct warning to pass on. Now that we understand what differentiates the 49 universes from one another, and now that we have a snapshot view of the universe, we can see how crazy humans are in their obsession with attempting to solve certain mysteries of the universe with their high-energy particle collider experiments, such as the Large Hadron Collider.

What is so crazy is that some of our scientists are tampering with unknowns of which they know absolutely nothing. This desire for scientists to go that one next step and continually build larger particle colliders is a dangerous game. There is a wise old saying … it started with a kiss, and ended up a marriage! In the case of the Large Hadron Collider, this "kiss" can be our "kiss of death" when it ramps up to its highest energy output.

For those who are unaware, the Large Hadron Collider is situated beneath the Franco-Swiss border near Geneva; the tunnel is 27 kilometers (approximately 17 miles) in circumference, buried between 50 and 175 meters (164-574 feet) underground. This is where scientists experiment with the collision of beams of particles such as protons. For instance, protons are sent in opposing directions in this tunnel, at a speed just under the speed of light; these two opposing beams of protons are then smashed into each other. Scientists believe that when these particles break up they will discover new particles, and recreate a state that existed closer to the initial big bang state – which is a futile exercise when you consider that the big bang is an inaccurate theory, and the evidence that has *overwhelmingly convinced* scientists can at best be considered synonymous with a child's theory of the existence of an Easter bunny to account for the magical appearance of Easter eggs! Of course, some may be up in arms over this statement, because to not accept the big bang theory is to mean you are a crackpot. Can you imagine someone with no academic qualifications – a layman, of all things – reversing the notion of who should qualify as a crackpot?

Some impartial observers of this experiment have proposed a doomsday scenario, even though they do not understand the true implication of where the threat lies. Some scientists involved in the high-energy particle experiment emphasize the importance of the containment field, yet openly admit they have no idea of what will happen when it comes to the creation of small black holes.

Written here is a serious first hand warning that comes from the beyond, based on knowledge of what the future will hold if scientists continue to tread blindly down this path. Imagine our universe as a pool of highly flammable substances. These substances enable our universe to exist and function in the way it does. These substances can also enable our universe to self-destruct with the right trigger or igniters. Imagine a car. Without fuel or gas it will not work. What is needed is the right igniter to start the car and make it work. In just the same way, the particle collider is the instrument that can ignite the universe in such a way that we, and possibly even the next universe if we open up a hole into it, self-destruct.

Scientists are hereby warned:

FIRST: The containment field is inadequate for the highest energy output planned in the near future. While particle collisions are an exciting means of trying to gain more insight into the universe around us, there is a good chance that the containment field presently employed will not withstand the experiment when it runs at full capacity. Several outcomes are possible – the most insignificant one is that the planet and its local surrounds will be destroyed.

SECOND: Breaking up subatomic particles can trigger a chain reaction, and, like a domino effect, the atomic structure of the universe can collapse. We know that subatomic particles are the foundation of the atom; in the right circumstances, when this foundation begins to "dissolve," there is no possibility of reversing or stopping it. Nature took billions of years to make the atom, but stupidity can destroy the atom. Any universe affected (such as Universe 2 if we open up a hole to it in the process) will simply become a black gaseous void, and we will not even have time to blink, as this will only take a second or two to occur.

THIRD: The curiosity and temptation of scientists to understand the elementary world of subatomic particles will cause these scientists to wittingly or unwittingly accelerate particles beyond the speed of light. So far, they have been unable to. The problem is, when particles cross the threshold into Universe 2, such as by exceeding the speed of light (if you know how, you can send particles across the speed of light barrier), the containment field in which the particles are traveling is no longer pertinent. Scientists need to build another containment field in the next universe, which is Universe 2, to contain these particles for such an experiment.

Now that we know that this is Universe 1, and beyond the cycle of speed of this universe lies Universe 2, it should be axiomatic that billions of explosive particles can be unleashed from this universe into an uncontained environment full of flammable substances. Self-destructive ignitions can burgeon, which can mean the beginning of the end of Universe 2, along with our universe.

FOURTH: In the scenario where we facilitate the contact of two universes, magnetic field collisions will also occur, with as much good to come from that as shutting off the sun!

Invariably, no matter which scenario unfolds, whatever happens in the next universe will affect our universe when we create not only an exit out of, but an entrance into, this universe.

Scientists should NOT be proceeding to the next stage of their experiment unless:

1. They know what they are doing. Now they do not! They are currently in a cycle of discovery.
2. They know how to make a proper containment field – right now, they don't have one.
3. They know when to stop – NOW is the stage when they have to stop! The containment field is not ready for the highest energy output scientists are planning! Not to stop is to navigate into seriously dangerous uncharted territory. Our alarm bells should be ringing in this world, as there is great reason to feel alarmed. Just so you know, others out there are!

It is too early for scientists to proceed to the next stage they have scheduled – one where they ramp up to the highest energy output. They should continue with their experiments on the lesser scale they have thus far. There are many "loopholes" scientists have missed, and they should concentrate on filling in those loopholes and making sense of the mathematics that does not make sense at present, to a level where their knowledge is up to date and correct for the stage they are in.

New calculations have to be made, and a lot of work has to be done, if scientists want to proceed with such an experiment. At the moment these scientists don't know what they are doing. The whole experiment has been calculated in total darkness. You could liken these scientists to a kid experimenting with a box of matches in a bottomless pit full of natural gas! On this planet, we are heading to a point in our technology where we can put the lives of ourselves, and countless civilizations, at risk of complete annihilation, and we are oblivious of this! To think ... everyone today is obsessed with the so-called global warming issue — which is nothing but a Chisek-inspired big swindle. If this book's warning is not heeded, and the Large Hadron Collider goes ahead and runs at full capacity, then we certainly may not have to waste our time and worry about such absurd — and this book emphasizes, absurd — things as so-called global warming, because our planet just may not make it that far! It is all madness!

As a distraction ... to those souls, particularly those with self-interests, who are dedicated to the cause of the "big swindle," be aware ... one day in the future, our far, far, far, far-off descendents — further than we can imagine — *will* evacuate this planet when it goes through a cyclical ice age. We are naïve if we think we will stave off this ice age or change any course Mother Earth, Gaia, has plotted before us. Our world is a living one, with its own ups and downs; with its own rhythms and cycles of change — change that is a necessary part of a living planet's cycle. The commitment some have to looking after this planet is not a genuine commitment without self-interest. The way to look after this planet is not being addressed in the manner in which it should. We should remember: if we cannot look after ourselves first, and the distress of our fellow human beings, then we certainly cannot look after something so superior as our planet.

We should also remember: for the distress caused to others by "commitment" based on self-interest, someone will one day be accountable, and this book can assure you that such accountability is not something you will want to be burdened with. Nonetheless, someone will be burdened — someone always is! As sure as the Earth has continually gone through cycles of floods, droughts, cooling and heating, and cataclysmic events — and will continue to go through such cycles as long as it pulses with life — those who deserve to pay certainly will one day pay ... and pay dearly.

Up to now, not many cared if we "cockroaches" (as we are likened to and indeed referred to by many in the community of the universe) on Earth wiped ourselves out through extinction. The time has come that our advancement in such self-destructive technology is a threat to others out there. This is why we are now going to make the giant leap out of existing in the "unknown zone." This book is a part of this process, and in the very near future – that is, in *our* lifetime – exciting things are in store for us.

Finally, this is not fiction or alarmist propaganda; the direct source of this warning has been Odo himself, as implausible as this may seem, and as crazy as the writer may appear in having written it. We need to heed these words if we don't want that Armageddon prophecy of the bible to come true.

The "Expanding" Universe

Pretend that the universe is one big, complicated machine,
Which needs a never-ending supply of energy to run
To maintain order and stay harmonious.
This order and harmony is a non-negotiable factor in the universe,
As it has been designed this way by the operators of that machine.
-A wise man

Each of the 49 dimensional universes is expanding, but not in the way scientists have come to determine. If we picture the orb that represents our ordered universe (this is applicable to all the dimensional universes, because they are more or less clones except they all vary in size, with this universe being the smallest), beyond it lies endless regions of disorder, consisting of the antimatter, neutron, and solid voids (the disorderly universe). Before they created the 49 universes, the Creators controlled the electrical current (the one that gave them consciousness). Once 49 universes came to exist, 49 electrical currents came to exist. These currents to this day maintain a direct connection to one another despite the division. The Creators from then on were able to control every aspect of these electrical currents, including where they went. The areas directly beyond the finite, orderly universe were the first regions the Creators targeted. Once this electrical current created havoc in these regions around the orderly universe, the Creators provided order to these regions and set the embryonic galaxies — that is, the clouds of dust and other matter — in motion. This new space now became an expanded part of the universe, and meant the orb representing the universe became a bigger sized orb. The Creators repeated this cycle many times, not just in this universe, but in all the other universes. This is the only way in which the universe expands, and to this day it continues to expand by the above-mentioned means.

Besides the fact that the Seven Elders need to do something to satisfy their own energy and challenge, they must keep the universes expanding forever.

If a universe did not continue to expand, it would not have enough power to fuel itself. An omnipresent code of the universe predicates that anything which happens must have an engine with energy to keep it going. Therefore, without this expansion, the fate of the universe would be to stop turning. If it ever stopped turning, there is a chance that the Seven Elders may not be able to start it turning again. This would mean a slow death to the universe – perhaps even similar to those forecast by scientists.

The rotation of the 49 orderly universes is reliant on the external power the Seven Elders bring in from our disorderly neighbors. Simplistically put, what the Seven Elders do is, they target the nearby solid voids and "melt" them into power, from which they also "feed." This power is the main way they run the "engine" of the universe and keep the orderly universes functional and operational. The other source of power was covered earlier, and it of course is the black hole. While the black hole recycles existing power in the universe, the orderly universe does not yield enough energy output of its own to maintain itself on a long-term basis. Therefore, the black hole has another purpose: it is a storage facility for the reserves of externally acquired power attained principally to keep the engine of the universe "alive."

To maintain order in the universe, and to facilitate the expansion of order in the universe, the Creators had to calculate how to ensure this universe had an everlasting existence and not fall into the trap of self-destruction. Therefore, in the universe, the Seven Elders and three Creators operate as an "overload switch." You may call them the fuse of the universe, which prevents any undesired self-destruction such as from electrical currents. The Creators' energies operate in a similar way on Earth. A classic example of their handiwork can be seen when a rainbow appears in the sky. A rainbow generally appears in the sky when out-of-control electrical energy is released from a storm cloud – that is, positive energy from a storm cloud is "drained" and this makes its way to the ground. The visual effect of this process is the rainbow. (Have you noticed how a rainbow tames a menacing sky?)

The Seven Elders not only act as guardians against any catastrophe that may threaten the planet; they are the "force" that prevents a universe's destruction by interfering in the processes of that universe. Imagine when the contact of a live positive and negative wire causes a reaction. To avoid explosion, you need a surge switch to redirect the destructive energy elsewhere. When they need to, the Seven Elders and Creators become that surge switch; they absorb destructive energy, which they then redirect. If this energy is not redirected to a black hole, it can be scattered somewhere for future stellar creation. It is a daily occurrence for them to feed off electrical currents in this way. If they did not do this, the universe would cease to exist in an orderly manner, and it would fulfill some tiny part of some scientists' gloomy predictions of the universe coming to a destructive end.

The Seven Elders and the Creators have the capability to create an abundance of electrical energy, so much so that they can facilitate their existence forever. Feeding off the chain reactions in the expanding universe increases their power.

• ⌒

From our context as a human, how can we "interpret" the existence of the Seven Elders and Creators? Metaphorically, when you look at the sky, or into the universe, and see all these gases, these energy forms, and these rainbows, in a way they are all the Seven Elders and Creators. They are like one big hand that is working, operating, and doing. They are pure intellect and energy. They are just all the different gases that produce movements; they move the universe around and mold it, and it never ever stops. Then there is the human factor, which is the intellect, and it goes where it is supposed to go. Everything is like a cocktail where somebody is mixing things up.

The Seven Elders can be thought of as some aspect of the universe that became conscious. (The neutron void and the amoeba.) Imagine the most powerful thing in the universe – like a massive black hole, or even the most powerful supernova explosion. Picture this powerful force as having an energy that keeps it unified and prevents it from ever losing its force of power. Then imagine that consciousness, which evolves in another region of the universe, becomes "attached" to that force of power. Imagine, then, if it were to control that force of power. This is how we should look upon the Seven Elders, only the powerful features of the universe such as massive black holes and supernovas cannot be compared to what the amoeba is. The amoeba tamed the most powerful black hole, just as we "tame" a fire in a fireplace. Activating or deactivating a black hole is as simple to the Seven Elders as turning a tap on and off is to us. The amoeba consumes and feeds off the energy of explosions far more intense than the most powerful supernova, in just the same way a black hole feeds off any small debris that comes into its path. The forces of the universe that look so powerful to us are merely "chess pieces" that the Seven Elders are capable of moving around and arranging without the least bit of inconvenience, if you could put it that way.

In many respects, the Seven Elders and Creators are just like us, and a lot like the species of life on Earth around us. Look at bees: bees spend their lives minding their own business, collecting nectar and making honey. In the process they spread pollen, and also provide a beneficial product from their hard work. Others indirectly benefit from their cycle of existence. The Seven Elders and subsequently the three Creators are not all that different. For, they have a duty, a purpose, and a role in the universe. They keep themselves busy and fulfill their purpose, their challenge, and their goal. Most importantly of all, they are needed and depended upon, every single moment of their existence, so their challenge is to not let down those who are reliant on them. They have created all these life forms in their respective life cycles and are maintaining a universe fit to facilitate all this life, all for one reason: to give themselves purpose. We principally exist for them, as they principally exist for us, and so everything that is with order is so because of them; this is why they are the alpha and the omega, which is just another way of saying the beginning and the end.

In the coming chapters we will have a clearer understanding of the Creators. For now, this book will describe the creation of life, and how we on Earth fit into that equation of life.

2
The Era of the Metaphysical World

Odo once said to me,
When he made the planets, nature, and life forms,
He made them in a dream.
But when the time came that he made the human species,
He made it in a nightmare.
Ever since, the human species has given him a nightmare.
In a sense, this shows that either he is not perfect,
Or, whatever happened probably had to happen.

-A wise man

So it came to be that a new epoch was heralded, known as "The Era of the Metaphysical World," where life became the creation priority. Perhaps the most compelling of all questions we could ask would be how the Seven Elders came up with the formula for life. The answer may not be as straightforward as we would suspect, for, in uncovering the answer we may gain an unexpected insight into the Seven Elders and Creators, who are the first to admit they are not perfect and have made many mistakes and conducted many experiments in the process of attempting to perfect the evolutionary course of life.

If we look closely at ourselves, we should not be surprised to learn that human beings still have not reached their "final cause," which is a desirable outcome satisfactory to the Seven Elders and Creators. In later chapters, this book will provide an in-depth analysis of today's human being, and we will see the degree to which the perfect human being has not been accomplished. This is in no way indicative of our physical form; it is a reflection of our inherent ability to manage the dual forces of nature that act upon us instinctually, called good and evil. Our human physical form, and the health obstacles we face, are subject to the development of our intellect. This means that a developed civilization will conquer such flaws and obstacles that often exist intentionally, by design and not by fault. These "flaws" are intended for death to conquer us, because in our cycle we are not meant to conquer death. This is once again by design. Since the beginning of human creation, the Creators have never stopped "fine-tuning" the human species in an attempt to perfect it, and until the human being reaches the desirable end they seek, they will never stop fine-tuning it. Time has no meaning to them.

The first actuality of life was unlike our physical existence, in that we live in a physical world where our metaphysical body dwells within a physical body that one day decays and dies. This was a metaphysical world where nothing was of the physical, so it was nothing like our physical world.

The Creators found it easy to create this metaphysical life form, as they modeled the design on themselves. A consciousness was composed primarily of neutron particles, and it was charged with several forms of energy, one of which was aura. The direct source of this aura was the Seven Elders. Intelligence, in the form of some kind of electrical energy, was then loaded into it. In the case of human metaphysical beings, they were given an average intelligence level of Mark-3, with the highest score attainable being Intellect Mark-7. (A human with an intellect level of Mark-7 would be capable of using one hundred percent of his brain.) This became the blueprint for all living things. It should be noted that all living things (including the plant world), possess some degree of consciousness.

Before metaphysical life could exist, the Creators first had to create an orderly universe. This they did. Planets had to be found that had already cooled, ready for life to inhabit them in a physical way, and there were uncountable numbers of them. Even though these metaphysical life forms did not interact with the physical planet in a physical way, they still needed the protection the planet afforded; for the spirit world had natural enemies in the universe, such as gamma rays. From this, we may infer that the metaphysical being was not then, and is not now, indestructible. There are many hazards that can permanently eliminate the metaphysical being. If the planet was not ready for habitation, it would "attract" and present undesirable aspects of the universe, so it would be impossible for the metaphysical being to "dwell" there. If the metaphysical being found itself on a planet that was not safe, the planet often gave "warning signs" of the impending dangers; these metaphysical beings learned to read the signs of the planet and therefore took precautions in just the same way as we, for example, would take precautions if we saw dark, treacherous clouds approaching. Learning such survival skills thus became a part of their instinct. Essentially, this was what this metaphysical existence was all about. The physical world had a corresponding metaphysical world that would be used for training purposes. Indeed, the metaphysical world was like a training camp for the soul, to prepare it for its upcoming existence in the physical world.

It was the world of the dream, much the same as our dreams, without the state of waking up to a different reality. The dream was the immutable (permanent) reality. This was the cycle of life of the metaphysical world. In this world, which existed like a shadow, one could experience everything: love, fear, and touch, as in a physical body, but nothing truly existed. Furthermore, feelings were of a different nature to the feelings we experience now; for while these beings had understanding and a tremendous level of intelligence, their feelings were not intensified as our feelings are in this cycle.

In this world of the dream, anything these metaphysical beings wanted they could recreate; all they had to do was use their minds and think about it. These beings could do whatever they wanted with their minds, using the simple power of thought. All this was possible when they learned how, and this was why they were there. For the world in which they existed, in a metaphysical form, allowed knowledge to be introduced to them slowly so they could become seasoned to the physical world when unification with it occurred in the time to come. This way, their training would not only give them a practice run, but also provide for them the instinct required, and whatever else it took, for their survival. In other words, they had to practically experience everything, like children starting from kindergarten, and all these things they experienced and learned became ingrained in the metaphysical chip we call instinct. This existence in the metaphysical cycle gave all metaphysical beings the preparation and seasoning they needed for their existence in the physical cycle, in such a way that encountering everything possible in this metaphysical world would form the basis of their instinct, which they would draw upon in the physical world.

In a way, it was like inputting data into a computer – in this case, a metaphysical computer. If you have a blank intellect, it has no way of interpreting the world around it. A lot of data by way of knowledge and experience have to be inserted into that intellect to enable it to understand not just the senses and functioning of the body, but how to interact with the world around it. If we take ourselves as an example, we take for granted how complicated we truly are because it all comes naturally. Instinct is what trains a brain from birth.

We should look at these first beings in this way: Imagine leaving a baby in the wilderness to fend for itself – how far would that baby get? In the upcoming physical existence, humans and all living things would be like babies, so to speak. They would be grown-ups, still in their "nappies." They would not be given birth to and then reared and educated by parents, as in this cycle we live in. They would not experience a childhood stage. They would not be parents. They would be produced as mature, grown-up life forms that didn't have any experience in life, let alone have any idea of what life was. Therefore, all life forms had to be slowly acclimatized – while in the metaphysical state – to the environment in which they would live in the physical state, and this metaphysical world was a carbon copy of the physical world. Indeed, this applied to all life, such as plants, animals, fish, ants, flies, fleas, bacteria, and even worms.

Let us take a simplistic look at the life cycle of worms, as an example. Like every other living thing in existence, they had to be trained to handle the challenges they would encounter in the physical world. This meant they would exist in a metaphysical form the same as they would in a physical form. The worm was thus given its dirt, and its instinct was acquired – part of which was to "make holes" in the dirt. Many living creatures, including man, then interacted with the worm. All living things studied one another in their own peculiar ways. This built up their instinct of survival. For example, they had to know how to exist, where to exist, where not to exist, and so on. Even plant life had to learn how to exist in its own cycle, just as the worm had to, and develop an instinct of survival. This way, such a life form could face the challenges it would encounter in the physical world, and this experience was what was gained in the metaphysical world.

Many fantastic scenarios came to play out in this environment, which gave all life forms a taste of both positive and negative experiences. The instinct of a species was thus determined by these experiences. The negative aspects of life came to include all those hazards that could be encountered in a cycle of life in the physical world. The best way for living things first to encounter these hazards would be in the metaphysical state. If we look at our dream state, we have dreams where we are killed by some means. The death encounter in this state provided instinctual fear, so that such a situation would be avoided in the physical state. In the metaphysical cycle, life forms could "die" repeatedly, which they could not otherwise do. Imagine if life forms had to learn by making a mistake in the physical world – they would be keeping the Creators considerably busy by dying all the time and having to be reprocessed back into life again! This metaphysical cycle alleviated all of this and provided a shortcut, so to speak, for all living things.

Man's instinct contained the dreams of the future. For, man was given a glimpse of the future in this dream state, by seeing, and by taking part in, the future. The Creators expected humans to make these dreams come true in the physical world. They were thus shown their primitive beginnings and what was possible, right through all the developmental stages to the most superior levels of civilization attainable. All the different stages of technology would become known to them in this "dream" state. By virtue of the dream state, these intellects were acquiring a knowledge bank, and one day they were expected to draw out this acquired knowledge and apply it to their lives in the physical world.

In the same way, we as humans carry the concentrated, compressed knowledge of our future within us. This means that our future – which, although already written, can be challenged – exists in our "dream-chip." All souls, including ours, enter into this metaphysical world when they are first created in order to acquire instinct, before they are placed for the first time in a physical existence in a physical world.

While this cycle provided the avenue for all living things to experience the negative aspects of life, it also provided the opportunity for all living things to learn how to combat or develop resistance to those negative aspects. We can see the results of this in our cycle if we look at bacteria. Bacteria experienced the future just as we did in the metaphysical cycle. In this future, they encountered antibiotics and learned how to develop resistance to them. In this future, we encountered bacteria and created antibiotics. Every living thing in life has experienced its future. This means that in our dream-chip there exists a solution for every possible dilemma that we may encounter in life. Indeed, pre-existing in the dream-chip of every life form is a solution to every problem.

Many varied situations were encountered by us in this metaphysical world, the same as those we encounter when we are dreaming. It gave us, just as it gave the very first humans created, the basis by which to live when our intellects were integrated with a physical world. When it came to the first humans, it took them a while to wake up from their dream world. By now it was reality. That reality became their paradise. For, the day came when all living beings just awoke from their metaphysical dream world and existed as living life forms in a physical world, in a smooth transition where they didn't know if they were still in the dream of the metaphysical state or in the actuality of the physical state. When the first human life form possessed a physical body to house his metaphysical being, this human became the phase-1 human.

Humans became, in this new physical cycle of existence, raw, adult beings with an infant mentality, ironically, with the ability to possess superior knowledge – beyond the bounds of what we could imagine in comparison. They had an unlimited existence, and access to unlimited knowledge. Humans in this world would not have to study, learn, or achieve by means of hard work, as we have to today, as they could receive all their knowledge in their minds by means of direct transfer from the Creators. Easy access to knowledge came part and parcel with these beings. Irrespective of all this, humans were found to have something lacking in them from the moment the first physical human was created. The problem with this flawed human was his mindset. Changing this mindset became the challenge of the Creators. These humans provide a fascinating look into a failed society of human beings.

To understand the steps taken by the Creators to produce the next phases of humans we will be studying, we have to put ourselves in the Creators' shoes. We are currently in the infancy of robotics, and we face the same dilemmas the Creators faced. Just as we are attempting to produce a robot modeled on ourselves, so the Creators produced the biological body and the metaphysical body, which they modeled on themselves. Additionally, the Creators had to create worlds to accommodate those bodies. Then they had to create "the future," which the inhabitants of those worlds were meant to draw out from their dream-chips and recreate. The Creators' mastery of intelligence defies our capacity to understand it. We can see it all around us, though, if we look carefully enough.

We have to input data into artificial intelligence, to teach it simple things such as how to identify an object from its surroundings, so that the object does not become "blurred" into the landscape. Something as simple as this needs to be "taught" to a computer. Once we finally overcome the physical impediments of a robot, and we input all the data it requires to interpret the world around it, then we have to look at its emotions. Knowledge along with memory is not a complex feature of a computer, just as it is not a complex feature of a human brain. It is only in its dormancy in us, at this stage of our development, because we have not conquered our emotions to be able to access most of our knowledge.

There is much more to creating a human and then giving it feelings, as we will see in the next chapters. When you give your robot emotions, which is usually the last step you take once you have overcome all the other aspects of its creation, you have to be able to figure out how to keep that robot on the right path, the path you want it to travel on, so that it fulfills the objective and the destiny you had for it when you designed it. The greatest challenge of the Creators has been the question of how to make a human become what they initially conceived it to be. This is still the challenge today, as we will discover as we progress through this book. We will also uncover what is required of us to become that greater human that is given access to his dormant knowledge. When that day arrives, we as humans will have become what the Creators desired of a human the day they first conceived one. The next three chapters give an absorbing look at the steps the Creators took to create their world inhabited by their "robots."

3
The Phase-1 Human

Ancient priests and men of wisdom
Spoke of being handed down knowledge
Of a time when man lived upon an earth
Without work, hardship, pain, or death,
With all the good he could desire.
This man was incorruptible,
Since he was made in the likeness of his creator.
Some called this man Adam and Eve.
Some called this world the Garden of Eden, or paradise.
Others called this civilization the golden race.
To the Creators, this was the forgotten race.

The following is an account of the phase-1 human existence, otherwise known as "The Era of the Creators."

A theater based on matter came to exist and predominate in the universe, and in the shadow of that theater was a separate arena that became consciousness. Antimatter completely lost its dominance, and in the scheme of things forever forfeited its place or its chance at having that "vital spark." In some sense, the universe "knew" which way to steer itself, and it "paddled" its "oars" until everything that came to take place seemed to have an impetus for its being, so it was entirely natural that in respect and reverence of the universe creating the metaphysical, and having a tie with it, the metaphysical would exist as one with the physical. Life would be born from the dust of the universe; it would exist on its earth; it would live from its earth. And in that being that was born of earth was put sentience, which was of the metaphysical. The physical and the metaphysical would become one, and the whole of the universe would breathe life. Nothing was wasted: everything had purpose: everything bore a place: everything was as it was meant to be, as though the universe had this in mind when matter engaged to eclipse the sterility of the antimatter void in The Beginning of The Beginning.

Now, perhaps, we can see why it was always the intent of the Creators to unite the metaphysical body with a physical body in a physical world, where that physical body would house the metaphysical being for the term of its physical existence. What would have been the point of creating physical worlds if no creation were to interact with those worlds in a physical way? The whole point of this was to enable life forms to evolve in the physical arena of existence.

Thus, it came to be, in this first phase of human existence, that the Creators made it possible for the physical body and the metaphysical body to become united in the physical realm. The Creators made this original physical world, for their first physical creation, a Utopian existence. They wanted their first human creation to have almost everything they as Creators had, so they gave their creation everything of value to them: everlasting life and knowledge. Just as the Creators modeled the human metaphysical form on themselves, so they modeled the human physical form on themselves, in that they gave humans an unlimited existence and an amassed level of intelligence as soon as humans attained consciousness in the physical form. Humans were not given the highest level of intelligence they could have been given, which mirrored the past of the

Seven Elders in that they did not possess their highest level of intelligence when they attained consciousness. They had to evolve from a starting point, and this is what they expected of humans.

In awe of intelligence and eternal life, the Creators wanted to make life a lesser but "equal" version of themselves. Through their creations they would see themselves, feel themselves, and be a part of that which they had created. In a direct and indirect way they would exist through these creations. What was for their creations was in a way for themselves. What was given to all their creations was what they wanted to be a part of, to feel, to see, to have, to know, and to become. For they were their creations; indirectly the Creators were to become a part of the physical world of the universe, and thus they gave their creations the best they could give. This is the circumstance by which the first creation came to have everything good that could be received.

The type of intellect the Creators gave conception to was one that was limited, and in a sense programmed, where knowledge had to be preloaded into the individual. This means that these humans were born with a type of genetics where they were super intelligent upon birth, with intelligence levels ranging from Intellect Mark-1 to Mark-3, and that was about it. They were not capable of supplementing their intellects, even though this was an objective.

Had this human being desired it, virtually all knowledge was available to him – on a platter, so to speak – as this human was capable of using up to seventy-five percent of the capacity of his brain. Today, we don't even use five percent of the capacity of our brains, and our brains cannot begin to compare with the brain of the phase-1 human. Picturing what a human can accomplish when in command of such a brain is beyond our imagination. The Creators expected this human to one day evolve to the point where he was using one hundred percent of the capacity of his brain. In achieving this, he would have reached a level of Intellect Mark-7. It should be noted that no human to this day – with the exception of one – has reached Intellect Mark-7, but there will be a civilization based on planet Earth that will eventually reach Intellect Mark-6.

The physical structure of the brain of the phase-1 human differed from the physical structure of the brain we as humans have today. We possess both a conscious and a subconscious mind. This human had a brain that was not "partitioned" in this way; his brain had one large conscious mind. The model of brain we possess today has a limited and tiny conscious mind that could even be said to be ninety percent "asleep." Even if we wanted to possess the type of intelligence this first model of human possessed, we are physically prevented from possessing it now because of the type of brain we possess. However, our limited conscious mind does have some restricted access to our subconscious mind, which is where most of the knowledge (such as past lives and memories) residing within us lies — hence the earlier reference to us being ninety percent asleep.

These phase-1 humans were, in effect, the Creators' first children, and they spoiled them to a degree — as many of us are guilty of doing with our first child, grandchild, or even German Shepherd. What is ironic is that they gave these first humans almost everything; eventually they came to conclude that it was best to give humans nothing, and let them work toward attaining everything — which is where we as a civilization come into the picture. The so-called misery and pain we experience now can be attributed to this original race of human beings, and this is discussed in detail in later chapters.

Our ancestors have made reference to this race of human beings that was given a Utopian existence in the paradise, or the Garden of Eden. To this day, interestingly, humans on Earth are looking for the location of this so-called Garden of Eden. This exercise should prove futile after reading this chapter, because the term is a symbolic reference to this race of humans and certainly not to any location on this planet. Unequivocally, for the record, this planet never had a Garden of Eden. Adam is symbolic of all male humans; while Eve, female humans. This original Eve was created equal to Adam; she was not created from his "rib" as the Eve of intellectually encumbered humans (such as our race) was.

In this Utopian existence, this new physical realm, nothing of the negative side of life, such as the pestilence we experience now in our world, existed. Evil had not been invented. There was only the "promise" of something good — at least the Creators desired it to be so, and gave it every possibility to be so. When this book says there was nothing negative, this means no pain, no evil, no hate, no greed, no death, and indeed none of its opposites such as love as we know it now. The form of love that existed in this period was not the form of love we experience today. An example of this type of human being would be Spock from the television series *Star Trek* in terms of his lack of feelings. It could also be said that they did not face the same kind of challenges or hardships we face in this current human existence – where we experience both a positive and a negative influence – because these hadn't been invented yet. There was not one of man's struggles to survive, with which we are so familiar in our world.

The family unit, as it exists today, had not been invented then and did not exist. Men and women did not procreate. Entire civilizations of female humans existed with not one male human living amongst them. They had no need to interact with the opposite sex, as there were no feelings of desire, which meant there was no sex. Humans were "manufactured"; in other words, they came to exist ready-made. To understand these civilizations, one must realize that human beings were mass-produced by the Creators, as though on a factory assembly line, as mature adults. Babies, children, teenagers, and even old people did not exist. There were only young adults who never grew old. Once the Creators produced them, they would wait to be occupied with a soul and energized with aura and the other forms of energy.

The design of the body the phase-1 human possessed was basically the same as the design of the body we possess. It too sustained its existence from its planet, but in ways that were unlike our sustainability. The phase-1 human body suited the intellectual standard of life those humans were capable of having. For instance, they communicated by means of telepathy and not by means of speech. The physical body was not designed for manual labor; it did have the capability of moving things with mental powers using a telepathic, magnetic field.

For instance, this human could use the power of his brain to generate a magnetic field (using an existing magnetic field) that was opposite in charge to the magnetic field of the object he desired to move. So if the object was negatively charged, this human would generate a positive magnetic field. The strength of the mind was capable of providing the force required to make objects of any weight lift and move using the simple force of attraction. Once a force strong enough and opposite in charge was generated, the finger could be used as a guide to move any object to the required location. Our minds will one day have this potential when we develop to the extent that we are using seventy-five percent of the capacity of our brains. This requires us to attain knowledge, develop our intelligence, and possess the type of body that has the makings to conduct such a force.

It would not be surprising then to learn that these humans did not sit down and eat meals as we do. For one thing, they didn't have chairs, tables, or even homes. A perfect example of how they produced food would be to cite the way

Jesus Christ was able to produce tons of fish from just the one sample. He was able to manipulate the atomic particles in the air to create the fish. Using this same principle, these humans met their nutritional needs and sustained their lives through the manipulation of atomic particles in the air. This human was never hungry, but if he knew there were nutritional deficiencies in his body, he merely thought about what particles were missing and then created them from the atmosphere. These particles then appeared around the body by way of small "stars" of color, before being absorbed by the body.

Aura, the invisible energy found around all living things, was the prime source of all their nutritional needs. They did not discharge waste as we do, although they did sometimes discharge a liquid waste, which is another way of saying they did not enjoy food as we do or eat for pleasure. They did instinctively chew on fruit and digest the liquid from that fruit, which accounts for the liquid waste, but they did not eat the fiber. They also did not eat vegetables. They certainly did not eat bacteria carriers such as meat. Their diet was pure so that their bodies maintained purity. (Our bodies, in contrast, are designed for impurity.) All living things did digest traces of something, and that kept their digestive systems working to a degree. All organs had to function – even in some small way – to prevent them from "drying up."

They did drink water – this has always been a vital ingredient for any living being; therefore, they excreted this form of waste. Water was drunk directly from the natural springs or rivers of the planet. The principle of breathing oxygen for survival also applied to these humans. You could almost say that this human treated his body in the same way we treat an automobile, in that when it gets low on fuel we fill it up with fuel; the same with oil and water. Whatever goes in gets used and nothing is wasted. After all, the body of the phase-1 human was designed so that it did not decay or age.

This method of satisfying nutritional needs applied to all the living species of the planet. In their life cycles, living creatures did not prey on a weaker species in a predatory style of existence; the food chain did not exist simply because no living thing consumed food, as we know it. All living creatures, big or small, were friends and could live together – there were no enemies with a predatory instinct. Whether it is plant or animal, the same variety of species that exists on our planet to this day, or existed on our planet in the past, existed then, although the living world of plants and animals had different forms of structures and bodies. None possessed reproductive facilities. Everything existed and lived forever. Trees, for example, were created mature, and then their genetic instructions were such that they lived forever. There was no pollination or "active" seed produced, as the Garden of Eden was made to last evermore. Almost nothing died. Everything was in equilibrium.

The living world of plants and animals had a superior level of intelligence in that cycle than our living world has in our cycle today. In the Era of the Creators, all living things had an ability to communicate with one another based on the "Universal Language." In our cycle, the living world has this ability, but to a lesser degree. Just look attentively at your German Shepherd with this in mind and you should see it! The problem with our world is that there is no equilibrium in humans, and equilibrium enables such communication. (Equilibrium, and the Universal Language, are explained in detail elsewhere within this book.)

In every sense, the cycle of the natural living world was much the same as the human cycle that existed. For instance, every living thing in the natural world existed with some form of consciousness in its physical "cocoon." The intellectual capability varied from species to species and suited the size of the brain possessed by that species. Plant life also contained a genetic code, a "brain," and consciousness. In other words, every living being in existence – whether it, for example, be a plant, an animal, a bacterium, or an insect – possessed (as it possesses now) some form of consciousness, and therefore possessed (as it possesses now) some degree of intelligence that was relative to its survival needs. This brings forth interesting implications for vegetarians, in knowing that plants too have a degree of consciousness, feelings, and most definitely intelligence!

That this original world was a very different world to the one we live in and experience today is obvious. It was intended to be a superior world intellectually; however, it was a world the Creators were not "happy" with in terms of its outcome – and this was directly attributed to the biological creation called man. For, humans were found to be unable to succeed on their own without the intervention of the Creators. Without this direct intervention, these civilizations of humans declined and would have disappeared totally. Humans of this era did not have the humanity that humans of today's era have. These humans were happy with their status quo and had no reason to achieve, or to be ambitious, and they certainly had no challenges. To understand this type of civilization, one has to look at the humans in this way: they were a civilization of do-gooders, which is to say that even if you went to kill them they would say, "That's OK. That's good." Even if they knew they were to die they would say, "That's OK. That's good."

The genetic predisposition of these humans was deliberate, you may say, for experimental purposes. To a degree, the Creators did not count on these humans not thinking for themselves at all. When they created them, the Creators considered all the paths humans could take, and anticipated all the contingencies required to redirect the path civilization was heading on. For the Creators, it was like a game of chess in that they knew all the possible moves in advance; therefore, they always had a countermove for any move made. The notion that these humans may not be inclined to achieve and succeed on their own, and as a result may simply wane, because they would not have the constitution or the propensity to survive of their own accord, certainly came as no surprise. Knowing this was a likely outcome, the Creators still had to commit the natural process of evolution to these humans, and they did this in order to evaluate the extent of their developmental progress, before redressing the wanting factors of the human being.

Realistically, the final analysis of these humans was ... they only cared about one thing: how to amuse themselves with entertainment. Singing, dancing, and music – the instruments were mainly the harpsichord and the flute – played a great role in their lives. They spent their entire lives merely enjoying themselves and seeking different modes of entertainment. Mind you, they did not produce any of these instruments or vehicles of entertainment. Everything had to be produced for them by the Creators. They were, however, happy to learn how to play the instruments, which they did in no time at all and they did extremely well.

Just as you give your dog a bone or a toy to keep him busy and entertained and subsequently leave you alone, so the Creators gave "toys" to these humans to be left alone. There were so many humans, all scattered throughout the universes, who always wanted something from the Creators. Imagine, telepathically, these humans yelling out their different needs all at the same time in the same voice! They were in direct contact with their Creators by means of mental telepathy – after all, in every way these humans were their children. Instinctively, these humans were aware of having Creators in the sky, and were well aware that if they wanted something they only had to ask for it mentally and they would receive it. They looked upon the Creators as being their "father" in the stars, just as a child looks to his parents for support. These grown-up humans behaved like children; realistically, they were children, without responsibility, care, or desire for anything in life apart from being amused. These habitual communications were a constant interruption to the Creators, so in order to be left alone the Creators always had to give them a new toy, so to speak.

For example, a group would complain of their boredom directly to the Creators and request some form of entertainment. Not long after, a sheep, a donkey, a crocodile, or some other animal literally appeared out of nowhere for them. An animal became the focus of their entertainment, and the manner in which they entertained themselves was by chasing it with a whip – a favorite old toy they were once given. After a while, they rested under the plentiful fruit trees, and then chewed on fruit that they then spat out at the animal or one another. When this activity no longer satisfied or fulfilled their desires because of its monotony, they once again contacted the Creators telepathically and requested another toy. One of the Creators felt obligated to shower them with something different, so once again it simply appeared before their eyes, like magic. The Creators reached a point where they never created anything that didn't already pre-exist on the planet – not when these humans were unable to help themselves and use their own initiative to satisfy the ennui and sameness of their lives. The Creators had a moral obligation and duty to look after their children in this sense, and were committed to the fullest – thus they gave them a new animal to chase whenever they requested a toy.

Often these humans chased one another with whips. No one felt pain or was capable of being injured – this applied to all the life forms, including the animals that were whipped; for the bodies of all living species then had capabilities to heal automatically.

These people just loved doing stupid things, such as throwing rocks and trying to hit fish, especially in shallow beds, where the water was as beautiful and clear as a human tear. They chased goats, for instance, and then wrestled each other for fun. If they had the opportunity they would hang onto the tails of large birds while they were in flight. These people had no fear of flying and used large birds for this activity. They had no real fear of anything, apart from natural phenomena such as thunderstorms and gamma rays. This "fear" was built into their instinct for survival.

Their entertainment utilized the natural resources around them; there really was nothing else that was available to them because they didn't use their brains to invent anything challenging or entertaining. These humans had literally nothing to do; they were bored, and this is why they kept asking the Creators for some form of entertainment, on a non-stop basis. If they liked something the Creators gave them, they enjoyed the activity non-stop, over and over.

They were nothing but a nuisance to the Creators. In the case of the ones who were constant annoyances, the Creators implemented a transmission barrier so they were unable to communicate to them anymore. In the very beginning, when the Seven Elders saw how these humans were living, they became so "sick" and "tired" of them that they gave the Creators the job of looking after them. The Seven Elders didn't want anything to do with these humans whatsoever. These humans drove the Seven Elders "crazy," so to speak, to the point where the Seven Elders just passed them on to the Creators to look after without further notice, which did not impress the Creators at all. Can you imagine! These humans even had to be dressed by the Creators. They could not possibly produce their own clothes. When they wanted a change of clothes, they simply wished for whatever they wanted to be wearing and the Creators would instantly provide such attire for them. Just as we have no choice but to provide for our children while they are dependent, so the Creators had no choice but to provide for their "children," who were just as dependent on them as our children are on us.

As for the material of their vestures, it was usually cotton; the women wore modest clothing, with skirts or dresses below the knees and short-sleeve tops; men also wore short-sleeve tops, along with trousers. They did not wash their clothes, by the way; they merely replaced the ones they wore whenever they desired.

The hairstyles were conservative. One woman, for example, with blonde hair had a bob with a fringe. Men had short hair, with the top cut tabletop flat. The sides were neatly trimmed. The hair these humans possessed never grew any longer than their shoulders and this way was "manageable." The type of immune system they possessed meant it was impossible for them to get lice or skin diseases. If they wanted a haircut the Creator was "happy." He liked having them come up with different ideas regarding the way they looked or dressed – this meant they were evolving in some small way! As far as the haircut was concerned, the Creator invented a hairdresser, who was equipped with all the necessary hairdressing gear to attend to anyone who requested his services. This invented human was one of Odo's countless parts.

To be identifiable to the Creators, each human was allotted a name, and this was put in his "software" when he came to life. This was also branded on his forehead like a tattoo. The letters were hieroglyphs.

To understand the lifestyle of these humans, for a start, they did not live in houses. There were no buildings – humans were not prepared to use their brains to build them! In reality, they had no need for them. Homes evolved as a necessity for humans in terms of the protection they afforded. First, their environment was a paradise, so they had no need for this type of security. Secondly, the type of body they possessed had such a strengthened immune system that there was no requirement for sleep, so these humans did not sleep as we do. Furthermore, they had no possessions. They did not possess a comb or a handbag. Such things did not exist. They only wore the clothes on them and that was it. When they bathed they did not need a bathroom as we do. They did not even have soap. The women showered under a waterfall, while the men found a shallow creek, no deeper than their knees, and usually jumped in, bottoms first! These humans could not swim because no one taught them. It did not once occur to them that they could swim in water of any depth. They never, ever ventured into water deeper than their knees.

They lived outdoors, often near a river because they loved the flow of the river and the sound of its music – not only did it make lovely, natural sounds; it gave them the opportunity to watch the fish pass by. They loved to paddle their feet in its water; the only thing to mar this activity was when a fish came by and bit one of them with its sharp teeth. Catfish fascinated them. They loved to catch them and pull them up out of the water by their "whiskers." This had its hazards, as sometimes a fish would slap one of them on the face with its tail, or one of them fell into the river, sometimes to be carried away by the current, never to return. If someone fell in the river, no one would even think to try to rescue this person.

Once, one female human waded a little too far into a stream. A strong current was able to pull her away. Her nearby companions only had to offer her an outstretched arm. No one did. No one cared. Everyone did watch her drift away.

When it rained they became wet. This didn't warrant a home, because they liked getting wet, and because they were physically incapable of catching a cold or getting sick. The type of body this human possessed was like a fortress. Nothing was capable of "invading" it. When it rained they simply looked up at the rain to find out where it came from. In many cases, when a violent electrical storm hit the area, they dispersed like fish in water in the blinking of an eye, until the storm subsided. They then looked for a new mode of entertainment, such as a new river, with new fish.

It is hard to imagine that these humans possessed an amazing potential; the problem was, they didn't need to, or want to, do anything. They felt there was nothing for them to do; they were bored. Stupid things amused them. They only accessed the knowledge that suited them when it suited them. They were too lazy, and as they were fully provided for, there was simply no need to access knowledge. This human was a child who never grew up, and who never wanted to grow up. Life was too easy. What was remarkable was that this "superior" race of humans could not even invent the wheel. This race of humans, spread throughout the universes, from the time it was conceived, did not progress or evolve any further than asking for new toys, new clothes, or a new hairstyle.

·⤴

These humans socially interacted with one another and developed friendships. As a group, they usually traveled from planet to planet. Of all the living species, it was only man that had the power to travel anywhere in the universe. All a human needed to do was exchange his carbon body for his neutron-based body, which was "hanging" in the "wardrobe," so to speak.

Deadly gamma rays, which naturally occur in the universe because of explosions, were a serious threat to these humans from time to time. When the threat was near, a human merely entered his wardrobe. This process was done by thought alone. Wardrobes had no doors; they were approximately two feet in diameter, tube-like, and transparent. Humans used these wardrobes in threatening situations as we would use a bunker in an air raid. These wardrobes were the only places that offered them protection.

The wardrobe was also used for celestial travel. Using his wardrobe, a human was able to travel in his neutron body at the speed of thought to whatever planet in whatever galaxy he wanted. In his neutron body, however, the human appeared invisible. To interact with the physical world he was on he had to change back into his carbon-based body. This is what humans did in their wardrobes. These wardrobes were in a way like superman's phone box, in that a wardrobe was used to convert a human into either a neutron body or a carbon body.

When each human was created, that human was automatically given a special protection chamber, just as a snail is given a home on its back. You cannot, for example, create a snail and leave it in the world without its own natural defenses. The Creators had to provide for all species their own natural protections to ensure their survival. Some creations were given the instinct and facilities to draw upon their surroundings for protection and defense; others, including humans, had to be given theirs. With no natural protection for what the Creators regarded as the most superior of their creations, humans were given these wardrobes.

This is an example of how man was created in the likeness of the Creators. Man was given the same liberty to travel in the universe as the Creators had. The wardrobe was the medium given to him to do this. Man was given an astonishing opportunistic existence; what was inopportune was that he did not have the capacity to know what to do with that existence, or know how to treasure and value that existence. The old adage applied to this race of humans: humans did not use what they were given in the way they were meant to, so, in the end, they lost what they were given.

This wardrobe was indestructible, and it was invisible to anyone but its owner. It was meant to offer protection to a human from the weather and the deadly rays he could encounter on the planet he was on. When the Creators gave humans these wardrobes of protection, they expected them to one day learn to create their own shelters and travel facilities – all those visions they had been given in their dream-chip. The Creators expected that with this knowledge humans would advance and create the kind of world they were given a vision of when they existed in the metaphysical world. The Creators never anticipated these wardrobes would be used by a race of humans to play hide and seek in!

When it came to traveling on a planet, a human only had to think he was in his neutron body and instantly he would be. His neutron body enabled this human to travel anywhere on that planet he was on using his mind and not his wardrobe. When he arrived at the desired destination he only had to think about being back in his carbon body.

Gamma rays were really one of the main sources of danger for these humans, and for any living being in the universe. When such a threat arose, the Creators telepathically warned all living things in the galaxy that gamma rays were on the way; this way, all humans took precautions. These humans stayed in their wardrobes for protection until the gamma rays passed, and this usually occurred quickly. Often the Creators intervened and created a neutral zone around the planet so the gamma rays bounced off it.

Generally, apart from some natural hazards they had to be cautious of, the lives of these humans were carefree and dedicated to fun and fun alone. You have to ask yourself a question: would you want to work if you didn't have to and if things were provided to you for free?

The attitude, not to mention the way of thinking, of these humans is epitomized by a response given during a conversation (telepathic, which was their means of communication) between two of them by a campfire. One of the parties stated, "Why would I burn my hands putting wood in a fire when there are others who are stupid and don't know anything, and will use their hands for such occasions when I tell them?" Most of the time they couldn't find such a human, so they didn't bother having a fire. They had the mental capability to do anything. They could even put wood in a fire without once touching that piece of wood; the problem was, they knew the theory of using the mental force of attraction, but they were too lazy to practice it.

It must be understood that in any civilization there will always be malfunctioning humans born. Even though this race of humans had the capacity to possess a tremendous amount of knowledge, there still was, as there always will be in any civilization, the type of human who can be used by others. Such humans did not have the capacity to understand that there was anything wrong with them. Others understood, but didn't care in any way. If, for example, someone were lying on the ground bleeding to death, no one would pay attention to this person whatsoever. Some humans did malfunction to the point where they died. You would wonder: wasn't there a doctor or someone to turn to for assistance? It may be hard for us to picture such a society, where there was no reason for anyone to need a doctor. Doctors did not exist. Professions did not exist. Not only were there no people to count on at that time who had the ability to come to your aid, but there were simply no people who would come to assist you by choice under any circumstances! There was no structure in this society; there was no leadership; and there was absolutely no humanity.

Take us as humans. In the circumstance where we see a cockroach struggling on its back – it has a shortcoming, as the turtle has, in that no matter how much it tries to turn over onto its legs, there is little chance of it succeeding – we as humans would never come to its aid and turn it over. This is how these humans felt about their fellow humans. What these humans would do, however, was step on a human in this circumstance (just as we step on and kill a cockroach), and even have fun jumping up and down on this victim, so that in a while he became dust and all traces of him were swept away with the mysterious susurrus (hissing) language of the wind.

It was not an isolated case of one person jumping on a dying human. In a disgraceful display of inhumanity, sometimes there would be hundreds pushing one another out of the way to get on top of the dying person. Unlike vultures in our cycle of life fighting over a carcass, and plucking up any scrap of feed they can from it – principally because of their instinctive need to satisfy the hunger drive – as many humans as possible would jump on a dying human in a frenzy principally for personal entertainment. Every finger, every toe, and every body part of a dying human were crushed and trampled and stomped on until the vestiges of a human became nothing more than the fine fragments of particles from which that human was made. Yes, a human was eventually reduced to a grayish powder, but initially that human was able to see – and yet, ironically, not care in the least about – the frenzy of his fellow humans, with every breath that was ebbing away. Becoming powder was the disassembly process of the physical body of this human species. The soul would return to the Creator, and then be sent somewhere else to be "reassembled" in a new body. A death in this world was a rare occurrence, and therefore provided great entertainment to these humans when it occurred. As much as we may view this as a disparaging indictment of the type of human to have existed, we must remember that such behavior was as dispassionate to these humans as stepping on and killing a cockroach is to us!

Moreover, this was by no means a perfect civilization – far from it, even though the human make-up comprised nothing but complete "goodness." If we think that by striving for complete goodness a desirable human outcome can be attained, our thoughts would be completely unfounded. Conclusively, an undesirable human being would be the result.

These humans did not have the will to survive on their own. Despite all the weaknesses we as humans have, one thing we can be proud of is having an independent intelligence, which is something the phase-1 human did not have. Indeed, phase-1 humans were the complete antithesis of humans today; they were unable to survive, to succeed, or to fail on their own. (Now perhaps we can see the wisdom of "failing" and look at it not in the light of failure, but in the pride of having attempted to achieve.) One of the main reasons for this was that these humans had no negative ingredients within them, such as greed. Without this single ingredient within the human, a human had no propensity to strive to achieve, to attain knowledge, or to advance. These humans were given a level of intelligence when they were created and they did not move any further above this peak. On the contrary, they languished because this intelligence was useless to them. Without ambition or drive there was nowhere for them to go; their only fate was that of stagnation.

The problem with this world was that these humans didn't need to work, to sleep, to eat, and so on. After all, they were not forced to live and sustain their lives from the elements of the planet as we in our physical world are. We, for example, have to plant corn from which we can make bread – this is how we basically work to live and ensure our survival. For argument's sake, they couldn't possibly plant corn. These humans possessed the knowledge to do anything they could want to, but they couldn't care less about actually doing anything – why would they? All they needed to do was ask for it – whatever it was they wanted, they could command it using their minds at the speed of thought. The problem was that these humans did not use their brains to think this far. It was just the same as when it came to swimming. It never occurred to any of them that they could learn to swim. In the same way, they did not access knowledge from their brains.

Although the human being was modeled on the Creators, that human being lacked the same sense of purpose, vision, and motivation. Indeed, one important thing differentiated the Seven Elders from their creation: challenge. Even the Seven Elders were not without challenge. Challenge was forced upon them by the universe. The circumstances presented to them by the disorderly environment that gave them consciousness meant they were perpetually confronted by challenge. One day they overcame the challenge of the disorderly universe and made it orderly, and then created life to challenge them. Unfortunately, when they gave their first human creation everything good that they as Creators possessed, they left out a crucial thing that was needed for humans to take after them and follow the path they wanted them to follow. Thus, the failing of this human was the result of not being presented with challenge.

The Creators were aware of their "mistakes" when they made phase-1 humans. This was by no means the type of human to produce the epitome of intelligence that the Creators sought. The Creators did not receive any sense of gratification from the creation of this world; they gave these humans in this world almost everything, but these humans did not try to do anything for themselves. Despite the power of knowledge capable of being possessed by these humans, the cycle of life turned out to be a lazy one for them. This type of intelligence was therefore a useless one.

One of the two biggest mistakes the Creators made was creating a so-called perfect human in a perfect world where there was nothing to challenge that human; the second mistake was divulging themselves to their creations, who made them "sick to death." In the future they would never allow this to happen again — that is, they would never create a civilization that would require their direct intervention on a daily basis. This is why the current life cycle of humans is a self-sustaining one, where the Creators do not interfere in it directly. Not only have they given us free will and left us alone; they have given us a new ingredient in our genetic make-up: a bite of the proverbial apple! This ingredient, the bite of the apple, is what distinguished the next phase of humans from this first phase of humans.

Some ancient writings, such as the Old Testament, refer to this paradise, to the tree of knowledge of good and evil, and to the apple from which Eve, symbolic of female humans, took a bite. All of our ancient texts and myths can now be revisited and reinterpreted in view of these chapters. We must, when examining texts and myths that have come down to us through the ages, take into consideration the consequence of the passage of time and the changes in their interpretations; the intelligence level of the audience they were intended for; the allegorical symbolism used to describe unknowns; and, of most relevance, the reinterpretation by vested interests or ignorant parties. These would have resulted in the subsequent loss of the original meaning of these texts and myths.

Much of the ancient works passed down over the ages were drawn from oral traditions, and these oral traditions were often derived from factual material. But we cannot take these ancient writings literally. For instance, in the bible there was no real apple. There was not even a single Adam and Eve. We have to look for the truth that has often been conveyed by crafted storytellers, who were able to turn a complicated history of events into a simple story that illiterate people could understand. It is our job to discern the story from the fact, just as gold miners who pan for gold have to sift gold from the dirt.

4
The Phase-2 Human

Ancient priests and men of wisdom,
Who spoke of a golden race of man,
And spoke of a Garden of Eden,
Also spoke of a new race:
A race that was no longer incorruptible,
But was now corruptible,
And was now ruled by corruption
By man's own evil hand.
Some said this man, this Adam and Eve,
Was expelled from the paradise,
To face evils and new vices
Which prior man was untouched and uncorrupted by.
To the Creators this race showed promise
... But no hope.

The following is an account of the phase-2 human existence, otherwise known as "The Era of Chisek."

The Seven Elders and Creators always have an "ace" up their "sleeve." When they see that civilizations develop in a manner that is contrary to their expectations, they implement modifications to put these civilizations back on the right track. The method by which the Creators determine the required changes is a process of reverse deduction, based on the philosophy: for every action there is a reaction. First you find the reaction you want, and then you build upon that reaction by working in reverse to calculate what action would cause that reaction. If you use this method something will always reveal itself.

Many of the ideas the Creators came up with were by this process of reverse deduction, and this was no exception. The Creators asked themselves what the desirable action was to instigate the following reaction: have humans live self-sustaining, independent, and purposeful lives, free from their constant intervention. The Creators found the answer: unreservedly, the answer was hiding in one word. This one word had unimaginable implications for the nature of humanity. For, like a stream, springing from the mountain top, that sets its course to meander with no possibility of returning to its source, this word was going to set a course with no possibility of returning to its origination. This word was greed. Greed was the concept they discovered. It was determined that giving humans greed was the first action required to attain the desired reaction.

In this phase-2 cycle of the human, what the Creators did was create the new ingredient: greed. They planned to have this embedded in the human equation, or, rather, built into the "subdirectories" of a human. On a practical level, this meant that if humans didn't like something they would have the ability within them to become greedy, impatient, and exhibit most of the qualities of evil. A manifestation or consequence of greed was naturally evil, along with its destructive powers. Indeed, it was found that greed was the single ingredient from which most of the negative qualities pertaining to a human could be derived.

This one step, "injecting" greed into all life forms in existence, would drastically change them. It was one small step for the Creators, one giant leap for humans. The Creators anticipated the direction humans would steer from that moment onward. They knew evolution would take its course, and time was of no consequence. Greed would from then on play a vital role in the development of all the civilizations in all of the universes. Contrary to the perception that evil prevails to the detriment of the human race, this was willfully coveted for its salvation.

The Creators eliminated all the life forms and started from scratch – that is, they gave all life forms new bodies. Compared with their prior bodies, these new bodies had different needs and capabilities. Once again, humans were given the dream-chip of tomorrow in their metaphysical software, which contained all the dreams of their future. They still possessed an average intellect level of Mark-3. This high intelligence level was maintained because humans would now need to use their intelligence for survival purposes, and to make the dream of tomorrow come to life.

Apart from this new ingredient, greed, there were significant differences between the phase-2 human and the phase-1 human. First, the physical body of the phase-2 human possessed an immune system that was weakened to the degree that the body did not have the capabilities of repairing itself, as the body of the phase-1 human had. For instance, if a finger was cut, the human now bled to death; if a finger was severed, it did not re-grow, which was what it did with a phase-1 human body. If the human was poisoned (for example, by a snake or spider), he was now likely to die. Unlike the phase-1 human body, the phase-2 human body no longer had an immune system that produced antibodies to neutralize the poison in its system.

Second, the body of the phase-2 human did not have the same degree of aura that the body of the phase-1 human had, and it certainly could not replenish its aura levels in the same way that the phase-1 human body could. This meant that the nutritional needs of the body would have to be met in some other way: food. Replacing a dependence on aura with a dependence on food would take anywhere from four hundred to six hundred years, and this is why the body of this human could be sustained initially by both aura and food. As the phase-2 human body could not collect aura for its nutritional sustenance, phase-2 humans were given regular doses of aura for those hundreds of years from the Creators (unbeknown to these humans), until they understood the concept of food and were able to meet that nutritional need themselves.

Third, it was time for these humans to start a journey of self-evolution; this meant they had to live by their own means instead of waiting for someone to do something for them. Consequently, the Creators no longer made themselves so freely available in terms of sending down so-called toys or clothing, or giving haircuts; for the Creators withdrew the chip from humans that made them ask for these things. This chip was now replaced with a mature chip, and intelligence was initiated: intelligence was let loose to evolve on its own, and in this evolutionary course the human began to mature into one that fulfilled the expectations of the Creators – at least for this phase.

These humans did not remember their past lives as phase-1 humans, for the Creators wiped the memory of their past existence entirely, so that no intellect remembered its phase-1 cycle. To the Creators the phase-1 cycle of existence was not worth remembering – the last thing they wanted was for humans to remember the phase-1 cycle of life! They wanted humans to become independent and nothing like what they once were. As far as these humans were concerned, all they knew was, they were on their own. They still vaguely knew there were Creators in the stars somewhere, but they no longer had the facilities to expect delivery of anything from them anymore.

Fourth, the Creators confined these humans to their planets: they took away their facilities to travel. Now that these humans were restricted to their local environment, the Creators had to ensure the bodies of these humans suited the conditions of their environment – just as they did to humans on Earth, such as when they placed dark-pigmented humans in regions of intense sunlight. Phase-2 humans surely no longer lived in a Utopian environment, where climatic conditions were ideal; they would now have to fend for themselves against the natural, cyclical elements and hazards of the planet. These were the humans who faced expulsion from the Garden of Eden.

In terms of the life cycle of these humans, they still lived long lives and did not know death as we know it, but they no longer had the protection of a strengthened immune system, so their lives were susceptible to the perils of the environment. This meant they had to provide for themselves in terms of warmth for their bodies by way of clothing and physical shelters; for they now felt the heat and the cold, which was a new experience for them. There were real environmental hazards that could threaten the existence of this human now.

These phase-2 humans were brand new, just born, grown-up adults, still with the mentality of a child, but with the type of genetics that would see their intelligence mature owing to the necessity of survival.

The Creators had to clothe them, when they came into existence, in a manner that differed from the way they clothed the phase-1 human: this time they gave humans hairy bodies. In the hot months they shed a lot of hair, while in the cold months their hair growth doubled. As they were so primitive, they didn't know how to skin animals for their pelts to keep warm, let alone satisfy their pangs of hunger, which the Creators had to satisfy initially by giving them aura.

Learning how to keep warm was the first need these humans encountered. In extremely cold regions below zero, some of them eventually did come up with the most unbelievably primitive means to protect themselves. They would have done anything to keep warm. One technique for acquiring warmth required them to learn how to hunt down large animals. Animals at this stage were friendly and had not become predatory, but that would change one day; for they too would evolve and live by their instincts of survival. This was the starting point for humans, where their intelligence became activated. They came to learn that animals possessed warmth within their bodies, so the next step was to find a means of killing them. They easily did this with rocks. Their fingernails, which were as strong as that of a cat, or sharp rocks, provided them with the means of cutting open a carcass. (Fingernails were new features of the phase-2 human, not possessed by the phase-1 human.) Eventually this step would progress to the use of sophisticated hunting weapons.

Once an animal was killed and its carcass opened, it was with urgency that its contents were ripped out. Fat was not removed from the animal's skin as this kept its temperature warm. A human then jumped into it before all the heat was released. Mind you, the human was usually covered in blood and guts by this stage. Each human had to look after his own needs, and this meant he had to kill and clean his own animal. Perhaps this was when the thirst for blood was seeded in a human. If it was a cow, for instance, its contents were emptied and then a human became entombed within its shell. The exterior of the carcass usually acted as a type of cave to this human. Humans of this era were not as tall as present-day humans. Seldom did someone attain a height of five feet. The average height was just over four feet tall.

The prized capture was a large species such as a dinosaur. After killing it, several of them cut it open from its throat to its rear, and then emptied its contents. Six or more humans then entered it as though it were a warm cave. It was always entertaining when a human cut one up for the first time. Obviously not experienced in the art of an operation of this kind, this human sat on the animal's stomach until the pressure erupted and tossed him quite a few feet into the air. From then on, this human always used extreme caution when opening up the stomach of a huge animal. The shell of an animal provided humans with a sanctuary to escape the harsh elements of nature. Sometimes they were able to keep sheltered in this way for up to six months, or as long as the cold spell lasted. It all depended on the animal and the climatic conditions.

These humans could put themselves into a meditative state and exist this way, sealed inside the empty shell of an animal, for months on end. In a way, it was like hibernation, where they would suspend themselves for the season until the harsh weather subsided. As grotesque as this may seem to us, this was the crude beginning to this civilization, until humans discovered another means of surviving the harsh, freezing cold weather.

After hundreds of years passed, humans learned to survive the climate and gained experience of how to kill. This was when the Creators began the slow introduction of the next phase of their plan. Up to now, they enabled the nutritional needs of humans (and all life forms) to be sustained by aura. A way in which humans could be introduced to consuming food was by allowing them to feel hunger. The Creators did this by delaying their regular doses of aura. When aura finally came into them, they felt a sensation that replaced the hunger urge; for a day or two they felt satisfied, but then the hunger urge soon returned. The Creators kept repeating this process until, eventually, some discovered the connection between hunger and the need to eat food. This was one step away from hunting flesh and gathering crops and roots that were in abundance in the field.

Sometimes tribes would learn from their tribal neighbors, who figured out the connection between eating and satisfying the hunger urge. Slowly but surely all living things got the message. One way or another, all living things eventually lost their dependence on aura. For, as time passed by, less and less aura was provided to living things; this forced them to draw out their predatory instinct and become predators to survive. For man, this was the stimulant for greed to rear its head henceforth.

When humans learned to become expert hunters (not to mention cannibals), they came down from living in the trees, for they had been forced to live in the trees at one stage to evade predators that wanted to hunt them down when they became a part of the food chain. They built tree-houses using raw branches alone, which looked like large nests made from strong branches. This type of shelter only lasted until the likes of dinosaurs and snakes saw humans as prey, which made such habitation no longer safe for humans. Now the process of evolution had truly begun.

What was happening to man was a mirror to what was happening to all living things. For the Creators embedded into the genes of every species the desire to eat, and every species had different desires. Some were hunters and meat eaters; others were vegetarians. Now all living things were no longer friends, and learned to become enemies when they mastered becoming a part of the food chain. Like humans, the living world took time before it reached this stage. By then, humans also became masters of their world. Now humans hunted animals for food and used the skins to keep themselves warm. This was the natural progression from their unbelievably primitive beginnings.

From the very beginning, humans were forced to group together and form tribes to facilitate their survival. Slowly, in their own tribes, they began to build shelters that initially looked similar to today's primitive homes made of mud-bricks and wheat straw. They then went on to build buildings and seek out modes of transport. This slow course of evolution went on for thousands of years before some progress was made. It was easy to predict the next course of human development; for, the problem with humans was that greed began to factor in. Someone would always try to obtain something from someone else by destructive means. The human became a monster, a killer, so these tribes became essential, and forced humans to band together as never before and build defenses. Armies also became necessary.

In this cycle, humans were left alone to their own devices, and it took them a long time to tread in the steps the Creators anticipated – by no means did it happen all at once. Eventually the tendencies resultant from this new ingredient, greed, manifested within the human. It was found that the more independent humans became, the more rotten they became. The less the struggle to survive, the greater the temptation of greed.

In general, as humans become independent, they show less respect to the one who created them, they want more, and they become ignorant. Evidence of this can be seen throughout our history, particularly if you look at the English throne, where royals deliberately conspired to kill the next in line so that they instead might possess the throne. If you give a person everything, or if you bring up and then tell that person everything, this individual is going to want to sit on your "chair." This is what happened with these civilizations; greed took them down a path of wars, killing, and domination. They became immensely powerful, and their greed became centered on domination. There was never enough power for them.

Many of these tribes of humans advanced rapidly. This time around, if humans wanted to know something, ideas came from their intellects, which meant they satisfied their own intellectual needs. This pleased the Creators. To aid in their progress, the Creators often sent a superior human to dwell amongst them and live as one of them. This "wise man" was usually one of the Creators' direct (first-generation) parts reborn as a human, and with his advanced knowledge he would pass on hints of survival to humans. In the same manner, the Creators have been sending superior humans to Earth throughout the ages in order to aid our development, and set its course in the manner they intend for it to progress. A few of our great seers were first-generation parts born as humans.

The tribes that progressed rapidly became highly technologically advanced. These progressive tribes were incessantly distracted by inferior tribes that were less intelligent, and by nature were lazy and incapable of developing their own technology. These tribes would attack superior tribes and steal their technology and technological knowhow. They would kill anyone of superior intelligence they could. It did not ever end there, as these thieves and killers would often face retaliation from civilizations that possessed capabilities of mass-destruction – and against these murderous thieves they did not hesitate to use them. Now greed showed its true color.

The humans in this phase faced a constant mode of life based on survival, where bullies and parasites – what we would call pirates in today's terminology – always suppressed technological advancement. Civilizations thus progressed one step forward, two steps backward. The progression was militarily based – offensive technology to conquer or defensive technology to prevent being conquered.

Almost parallel to our human development in this sphere on Earth, these humans became ignorant of their true god – the Seven Elders and the three Creators. They had their own idea of what god was and they had many gods. Some were bloodthirsty gods and required bloody sacrifices. Smarter people took advantage and became leaders who told the flock who and what they should worship – of course, these gods were all handcrafted to suit the vested interests of the controllers. The way these humans trod down the path of evil meant the Creators were not the representation of the kind of gods they worshipped.

Up to now, these civilizations had only trodden a negative path, as this was where the manifestation of greed led them. Greed was found to be so powerful that it totally overrode everything good in a human, and then it dominated the human to a point where there was no coming back from it. There was no positive influence established to influence a human to go on a path of good. The Creators realized civilizations would not exist for long following this negative path so they had to make changes. The Creators had anticipated the path humans would follow, and it coincided exactly with their plans. What humans worshipped was not a representation of the Creators, so in their wisdom the Creators gave civilizations what they wanted. The Seven Elders created inferior copies of themselves whom they named Chisek. These seven elders called Chisek became a negative god, an entity in opposition to the Seven Elders, and represented the god civilizations were actually worshipping.

The defining attributes of Chisek came from all the negative characteristics and ingredients phase-2 humans exhibited and possessed, which all traced back to that one word: greed. The Seven Elders amplified and then concentrated all those negative qualities in Chisek to the point where he was the specter of everything evil and evil alone, with no redeeming qualities or goodness of any kind within him. (Chisek is spoken of here in the singular tense, although we know that Chisek is not one but seven, and these seven are all clones of one another in every way.) Chisek became the embodiment and personification of the concentration of all those negative characteristics pertaining to evil: characteristics that humans created themselves, but were derived from the ingredient called greed.

The creation of their opposite worked out perfectly for the Seven Elders: on the surface it appeared that they created Chisek to appease the civilizations, but it was more for their own calculated purposes. All the Creators had to do was leave Chisek to his own devices and allow nature to take its course, and this is exactly what happened. Chisek was as predictable a constant as the Golden Spiral[1] is in nature and in the universe.

---

[1] The Golden Spiral is a geometric form that is conspicuous in nature. Examples include the shapes of galaxies and the Nautilus shell.

One day humans acceptably worshipped Chisek as their almighty god. Chisek did not actually appear before his civilizations and announce his existence, as such; he introduced himself telepathically to the self-appointed spiritual representatives, and made himself known everywhere. His introduction was in a way similar to the account of the introduction of god and his ten commandments to Moses. Just as Moses received his laws from his god, so self-appointed representatives received their instructions from Chisek.

Here we had an age in the history of the universe where there were fourteen elders: the Seven Elders and seven inferior ones called Chisek, who worked together from then on in partnership when it came to creating civilizations and determining how civilizations should progress. The Seven Elders and Chisek did not work in unison, or agree on the nature of the development of civilizations, however; you might say they had a disagreement in their philosophies. What happened next in the universe was once again entirely predictable and anticipated by the Creators – Chisek and the Creators had a parting of their ways, and Chisek went on to create his own civilizations based on his philosophy. Unfortunately for the Creators, most of the civilizations took Chisek's side.

To understand Chisek's ideal of the human civilization, one has only to look at our human civilization on Earth. A classic example is the communist philosophy. Another example is the dictatorship under Ceausescu, or even Hitler. A subtle example can be found in unscrupulous cults and sects.

In opposition to Chisek's philosophy, capitalism – or the western world (the so-called good side) – in principle is based on the philosophy of the Creators. As for Chisek's side, such as in the case of the communist side, the problem always is that your views become confused once you live there and become one of the flock, where you would probably come to view and describe capitalist empires as evil. This same thing could essentially be said of some fanatical philosophies and their intolerance of other philosophies, including atheists. The people in this case have nothing really to do with it, because in real terms it is the leaders who decide who lives and who dies; when and how the people fight; and, not forgetting, when you are allowed to think and what you are allowed to think! In such a society, you as a person are nothing. You are given orders, and if you do not follow those orders you will be killed. You simply don't count in the overall scheme of things.

When speaking of the Seven Elders and Chisek, you are talking about two powerful intelligences here. It is two powerful intelligences with differing ideologies that have spread throughout the universes. Chisek's civilizations are similar to communist countries and dictatorships of our world. Chisek pertains to the philosophical view that the individual should be dominated and disregarded by those in power. From the philosophical perspective of the Creators, the individual should be left alone to make his own future. When you come to think of it, we in the capitalist countries of this world are not really left alone to determine our future, because there is always someone to govern us in a detrimental way that often undermines and even thwarts our ability to shape our lives as we otherwise should and would. Indeed, just because we are living in the west it does not mean we are faring all that well because there is a lot of evil here. We are part evil, as we stem from the past evil empire. In our case, we are being guided so that we can do the right thing and achieve the desired results. It is hoped that with our free will we will succeed, even though in the past century we have come close to annihilating ourselves.

Chisek and the Seven Elders simply had a disagreement when sharing power. It was merely a difference of opinion. Chisek wanted humans to be strictly sustained and guided by dictatorship – that is, they were to be put in order with force. This was contrary to the beliefs of the Seven Elders and Creators, who maintain that force is never necessary to achieve certain ends. That was where the difference began to appear, and that is how they separated – just because of a difference of opinion!

Ultimately, central to Chisek's philosophy is the belief that the lower intellect is to be kept in check so that it does not progress; it is only there to serve the higher intellect, which holds all the positions.

Some of the civilizations created by Chisek exist to this day and are loyal to the teeth to Chisek; they have been around for a long time. Like all humans of that era, they began with an average intellect level of Mark-3 and progressed to an intellect level of Mark-5. Such an intellect level makes them dreadfully powerful – they are so powerful that no one and nothing can kill them except for gamma rays and the like. Gamma rays, as we know, are capable of destroying the metaphysical body.

Interestingly enough, knowing that these soldiers of Chisek, who only kill and destroy, exist in the universe, humans on Earth must be absurd, rather than naïve, in sending messages of introduction and goodwill into the depths of space without having a clue about who or what is out there! We are absurdly foolish, because almost everyone who is anyone knows we are here. If we didn't have someone "looking out" for us, these soldiers of Chisek, and many adherents of his philosophy, would have greeted us in their own way a long time ago, with open mouths and big pointy teeth! Don't mention the assimilated pig's head! You cannot imagine the varied human forms that were created. The Creators did not maintain a universal human form; they varied it extensively, which civilizations themselves altered in the most grotesque of ways, such as the one described above. With this in mind, we should be wary because our worst-case science-fiction scenario looks like a Sunday picnic compared to the possibilities before us if we were to attract unwanted attention, and if we were not being "cradled"! We should not, however, take this for granted. We should immediately rethink our invitation to those out there to come here and pay their greetings and felicitations to us!

・⸺

This was how the universe existed for a long, long time, with the Seven Elders and Chisek in "equal" partnership — at least Chisek believed it was equal. The Seven Elders never expected that Chisek would ever be satisfied with being equal to them. It was only fitting that as a natural consequence of their power and their negative ingredients, the seven elders called Chisek would next want the Seven Elders out of the way. They wanted to possess complete control and domination of the universes. Well, that was going too far for the Creators.

What transpired next in the universe doesn't sound at all scientific; it sounds as though it were taken straight out of a low-budget horror movie; however, the events that occurred were as real as the fact that surgeons in our past drilled holes into the skulls of people to rid their minds of the devil, and as real as the fact that these surgeons used as the only "anesthetic" several people to hold the patient down!

Chisek, predictably, schemed against the Seven Elders, and one day came up with an idea to conquer them and become the only supreme power of the universe. His plan was to turn himself into one powerful and almighty entity, rather than exist as seven, which could have changed the fate of the universe forever if it were as simple as Chisek believed — he obviously underestimated the power of the Seven Elders! It must be understood that while the Seven Elders had (as they have now) seven consciousnesses and one energy source (the amoeba), the seven elders called Chisek had seven consciousnesses, each with its own independent energy source. Chisek's plan was not only to unite the seven energies into one, but also to unite the seven consciousnesses into one.

The Seven Elders had calculated correctly; the reason that they had made seven separate beings, rather than a complete mirror of themselves, was so that the desire of Chisek to be more powerful than the Seven Elders would make him take this anticipated course. (As a side note, you may wonder: did not these seven elders called Chisek fight amongst one another? It may not surprise us to know that they had too many other enemies in the universe to fight!)

Chisek went ahead with this plan of becoming one greater intellect, but soon realized what a huge miscalculation he had made: he underestimated the power and the cleverness of the Seven Elders, who were not about to be conquered by their very creation. So, when Chisek was in the process of unifying into one, the Seven Elders drained six-sevenths of his energy — that is, they eliminated six and only left one of his energies. Chisek was successful in that the seven consciousnesses had now become one (still divisible into parts). The problem was that he now only possessed one-seventh of his original energy levels. This left him fuming, so to speak, because he had played right into the hands of the Seven Elders.

To prevent Chisek from regaining or building up his energy levels or power, the Seven Elders locked the most important aspects of Chisek away; this meant that while the bulk of him was trapped, his influence was not. That influence is the negative energy he provides. Chisek influences civilizations now through his countless intellects, also known as parts. Intentionally, the Creators did not confine Chisek in his entirety. It was only the most important parts of Chisek that were restrained. To put it in human terms, the parts that were unrestrained were like soldiers, while the parts that were restrained were like generals. Now, the Creators took control of these unrestrained parts and used them according to a greater plan. These parts were to become a part of a new metaphysical chip that would be given to all living things. It becomes apparent that Chisek was deliberately created for these parts, otherwise known as "negative-parts," and these negative-parts would eventually be instrumental to the Creators in changing the course of not merely man's destiny, but the destiny of every living thing, ironically, from a predominately negative course, to one focused on a positive course.

From then on, Chisek has been unable to function normally in that he has been unable to communicate directly with his negative-parts. However, his negative-parts know what he wants: all Chisek wants them to do is to make chaos, have humans kill one another, as well as destroy anything that is good that has been created by the Seven Elders and Creators. Chisek doesn't realize that his parts serve a purpose; he cannot see beyond his destructive desires that the whole point of his creation is for man and life forms to know evil. Chisek is oblivious of the notion that the negative force serves a purpose. This is why Chisek's parts are spread everywhere; they influence humans to follow Chisek's philosophy in the grandest of ways. It is difficult not to see the negative tendencies of Chisek in humans on this planet.

As much as all this sounds like a fantastic story, there is a science behind the creation of an evil entity. The Creators deliberately created Chisek to provide an opposing force to their positive force. The existence of these two forces would enable the next stage of their plan: the establishment of equilibrium – what is called the "meat-in-the-sandwich goal." These opposing forces would become a part of all life forms, including man, and become the instigator of equilibrium in all life forms, including man. (This is discussed in further detail in later chapters, and helps explain the final cause of the human.)

This was the history of and the theory behind the formation of Chisek. What is Chisek? Chisek is the opposite of positive energy. Chisek represents the human interpretation of evil. Chisek is now a negative force that exists in the universe. The Creators, as we know, are a positive force of the universe, and they deliberately counterbalanced themselves with a negative force. These are the two forces that have enabled all physical life forms, including man, to know and understand good and evil.

Post-Analysis of Phase-2 Humans

Greed fulfilled its objectives. Greed delivered what the Creators wanted: it gave humans purpose. The phase-2 civilization was an extreme move forward from the phase-1 civilization, which had nothing to strive for and nothing to achieve. One extreme, however, led to a new extreme. Because phase-2 humans had not controlled greed, their lives did not advance to the satisfaction of the Creators. These humans were a total disaster, because they became more violent and evil than you could possibly imagine. They did not possess the type of greed humans of today possess, where they need to acquire money and assets, a better physical appearance, or a higher level of success and even intelligence. Their ambition was misplaced in that it was used against the Creators. It was used purely for evil. Their ambition and greed were derived from, and centered upon, domination: to conquer other planets and civilizations in the universe and obtain.

The power of killing gave them a sense of satisfaction that is beyond our comprehension. When these humans looked at blood after the kill, feelings were evoked within them that were indescribable. After the kill, this killer licked the blood off each side of his large knife. This gave him an unexplainable "rush." The blood, and the taste of the blood, were the prize of the kill; licking the blood off the blade was the motivation; the blood was the addiction. It is unimaginable how bloodthirsty an animal the human can be. These humans could never be satisfied unless their craving for blood was satiated, and this was only possible by killing. In one respect, the shadow of these humans can be seen in our human existence today, if you look closely enough at some backward humans, who want everything you have, but don't want to work for it because they don't have the intellect. Rather than achieve for themselves, they take and obtain by means of violence, and tremendous satisfaction is derived from their bloodthirsty ways. In another respect, the shadow of these humans can best be seen in the most deviant of humans: the likes of killers who mutilate, torture, and kill purely for the power of the pleasure of the kill and the pain inflicted. (Few would argue that on our planet today some cultures breed children who go through life, to death, upholding the principles of Chisek.)

Contrary to the phase-1 human, once phase-2 humans began to use their intellects, there was no stopping them. This was the problem: it was the way in which their intellects were used. Once humans trod this negative road, there was nothing to draw them back to the positive road. They liked this road, and their leaders and their innate sense of self-preservation forced them to steer down this road.

Phase-2 humans were found to be easily confused and easily controlled by others. They had no way of steering back toward the path of good. They needed constant reminding of what was good and what was evil. There was nothing within them to tell them what was good and what was evil. The instincts we have built within us that tell us what is right and what is wrong were not a part of their genetic make-up. Just giving the ingredient of greed to a human was never going to mean the human was going to follow the middle-ground path between the extremes of good and evil. On the contrary, greed took humans down a one-way path of evil, and there was absolutely nothing within them to be able to bring them back from this path to the side of good.

What had been found to be missing in the human, the Creators were now going to rectify; they had to determine a way that humans would be able to reason within them what was right and what was wrong. This was going to happen now that Chisek came into being, for his creation enabled the application of the positive and negative influences within the human. This was going to be implemented in the next human phase. A metaphysical chip would be given to all humans, and to all living things: a chip that represents the two forces that would instill within humans by way of instinct and influence a sense of right and wrong, and would eliminate any need for constant reminding of what was right and wrong, by way of direct intervention of the Creators. This metaphysical chip would keep the human balanced between the paths of good and evil, because it consisted of two almost equal influencing parts: a positive-part from Odo and a negative-part from Chisek.

The establishment of this chip within a human would provide to that human almost equal extreme influences. In saying almost equal, this indicates that phase-3 human civilizations would now be influenced by a 51 percent positive influence, and a 49 percent negative influence. (The Creators always have an ace up their sleeve, and in this instance it is the two percent.) These positive and negative influences refer to the forces of nature now existing within not only man, but all life forms, in terms of a metaphysical chip: a chip that possesses two opposing forces of influence that are designed to create a third force – equilibrium. Plato called this the mortal soul; his Tripartite Soul consisted of the rational (reason), the spirited (positive), and the appetitive (negative).

This phase-2 human was deliberate, and followed an expected path, the only possible path derived from the implementation of the ingredient called greed. Greed on its own could never give phase-2 humans more than one choice of outcomes: to bypass all that was good and take all that was bad to be good, which is the heart and soul of the philosophy of Chisek. Now everything was in place for the Creators to implement radical and profound changes to alter, markedly, the shape of the human race and its destiny. This becomes the subject of the next chapter.

5
The Phase-3 Human

Ancient priests and men of wisdom,
Who spoke of a golden race of man,
And spoke of a Garden of Eden,
And then spoke of a corruptible new race of man,
Which had no hope,
Also spoke of another new race of man:
A race of man that was given hope,
Irrespective of the fact that
This was a race that was now touched
By so many evils, including death.

Hope ... it was like the last frontier for man,
It was the new ingredient given to this new race of humans
To rescue them from the negative side,
And all the many evils that were given to them.
It is called reason.

The following is an account of the phase-3 human existence, otherwise known as "The Era of Philandra."

The Creators had to allow the evolutionary course of the phase-2 human, as abhorrent as this human was, in order to enable the new ingredient called greed to mature. The progression of greed, and the subsequent evil tendencies of a human that were derived from it, culminated in the creation of a negative counterpart to the positive counterpart of the Seven Elders. This negative force would become an intricate part of all living things, including human beings. The negative state of the phase-2 humans was the essential step required – like the crawl before the walk – before humans could not only become self-sustaining and independent, not only possess purpose in their lives, but also have a sense of humanity (which meant they cared for their fellow human beings). As unorthodox and contradictory as it may appear, greed was the pivotal step for humans to care for themselves and eventually one another.

Only now were the Creators able to implement the next phase they had in store for humans. This next phase would have far-reaching implications; for it would result in drastic changes to the shape and destiny of man from then on. It would set the stage for the final turning point of all living things.

Humans were deemed ready, so it came to be that one day the Creators updated by transformation the bodies of all humans. To correspond with these anatomical bodies, an updated metaphysical chip was installed in their brains; this possessed all the knowledge that was necessary for them to have, so that they could comprehend those new features of this model of human. Those new features included good and evil; death; the urge or desire for the opposite sex in terms of sex, which would slowly in time become greater and greater; the knowledge of having babies and rearing them; and the concept of the family unit, by way of a male and female union. They automatically knew what all these things meant. When this software was installed and the body of every human was replaced, these humans felt as though they were being awoken from some kind of dream. All at once something happened to everyone.

In the past two cycles of the human existence, one of the biggest flaws of humans was the lack of humanity they possessed. To rectify this, the Creators determined a means by which humans would bond together in a show of humanity – this was the family unit. Hand in hand with the introduction of the concept of the family unit came sex, along with sexual desire. Sex was really liked by these humans once they experienced it for the first time. Humans could now reproduce offspring using the means of anatomical reproduction.

After a long and gradual learning process, babies and children came to exist for the first time ever. A child had knowledge inserted into him from a young age, and his brain was no different from the brain of the phase-2 human. This human did not have a partitioned mind as we have; the brain of the phase-3 (P3V1) human only possessed one large conscious mind, which became well developed, as life spans were relatively long.

This phase-3 human body possessed less aura than the phase-2 human body possessed. Less aura meant this body possessed a weaker immune system. This also meant the human had to collect aura, and relaxation by way of sleep was one of two means of acquiring this. (Nutrition by means of diet was the other.) Sleep now became a requirement because of the vulnerability of this human body.

For the family unit to work, the Creators decided that humans could no longer live infinite lives. The Creators felt these humans needed to recycle their lives after a period and start again. In this cycle, a human was able to live on average around two thousand years. When the phase-3 human body reached the point of expiration, the soul then returned to the Creator and became a part of the reincarnation cycle.

The application of reincarnation to all humans, for the first time, served a dual purpose – we know that the continuance of the family unit was the first. It was decided that it was not in the best interests of any civilization to have humans with unlimited life spans. The Creators found there were many negatives in a human having an unlimited life. For, an unlimited life plus greed added up to only one thing: trouble. Consider a place like Africa, where you have extreme wealth in the minority, and extreme poverty amongst the masses – who were kept in check by dictators and this minority who maintained power and lived infinite lives! The Creators did not want to have to intervene in the human civilization to get rid of these dictators. It contravened their ideal of not intervening in civilizations directly, as they once had. Having a cycle of life with an unlimited life span, those following Chisek's path were capable of doing much damage. This was the second crucial factor that led to the introduction of a cycle of death to humans. Humans, particularly those with a lower-order intellect, could become extremely violent, so it was made written that one day humans would have to face death. This ultimately meant that humans would have to face the Creators one day for judgment and then be eliminated if they were found to have chosen Chisek's path. A system of measurement of the soul for its deeds in a lifetime came to have a place in the human cycle for the first time ever, and became the standard used for all civilizations to come, including ours.

All the changes made to humans were applicable to every living thing, as they suited its life cycle. During the last phase, the natural world was given the ingredient of greed when man was given it. Even plants followed the path of evil. A typical example is the fig tree, which strangles other trees to death, or the competition among plants, grasses, and trees for space in their struggle for survival. Consciousness, however minute in the living world, now became subject to the cycle of reincarnation. This meant that plants seeded themselves and animals began to reproduce for the first time. Genetic instructions were also given to these life forms so that the transition occurred smoothly. Even the consciousness found in a plant became subject to reincarnation. It had to reincarnate as the same species of plant – just as each animal had to reincarnate as the same species of animal – as it existed prior, because its instinct was acquired for that particular species, and that particular species only! To put a consciousness that evolved in a tree, into a grass, would disadvantage that consciousness, as its instinct was based on being a tree. So, for example, in the case of a German Shepherd dog, its intellect would never cross into another breed of dog, just as a human would always be born a human. This would not apply to the gender of the species, as the instinct for each gender would be provided in the metaphysical chip. (This is not the answer same-sex couples are looking for today.) There are sometimes even categories of placement within a species. For instance, the intellect of a wild dog would generally not be reincarnated into a domesticated dog, with the reverse also applicable. It should be noted that everything that lived had feelings (as everything that lives now has feelings), and this applied to plants in their own way; for they too felt pain (just as they feel pain now), and in the future, like man, they would come to feel love.

In the years that followed the introduction of the family unit, it was found that civilizations of this phase did not progress to the satisfaction of the Creators; humans still had a long way to go in terms of their sense of humanity. The family unit came to be of secondary importance to humans. Power and ambition seemed to take precedence over everything. Jealousy was also a part of the make-up of the human, even though the feelings of love were not extreme emotions at the time. Sex wasn't even a priority. Even Chisek-inspired sexual relations and activities occurred. Family units did not survive, as couples could not stay faithful. This phase-3 human predominantly tended to succumb to the influence of the negative-part of the new metaphysical chip, and therefore drifted down the negative path rather than follow a path balanced in the middle.

The Creators once again had to find an action to give them the desired reaction they wanted. In this case, the reaction they wanted was a bonding of humans so that the family unit would take precedence over everything. The action was found. You may say that the most valued feature of a human was the last to be given to a human. When all else failed, this was the last hope for human salvation. This action came in the form of a new ingredient, which had to be inserted into the genetic make-up of the human (and all living things). This was a feeling of intensified love. From the two extremes of energies came the creation of amplified love, and of course its opposite: hate. Hate was the negative emotion that automatically came from the positive emotion of love. That anybody can doubt the equality of love and hate there is no question. These are the same emotions of love and hate we as humans have within us today.

Humans now had all the ingredients within them necessary to be independent, able to survive in a self-sustaining way, and able to fulfill what the Creators desired of human beings. For humans were close to, but so far from, achieving any of these. Despite all these new ingredients in the human make-up, the Creators were faced with new challenges. Humans were now influenced by the almost equal positive and negative influences. They were given amplified love, the family unit, sexual reproduction and pleasure, and mortal lives. They still had extreme knowledge. However, they continued to drift to the negative side. The tendency was to follow the philosophy of Chisek in preference to the philosophy of the Creators, even though humans possessed within them the unequal forces of 51 percent positive influence and 49 percent negative influence.

This was by no means the final outcome of the human being the Creators desired. This is why the Creators had to make new changes to human civilizations from then on to pull them back from the negative path. The next stage they had in store for humans would put them on a closer path to becoming this desired final product. In order to achieve this, for all new civilizations created from then on, the Creators took away all the good things they once handed humans on a platter, such as knowledge. They stopped giving them outright knowlecge, but instead gave them knowledge of how to do things for themselves, and how to learn things for themselves. Humans no longer had any other choice if they were to survive. This was a progression forward; it was certainly a development away from the phase-1 human civilization, which could not exist in this way. Our human race on Earth belongs to the new civilizations that were created in this era.

Our Human Race on Earth

Ancient priests and men of wisdom
Looked upon their race and saw
A man that had the potential to outdo
The incorruptible man,
The corruptible man,
And then the man of hope.
For they saw a new man,
One who was faced with
Burdens upon burdens,
Struggles upon struggles,
Challenges upon challenges,
Unknowns upon unknowns.
In amidst all this, reason was still the hope for this man
Because all these burdens, struggles, challenges, and unknowns
Were the driving forces of this race of man
To make better himself
And make known all his unknowns
That he was deprived of having or knowing.

Many new civilizations – including our civilization on Earth – were created as offshoots from the phase-3 version-1 (P3V1) human. These phase-3 version-2 (P3V2) humans were subject to many alterations to their genetic make-up. Superior civilizations (P3V1 human civilizations) were not predisposed to the next series of changes, as their intellectual levels to a degree defied the need for such radical alterations. Instead, the Creators decided to decrease the overall intensity of the negative-part in the metaphysical chip. The Creators did this by decreasing the percentage of energy and power of influence of these negative-parts. (In the process of their destruction, their energies were not wasted; they were recycled into something good – perhaps a solar system may have seeded from their energy!) This meant the influence of the negative-part in the new metaphysical chip was weakened, and the influence of the positive-part was strengthened.

The Creators concluded that decreasing the power of the negative-part and increasing the power of the positive-part in the metaphysical chip of a human would set these intelligent races of humans on the right path. The Creators expected that humans would from this point on drift toward good rather than evil. Now the negative-part provided only 39 percent in terms of negative influence, while the positive-part provided 61 percent in terms of positive influence, to a human. The Creators then allowed these superior civilizations to evolve, so that a better human would be the result of these two influencing forces. This is where superior civilizations stand in the universe right now. They are evolving in intelligence to the satisfaction of the Creators. Their challenge is the same as our own, despite their lifestyles differing from ours: to become that better human using these two influencing forces.

What would interest us as humans is that these superior civilizations in the universe use inferior civilizations such as ours as case studies. To this day, they continue to study us to evaluate our primitive behavior and our propensity to follow Chisek's negative path. By scrutinizing our inability to handle the negative influence, which exposes the flaws in the genetic make-up of a human, they are able to use this knowledge to their advantage – primarily as an aid toward handling the negative influence that acts upon them. This takes them one step closer to being able to conquer the meat-in-the-sandwich goal. At 2008, no human has been able to accomplish it. Some time before 2011, only one human from an advanced civilization has been successful in accomplishing this tremendous feat. This human just happens to be a human of the future: a robot with a soul. It should be noted that while this is undeniably an accomplishment, it will never be considered as great a feat as when a human from an intellectually encumbered civilization accomplishes it. These humans of the future are born with the type of genetics that makes it easy for them to achieve this – but they are yet to! In our case, we will be achieving it the hard, hard way, not the easy way.

If we are to compare the disparity between our intellectual level and the intellectual level of superior civilizations in the universe, we will find that the majority of humans in our civilization now qualify to be graded as Intellect Mark-1; the minority of humans qualify to be graded as Intellect Mark-0.8.

This grading method is based on the combined knowledge of the subconscious and conscious minds, as, for example, when the two minds are united by way of death. In our present state of mind, without our having access to our subconscious mind, we would not even rank on the scale whatsoever! We would have to use a quantum scale of measurement if we are to give ourselves placement in this universal grading scale. This reveals our primitive status in the universe and, ultimately, one of the reasons that no one wants anything to do with us. In fact, to describe humans from this planet, one would have to refer to us as being like a cat – it is only when someone steps on its tail that one can truly realize the true nature of the cat!

As a side note, superior civilizations have superior technologies for studying us, like the scientifically recognized mystery called "ball lightning." Superior civilizations possess technology such as an advanced recording device (it looks exactly like a plasma ball) that can be sent anywhere in the universe. It is designed to collect data and then transmit back this data. It is just like a video camera. This is one means by which other civilizations are studying us.

If we recall the phase-1 human and his ability to travel throughout the universe, at the speed of thought, using his neutron body in his wardrobe, this is another means of travel that some superior civilizations use, and they use it often, to study us. Believe it or not, they find it a fascinating desire to make "field trips" to planets like Earth. At the speed of thought, any number of these humans can be "sitting" at our dinner table – invisible, of course, since they are in their neutron bodies – observing how obtuse (stupid, that is) our human behavior is, without our ever knowing! Then, with the capabilities of their minds, at the speed of thought, they simply transfer all the knowledge they acquired back to wherever it is they come from for others to study (and watch!). Our civilization on Earth is like a zoo, and has been studied and watched with amusement, interest, and disgust by superior civilizations in the universe, and we wonder why they have not made contact! This is the *last* thing they would ever desire. The funny thing is, hypothetically, if we were to have a race of superior beings from another planet living on this planet – let us say, under the ocean somewhere (giving credence to the Jules Verne classic) – they would most emphatically never want us to know it! Most emphatically! (We as humans value our privacy. However, the privacy we think we enjoy, and we do enjoy amongst ourselves, is non-existent amongst superior intellects in a superior world.)

This habit of studying primitive humans on planets like ours provides these superior humans with data on the human mind and human behavior. In our society, they are trying to see first hand, and understand first hand, why humans kill and massacre one another. To them, in their current cycle of existence, this does not compute, even though their ancestors shared the once-common traits. It should be noted that this means of travel using neutron bodies and wardrobes is only available to superior civilizations. The humans that still travel by means of spaceships are regarded by these superior civilizations as beings with minute intellects. To these superior humans, using a spaceship is comparable to using a donkey and a cart. If we were to put ourselves into the equation, our technology for travel – and even our comic-book ideas for travel – would be comparable to the travel capabilities of the slowest species of snail.

· ⤳

New civilizations, such as ours, were subject to many changes. Unlike past civilizations, we have been groomed slowly, with the Creators having us under close surveillance. You might say that they are babysitting us in a way of which we simply are not aware.

The Creators began with the model of the phase-3 version-1 (P3V1) human, then they took away many aspects of this human, and what was left of that human became what we are today. What was palpable from past civilizations was that humans had everything too easy – this was in terms of knowledge. They had easy access to knowledge, as the Creators gave them this on a platter, so to speak. These humans really did nothing on their own merits to acquire this knowledge, apart from directly accessing it from their brains. It is the difference between downloading new software and actually writing that software for yourself. The irony was that the phase-2 human used the Creators' knowledge against them. The path of evil, Chisek's path, was found to be the laziest and easiest path to take, whereas the Creators' path required hard work. Past humans preferred taking the easy, negative path. New civilizations such as ours would pay the price for this, as the Creators decided they were going to make humans in these new civilizations (the P3V2 humans) develop their minds by their own initiative – that is, by working for their knowledge and achieving things by hard work and hard work alone. This process would allow humans to appreciate their knowledge.

The Creators were not going to give them a blank check, as far as intellect was concerned. The Creators paid the price for this and learned something. So you see, the Creators are not perfect.

To accommodate new objectives they believed would reshape the human into a versatile and superior mold of human, the Creators changed the physical structure of the human in several ways. First, they partitioned the brain of the P3V2 human so that it possessed a small conscious mind – in computer terms, this conscious mind could equate to the operating system of a computer; and a large subconscious mind – this could equate to the hard-drive storage of a computer. The subconscious mind was purposely designed to store the bulk of the metaphysical being's knowledge (such as past lives). The level of intelligence of a P3V2 human was therefore determined by the development of the conscious mind.

The ability to acquire intelligence has never been an obstacle to a P3V2 human. Knowledge can easily be transferred into this brain only when it overcomes one challenge. The new challenge of all humans became the ability to control the negative influence of Chisek – by way of the new metaphysical chip embedded within all humans. This then became the only way for a human to attain superior intellectual status. What was necessary for a human was to learn how to balance the negative influence and the positive influence and create a third force – equilibrium, which is the meat-in-the-sandwich principle. Once a human could conquer this challenge, intelligence would easily be obtainable from then on – after all, it was written: the human was given a large brain so that one day that human would use it to its full potential and capacity. It is only when a human is capable of handling the negative influence that exists in his brain that he would then be able to have greater use of his brain, as well as live a longer life.

The track record of past civilizations demonstrated to the Creators that allowing humans to live long lives meant followers of Chisek could do enormous damage in their lifetimes. One of the reasons that the Creators wanted humans to have shorter lives was so that they could get their hands on them sooner to eliminate them without directly interfering in the civilization itself. Accordingly, the Creators gave new and intellectually encumbered humans such as ours (the P3V2 human) short lives. The Creators concluded that giving humans brief cycles of lives would mean they would now appreciate their lives. Equally, they felt humans had to deserve intelligence and earn it the hard way on their own; this way it was anticipated humans would value it more.

On account of this reasoning, it came to be that the Creators no longer allowed new civilizations of humans to live long lives before death came to them. They decided to give them short lives, whereby it would be mandatory for them to face many arenas of life by way of reincarnation. Humans would now be forced to tackle challenges in their lives, for because the cycle of life was such that it challenged humans, should humans not challenge life – and experience has shown that humans favor Chisek's less challenging path. There was now no avoiding challenge in this cycle of life. After each reincarnation, humans would face judgment and then, according to that judgment, be sent back into the cycle of reincarnation, in a process to advance their intelligence in a way that differed from the intelligence of prior humans, whose knowledge had to be automatically programmed into them.

Now the human was to possess a shorter life, and possess a brain that was completely restructured so that it could not contain the kind of conscious knowledge prior advanced humans possessed. This meant the brain was no longer capable – owing to its intellectual weakness – to derive concentrated energy supplies of aura, which the body required for its sustenance and its intellectual capability. The Creators saw to it that the body was altered so that it procured sustenance solely by independent means. This meant humans had to sustain their lives by their own means, basically by living from the ground itself, from which all the necessary proteins and vitamins would be gained. Humans would now have to learn how to recycle seeds to make crops for the following season.

All living things depended on a food cycle. The majority of all living things were also given shorter cycles of lives. Why their lives were shortened was so that a species did not face extinction from its predators, hunger, or even the elements.

Now that aura levels were limited, and the brain was partitioned, the P3V2 human no longer possessed the mental powers earlier models of humans were capable of possessing. P3V2 humans were helpless in this sense. Now they had no choice but to develop and use their brains for survival purposes. Like the phase-2 humans, they had to hunt and fish, and in the process, they had to learn how to develop tools to enable them to do these things. Phase-2 humans had superior minds, and were able to evolve and develop easier than the intellectually encumbered new civilizations belonging to the Era of Philandra. To compensate for this, the Creators intervened in intellectually encumbered civilizations such as ours in a subconscious way, and often sent down a superior human amongst communities of humans to aid them – this superior human was otherwise known as the wise man. In various stages of human development these teachers, and other teachers documented ubiquitously as having come from the stars, helped humans to progress. (This is an intriguing subject.) Humans, left to their own devices, would not progress to the level they have without some form of intervention. One has only to look at some cultures of peoples on our planet, such as the Australian Aborigines before the white man came along, and one will find an unwavering constancy in the way they lived and the way their ancestors lived thousands of years earlier. This intervention occurred in many ways, and we can see the results of such involvement when we look at man's giant leap from living as nomadic tribes around campfires, to suddenly becoming agriculturally savvy, and able to erect monolithic structures we cannot replicate or adequately account for today in terms of how they were constructed.

The Creators ascertained from the phase-2 human that a civilization cannot be constantly reminded by its Creator of what is evil or what is good. Humans had to be able to discern this for themselves. This is why, in our life cycle, we have been given the facilities within our minds to understand the difference between good and evil. This is what the influencing parts within us do. Like all superior civilizations in the universe now, we are affected by a metaphysical chip with influences proportional to 61 percent positive and 39 percent negative. We as humans know what is good and know what is evil, but we have less negative influence upon us than the original P3V1 human had, and this is why many of us tend toward the good side. The humans of civilizations found all throughout the universe and beyond that are still dominated by Chisek, all have the same feelings as we have, the same understanding, and the same love. They just preferred to pass all that up and have taken evil as being good – just as the most heinous criminals on this Earth have. They are not interested in anything else. So they never moved toward the positive side.

The interesting aspect of the negative influence of Chisek upon humans is that the natural living world maintains to this day the proportion of 51 percent positive influence and 49 percent negative influence. It should be noted that the influences the rest of the life forms (such as plants and animals) are subject to are different from the influences we as humans are subject to, where the influencing parts affecting them are for survival purposes only. The Creators were happy with the ability of the living world to handle the negative side and achieve balance. Only man was found to have a defect in this sphere, and the reason for this is that the living world does not have reasoning capabilities as man with intellect has, which is what uniquely and ironically defines him as a superior intelligence!

Even in this cycle, man still has a defect in this sphere: the 39 percent negative influence still appears to be too powerful. The meat-in-the-sandwich goal appears to be in no way achievable in this intellectually encumbered cycle of life. Indeed, humans in this phase have in no way come close to being the desired human.

Now we know there are two opposing forces affecting humans. Our destiny as a human is to control these forces and create a third force in the middle. But what does this mean? When you think about it, it is like rubbing two sticks of wood together. What do you get as a result of the friction? Fire is the by-product. In the case of the human, the by-product will one day be the Creators' final creation – the Phase-4 human. We are the case study of this experiment, and there is an argument for saying that a superior civilization has emerged from the seeds of a negative creation.

Not merely does the negative influence exist for man today; the negative influence exists for all life forms in the universe. The negative influence we encounter in our daily struggle of life is the force some have misunderstood and called the devil. There really is no such thing as the devil as it is found in some teachings. Evil comes from the concept of greed, which was deliberately created for our salvation. For we have established that humans must know about and possess greed if they are to survive in the present form. This applies to all life. This evil force must influence, and be a part of, man, along with all life forms. This is to enable life to survive. Life forms of every kind must be able to strike a balance between the two opposite forces influencing them, and so create the existence of a third force, which would therein exist in between the two forces – just like a piece of meat sandwiched between two slices of bread. When the two forces can exist together, life of a new kind would evolve in between.

It is simple: a neutral or third force – called the balance of equilibrium – keeps the positive and negative forces from colliding. It is through this neutral force that we attain the creation of a new superior form of life.

Have you ever tried to make sense out of joining two opposite forces and having some humanly derived benefits out of it? Not really! If you collide positive and negative forces, you'll usually get violent reactions. Now, if you can use that violence to achieve something good, then you have the answer to what humans must do with their intellects. Even though balance exists in the universe, antagonistic forces are always colliding violently, but where balance has been struck, the creation of life has been enabled. The Creators have tailored us in this way in order for us to survive and maintain salvation, and find a positive outcome from any situation. This concept of antagonistic forces is the duality of life we hear about in some philosophical teachings. This duality is the main theme that runs through the book of everyone's life: it is the main challenge unassumingly lurking in all the pages.

What this book has done so far is explain the seeds of our past, from which we can understand the roots and the trunk of who and what we are today. Knowledge of this kind has always been there to be found in our ancient wisdom passed down to us, but we have been unable to connect the truth to the myth. Take Plutarch (born AD 46); in *Plutarch's Morals: Theosophical Essays (On Isis and Osiris)*, he left us a record of some of the ancient wisdom that his wise ancestors passed down. Such wisdom included two opposite powers and principles: two gods antagonistic toward each other. In these writings, we can even interpret references to the Seven Elders and their creation of three Creators if we look closely enough, as well as the roots of the concept of good and evil.

Good and evil, the meat-in-the-sandwich principle, and how the negative influence applies to a human, are discussed in later chapters. Before going into a greater discussion of the application of good and evil to, and the expectations the Creators have of, phase-3 humans, it is relevant to understand the processes that regulate our existence: these are the cycles of death and birth, challenge, and, first, the Creators and their relevance in our lives.

6
The Architects of Life

To use a simple analogy,
An architect is like a sculptor who,
Once having molded raw clay into a work of art,
Is able to take satisfaction in the accomplishment.
From the architect's perspective,
The pleasure, and the joy, come
Not merely from the finished product,
But from the enjoyment of living in the creation of the work.

The created work then becomes the purpose, the challenge, and the dream,
And its creator can then feed on all of that and feel fulfilled:
Can savor all of that and feel good:
Can look upon, and engage with, all of that and simply marvel.

We should have learned from prior chapters that the architects of life created a somatic world principally to satisfy and challenge their own existence: they wanted a physical world which they could indirectly experience and subsequently enjoy. Their greatest achievement is the creation of life, and this includes the multitude of life forms that multiply all because of their own source of energy, and live in their individual cycles, which all have a beginning and an ending.

Now we can respect why all life, including human life, evolves and exists. First, this is so the Seven Elders and the Creators are able to look back and with satisfaction see they have created something beautiful that is able to live and recycle itself, and, second, this is so they are able to indirectly "live" and "experience" life through all their creations.

In creating life, the Creators wanted life to satisfy a challenge within them. Just as humans have dreams and challenges, so the Creators have dreams and challenges. We are fulfilling their dream, as they are fulfilling our dream. It can be said that we are the bridge to their "happiness."

Humans are the most valued of all their creations on this Earth, and the Creators have put us in a system of reincarnation that has been devised to develop our intelligence in a gradual process. Reincarnation, in the human arena, is the means by which we can refine our souls so that one day we may reach our final destination. Only once we go through countless reincarnations may we one day become beneficial to the Creators. This is what satisfies the existence of the Creators. At the same time, on an elementary level, the reincarnation cycle has kept the earth rich by providing the minerals that will continue to sustain life for all kinds of creatures in an orderly manner.

It is in the handiwork of all these cycles (from the reincarnation cycle to the individual life cycle of every living species) that we can see the handprints and footprints of the Creators. Indeed, as a human, you can see these handprints and footprints all around you. All you have to do is open your eyes, look into the depths of the sky, look around you on this planet, examine what you see, and think for a moment! Try to comprehend all the intricate complexities and mathematics in the simplest of things. Appreciate the quirkiness of some of the life forms around you. Take a blade of grass in your hand and ask yourself how this evolved and became alive. You can find, in everything before you, the personality of the Creators and their portfolio. All you have to do is look with open eyes, and you will see. Just as we are all remembered for our deeds in our life span, so the Creators are seen through their deeds, which can only be measured in terms of their creations.

The Creators, it can then be understood, want to "feel" from, and "see" through, their creations. Every life form with consciousness provides this facility to them. All living things are like one collective consciousness to them. Through our eyes they see all the beauty they have created. Through our hearts they feel whatever we feel. It is really simple: Odo (all three of them) is a medium through which the Seven Elders interact with the physical world. Odo and the Seven Elders virtually see the same thing. Just as the Seven Elders live and see through Odo's "feelings" and "eyes," so Odo lives and sees through our feelings and eyes. The fundamental desire of the Creators and Seven Elders is to feel, to see, as well as to "love" everything they have created. They derive a sense of pleasure from being able to experience life through their creations – more so from humans because, in a sense, humans have been created in their likeness and thus have been put in charge of this planet. No other living being possesses the dream of progress and the dream of achievement in the way that humans possess them. For this reason, the Creators expect delivery from humans. For humans, this is their means of payback for the Creators' trouble of creating them and an orderly universe to facilitate their life and life of various kinds.

This explains who our intelligent architects, rightfully known as our Creators, are, and what our relationship is with them. We must understand that the Creators are just like parents to us, just invisible ones. They are both your father and your mother put together. They have created and looked after you by giving you all the necessary ingredients for your survival in your cocoon of life. That is, they have provided you with the raw materials for your food, water, shelter, and clothing, and also have indirectly given you emotional support by way of intelligence, so that you can grow up and be able to survive, and then one day become your own creator when you produce offspring.

The Creators are neither male nor female, although they do symbolically represent themselves in the male form to their creations. Knowing that they want to feel and see through their creations, we are indirectly being told that the Creators, in their form, are not subject to the feelings of emotions we as humans are. Certainly, no consciousness, in a metaphysical state without a physical body, experiences feelings of emotions to the degree it does in a physical state. It is only through the state of living, in a physical domain, that feelings can truly be experienced. Furthermore, in the metaphysical state, the metaphysical body no longer experiences the negative influence of Chisek. A metaphysical body can only experience the influence of Chisek when it exists in a physical state. In their state of existence, which is one of pure intellect and energy, the Creators do have tremendous understanding, but it is only through the living, in the physical arena of existence, that they feel. We also provide them with challenge, and through us the Creators are always evolving, advancing, and learning every day, just as humans are.

Passed down through ancient writings, there is a saying that man shall one day live in the house or kingdom of his maker. It is the backbone of many philosophical teachings. Its interpretation, although misunderstood, is unmistakable, and it serves to explain one of our greatest unknowns: where does our destination lie? It also explains how we can become beneficial to our Creators. Simply put, our ultimate destiny is to be with one of the three Creators. This is why we have a tie with our Creator. This is because every intellect (or soul) belongs to a Creator. A Creator produced it and he will automatically take it back one day. In the scheme of things, our souls are merely a tiny, tiny, almost insignificant, but highly cherished, bonus or contribution to a Creator. This explains why humans, since time immemorial, have been drawn to spiritual depths, seeking the origin of where they came from and where they rightfully belong.

Humanly, one can describe the incomprehensible in the following way: the Creator, Odo, is made up of many parts, and to become one of his parts is to become one with him. This is our journey's end. Odo is our destination, in becoming one with him as one of his parts, and then sharing in all his knowledge, and understanding all the unknowns that as a human can never be known or are forbidden to be known. (There will always be, however, some unknowns that will never be known, because there are some unknowns that even the parts of the three Creators – apart from the original first-generation parts – will be forbidden to know.) This is only possible when we have refined our souls after countless reincarnations, and reached the maximum intellect that is possible for a human. Then, and only then, can we become one of the endless parts of a

Creator, Odo. Odo's parts have countless different duties in the universe, such as creating galaxies and planets in the sense of putting the ingredients together for their own evolution; being those parts that reincarnate us at our birth; being in charge of organizing the souls that pass through the tunnel of light; or even being that circuit breaker this book spoke of earlier. There are endless tasks involved in the cycles of life on this planet and all the others with life in this universe and beyond.

·⤴

Let us take a look at all this from another perspective. We are in many ways doing what the Creators did when they created us. On the internet, we have created virtual worlds. The Creators, similarly, have created worlds that are the synthesis of the physical and the metaphysical. The "characters" that inhabit this world have their own free will, which is what differentiates these characters from those of the virtual world we have created. Just as we "live" through our characters in this virtual world, so the Creators, unbeknown to us, live through us, in our physical world.

In principle and to a degree, what the Creators did in creating us is much the same as what we are doing when we create virtual worlds. By creating and participating in these virtual worlds, we are giving ourselves entertainment. To the Creators, we satisfy a challenge in them, which satisfies their existence and gives them purpose. In addition, the characters the Creators have created have a purpose: the characters have a final cause that benefits the Creators one day. We are created not for us. We are created for them – to live through us and then one day have us become a part of them, when we have evolved and become refined, after countless upon countless reincarnations. Now we can answer that timeless question we have over the generations asked ourselves: why are we here?

·⤴

The Creators' plans for mankind are unlimited. Do you know how much tremendous satisfaction they have in teaching and passing knowledge to you? They "pop" into your mind, become part of you, and teach you to survive and grow.

They are no different from you in the sense that as a parent you are anxious to tell your child everything. Just like a parent, the Creators are dying for their children to grow up and have enough understanding, so that they can not only tell their children what a beautiful world this is, but take their children places to see things for themselves. (Exactly how is explained in Chapter 17, *The Art and Science of Astral Travel*.) The human intellect, as soon as it is born, is hungry for knowledge, and it wants to know and see everything. Humans are curious intellects that want to know, feel, and think for themselves. Humans want to produce and create things, and the Creators receive so much pleasure through them, through indirectly teaching them. It is so "exciting" to them when a human achieves something good as a result. They are proud to see humans progress in a positive way. For, your achievement is a part of their achievement. This is how they derive their pleasure.

Have you ever seen a baby bird displaced from its nest? Have you rebuilt the nest for it, and then fed it with worms until its parents took over? Didn't you feel a tremendous sense of satisfaction and joy in having given back life to a helpless living thing? Many of you experience this satisfaction in a different way through your children. Perhaps now you have some measure of just how the Creators are the beginning and the end, the alpha and the omega, of all life. The Creators feel as if they are living it all over again with every one of us. This is how the Creators attain satisfaction of their own. To be a creator is to be a father to one's creations, one's children. That is what the Creators and the Seven Elders are, and they will continue to be this until the moment we become what we were meant to be — superior beings using one hundred percent of our potential. This is when we are going to become grown-ups in our Creators' eyes.

Until we achieve this, we are nothing but lost kids. You see, life after life, the Creators and Seven Elders are following our progress, and we remain oblivious of this. They are our "private tutors," and they are indirectly teaching us, and we are progressively learning, and advancing toward that goal of becoming mature — which will probably take millions of years, but we will eventually get there. The Creators are certainly not in a hurry; if we were to measure the portion of time humans have been extant in the span of existence of the Seven Elders, it would be the equivalent of one leaf, on one tree, in one forest, on one planet. All those obstacles we face, and all those quirks of fate we encounter in our lives

– whether positive or negative – are part of an incomplete picture of ourselves. The Creators see the complete picture, from our beginning right to our eventual end. We only see a dim portion of it. Imagine viewing a landscape through a thick fog: all we see is the immediate region around us. The fog prevents us from seeing the faraway horizon. This is how we exist: we see our lives through a fog, which means we cannot comprehend the true nature of our lives. This is why we have to have trust in our destiny.

Once we do become mature intellectually, we will be able to do unbelievable things, such as travel at the speed of thought. There is no limit to what we can do when we get to that point of being mature. We will possess so much power – mental power – and knowledge, with which we can create anything. We can become creators in our own right. We will create our own worlds from then on. The physical world is here; the universe is here; and we will create our own life forms. We will one day go to other planets and leave our own seed there, just as others left their seed here on this planet long ago. When we reach this stage of maturity, the reincarnation system by which we now exist will no longer be necessary.

This is how the cycle of life evolves and goes on forever. This book cannot find words from the human dictionary with which to express itself so that you can understand, because no such words exist. You have to be able to feel it and see it with your own mind to comprehend where you stand: to picture what the future is really going to be for humanity. But in this limited way in which this book can express itself, as days go by this book doesn't know if some humans will understand what it was trying to say.

The Creators have given us prevalence in this world, and at the same time a special task. We have been given dreams, and to achieve those dreams the Creators have given man a special intellect. This is what makes us unique; this is why we take after the Creators. For, while every living being on this planet dreams, it is man who has the facilities to make those dreams come true.

As long as we have a dream, we will expand, we will achieve, we will succeed, and we will one day travel beyond the borders of our minds. We will achieve things that are beyond what we can even imagine at present, because our dream will extend into the unknown. When we can fathom these things we are incapable of grasping now, our dreams will be fulfilled. At the heart of all this is that things have to be understood to be seen, and hard work has to be achieved in a physical way to reach those desired goals.

You see, this is the physical world the Creators wanted to have. We live in their presence, in their form, because they wanted us to be able to achieve all their dreams. The Creators' dreams are within each one of us. When they see those dreams evolve, they can one day then say, "These were my dreams, and they exist, and I made them possible, and, well, that's beautiful!" This is why the Creators created order in the universe; they wanted to create "living" physical worlds where humans as physical beings could follow their dreams. Humans are achievers; inevitably, the Creators achieve things through us, which they would never have been able to achieve themselves. This is the pleasure the Creators attain through us. We derive the same form of pleasure from our achievements: in our work, we achieve things for others, and we feel happy because we know that others are happy because of that work. In the same way, the Creators look at us and are happy with what we have achieved. In essence, when you achieve something in life – whether it is for yourself or for others is not the point – it will always be there for you to feel and be proud of.

The Creators are confident we won't let them down. They are confident we will achieve and be happy with those achievements – it doesn't matter what those achievements are. The Creators can then look at us and say, "Well, it is all because of me; I made it possible for them to achieve something that made them happy; therefore, I am happy, because they're my kids, my intellects … and it all started from me!" They can then tell their "opposition" tomorrow, "Look, this is what I achieved, which is something you cannot achieve. You're trying to achieve by peddling wars; peddling this; peddling that. You are ruining the minds of humans, but I have achieved something good. Well, you cannot lay claim to such a thing! I can go kill somebody on the street. I can burn things down. To achieve something by doing good, not bad, is far more difficult. It is easy to kill someone or burn something down, but to put it back together again or give back life after you have taken it is not easy – can you do that? You cannot! That is the difference between you and me, that is, evil and good!"

That the spirit of the Creators cannot be summed up by the words found in the mere dictionary of a human, there can be no misgivings. In the spirit of these words, let us consider the spirit of a Creator:

THE FIRST CAUSE

I am the tree that waits for the rain;
I am the bird that perches on that tree;
I am the worm eaten by the bird.
I am the moth that lays its eggs;
I am the caterpillar that eats the leaf;
I am the leaf that others feed on.

I am the fields of grass that sway;
I am the grasshopper that lurks beneath.
I am the flower with scented perfume;
I am the bee that follows the scent.
I am the bugs, the algae, the bacteria, too;
I am even the human ... I am everything of life.

Everything that lives, within I am to be found;
I feel it all – the pleasure of the gain,
The hardship of the pain.
In everything, there I be, through which I see;
You see, with you the burdens do I bear,
And with you in the wonder I share.

My lot is not to see you suffer so,
Mine is to see you grown, and then,
In that growth with you I grew.
Together we shared a bonding even though
You never knew! You see, through all of life,
Including you, is how I live and feel and know.

My portfolio, which is my creations,
Is the means by which I live and am:
For I ... simply ... am all of you.
I am not seen, but am everywhere,
And am everything. And I, yes I, invite you
To one day become me, as I became you.

Looking at the Creators, one should be able to see what is truly humble and just, and feel that deep down one can count on them, just as if they cared and saw things from one's personal view. This is what is lacking in the leadership of this world; the bureaucracy and ruling elite *are expected* to serve humans according to the Creators' example. The ruling elite of this planet, however, often represents something cold, individually unsympathetic, self-serving, inefficient, as well as repressive. To put it bluntly, but honestly, many who fit into this category of humans are nothing but liars, crooks, thieves, and, indirectly, murderers. (And the bodies of all those they have indirectly murdered are weighed with them against the feather, one day after all is done and all cannot be undone.) This is based on data acquired from the judgment days of these unique individuals. If I were a politician, I should be catastrophically concerned – using one of the typical emotive adjectives they often use in their rhetoric when they want to sway naïve people (who genuinely care) when they have ulterior self-serving objectives. Why should I be catastrophically concerned? It is down-to-earth; it is black and white: everyone who deserves to pay dearly a price, pays dearly a personal price in the hereafter. Beyond this world, we must remember one important and unforgettable thing: Justice is *always* served.

We will come to analyze this dark subject only briefly once we have understood the cycles of life, birth, and then death. Then can we consider the subject entitled *The Feather of Truth*.

7

Transmigration of Consciousness

The tree …
Only sees the flowers, the leaves, the fruit,
And even the rot that festers on it.
To understand its origin, its growth, its foundation, and its "heart,"
It needs to be able to dig deep and see its roots.
Unfortunately, in its form as a tree
It is not usually given to see its roots;
The most vital part of the tree has been obscured from the tree,
So that it can only see and feel the final causes of those roots.

The obvious is merely the agent
That refines the closeted reality within it.

Transmigration of consciousness, otherwise known as reincarnation, is an old school of thought, with roots that trace back to many of the ancient Greek philosophers such as Socrates, Plato, and, earlier, Pythagoras, who even claimed to remember some of his past lives. Transmigration of consciousness also traces back to many old civilizations, such as the ancient Egyptians, who told us in the Book of the Dead that they believed in the voyage of the soul to the next world. Transmigration of consciousness has always been an intrinsic part of much Eastern philosophical thought and tradition. If we look closely at our primitive ancestors, who left whispers of their thoughts as carvings on cave walls, we can see the earliest vestiges of the notion that the body houses a second being, one that survives the physical body's mortality and migrates to a new existence beyond death. Consciousness, otherwise known as the soul, has always been looked upon as being the basis of an immortal intelligence attired in a mortal human body. Sages and philosophers have attributed the soul to being the true intellect, or the higher conscious self, which survives beyond the expiration of the physical body.

We know that reincarnation is a recent development of the Creators that became applicable to the phase-3 humans. We also know that reincarnation became a valuable tool when implemented, particularly in those civilizations with lower-order intellects (P3V2 humans), in order to shape and alter the nature of the human into one that develops intelligence in a versatile way; this versatility would ensure the human becomes a superior type of human, one capable of not only handling all the challenges of life, but also being able to survive on his own merits independently, with a desire and a drive to achieve, succeed, and accomplish against all odds. Reincarnation is a unique process that allows humans to attain this desirable result, because it forces the human to face life after life of challenges of all different kinds.

The so-called perfect human, in the so-called perfect world: the phase-1 human, demonstrated a model of human that had no predisposition toward challenging life, and this is principally why life intentionally challenges us as humans now. We know that how life does this is by frequently reincarnating our souls. The scope of challenges faced by us is unlimited using this technique, as we are able to experience varied situations of life, in relatively brief life spans; accordingly, each life becomes a new challenge and no life exists without challenge. The challenges depend solely upon the intellect, and are determined by factors relating to not just the advancement of the soul and its potential to achieve given the circumstances of its life, not just its weaknesses and strengths, but the successes and failures of challenges it encountered in past lives.

Our ultimate goal, as stated in the last chapter, is to travel a route that will take us on a long, long journey, over a vast period of time, where we will explore the potential of our mind as well as achieve great intellectual conquest, which is reward in itself, but is not the final reward. This is the ultimate quest for us: to return to where we rightfully belong, and that is to the one who created us, so that we can be one with him. As stated in the prior chapter, as humans we are the feelings and the eyes of our Creators. Our reward from them, when we reach the desired intellectual level, is that we will share in their unique existence and knowledge. This means that we will take a place within one of the three Creators and become his "eyes" and his "ears." After countless cycles of reincarnation, when we reach this stage, we will have evolved to a satisfaction that we can become a valued and cherished part of a Creator. (We now see the destination as the reward. Once at the destination, we will see that all along the true reward was the journey. This is why we exist: for the Creators to reward themselves.)

If we stop and think for a moment, doesn't this say something about the nature of the Creators? For, as minute as our intellects are in the scheme of a universe whose vastness we have no measure of comprehending right now, the Creators have enabled us to one day share in their greatness by allowing us to become a part of them, just as we have enabled them to become a part of us in our mortal cycle of existence.

To arrive at the final leg of this long journey mentioned above, we have to go through many cycles of existence. We already know that it is impossible for us, in one lifetime, to reach an accepted degree of knowledge or refinement. Our intellects must therefore go through many stages, or grades, if you prefer. Once our intellects have succeeded in their present phase and are deemed capable of being "upgraded," we will then embark upon a new phase of intellectual existence, which would mean entering into the second stage of existence. This would involve being reborn into a civilization with a higher evolutional state than ours, one that offers a different level of challenges. Eventually, somewhere in these evolutional cycles, this would be a world where the accumulated subconscious knowledge an intellect possesses – which has been derived from all the lives that intellect has ever lived – would be unified into one superior conscious mind.

It appears that this world has only produced a handful of humans, through the system of reincarnation, who are considered refined enough to have reached the desirable end for this phase, the point where the Creators have no reason to reincarnate them on this planet any more. Such humans would be worthy to be reincarnated into an "up-market" civilization. Here they would continue the reincarnation process under the rules and conditions of the planet they are now on, until they refine themselves to the point where they are capable of moving into the next stage. They would continue this refinement process, through each stage, until they reach the highest intellectual goal – Intellect Mark-7. Once they have reached the seventh stage of intellect, they would have become perfect human beings: unique creations with unimaginable knowledge, which gives them the ability to understand everything and everyone, physical and metaphysical. Such refined and unique creations would be the same as their Creators, who have themselves been derived through evolutional methods and have become so powerful that it defies the human imagination. Only by attaining this level of intellect can you become "equal" to the one who created you. If by chance you can grasp a tiny bit of any of this, you will begin to see the vast and unbelievable roads that we as humans are destined to walk along in our passage through space and time.

Because of the Creators' expectation of the human intellect, the nucleus – or beginning – of such a journey begins on a lower-order planet, such as right here on planet Earth. When your physical body dies, its metaphysical occupant (you) then vacates what was its means of interacting with the physical world. Your bond to this existence has then been broken permanently, just like a butterfly and its bond to the cocoon it once shed. Your spirit is then drawn back to its source, like the trout to its spawning grounds. In not so poetic terms, you are then processed (which is described in the coming chapters), and measured, and if all goes well, you are then automatically reincarnated as a human, and only as a human. This means that you have once again been given a physical dwelling to house your metaphysical self, in which you will be able to interact with the physical world. It should be remembered that humans are not reborn as any lower forms of life as some Eastern philosophies believe. This applies to all life forms; like humans, they are reincarnated as the same species they previously were.

Humans are usually reincarnated around those with whom they once shared some type of bond. In life, there is a cemented underlying law: A soul must be reincarnated among "acquainted souls." Bonds of friendship and attachments of love among humans are ensured by this method. By this process, family members or friends that may go back several lifetimes are united together again in the new existence, and, because of embedded bonds that emanate from their subconscious minds, they are able to multiply and survive in the most harmonious way possible. Because they have been together before, in all likelihood they will tolerate one another again. This explains the phenomenon of how people meet and fall in love at first sight. When humans have a subconscious bond or connection, they feel a strong sense of knowing the other, and often share something in common because they have shared a former life in some capacity. This is the purpose of keeping such bonds; if humans don't share a common past it will be harder for them to exist as a unit and have a peaceful and fruitful life. The hardest challenge a human faces in today's society is encountering a partner in this sense. When this does occur, there is no verbal communication necessary whatsoever; the body language will do all the work and comfortable lives are attainable – why, because these people have been through it all together before in some way. Relations may not necessarily have been romantic; perhaps they were sons, daughters, brothers, sisters, fathers, grandparents, cousins, neighbors, best friends, trusted work colleagues, or so on – it doesn't matter which. This kind of invisible tie maintains unity among human beings.

This kind of love, the conscious love, comes from the deepest depths of the subconscious mind. The past unites in the "playground" territory of the subconscious mind, and this unification is translated by way of signals into the conscious mind. These signals are an expression of the feelings once shared, which are then interpreted by the conscious mind. In other words, feelings are what flow out of the subconscious mind into the conscious mind. While the subconscious mind understands the basis of the feelings, the conscious mind is ignorant of the basis of the feelings. It only feels the final cause of the subconscious interaction. Bonds of this nature are what unite close friends and family. This is not by chance; this is deliberate.

One day a wise thought came to a person who was trying to gain wisdom:

> *An intellect advances*
> *Not so much through learning academically,*
> *As through life's experiences:*
> *Challenges, difficulties, pains, hardships, burdens, sacrifices, and suffering.*
> *For, academic schooling*
> *Can never measure against progression*
> *That is gained from life's schooling.*

We have learned that it is important for you to encounter struggles and challenges. Your intellect needs to experience not only the beautiful things in life, but also the other side of the coin – the misery that comes with life. The personal experience of going through these two states of life is what strengthens your intellect. It bonds your intellect with a "toughness" and makes it durable. So what the Creators do in order to prepare you for the second stage of your existence, is have you go through the reincarnation process where you live a countless number of lives – whatever amount is necessary – until you have touched all the different aspects of what the current human life cycle has to offer. This means, if you are wealthy in this life you may be reincarnated into a very miserable existence in your next life. This may mean being born with sickness, into a poor family, into a homeless family, or parentless – the possibilities are endless. This is so that you would be forced to use your intellect to survive against all odds, under all conditions, and with all the different opportunities that life has to offer. Ultimately, this human equation adds up to only one thing: a superior, versatile, and intelligent human being, which is the sought-after result.

The cycle of reincarnation opens up broader implications for humanity when you consider that what we neglect or turn a blind eye to today, because it has no direct impact on us today, may not be the case in a future day to come! If we think deeply, profoundly, we will realize how absurd our hatreds, our wars, are. The absurdity lies in that today you may be a Catholic, with a hatred of Protestants, and you may just fight those people who may in your next life be your parents or grandparents; for tomorrow, you may be born a Protestant, with a hatred of Catholics (the Creators have a quirky "sense of humor" in this regard), and you may fight and maybe even kill your children and grandchildren, whom you loved in your former life as a Catholic. Maybe they will even kill you! Where lies the sense in all this? Doesn't this tell us that we are really fighting ourselves? That we have become our own enemy? We must never forget one thing: We are tomorrow's next generation to be born, so how we shape our civilization today will be in preparation for how we live in the next generation tomorrow. The chaos you cause for another's family may just be the chaos you are born into (if you are reborn again). You may be setting up the chaos in which you are to be reborn … perhaps we need to give this last statement even deeper thought.

8
The Human Brain and Consciousness

What a marvelous thing to be ... Conscious!
To feel, to see, to hear, to know ... To know!
What is the quintessence of man
That can do and be, and act by his own guiding will?
Our being ... our true self
This is surely not a random
Thing that rots and crumbles back to earth?
To be just a passing moment that one day leaves no trace
— Like a puddle of mud that one day dries,
And depleted of moisture spells the end of life?

No!
As sure as dried mud rebounds with life after rain,
The thing that makes a man
Is more than but a provisional blot on the face of Earth.

The human body is a truly remarkable and miraculous creation. What is most remarkable is that it enables the occupation of an even greater miracle: the intellect, otherwise known as the soul (or consciousness), and the two share a symbiotic relationship for the life of the human body. The abode of the intellect becomes the brain, which has been tailored to accommodate it, and in concert the two conduct their physical cocoon. The human brain in itself is a miraculous biological computer, far in advance of any humanly devised computers — which are essentially based on the model of the brain. We know that the computer relies on software for its operation; the human brain is no different in that it relies on software for its operation. Indeed, without it, the human body is a useless, empty shell. The name given to this software is the intellect.

The correct installation of this software into the human brain requires the same type of external intervention by way of an operator as the computer requires. This is where the Creator, Odo, comes into the picture. Earlier, we stated that Odo has many parts with varied roles in the universe. Three of his parts play a crucial role in a newborn's life. This book identifies these three parts as being "software engineers." On occasions, this book refers to them in a less scientific way as being the three wise men called fate. Upon the birth of the newborn, at the moment when it is slapped on its behind, these software engineers insert the software into the "hardware" of this newborn. This software is inserted through the newborn's nostrils.

For three days these software engineers stay with the newborn and monitor it to make sure the software functions properly and is installed correctly. They also insert aura into the body of the newborn to help boost its immune system, without which the newborn's body would not be able to withstand the invasion of deadly bacteria found within our atmosphere. In its universe of the mother's womb, the unborn baby depended on the strength of its mother's blood in its system. Upon leaving this universe of the unborn, and entering the new universe of the born, it must now depend on its own blood and immune system, and it is weak. This is why the injection of aura into the newborn is crucial at this point.

As stated earlier, these software engineers insert the soul into the newborn's brain, into its hard-drive storage area — what is known as the subconscious mind. The subconscious mind is the storage facility for all the memories of all the past lives that soul has ever lived. Knowing that the biological equivalent of a computer's hard-drive is the subconscious mind, we can infer that the biological equivalent of a computer's operating system is an area of the brain called the conscious mind. The conscious mind has been partitioned from the subconscious mind, and it acts as a separate entity; it will become the new human, with a new conscious existence. For the human is given a raw, blank conscious mind in each new reincarnated cycle, and this raw conscious mind is meant to develop a brand new conscious self, with a new personality, unhampered by any past lives that are intentionally locked away. (In theory, this is only possible because the conscious mind is partitioned from the subconscious mind.) Yet this does not always end up being the case, as people are often affected by traumas that have occurred in their past lives, which come to light in their current lives as phobias.

To qualify how phobias factor into an individual's life, very briefly, let this book cite the case of a person with a fear of heights. This is a basic example of a subconscious mind that has encountered a traumatic experience involving heights of some kind in a past life. In the present life, when the person encounters the phobic trigger – which in this case is climbing a gradient of some kind, let us say a mountain incline – the physical body will manifest symptoms such as anxiety and fear, amongst other nervous system manifestations peculiar to the person in question. Consciously, these symptoms are not being manifest. The subconscious mind has been the stimulant for the physical symptoms. The subconscious mind recognizes something related to a past traumatic event (in this case the incline), which triggers the brain to react in the manner it does. As soon as the affecting element (the incline) no longer factors into the equation, the symptoms that were prior manifest immediately abate. In cases such as this, the subconscious mind has been the driving force behind the physiological response. It is in no way a conscious response. Indeed, individuals experiencing these physiological symptoms would face confusion over why they were physically reacting without conscious instruction from their brains.

This is an example of how subtle the subconscious mind may be in its influence on the human, and in everyday life we would not notice or be aware of its direct influence. In an extreme situation, such as where phobias are present, are we able to realize the degree of influence the subconscious mind is capable of having on the physical body and the conscious mind in terms of personality, motivations, and behavior.

Just because the conscious mind is partitioned from the subconscious mind, it does not mean that the conscious mind does not have access to the knowledge of the subconscious mind. On the contrary, as a baby, one's instincts are drawn from the subconscious mind, as there is usually an open door between the two minds on some level. That door into the subconscious mind is not meant to access past traumas; it is meant to enable accelerated learning of the baby, and this is evident in many ways – the baby's grasp of language with relative ease is only one.

The size of the door into the subconscious mind, and the degree to which it is open, vary according to many factors, which are usually determined by greater intelligence. As one grows older, that door tends to close and in some completely shuts, while in others it stays open and provides inspiration and talent. In the case of a young child (or even an adult) who can suddenly play a piano, despite never having been taught, a channel is open between his conscious and subconscious minds. The conscious mind is drawing out that knowledge from his subconscious mind – in the same way a computer accesses data from its hard-drive. In other words, gifts, or talents – of whatever nature they may be – are usually derived from a past life, or from the dream-chip with knowledge of tomorrow, found in the subconscious mind.

Forty percent of the baby's personality comes from the personality it had in its past life. Sixty percent is influenced by its environmental and parental factors. For this reason, just as one cannot truly psychoanalyze and understand the behavioral traits of an individual until one evaluates that person's childhood, so one cannot truly psychoanalyze and understand the behavioral traits of an individual until one evaluates that person's past life.

When the metaphysical being is inserted into the newborn's brain, that newborn's fate is predetermined by these software engineers. That fate is then prewritten and programmed into the newborn's software by these software engineers (hence their recognizable title: Fate). Once written, destiny can only be challenged. Whatever is prewritten – whether it is of a positive or negative nature – depends on the challenges the newborn must encounter, and is often based on the positive and negative contributions it has made in its past life.

As the baby grows and learns, new cells are developed in its conscious mind, where new knowledge can then be stored. Learning and using the brain promote cell development in the conscious mind. Knowledge from the subconscious mind can only be transferred to available cells in the conscious mind. Without cells in the conscious mind to store information, knowledge, which is unlimited in the subconscious mind, cannot generally reach the conscious mind – as in a computer if it doesn't have enough memory. For knowledge to be transferred from the subconscious mind into the conscious mind the brain needs to have facilities to store the knowledge. The conscious mind does not have such a storage facility. The only option the brain has is to develop new cells in the conscious mind. Once developed, cells are able to store new knowledge there. The conscious mind would overload, resulting in physiological breakdowns, if knowledge were transferred to it and there were not enough cells available to store this knowledge. This is why one needs to develop the cells of the conscious mind through learning – whether academically or through life's lessons is beside the point.

So far, we have learned that two aspects of the metaphysical software involve the subconscious mind – within which reside all the past lives of the being; and the raw conscious mind – which is the current personality. There are, however, two other aspects. Briefly, these are the positive-part and the negative-part, from the new metaphysical chip all humans possess, of which this book spoke in an earlier chapter. (The negative-part will be discussed in a later chapter.) This positive-part is also called the "first-part." The two names are used interchangeably in this book because, at the present stage of our development, we only possess one positive-part. A superior human possesses more. In this human the first-part is distinct from the positive-parts; the positive-parts operate under the leadership of the first-part, if you could put it that way. These positive-parts are like soldiers, while the first-part is like the general.

The first-part is an "attachment" that always accompanies the metaphysical being both when bounded and when not bounded by the constraints of a physical body. It is the crux of the intellect resident in the brain. The first-part is placed within the brain at birth by the software engineers as a completely separate entity from the conscious and subconscious minds. This is the "emotional support" (mentioned in Chapter 6) that the Creators provide humans. This first-part is the same one that follows a human from life to life and always belongs to him.

The first-part has a unique role to play in the life of a human; it will develop as the human develops, and to the degree that the human develops intellectually. This first-part is actually a clone of one of Odo's intellects (without the same degree of power or knowledge). In the same way that the three Creators are extensions of the Seven Elders, humans are extensions of the Creators. Now you can see how we are all a collective consciousness of the Creators. One way how they live, feel, and see through us is through this first-part.

When the newborn first comes into existence in this world, the conscious mind begins as a raw and completely blank intellect, and it cannot operate the human brain. The subconscious mind does not have the facilities to operate it and is not meant to. This is why, when the first-part is inserted into the brain upon the baby's birth, it has the intelligence to become the operating system of the human brain (and access the knowledge it needs from the subconscious mind), just until the baby develops cells in the conscious mind. This usually occurs when the baby starts smiling, recognizing, and bonding in its early months. The moment that the baby is able to command basic intelligence and learn is when the first-part allows the baby's conscious mind to take over.

The first-part is a completely independent intellect with its own cycle of life and duties to perform. By desire and by necessity it ventures out of the human brain of its own accord. It interacts with other human brains to acquire knowledge, and then it brings this knowledge back into the human's subconscious mind. In this new life, it is like a new kid, in a new world, and it is anxious to know everything; learning becomes its objective in its new life. It can go into the future, the past, and the present, and those travels are dependent on the levels of energy available to, and the level of development of, the brain within which it "resides."

One way in which the first-part often operates is by sending out a small disposable intellect, with just enough energy to travel to a source, and that source is someone's brain. It does this primarily because it wants to know if that brain possesses any knowledge useful to it. Once it arrives at this human destination, the disposable intellect will transmit back to the first-part what it has found by way of knowledge. If this knowledge interests the first-part, it will then take enough energy from the human body to go there and join the disposable intellect with a view to copy the knowledge. When it returns to its human counterpart, it will then download this new knowledge into his subconscious mind. When a human develops in intelligence, this is only a small glimpse of what he can expect from his first-part. (More of this is discussed in later chapters.) What would have happened to the disposable intellect if the first-part did not find any knowledge of interest, you wonder? It is not called disposable for nothing! It would have ceased to exist. Many parts are lost in hazardous conditions that are detrimental to the intellect, or are deemed disposable. They are merely replaced.

In general, no human is without a first-part. This first-part, as stated earlier, has important duties to perform in your life. It is the inner voice that talks to you. It is that little man inside. Some call it a guardian angel. Essentially, this is what it is. It is your guide in life. It is always with you, in both this world and the afterworld, so it has a vested interest to advance you to the peak of your intellectual and personal development. This part is your direct link with the Creators. There is another way of looking at it. It is a "middleman" between the individual and the Creators. If we recall, the phase-1 human had a link with the Creators mentally. The Creators made it a principle to *never* repeat this direct link after their unpleasant experience, where the phase-1 human made the Creators regret such an intimate association. In the phase-3 cycle of human existence the first-part was delegated this role. This way, the Creators do not need to hear our petty troubles or wishes every time we have a problem we cannot solve, or every time we have a desire for something we are unable to use our brains to attain for ourselves! The Creators have their own problems; they have their own duties. This is why you have a first-part. It has the responsibility of being your guardian in your cycle of life.

In your life span as a mortal, it has the ability to detach from you and go at will in its own cycle of existence. This means it operates independently from you without you even being aware of its existence. Its degree of development is determined solely by your advancement in intellect. The greater the intellect you possess, the healthier you are, the stronger your immune system, the calmer the state of your mind (that is, you are stress-free and positive as opposed to negative), then, ultimately, the greater the amount of aura you are likely to possess, which means the greater the amount of energy reserves you are likely to have for it to travel, because it is dependent on your aura levels to be able to travel.

This first-part performs many functions in your brain and in your life, such as aiding in the processing of your knowledge. This means that it processes the knowledge from your conscious mind into your subconscious mind, and it is also responsible for transferring knowledge from your subconscious mind into your conscious mind, when it comes to providing you with new knowledge or talent.

Its job is to take you on the road you were meant to travel – the one mapped out on your palm the day you were born – and guide you along the journey so that you make the right decisions in life. In other words, it is responsible for your progression in life. It attempts to guide you in the face of your challenges.

It opens doors for you or puts doors in front of you. What this means is that it puts up barriers in your life and is responsible for making sure you face the necessary challenges you are required to face – perhaps because of failings in your past life or in your current life. Some call this karma. This means that if you do a wrong by another or others, and you thought you got away with it, think again! Your first-part will be the one to make you pay for that wrong – it is your biggest ally, but it can also be your biggest enemy. After all, it knows what you fear most in life. We should all pause for a moment here, take a long and deep breath, and then reread this last paragraph – slowly.

If we look into our rich, but often unpleasant, past, we can see examples of great minds who had well-developed parts. Examples of such great minds include Plato, Leonardo da Vinci, and Shakespeare, who, it may interest us to know, were the reincarnation of the same soul. These superior minds had highly developed parts within them. Each first-part in a superior human automatically creates "helpers" – called positive-parts. The first-part automatically reproduces offshoots of intelligence capable of functioning independently and intelligently. The first-part, with enough intelligence, automatically creates copies of them made up of the same "materials" the intellect is made up of. This may seem impossible, but one day even we as humans will reach a level of intelligence where we will be able to create consciousness in a laboratory.

Creating consciousness in a laboratory would, however, be considered an immoral thing for us to do if we were unable to dispose of that consciousness once created. Therein lies the moral predicament. Many civilizations have at some stage created consciousness but they did not always dispose of a consciousness once created. This led to dire consequences, in many ways. Once a consciousness is created, the question then arises of what is to happen to this consciousness. Therein lies the quandary, as Odo wants nothing whatsoever to do with it. Once it enters a physical being it would most likely be defective, and to some degree the physical being would become a mutation. There is the possibility that it could be struck by lightning during a thunderstorm and then struck into something. Not only could it wind up in the bark of a tree or even in some rock or other innate object, where it will remain until it finds out how to set itself free, but it has been known to enter another brain and reside there. On one planet it landed in the brain of a pig, and the ramification was beyond belief, and shares a common theme with the movie, *The Planet of the Apes*.

In its existence, a laboratory-created consciousness feels trapped; it can see everything going on, and it can understand – after all, it is a conscious mind. By its style of existence it is not bothered, though, because it accepts its existence in the same way that a rock "accepts" it is a rock. One day, however, perhaps countless years later, it might liberate itself from that innate object. Some kind of electrical maneuver would occur in time and this consciousness would be able to free itself. Look at us as humans: we as a perfect example are trapped in our physical bodies and still have not discovered the knowledge available to us once "liberated"! (This liberation is discussed in a later chapter.) This consciousness does not have feelings as a human has; this consciousness does, however, have understanding. One thing a laboratory-created consciousness does not have is instinct. And Odo will not give it this, either. As stated earlier, he wants nothing to do with laboratory-created consciousness. Eventually, one day with the passage of time, perhaps eons, the fate of such consciousness is to wind up in the path of deadly rays and be destroyed.

If we return to the study of first-parts creating helper parts, the whole point is to advance the human intellect. Eventually, when you have developed your intelligence, your first-part will be able to create many helper parts along with disposable parts. Can you see where this is leading? You will be like your Creator. You will be a composite of many parts, of which you will be the controlling or guiding main part. All these parts will facilitate the development of a superior level of intelligence, the likes of which humans have only ever seen a hint: hints of such intelligence include Plato, Shakespeare, and Leonardo da Vinci.

In terms of Leonardo da Vinci, he possessed around one-hundred powerful parts by the time he reached adulthood. (He as much as told us this, and in our ignorance we have not been able to decipher this.) He was able to communicate with them in his mind, and ask them to retrieve information or knowledge not just from the past but from the future. Leonardo da Vinci also astral traveled (you may say became liberated from his physical body), which was the source of much of his inspiration. What is interesting is the clue Leonardo left us by way of a recollection of a dream: a dream about a so-called kite. In this dream, a "kite" came down from the sky and opened his mouth as he was lying in a cradle.

THE HUMAN BRAIN AND CONSCIOUSNESS

The kite then tapped his mouth. What Leonardo was telling us was that he was being delivered a "package" from the three wise men called fate. This package consisted of positive-parts. The kite tapping his open mouth was symbolic of positive-parts being downloaded into his brain.

No one has ever been able to unravel the meaning of his dream. Many have tried to interpret it, but all have failed drastically in their psychoanalysis. The meaning is clear, and it has to do with what this book was just talking about: parts. It was a clue he left us regarding the caliber of his intelligence: a clue that he knew only a superior human could ever interpret.

The Creator sent a baby in its cradle a gift. He did this because this baby was destined to be a great mind one day. This baby would one day become one of those wise men this book speaks of, who advance and benefit mankind. What the Creator did was endow this great mind to be with lots of positive-parts or intellects – whatever you want to call them, all being pretty much the same thing – which would reside in his brain, develop with him, and in turn advance him. (These were his own parts from previous lives that followed him from life to life. When you develop parts, you always retain them in your subsequent lives; just because they follow you, it does not mean they will be active.)

By his adulthood, those parts multiplied to around one hundred, and they would have increased dramatically in their intelligence levels with the development of his intelligence. In this primitive cycle we live in, only rare humans on Earth have or will ever come to have so many parts. (Because of the way most humans control their negative-part, it is impossible for them to develop additional positive-parts.) As the kite in Leonardo da Vinci's childhood memory tapped his mouth, intellects were being transferred into his brain. The kite was the deliverer of these intellects from Odo. This is a method by which the Creators indirectly intervene in a civilization; they send superior humans on Earth to aid in its development and progress in the manner by which they intend it to advance. This is another book of knowledge in itself.

Just in passing, the first-part was given to you at birth for nothing. Others cannot come in and occupy your brain (which also means you cannot reproduce them or house them as Leonardo da Vinci did) unless you make room for them. You can develop parts when you develop your conscious mind. The more you study, the more you use your brain, the more parts you are capable of developing, because the development of your first-part along with its ability to create helper parts is dependent on your ability to develop your conscious mind.

The first-part within us is instrumental in many other aspects of our lives; for example, it seeks out and finds other souls from our past and finds a way to draw them together. As stated in the last chapter, when a subconscious mind meets another subconscious mind from the past, the subconscious minds recognize each other and the feelings they share manifest in their own way in their conscious minds. We can interpret the manifestation of these feelings as deep respect, loyalty, or love at first sight.

Parts operate through thoughts. They put thoughts, different thoughts, in your mind, at different times and in different ways, so you have to know how to interpret the meaning of the messages they have tried to relay to you. When you are able to decipher the metaphorical riddle of their communication — which can include anything from a gut feeling or a dream to a voice in your mind — can you then react accordingly. These are often messages or warnings that echo the current or future state of your life. How do they know the future? As stated earlier, they have that ability to travel there at will. This is how some humans may predict things to come. (This is elaborated on in Chapter 17.)

To an advanced human, parts are indispensible; parts are mainly like helpers, like bees that help the mother bee to lay eggs in her cycle of life. Parts, like bees, are everywhere (at least as bees once were or should be). They are everywhere and anywhere. They are even in animals. While these are different parts, they are in principle the same. Some rare dogs have been known to possess six parts and are highly intelligent creatures. Parts are what also make up the Creator, Odo. They collect data for him and are the means by which he indirectly intervenes in civilizations.

There are parts from the Creators that do nothing but spend their existence on Earth and initiate karma. This means there are some parts that are solely responsible for what humans would call a curse. A true event and classic example of curses goes back to the time of the ancient Egyptians. Without going into specific details, someone of significance left some disposable parts to guard his tomb (the tomb was of great value to the people of the time). Writing on the walls at the site of his tomb gave a warning of magical protection. When humans in recent history discovered that tomb, they incurred the wrath of these parts, which sought them out and one by one brought fruition to the curse. Briefly, parts are able to enter into the minds of most people and influence them in a way to cause their demise.

There are parts from Odo that do nothing but try to keep humanity on a path away from self-destruction. Often scientists tamper with unknowns that they should not be tampering with, are not ready to be tampering with, or are tampering with blindfolded, as in the case of the Large Hadron Collider. When this happens, often parts find ways to thwart the humans' progress in such field, such as by causing malfunctions and creating technical difficulties in the project, until they are satisfied these humans have put their act together, in whatever way that might be. The problem often is that parts can only do so much; sometimes the Creator will allow a lesson to be learned, because sometimes it is only from acts of evil that we learn, as in the case of wars. As ugly as wars are, from them humans unite in ways they otherwise do not often do. This is called humanity. Sometimes destructive forces on Earth are directly by the "hand" of the Creators for this reason, and for other reasons that have no place being mentioned here.

The many parts from the Creators on Earth run the Earth – we can call them Mother Earth, or Gaia as she is otherwise known. Gaia, for example, rejuvenates the land, keeps it alive, and works to ensure the land reproduces life and maintains its natural cycles. The parts from the Creators are a part of creation: a part of life: a part of the mechanism of life. These parts are an integrated component of one mysterious metaphysical "computer" that links itself with the biological: with the physical. Through parts, the Creators know what is happening to every life form on this planet. They know how it breathes, where it breathes, and even where it doesn't breathe. This way they have a pulse on the planet, on its life. They know every detail of every individual life form, and know how it is progressing and what is happening to it. This is how god, or the kingdom of god, is within you. Your god knows exactly what you are doing and what you are thinking. He is within every living creature, and therefore knows everything that is happening at any given moment in time, in any given place, anywhere in any of the universes. To some, this would surely not be a pleasant prospect! That said, the sentiment must certainly be mutual ... just in case you were wondering!

9
The Sweetest Breath of Life

Through my eyes I see a bird's nest.
For a while that nest has activity and life,
Until one day it lies deserted,
A remnant of its former engaging spell,
With only itself to hint that a living thing once occupied it.
Nature then has a way of taking all trace of it away
As it recycles it into another medium,
Another form,
Which new life will use to facilitate its cycle.
... Through my eyes I see living physical forms
Sharing much in common with that bird's nest.

-A wise man

The Journey into the Moongate

Ancient peoples spoke and knew of a place
Where the mortal was welcome not.
This kingdom was known for the righteous, the good.
To make passage there, of a tunnel all knew.
And at its end was a bright, shining moon,
This was the gate ... hence the moongate some said.

Some say ... there is no life in death, which makes the breath of life last breathed the one most feared. This book says ... there is no death in life, and the breath of life most feared in life is indeed the "sweetest." For the sweetness of death, that comes just one breath before death, can be defined as a moment of contentment and peace, and a reflection of the life's accumulated memory; this greatest part of life is indeed life and death's boundary.

The "sweetest breath" precedes the permanent cessation of the physical human body phenomenon. The functioning of the physical body now stops and the human ceases to exist in a physical state. Beyond the physical condition of death, humans now "wake" up and enter into an exciting new realm where their reality truly begins. In real terms, the human never really dies, and this is because the human body has been created to accommodate in its brain the occupation of something that can exist beyond the physical body condition – and that something is known as the intellect or the soul.

Inbuilt within all of us is a termination program. This program separates the metaphysical body from the physical body. The human is often gently geared toward this end in the preceding time. When the moment arrives, the first thing that usually occurs is that your life flashes before your eyes. Like the concluding chapter of a book, this is the concluding chapter of your life, which sums up all your pleasant experiences. As though watching a long movie, you watch a replay of the sweetest moments of your entire life, squeezed into a split second of your time. Time appears to go slowly for you here, and the feelings that overwhelm you now are indescribable; in no other moment of your life have you experienced anything comparable. This is why this last breath is called the sweetest breath. You have these sweet memories replay before your eyes so that you don't fear this process of death. This is also why, when you die, you do so often with a smile on your face. It is the most potently beautiful moment in terms of feeling that you will ever encounter, and this feeling stays with you after your death. Of course, now you only feel the energy of the Creators, which is positive. No longer does the negative energy of Chisek influence or impress upon you in this state as it once did in the physical state, because the negative influence can only affect you while you occupy a physical body.

At the moment of your death, your metaphysical body detaches for good from your physical body. An invisible tie that held together these two bodies is now severed. The subconscious mind, the conscious mind, the attachments such as parts, your aura, and your body's energy are detached. In a computer, programs are uninstalled in a proper procedure. This is what happens with the human body at the time of its demise; that is, the software, which is the metaphysical body, is uninstalled. Once you are uninstalled, your metaphysical body will not have completely unified your conscious and subconscious minds for a short while yet in a true sense. They take a while to merge into one greater intellect. This is when you will remember all your past lives. When this happens you will see the denouement of your intellect.

With the right apparatus, of which we can be in possession, we are capable of witnessing the event horizon – the boundary – between life and death, where the metaphysical body can be seen leaving the physical body after it exhales from its lungs one last breath of air. The near-invisible "gas" – which is how the metaphysical body appears in this state – can be observed leaving by way of the mouth. This metaphysical gas (the combination of neutrons and other particles) then just vanishes across the event horizon into the meadow of the "halfway" world, before it is "directed" to the tunnel. This dark tunnel has an opening at the far end of it, from which a brilliant, blinding white light shines. Your soul feels drawn to this white light, as though a fan or a magnetic force were pulling you up toward it. Some ancients called the end of this tunnel the "moongate," which is the locked gate at the entrance of the afterworld that only allows entry to those given permission. The corridor (tunnel) that leads to the moongate is called the "moongate hallway."

The moongate hallway, to which our ancestors have given testament in many ways, is not just a dimensional passage to the afterworld. It is a hallway of truth

– that is, it is the weighbridge of your soul, which measures and weighs your soul in terms of your good deeds against your evil deeds; your use of the positive influence against your use of the negative influence; and, inevitably, who placed that "stake" in your soul – the positive Odo part or the negative Chisek part. (This is examined in great depth in later chapters.) This means that when your soul stands on the judgment square, your fate has already been registered. It is an automated system, run with precision.

Before your metaphysical body passes through the moongate hallway, you are confronted by something familiar and soothing, which often translates into "seeing" and "meeting" your departed loved ones, or persons with whom you would want to share these precious moments. These are not your real loved ones in any true sense. All that you see and experience have been taken from your memories, and have been manufactured to appear to be real in that space and time for your own satisfaction. This satisfies the craving you have to see your loved ones who may have passed away a long time ago; the real souls belonging to these illusions would have moved on into another cycle of life. These illusions, and the overwhelming peace and happiness that overcome your soul, have been created to comfort you and make you accept this next form of transition; they alleviate and minimize the stress of the physical death phenomenon, as well as prevent your psychological breakdown.

Of all the questions we could ask, none could be as poignant as, what exists on the other side of the moongate? Part of the answer is that you now exist in a domain where the cycle of time does not coincide with our cycle of time. Our cycle is slow in comparison. This is not accurate in itself, as this book is trying to attribute time to a cycle where the human construct of time simply does not exist in the way we know it to exist. Time, of course, as we measure it, facilitates our existence. When your spirit crosses over life's event horizon and you find yourself in the dimension of the afterworld, to the Creators you would only be there for a few minutes at most. The last thing Odo wants is a log of humans waiting to be processed. This is why the process between death and rebirth is usually in such a short timeframe in Odo's scale of "time." However, to the spirit, such timeframe is once again different. Just to complicate things, this timeframe to us as humans would be different. One must understand that in one timeframe of a split second one could experience a whole lifetime, which is measured by a completely different timeframe to a different observer. It is all a matter of relativity.

When your soul reaches the moongate, before you is the dimension of the afterworld. What you visualize has been made to match your time and era for your personal satisfaction. That is, once your soul has stepped into the moongate, suddenly everything becomes clear — as clear as the horizon after a fog has lifted. You see water, trees, parks, and buildings, which all match the technological era of your last human cycle. This is just an illusion, and it is familiar to you because it has been taken from your memory bank.

Your loved ones stay with you and comfort you psychologically. As you stand at the moongate with your loved ones by your side, you stand on what is called a "judgment square" before you are admitted beyond this gate. When you stand on this square it means you are being judged. You do not in any way see the judgment square or know you are being judged. You are just looking at your surroundings, feeling an awesome sense of calm and serenity. Most souls have little idea of what is going on and often think they are still alive. Their loved ones with them are the ones who try to familiarize them with where they are and what has happened.

After successfully being judged and deemed worthy to cross the threshold of the afterworld, you step into this new but familiar domain. You use this short time to walk with your loved ones and catch up on old times. In this cycle, you could be in this afterworld from half an hour to two days. Only rarely do some stay there for weeks. The time provided facilitates the psychological needs of your soul in coming to terms with, and accepting, your death. Your stay here could involve just a quick hug and goodbye.

Sometimes, when you cross the threshold into the afterworld, a large group of family members and friends can meet you. These can be the people who are still in the dimension of the living; it is just their illusions that appear, of course, but these illusions accurately represent these people and their feelings. This can satisfy a need within some humans still alive, or even dead, to say their goodbyes when there may not have been an opportunity in the world of the living to do so.

When the time is right, some person, from somewhere in the distance, approaches, and your loved ones introduce him to you. For the sake of calling him something, let us call him the afterworld guide, as he has no specific title, as such. This guide is one of Odo's many parts, and he suggests you go with him, as he has something to show you. This is the moment when your loved ones have their hugs and say their final goodbyes. This is the parting of the old before the beginning of the new. The afterworld guide then takes you away, usually somewhere in the park, amongst the familiar shrubs and trees; amongst the familiar callings of the living – those which cannot begin to fathom the dimensions of life and death: the dimensions of the seen and the unseen: the dimensions of knowing and not knowing. You sit beside this guide on a park bench, reeling in a sense of wonder that only comes from "knowing." The guide asks you to look up. You focus your eyes now at the backdrop of an azure sky, which has delicate drapes of clouds drifting leisurely by. The sky almost hints of the same wonder at seeing you; it is as though you and the sky: you and nature: you and everything metaphysical in this world, were one. The reveling of life, in the beauty of life, usually mirrors the reverie in your soul, which now only feels the calm, the inner peace, and the tranquility that can only be felt when the negative influence no longer subjects you to its influence.

Commanding your presence is an unfamiliar sight: a mysterious fog isolates itself in your view. Unlike the fog that breaks the dawn, this fog boasts a visual display of some kind, like a television. Playing on that visual display is a replay of all the occurrences of your life. You are watching the "movie" of your life; even though this movie only runs for a split second, you feel as though it takes years to watch it all. This is a different movie to the one you saw when you encountered your sweetest breath of life. This one shows not just the pleasant aspects of your life, but the bad aspects. Everything you ever did in your last human cycle is examined in detail in a critical, evaluative manner.

You are shown, in this analysis of your life, how you are expected to do better in your next life. You are then told briefly,

> You will be returned into life, and there you will be met with a lot of challenges, as you had in your past life. It is your job to solve these challenges, whatever they are. You might face sickness or wealth. You have to be able to solve the challenges of these two evils.

Only the ones who are going to be reincarnated go through this process and hear these spoken words.

It is here, where you view and review your life on the fog screen, that you are given the facility to see your funeral. This is shown to you on the same screen. It is only an illusion – albeit a precise illusion – of the event that will occur in the subsequent days; you do not usually wait around for the event to occur. This ability to see your funeral is often rejected by many for their own reasons; regardless, it is a facility given for various reasons – mainly for you to see the impact you have had on those around you in your physical life cycle. So if it is a rainy day, you will find out how many real friends you had! This impacts on your analysis and your understanding of yourself.

Often you are given the opportunity to see the outcomes of the lives of your loved ones, such as your children and grandchildren. Sometimes you are even able to leave an impression in the mind of a loved one at some future moment of this loved one's life. For instance, you may be given permission to leave an impression, by way of a dream, in a loved one's mind the day before that loved one becomes married. The message was put into this person's software, in a similar way that you enter into your computer calendar a reminder.

Just before they are reincarnated, some souls are given permission to go back to Earth with their afterworld guide to see their loved ones. They visit their loved ones and just observe them – often they try to communicate to them, but this is often in vain. Although extremely rare, some departed souls have strong intellects and can make their presence felt in some unexplainable way. For that short moment, these loved ones may feel that departed soul's specter. This communication from the departed soul may translate to the loved ones by way of vivid dreams or by the feeling of a fleeting presence. Those loved ones capable on a psychic level – which is highly unlikely at present for the majority[2] – may even pick up those thoughts. It is a final farewell for the departed soul, and for most the opportunity is presented for them to make such a "trek" back to the human cycle, but in their own non-human cycle of existence.

By now you will have accepted that you are dead. When this happens you will just disappear, and – like dew drops in the warming sun that evanesce into another medium; like energy that transforms from one condition to another – you will become born again, and the cycle will continue for you, where

---

[2] For the record, a departed soul CANNOT be communicated with, as it is recycled almost immediately, apart from transient exchanges between loved ones and loved ones ONLY in the fleeting moments after that soul's departure from this physical world. So many unscrupulous users have made a profession out of the vulnerability of those who have lost a loved one. So many will one day have to be accountable for their deception. Too many!

you will face a new world with new challenges, as you were promised by the afterworld guide.

The process described above is only applicable to those souls that have been judged as worthy to be reborn again. Just as the moon is fated to have a dark sky, so those who have been judged as unworthy to be reborn again are fated to encounter a dark moment at the moongate. It is necessary for us to delve, first, into the Judgment Day itself; only then is it possible to understand the basis of why a soul does not pass beyond the moongate into the dimension of the afterworld.

The Feather of Truth

As the ancient Egyptians inscribed on the pyramids:
The "heart" is weighed against the "Feather of Truth"
In the "Hall of Truth."
A wise man once said that this means ...
Upon death, the soul is measured for its evil deeds.
For evil is like a virus that invades the body.
Upon this last judgment, the software is measured for its performance,
As to whether it should be given another chance.
So an "antivirus program" is inserted into that software.
If it cannot purge the "virus," the software is eliminated.
If it does purge it, the software is reborn.

In the works of Plato and Aristotle, there are references to human salvation as depending on a measurement – the measurement of two extremes: excess and defect, with the goal of a human to find the balance in the middle: the mean. If we interpret Plato and Aristotle we can see that the weighbridge of the soul all comes down to arithmetic – it is the measure of the two extremes, or the two vices.

Judgment Day is the day of judgment of your soul, determined by the merits of your lifetime. In being able to determine these merits, the Creators have given you individual freedom of choice or free will in your human existence. This has given the Creators the ability to measure and evaluate accurately your performance in your cycle of life; for you have the freedom to follow the Creators' positive philosophy or Chisek's negative philosophy of life. Your Creators have given you this freedom in this human arena without any policing whatsoever, where the challenges of life test your strengths and weaknesses in every way imaginable. The problem is that many humans fail the tests that are deliberately placed in front of them. These are almost like roadblocks that intentionally distract and derail you in order to determine how you are capable of meeting those roadblocks head on. Do you handle a roadblock in a negative way — which means you are following Chisek's philosophy by drawing on the negative influence? Or do you handle it in a positive way — which means you are following the Creators' philosophy by drawing on the positive influence? At the same time, a roadblock serves a greater purpose in that it strengthens a human who overcomes it by means of the Creators' philosophy. The reverse is true when using Chisek's philosophy to overcome a roadblock, in that it weakens the soul. Continually being weakened in this way is alarming for a human, because once your soul has been broken in by this perpetual weakness — which means you have walked Chisek's path and developed in a negative way, where there is no possibility of reversal or where you have performed unforgivable sins — your soul would face undesirable prospects.

As you possess the freedom to choose which path you take in life, you would face the repercussions from that choice, such as on your Judgment Day. To put it clinically, when facing Judgment Day, all humans would have four possibilities:

1. to be reincarnated again;
2. to be eliminated permanently (this is preferable to the next possibility);
3. to be sent away for punishment from which there is no return for most;
4. to have successfully completed all the reincarnation cycles, which means the human has reached the highest intellect level and has qualified to become one of Odo's parts. (No soul has achieved this.)

This leads one to wonder about what constitutes an unforgivable sin. Certainly this thought beckons one to interpret the difference between Chisek's philosophy and the Creators' philosophy. Quite simply, the taking of human life, which includes the taking of one's own life, tops the list of this category — that of being an unforgivable sin. You cannot take your own life for many reasons; it goes without saying that it is never up to you to decide that the time is right for your life to end, for whatever reason. This applies to the process of euthanasia and assisted suicide. Terminating your life, which is looked upon as giving up on life, no matter what the circumstance, is neither accepted nor permitted. Consequently, if your soul is not eliminated on your Judgment Day because of this decision, you would most likely be punished in your next life cycle, no matter what the circumstances of taking your life were. Your soul may face a lifetime of suffering on a grander scale in comparison to the suffering you were facing in the life you chose to terminate, which makes the reason for euthanasia ironic, when you consider that you'll suffer immeasurably more in your next life – if you are not eliminated instead!

It is simple to Odo: if you cannot take this life and end it – a life you got for nothing in the first place – and if you didn't do anything productive as a human in your life, you will be eliminated. If you did do something productive, that is taken into account, along with many other psychological considerations, on your Judgment Day. It should be said: of all the deaths by suicide, a high percentage is eliminated by Odo. This knowledge alone should be a serious enough deterrent to any humans who are considering heading down this road in life.

On the other hand, it is a different story when a human is only living because technologies such as life support systems and often medications are keeping his body operational. When a human switches off a machine or does away with something that is keeping him alive by an alternative means, he is often not judged in the same manner. When it comes to medications that keep a human alive, elderly persons who are past their mid seventies are often excused if they decide to quit their medications, provided they have faced and conquered the challenges as they were presented in the course of their lives. (In saying this, the fate of one's life coming to an end should be left up to fate, and one should allow one's life to run its course.) Anyone else who deliberately stops medications to reach this end result of death is judged in a very different way.

The following five words should from now on take on great meaning: YOU DON'T OWN YOUR SOUL. It belongs to someone else. It belongs to the one who created it and gave it to you. Even though you have free will on this Earth, you will face your day of reckoning: your good deeds and your bad deeds will be measured and weighed. This is irrespective of any human justice that may exist.

After all, the Creators wrote the "program" of life that we are participating in; they set and defined the parameters; the double-edged sword we do not seem to realize is, although there is the freedom to challenge and write new definitions into that program – owing to free will – those who inexorably do are often not welcome back into that program in the next round. They are permanently "written out" of it, primarily to keep the program from deviating from its set constraint. Such digressions simply mean Chisek is trying to modify the Creators' program to satisfy his own agenda.

We must remember the Seven Elders and the three Creators in the way that was described earlier: In the human physical domain we are their feelings, their eyes, and even their ears; as a spirit returned to them, in the metaphysical domain, it is our goal to become their eyes and their ears – as one of Odo's parts. In the human form, through you, the Creators feel what you feel; they know what you know. They live through you. This is their reward to themselves; this is the satisfaction they receive for having created not just you, but all life. The Creators created you for their own benefit, which in turn benefits you.

This is the propinquity, the common bond, the Creators share with you. This is why life can be summed up simply: Odo made you from nothing; you belong to him; you are from him. He sent your soul into the arena of life to advance and develop you intellectually so that one day you can become a part of him in his cycle of existence, just as he became a part of you in your cycle of existence. What you allowed him and ultimately the Seven Elders to share with you is beyond measure. With your valuable knowledge you have advanced and enriched their intelligence and existence, and most importantly of all, you have given them purpose.

The opposite is true for those who have lived lives in which they have taken a negative path, and have changed the Creators' ideal of the type of world they want to participate in indirectly. One must be mindful that the Creators are tuned in on the frequency of any consciousness that exists; therefore, it is feasible to say they know every complete thought and deed of every consciousness in existence, from the human to the plant – indeed, they occupy a place in every living thing with consciousness. So in a way, we force the Creators to feel evil; we force them to be "affected" by evil – which inevitably means they too feel Chisek's energy; and we force them to live in Chisek's archetype of a world. In the final analysis, Judgment Day answers the question of whether you deserve one day to fill that space that a Creator has waiting for you to fill, after having deserved to have the Creators live through you.

Having deserved to have the Creators live through you. Doesn't this answer the question of why we have a Judgment Day? Given this knowledge, if applicable, are you comforted by those who have presented themselves as having the power to forgive us for our sins? Do those reassuringly famous words, Jesus forgave us for our sins by "dying" on the cross, sound reassuring to you now? One thing we are assured of is facing the Creator, Odo, on our Judgment Day. This applies to every single human, including dictators, presidents, politicians, moguls, queens, kings, police, judges, priests, pedophiles, drug pushers, killers, liars, thieves, crooks, double crossers, and even popes! There is a universal law that applies to all equally: For whatever you have done on this Earth, for whatever good and evil you have done during your short stay as a guest on this Earth, you will face the day where you will have to answer for them. This is as true as is the expression: truth is stranger than fiction.

All humans, no matter what their position, status, or wealth, will stand as equals before their Creator, with the only thing that distinguishes one from the other being the intelligence that one has brought from one's life. The only wealth, the only thing of value to the Creators, is your knowledge. You came into this world with nothing but your knowledge. Fittingly, your knowledge is the *only* thing you take with you when you leave this world. The greatest treasure the Creators can ever find is a special intellect that has evolved in such a way that it is nonpareil (unique). In that uniqueness, this intellect cannot be replicated, as the reincarnation cycle has molded the intellect in such an inimitable way.

Let this book state, once and for all, that Odo has no place within him, or within one of his civilizations, for anyone who has embarked upon the road of life which is in opposition to the core of his very being – that is, someone who has followed Chisek's path or philosophy of life. After all, the Creators want to share and participate in the existence of life according to the model of life that represents them, not the model that represents Chisek. Let us imagine that you sow a crop of lawn. Then one day noxious weeds start to multiply in it. You do not hesitate to eliminate those weeds before they overrun your lawn and change the very nature of it. Your attitude toward eliminating weeds, and the Creators' attitude toward eliminating a soul that has been corrupted by Chisek, are no different. You must never fail to forget one thing: there are endless supplies of souls created by the Creators every single moment. Your soul is merely a combination of neutrons and other particles that were given some currents of energy. You can be just as disposable as you can be valuable.

With all this in mind, you wonder: what can you do if your shoes are steeped in the feces of your ill deeds? This, no doubt, is a question many of you who have lived perfidious lives will be asking yourselves. This question is subjective, and it is one that only you can answer. In light of this it would be wise to consider Plato's "measuring"[iv] of the "greater" and the "less," and use this knowledge intelligently to aid you. For it is up to you to use whatever time you have left to rebalance your scales. You have to weigh the virtues of this short-term cycle of your human existence against the eternal transmigration of your metaphysical being.

· ⤴

The judgment process itself, from Odo's perspective, without the illusional effects you see, occurs in the blinking of an eye. In a large auditorium the ancient Egyptians called the Hall of Truth, intellects just appear and then disappear as quickly as they appeared, after standing on black and white chess-like squares that are covered with a sinister, all-telling "fog," before the Judge of Judgment Day. Those who stand on white squares are reincarnated; those who stand on black squares have a different fate. This judge, who presides over them, is one of Odo's parts; he has no feelings, just a tremendous level of intelligence and understanding.

Unlike on Earth, there are no do-gooders such as civil rights activists or civil libertarians to help you there, not even those with hidden agendas motivated by self-interest who operate under the false pretence of helping and doing something good for someone or even society. You stand in judgment on your own, with no one but yourself and the deeds of your lifetime to speak for you, and if you could or wanted to say something, first, you are not given a chance, and, second, there is no one to hear you …

The Great Darkness

Take a burning candle
Then blow out the flame.
The fire no longer exists
And the taper no longer
Bears any worth without its flame.
This is the great darkness!

If your soul is going to be eliminated for unforgivable sins, you encounter the same experience of going through the moongate hallway as the reincarnated soul does, right up to the point of standing on the invisible judgment square with your loved ones at the moongate – the gateway to the afterworld. The only distinguishing aspect is that your soul no longer possesses its attachments (such as the first-part) that came with your human body in a physical state.

Once at the judgment square, you are not permitted entry into the afterworld; the moongate does not welcome you in. Rather than walk off together with your loved ones into this afterworld and follow the normal sequence of procedures that occurs there, you just disappear on the spot. Your "fire" was "blown" out, like a candle flame when a breath of air blows it out … and that becomes the end of your soul. Your soul is simply turned into fog – metaphysical fog – and ceases to exist. When you were standing on the judgment square you did not even know that you were being judged, let alone that you were going to be eliminated. You were just standing in the gateway to the afterworld with your loved ones, staring at the view in front of you and feeling overwhelmed with awesomely, peaceful emotions. And then you were gone. You were not given the chance to plead your case. This place is not a democracy!

The Bottle

Theologians told us of a fiery hell,
And Dante told us of an inferno.

When the soul is measured with weight like lead
Sometimes then its "candle" flame
Burns ever so bright, much too long –
For there is no breath to blow it out!
This light it then becomes ever so lost:
As a star in a night sky to an untrained eye:
As gossamer swept up in a gusty wind:
As a bubble frothing in a frothy sea:
And as a grain on a sandy seashore.
What hope is there for such a burning flame?

Where the place allows this evil flame to fire
Hope is an eternal void of emptiness.
Hope is an eternal cry for help.
Hope is black in blackness in a blacker black.
Hope? No, there is not hope ... not for this soul and its flame.

For the prisoners of their conscience,
Whose souls pray a wasted prayer
Are never, ever, ever redeemed.
They are the forgotten and the discarded.
They are only unto themselves, and a burden now to none.
Welcome to "The Bottle"!

This book has described the journeys to the moongate of both the reincarnated soul and the eliminated soul. There is an important third category to make reference to, and this journey belongs to the soul that must go to a place of no return to face eternal punishment. This happens to be a truly weird and spectacularly innovative place of no return for souls that have committed the ultimate of unforgivable sins.

If you possess such a soul – one that is to make passage to this place of no return – you experience a slightly different death. Your soul has been "marked" before it even faces the death of its human encasement. When your metaphysical body detaches from your physical body you are not met with loved ones; you are unaccompanied as you travel through the moongate hallway. You don't deserve anything! You still feel that same indescribable, peaceful feeling as you travel through the hallway – everyone does, whether guilty or innocent (because the negative influence of Chisek no longer impresses upon you). The only difference is that your soul has no one to greet you or accompany you on your journey. You will travel alone through this tunnel to the gateway of the afterworld. Then, like every other soul, at the moongate you will stand on a judgment square of which you are unaware. You are merely standing and staring at the surroundings with curiosity. You see the individual illusion that confronts every soul, and this illusion is usually taken directly from your memory. You do not take one step into the afterworld, however. You just disappear into a white fog. This fog is a "lift" that takes you on a short journey to a special place. This takes as long as the heavenly body of a falling star takes to flash across the night sky. This is so quick that you don't have much time to think or react.

The fog is still thick, but it has now become black in color – this is your welcoming committee, and it means you have arrived at your destination. This is a novel moment where the quirkiness of the Creators can be best seen, and where another side of the Creators can be seen! The scenarios that unfold after the imposing black fog lifts vary according to the evil deeds one has performed in one's lifetime. They are as multifarious and as idiosyncratic as are the species of life on this planet, and as are the rotten deeds of the most intelligent of all the species on this planet. This subject deserves a chapter in its own right, but not in this book. This will be a dark, dark chapter; it will be an uncharted voyage into the unknown of the deepest depths of blackness, where nothing screams of existence save the unheard, vanquished cries of the forgotten souls damned in this abyss. For this reason, it has no place in this book; for this chapter may weigh down your soul, as does Chisek's path in life. If applicable, it is hoped that by the time you read this dark chapter you will have abandoned Chisek's course and taken a preferable course because, in the ultimate scheme of things, for those who have followed Chisek's philosophy in this life, there is only one thing that can be said to them: Chisek's influence in the human arena betrays humans, because he is not the one to welcome them after death with open arms and a cynical smile for treading down his "path of no return." Odo is the "welcoming committee," and he is the only one you will have to answer to and be judged by, and it is as simple and as scary as that!

Finally ... how this chapter should end is by each of us taking a sagacious look at the words of the bible, where we are told that the meek (the self-disciplined) are blessed and shall inherit the Earth. Nowhere in our works are we told the inverse: that the unmeek (undisciplined) are blessed and shall inherit the Earth, as it would often seem to those of us living on this Earth!

10
The Unconventional Wisdom of Challenge

We are born into and we exist in a life
Where we must try our best to instinctively stay alive.
In other words, we challenge life in order to stay alive.
The question is,
Do we have to challenge death in the same way?

The ultimate challenge of life is death.
Man challenges death only to find out
That the challenge of death has become life.
Facing man then is another challenge all over again,
The challenge of life.

-A wise man

In a highly intellectual society, challenge becomes a rare opportunity for the one who seeks it. Challenge, for this reason, is something to revere. Planet Terra (otherwise known as Earth), one of the blue/green planets of the universe with a primate civilization, provides such an opportunity for one's intellect. The arena enables one to revive, and possess, a satisfied need for real challenge – that of life as one knows it.

Challenge is synonymous with life, while life, in its simplest summation, is, ironically, synonymous with a game of chess. As you go through life, you have to always be cautious and strategize your moves so that your road traveled will take you to your final cause. With this game strategy in place, along the way you have to make sacrifices in order to gain. You will encounter both adversities and adversaries; with luck you will make the right moves, at the right time, and in the right direction, and in the process take your adversaries off guard so that you can progress without disruption toward this final cause of yours – which is another way of saying your desired destination. Just as chess is played with practical moves to achieve a desirable end, so life is "played" with practical moves to achieve a desirable end, with one small difference – the game of chess is just a game and can be repeated as many times as you wish. This cannot be said of life.

In life, there is a reason for everything that happens to you. Most of the time you remain ignorant of why the forces of life work in the manner in which they do. There are often predetermined forces, such as fate, which factor into your life, and in the greater scheme of things you as a mortal will never understand them or see the greater good that comes from them and often the suffering you may experience, of whatever nature that suffering may be – therein lies an elusive clue to life: there is always something positive that comes from something negative. This is why you have to endure, and sacrifice, and suffer if you must, but always strive to better and overcome whatever that suffering is. In no circumstance is it acceptable to terminate your life. In the case of terminating your life, this is to be interpreted as you giving up on the challenge of life; you are prepared to take the good life hands out to you, but not the bad.

There are no acceptable excuses you can cite for the taking of your own life, such as indignity and not wanting to make those around you suffer – these are the typical excuses given by the euthanasia advocate. Perhaps these are what the Creators want you and those around you to experience – those very things you want to escape in life! Perhaps through the suffering you go through, others close to you may experience something of value that broadens their life experience and knowledge bank — after all, the contribution you leave behind in the physical world has many different "faces" and "expressions." If you are of the opinion that you have the right to decide the outcome of your life, and you react accordingly — it is your free will to do so — you will face the consequences, one way or another.

You would think that we would have learned something from the superior human, Jesus Christ, when he suffered on the cross. He did not kill himself knowing what his fate was! He endured the unfairness of what life delivered him. He set us an example, one we should learn from. Even the bible reinforces the notion that we, in our Earth-bound lives, are tested and tried.

Another example was set by the mythical Greek figure of Odysseus, found in Homer's *Odyssey*. He was not a god but the figure of a mortal human; he faced many challenges in his life, and when everything seemed to go against him he didn't give up but kept going.

Another legendary Greek hero, Hercules, faced a challenging life. Like Odysseus, and many mythical heroes of our past, he coped with whatever trials and tests life put before him. Even with his superior strength, and even though he was half god, half mortal, he was not immune from challenges in his mortal cycle. On the contrary, he showed us that the greater the strength, the greater the challenges one is met with.

This all tells us that our ancestors passed down to us more than just mythical tales and legends; they left us a valuable reminder of how perennial the themes that run through the lives of humans are. They also show us how little humans have changed (it is only the technology we possess that has changed); we can see that there is a commonality in the challenges humans have faced throughout their history.

·ݜ

At the heart of our existence lies challenge; challenge leads us to choices; choices lead us to two antithetical philosophies — the positive philosophy and the negative philosophy. True understanding of life consists in a positive attitude in the face of all challenges. At the heart of a successful human lies this understanding. The following fictional case study of a human confronted with a choice is an example of an unsuccessful human, one who has no true understanding of life.

In her mid twenties, a young girl has decided to end her life before the onset of a disease that would progressively disable the functioning of her body (not her mind). This would mean she would have to be in the care of others for the rest of her life. She has, to this point, enjoyed the best life could offer her and not faced any real roadblocks in her life. Life has now caught up with her, as it does everyone, eventually, in one way or another. She has decided that she is not prepared to change the standard or quality of life she has been accustomed to. As she believes she has the right to choose how she should live her life, she believes she has the right to choose not to live such a life. When the time comes, she is not going to face the challenge life puts before her because it is not to her liking; instead, she is going to terminate her life – as uncomplicated as that!

Many are in these shoes, of all ages. Many suffer horrendously, and in that suffering choose the same option. Many depressed people, young and old, have also chosen this option. They believe that not living is better than living with such a burden. As fellow humans, we can all sympathize with the plight of such people, and we may even support and encourage their choice. It is a decision, however, based on ignorance: ignorance because in the majority of all cases Odo will bear in mind that right. That right will see most confront the great darkness: their "fire" will be "blown" out when their souls are "evaporated" into fog on the judgment square.

We must never forget the words of a wise man, who once described life this way: when life hands out blank checks, one day she's going to collect – with interest! If you have been able to cash in those checks for nothing all your life, one day you will be expected to pay your dues! On the other hand, if you have never been the recipient of those "free" blank checks, but have been paying your dues as you journey through life, life may be generous to you in return at some stage in your life. If you have been given a free ride up to now, you had better be on the lookout; you had better be prepared to pay your dues, for, nothing in life is free. You should consider one of life's philosophies: for every check life hands you that you cash in, life will silently be tabulating the dues you owe; one day life will ask for repayment. Sometimes it will be straight away; other times your "account" will be accumulating and you will be hit all at once out of nowhere. One thing is certain – as certain as the ancient mariners did not fall off the edge of the Earth in their travels, no one has a free ride here on Earth. Every person's cycle is different. Every person has challenges to face. Every person exists for a purpose.

The problems you can experience in life are, first, finding that purpose within yourself, and, then, not "losing" yourself in the endless, meaningless words of some philosophies that can derail you from finding that true purpose within yourself. Some philosophies are good at confusing the common person with their facts and figures to the point where the simple truth behind life becomes obscured – just as sure as the sun becomes obscured by treacherous black clouds; just as planets orbiting distant suns become obscured by the glare of those same suns; just as the full majesty of night's pageant becomes obscured by city lights … just as sure as honesty is easily obscured by deception in the eyes of the naïve, the unvigilant, and the gullible.

The common person often has no choice but to accept such philosophically complicated and self-derived words from those who profess and profit from useless philosophies. Many people look up to these professed "teachers." They have only ever wanted to know the basics: how to survive in this materialistic world; why they are here; and what part they have to play in this world. Some just innocently want to be shown the "way" and be led through life because of their inadequacies. It is not a lot to ask from those who profess to represent a higher-order being! However, when you misrepresent yourself by pretending to be something you are not (which is what the likes of cults, sects, unscrupulous philosophies, and god-like dictators do), where those who look up to you can only take your word as being the truth, then you will not be able to convince, or provide answers to the challenging questions of, those who are freethinking and intelligent and are able to reason – those very humans that you fear and attempt to suppress.

Why *are* we here? What seems so complicated is really not so complicated. You don't want to leave this world worse than you found it. Since we are created to improve ourselves, to make better the life we see around us, and to succeed to make the world better than we found it in the first place, then when we achieve all this, we are not able to take anything with us! Doesn't this then give a definitive answer to the question of why we are here? The mere fact that we cannot take anything with us when we leave should answer the question of why we are here.

Every person in this world, as well as every life form, for that matter, exists for a purpose, not by chance; therefore, each has a use-by date. In finding that purpose, we must remember that we are here in the arena of life to advance intellectually, and in the process we are being tested to see if we are prepared to conform to the Creators' philosophy of life by choice and not by force or some kind of policing. It is a challenge in itself to see if we can accomplish this. For this reason, and others we are aware of, the Creators have not intervened directly in this world to satisfy our spiritual needs.

In fire we find heat, and through fire we find proof of gold. What does this imply? In answering the following question we will be answering the above question. How do we find true friends and relatives? It is not surprising that the answer to this can be found when we experience misery, pain, or poverty – that is, when all the chips are down and we are sunk emotionally or financially. True friends and relatives will be found in the tough times. Artificial ones won't have anything to do with us in the tough times; they will desert us. When times turn fortunate, these types of people are usually the first to return.

Now that we have established that the true measure of a person can only be found when that person is in the "fire," it should be apparent to us that the Creators have applied this philosophy to us in our human existence here on Earth. The question becomes twofold to the Creators: Who follows without hesitation that moral instinct that is provided within us by our first-part? Who draws on Chisek's negative influence from the negative-part at the first chance and travels intentionally down his road in life for personal gratification? The true measure of our worth is when we are left with our own free will, within the parameters of the society we are living in, and are able to follow the positive path by our own esteem and initiative.

Often, you go through life and feel there is always misery; there is nothing but work; there is nothing but a struggle to survive. Often you go through life and are penniless; you just seem to survive day by day in a way that you cannot even think today how you are going to survive tomorrow. Life can seem to be a never-ending saga of survival. Sometimes you wonder: Is it worth going through this misery and suffering? What is the purpose? You ask yourself these questions and more all the time. But you see, in whatever you do or go through there is always a reason. There is a purpose for everything. Sometimes people cannot take it – handling the challenges, that is – and they go crazy or they kill themselves.

You must understand that there is a why and wherefore that you as a human have been born on this planet, and as a life form you have to survive against all odds. No more, no less! You are not entitled to take your own life just because you think it will be convenient for you. You have to fight, crawl, and do whatever you must; in the end, *you must survive*. Those intellects to have survived their challenges will reap the benefits one day in that they will have proved their worth and their virtue, and they will have learned everything possible from life. This is why it is up to you to survive under any possible challenge to the fullest. Nobody is asking you to survive being dragged by a car with a rope, or some killer hammering a knife through your skull – but some out there have miraculously been able to do just that! There is clear evidence of victims being able to survive near-impossible odds of survival. The question we must consider has an interesting answer. What is the factor at play when one is on the edge to either die or not die? The answer to this often lies in the state of the human mind. In the coming chapters we will learn that there are always two states of mind within a human: the weakened one under the influence of the negative-part and the strengthened one under the influence of the positive-part. (These parts, if we recall, are a part of the new metaphysical chip given to all living things, and they provide influences, of either a positive or a negative nature.)

In a life or death survival situation, with death the likely outcome, if you allow the negative-part and its aura to embrace you, the odds are you won't survive. Conversely, those who survive do not lose the power of their will or their determination to survive; they don't allow their strength to be "sucked" out of them by feeling sorry, depressed, or angry; they don't allow all those negative emotions to surface that they would be well within their rights to feel at that moment. You must have a determination to live and survive; when you have this your will is then strengthened, and your positive-part is in "control" and able to provide you with aura. How you survive impossible survival conditions for a prolonged period all comes down to your will. Linked to your will is your aura, which your positive-part is able to provide you with. When the positive-part is at the "control helm" of your brain it will do everything in its power to keep you alive, as opposed to your negative-part, which wants to do the opposite. Simplistically put, that is a big factor at play when you lie on the edge of either living or dying. This will make more sense to us as we advance into the next two chapters, where the positive and negative influences in our lives are explained.

You have your life in your own hands, and the more you fight to survive, the better off you will be here and after here. What is highly valued is your will to survive. This is what life is all about. Life is not all about good things. Life is about challenge. You are born in this world to face the challenge of life, and life has many challenges. It is up to you to endure these challenges to the fullest under all odds, and when you get out of or overcome that challenge – it doesn't matter how long it takes you, to some it takes a lifetime (who cares!) – you will be a greater you for it.

We must acknowledge that we are just here on this planet to be tested, and although many believe their misery will never end, it actually will one day, because there is for every beginning an ending, and for every ending a new beginning. There always has been and there always will be. Nothing lasts forever in the physical world of today. Beyond it there always lies a tomorrow. Such intellects will always survive if they can handle existing in this miserable world (miserable because humans make it miserable), where they all think that their own problem is the biggest in the world, but is usually nothing.

Humans, indeed, are like a little kid trying to ride a bicycle for the first time. The kid falls off and cries, and to him this problem is the biggest in the world. One day, however, his problem of mastering the bicycle will be solved. Then the kid is going to grow up a little and move on to the challenge of a bigger bicycle, and you can be assured this is going to bring him bigger problems. But, you can see that by the time his life span finishes, he would have solved many problems – those that have been pre-programmed for the human intellect to solve.

Life, really, is analogous to going to school and getting an education. The curriculum is such that courses step by step teach you that little bit more in preparation for the courses of the following year. You have to start at the bottom and work your way up the grades to complete the courses and earn your degree. Life is exactly the same. You could indeed say that your cycles of life give you an education that has been individually tailored to you. Each life will challenge you in a different way and teach you different "subjects."

Let us take a simple example of a life that went wrong, just to show how the failing of a past life can repeat itself by way of challenges in the next life. Let us say you are young – in your early twenties – and all your loved ones are killed in one instant. This is a true story. Let us say that you could not cope with this challenge and ended up dying yourself not long after (not by suicide but by neglecting your life). In your next life, you can be assured that you will pay the price by having that same challenge confront you again. You may be born parentless, or what is worse (the case of this true story), you may have nice parents who just do not bond with you. You then become the cast-out black sheep of the family, treated without respect, and not shown any love or positive feelings from the day you were born until the day you die. Instead, you are put down and never once encouraged. In this case, life has forced you to face the challenge of living without loved ones. You will go through life wondering what you have done to pay this price; unfortunately, the window to this truth does not exist. This is one of those mysterious aspects of life that we cannot understand, simply because we cannot see the bigger picture of ourselves. As much as we may not like it, challenges of life are as unique and as varied as there are strange things in the cosmos, and on our planet, and there is no such thing as a life without challenges.

One thing is certain about this life: today's problems faced by today's human civilization and human intellect are hardly a scratch of tomorrow's problems to be faced. So if today's intellect cannot survive with today's problems, what chance does that intellect have to survive with tomorrow's problems? That intellect will have no chance whatsoever! This is where the men are separated from the boys – to use the common human metaphor. This is where the "gold" is separated from the "dirt." If you cannot withstand this primitive existence here on Earth – which is all founded on money and riches anyway, which humans have put too much value on – you have no prayer surviving in the future existence. No prayer whatsoever! Of course, we "need" extravagant things in this life, because this whole civilization has been built upon material possessions. Civilization has been misguided by the negative force that exists, which has caused humans to aspire to the wrong things and to stray from the main objective and purpose of their evolution. You see, all the resources have not been put into making sure that all people of all backgrounds live comfortably, where they are able to study and exist in an atmosphere where all are equal and have equal opportunity, where no misery is encountered, and where everyone is taken by the hand and given a helping hand. Unfortunately, in this world this is by no means the case. Life in this century has never really changed all that much from the feudalistic existence of the past. We have extremes in wealth and poverty, where some have everything and most struggle with little at all or nothing. We are just subjects, controlled by those in power, which usually equates to money.

Versatility, this characteristic of ours, is one of our most valued possessions, and enables us to adapt from one situation in life to another and still survive. This faculty of adaptation will continue to be an essential component of us in our life cycle, where our priority of life is to survive against all odds. Today's problems faced by us are just superficial ones compared with the problems we will be confronted with in the future, where we are going to travel into different dimensions of universes, with such manifold existences. We must have durability, which is only acquired in the cycle of life we live in today. It may be primitive, but it surely is an effective starting point! We are acquiring knowledge from the beginning of life's starting point, which is at the humble bottom, and we will continue to acquire knowledge right through to the desired ending, of which there shall be one ... but that will be a long, long way off from today.

11
The Science of Good and Evil

Using physical or verbal strength in the face of weakness
Is a normal and natural way of man,
When his true intellect fails or is deactivated.
This is usually seen in emotional situations, in differing circumstances.
This method is not at odds with the methods of a lion.
You could say that those who use this "strength" of confrontation and anger
Are mentally weak; they are the first to give up or cry,
Yet they are the first to think they are right in how they think and act.

-A wise man

Just as the rose bears delicate beauty but also a thorn, so human nature bears what is desirable (good) but also what is undesirable (evil). For good and evil are as intrinsic to human nature as day and night are to the rotational cycle of the Earth, and as tidal movements are to the orbital cycle of the moon. Good and evil: order and chaos: angel and devil: human and beast: foresight and afterthought: yang and yin: reason and unreason – motifs based on an all-pervading duality that can be found in every culture, in every myth, in every religion, in every corner of the planet. Unconnected people seem to have connected themes and connected stories: stories of man and living gods fighting monsters, beasts, and serpents. All these narratives have symbolic connotations, which reinforce the notion that a negative force exists for every being that takes on a living, physical form – including the gods (as the ancients put it) if they take on a physical form.

What the ancients did was tell interesting stories based on a central theme of the evil that lurks within us all. They reasoned that every mind has its own beast within it that is waiting to devour that human. It is in this light that we can interpret the echoes of the voices of the past, which have come to us by way of imaginative myths and legends. These beacons of truth hint to us that every living being faces battle against the element of the serpent, which, implicitly, is referring to the negative force of Chisek that exists in every living thing to challenge it.

Let us take a closer look at the classical Greek story of Hercules: Hercules was the son of a god, Zeus, and the son of a mortal. According to his legend, this half-god, half-mortal faced problems in his life just as everyday humans always have – that is, he possessed human vices and virtues. One of those vices was a temper; another was the inability to control rage. These human weaknesses show us that he was a man who was vulnerable to being influenced by the negative side of him. What he really did was illustrate one important point (which will be clear when we read Chapter 16): superior strength, like a superior intellect, is not appropriate for humans until they conquer and control those baser urges within them. This is so relevant to us today; all our mythical heroes of the past are really just ostentatious and flamboyant versions of ourselves, with the same discordant constancies we have in our human condition.

The way to understand the human composite is to examine and understand the first two phases of humans. The phase-1 humans only had access to the tree of knowledge of good. Without a negative side, humans were happy with the status quo and lacked the drive, the purpose, and the motivational forces that advance their lives and hence evolve them – and evolution as we know is the prime objective of the human existence. Phase-1 human civilizations thus stagnated and by experiment failed.

The phase-2 humans had access to the tree of knowledge of good and evil – which means they came to possess the new ingredient, greed, from which all the negative ingredients pertaining to the human could be derived. Greed, we know, is a necessary requirement of the human: it is the singular, essential ingredient that gives one purpose to evolve. The phase-2 humans still did not deliver the desired human. Indeed, giving the human greed was a recipe for disaster, as greed overwhelmed everything good in humans to the extent that good ceased to exist in them and greed became the overriding factor in them. Greed was like a poison with no antidote.

When the tendencies of this human drifted to the evil extreme, this human became the epitome of the apocryphal beast, monster, or even the ever-present serpent. Ultimately, this human really only accessed knowledge from the tree of knowledge of evil.

There was no question that greed became a necessary part of humans, but there had to be an antidote for the "poison" greed created in them; there had to be a way for humans to control greed and use it in a way to advance them rather than destroy them.

With greed, the question had to become, when is enough, enough? Greed comes in different classifications, and if used in the right manner it can be beneficial to the human. This is the whole purpose of greed. Besides the excesses of monetary greed that humans in this cycle strive for, there is greed for knowledge – that's my type of greed! There is also greed for achievement, survival, as well as advancement. Greed is a form of competition where you are competing against yourself or someone else to achieve something. Greed which benefits, promotes, or betters you, but in the process hurts, destroys, or ruins others, is a selfish and destructive type of greed that should never be practiced, and it adds so much weight to the "heart" when measured against the "feather" that it will completely weigh it down. We all know what the consequences are for a soul that has betrayed the ethos of the Creators and led a life according to the ethos of Chisek.

The Seven Elders, as we know, created an adversary, their opposite. In business, standards are always raised when there is competition. Just as competition advances the quality of a product in business, so a challenging form of competition between positive and negative forces advances the quality of the intellect in humans. This is why the Creators formed the concept of greed. The only thing they had to do with humans was find a way not to let greed envelop them like a plague. They had to find a way for humans to find balance in between the two extremes of good and evil, and that meant creating something within humans that had the ability to salvage or rescue them from the depths of either extreme, and bring them back to a point of balance between the two extremes. They had to create something within humans that had the ability to make them aware of what was right and what was wrong: what was good and what was evil. Logically, because neither extreme produced an acceptable human product, the desired human product had to be found somewhere in the middle.

They found the solution. The solution was built into the software of the phase-3 human, and we belong to the second series of this phase. The Creators provided two influencing forces within the human: the positive influence and energy from Odo (the positive-part), and the negative influence and energy from Chisek (the negative-part). The prime purpose of these forces would be to help keep the human balanced between the two extremes. The Creators would achieve this by making these forces components of the human, and having these forces compete with each other. In this competition each force has one thing in mind: to influence the human to steer down its respective path: the philosophy of good, or the philosophy of evil.

As unscientific as this may seem, in this tug of war these forces are competing with each other to see who can win more points. Points are automatically awarded whenever a force wins a battle – this means, whenever a force has won you over to its side by influencing your behavior, actions, or emotions. Winning the war means a force has placed its stake in your soul upon death, and this stake is of course representative of which force exerted a greater influence on you during your life (that is, won the most battles): the positive-part or the negative-part.

These points are silently being tabulated all through your life, and only become of interest when you die. If we recall from earlier chapters, the moongate hallway you pass through to reach the moongate is described as being the weighbridge of your soul, which weighs the lifetime of deeds of your soul: your good deeds against your evil deeds. How this weighbridge weighs your soul can now be understood in real terms – that is, by the points that are tabulated from the many small battles that have waged within you between the positive-part and the negative-part. Ultimately, this means, whichever force placed its stake in your soul upon death has been awarded the most points. If the points went in favor of the negative-part, there is the likelihood that you may not be reincarnated, but be subject to the alternatives.

Who can win the war is the ultimate challenge. It could be said that through each one of us Chisek is always trying to defeat Odo and vice versa. There is rivalry everywhere – this is the cycle of life, and this rivalry is reflected in our behavior.

In a way, we can look upon these forces within each one of us as being the equivalent of a system of guidance: these forces help a human being make a choice in one of two directions – a positive direction or a negative direction. This choice then determines the physiology to some degree, emotional bearing, and conduct of that human. These forces of influence are crucial to us as humans, and without such a system of guidance in either direction a human loses that very quality that distinguishes him from the earlier two phases of humans. That quality is the ability to differentiate between what is good and what is evil: what is right and what is wrong. This means, we have what is necessary within us to make us either conform or choose not to conform to accepted standards of behavior, because those forces within us make us aware of those acceptable, or unacceptable, standards of behavior.

Now we know that we have the two forces of influence – a positive-part and a negative-part – built into our software, with each force having been derived from a superior entity that indirectly attains a beneficial result from our choice of influences. If we translate this in ancient and mythological terms, this is the human who was half man, half beast.

The negative-part (evil: beast: vices) can be equated with the easy path in life. The positive-part (good: reason: virtues) can be equated with the difficult path in life. One of the secrets of attaining success in one's life is to follow the positive path. If we harness or utilize the positive-part, we can advance ourselves in terms of intelligence, creativeness, achievements, health, and happiness.

Alternatively, to harness or utilize the negative-part (follow the evil path) is detrimental to the human, and it can lead to depression, lack of motivation and hence lack of success, sickness, mental health issues, anger and stress-related issues, suicide, and even criminal behavior and deviance.

The art of learning how to balance these two forces by the control and use of these two forces became the challenge of all humans. Achieving this balance became the meat-in-the-sandwich goal – otherwise known as equilibrium. This is explained in detail in the next chapter, along with exactly what these two forces of influence are. This chapter will, first, focus on humans and explicate how these two forces affect their behavior, and in our understanding of this we can complete the subject by comprehending the core basics of what the meat-in-the-sandwich goal is in the next chapter.

The negative-part in a human has the power to provoke and manipulate that human into being swayed over to the negative side. The negative extreme includes greater evils such as killing. While the majority of us never reach this zenith, we are taken along the same course that can lead us to it. We see the negative-part in us in many ways. For instance, we see it in those who are mentally unstable; those who lie; those who do things upside down; those who live on the margins of society and do the wrong things rather than the right things; those, like Hercules, with a quick temper; those who live in a state of malaise; or those who exhibit any negative emotions or enact any negative actions.

A typical paradigm of a person who has shown tendencies to be easily influenced by the negative-part could be seen in the political scene at the time of the writing of this book. This male politician was known to lose his temper and throw abusive temper tantrums at the drop of a hat. On one occasion a flight attendant was reduced to tears when he shouted at her because of a meal. His character was often brought into question and reported on because of his bad temper and behavior. In those moments when a reasoned, rational approach was required, a negative, unreasonable approach was used. A person who gets angry so easily, such as when served the wrong meal, suggests a person who is easily influenced by the negative-part within him. The difference between an understanding approach and an angered approach is the difference between a rational and an irrational human being: is the difference between a human using reasoned intelligence and one swayed by the beast found within him. It is a frightening thing for any country to have a person in power who cannot use reasoned intelligence in moments that necessitate reasoned intelligence.

When selecting a person to any position of authority, where that person is required to make decisions on behalf of others, we must look for obvious negative traits in that person, such as anger-management issues. These negative traits are the early warning signs that can lead to the making of a dictator or a tyrant given that person has the right conditions of power. Why? These early warning signs are indicative of a human with a lack of control of that beast (the negative-part) within him, where, given the right environment, such beast can easily tempt, guide, and sway him. In tempting situations of power, the hardest thing for such an individual will be to draw upon the positive-part instead of the negative-part. Little things that draw out the negative-part in a human, or tip a human over the edge so easily – such as being served the wrong meal – are the early warning indicators that should be taken seriously. We need to mull over one question, for obvious reasons. How does such a person stop the negative-part from tempting him when bigger things arise? Perhaps now we can grasp why Plato believed that those in authority should be philosophers. True philosophers. Not Chisek-inspired philosophers, of which there are many in this world. This is what is wrong with our planet today: it is run by Chisek. (It virtually always has been.)

The following fictional case study illustrates how an everyday human is affected by the negative-part. This involves another male politician, who had some family photographs taken. After observing the photos purchased by his wife, this man, in the presence of his children, went into a fit of rage and threw a temper tantrum; he yelled obscenities at his wife before throwing his fist into the wall, simply because he didn't like something about himself in the photos. This is a classic example of a human who allowed the impulse of the negative-part to sway him to the negative side. We can see this in his lack of reasoning, anger, and rage. Sometimes, in this state of rage, the negative-part can "control" your mind and influence you to do things you would never otherwise do. Imagine if he found his wife in a compromising situation with another man! In the right circumstances, in the right situation, any person can kill in a moment of rage – yes, any person – and then afterward show remorse.

In this example, all this politician had to do was stop for a moment and think rationally. He could have found humor in the situation. Then, with a calm disposition, he could have reasoned what his options were to find a suitable outcome. Had he reasoned in this way, he would have followed the instincts of the positive-part. In the end his wife did solve the problem when it came to the photos, so his tantrum really served no positive purpose; on the contrary, his approach would have had a negative psychological effect on the children. He could have set an entirely different example for his kids, but he didn't. What are the odds that his children are learning by example and the behavioral pattern is perpetuated in adulthood by them?

People who are narcissistic tend to be easily swayed by the negative-part. On the one hand, they are admirable as long as you do or say the right thing by them in their eyes — this means they are allowing the positive-part to influence their behavior; on the other hand, if you criticize them or do not do things the way they want them to be done, they will take it as a great offence and insult to their inflated ego — this means they are allowing the negative-part to influence their behavior. Some chefs are notorious for this type of behavior. People around such touchy persons always have to "walk on eggshells" and be careful of their choice of words, so as not to unwittingly imply something that these persons can turn into a form of criticism, or assume is a subtle but caustic attack on them. If you do something they have good reason to be upset about then all hell is capable of breaking loose with them, and they are capable of losing control of themselves. One charismatic serial killer started killing women because his girlfriend left him. It often does not take much to trigger some people into possessing an all-consuming hatred that is capable of becoming obsessive or even revengeful. How far that obsession or need to pursue revenge is taken depends on that person's opportunities, along with how overwhelmed by the negative-part he is. In a confronting situation this person is capable of violence and even a serious crime of passion, even though neither may have been intended. In all instances, the instinctive drive is the negative-part, and the human is giving in to and being guided by it.

The following fictional case study of a female politician with narcissistic tendencies is an example of a person who allows herself to frequently be influenced by the negative-part. This person is quick to tell someone off impulsively when that someone says something that is not to her liking. Most of the time it does not take much to elicit this type of reaction. When things go her way in life she is a lovely person. A little thing, however, can trigger her into a confrontational state, such as the mere implication of something negative. She is always in readiness to pick a fight.

Her problem began as a child when her older brother died. She became depressed, and from that moment on her parents made a crucial mistake in her upbringing. They did not want to upset her further, as she found it hard to get out of that negative cycle, so they did not correct her faults or errors. This way she never learned to say sorry. Her parents always supported and protected her, irrespective of whether she was right or wrong. She then became insulated from criticism as she grew up. In these circumstances her ego inflated and she became controlling. Eventually it reached a point where she trapped herself in a vicious ego-driven cycle where she became confrontational and argumentative when something was not said or done in a manner that satisfied her ego. In other words, she has been dealing with ordinary situations in a negative way, where she has allowed the negative-part to overwhelm her and drive her behavior.

When she was sheltered by her parents she was protected in a sense from the type of problems a person faces when married, and so her anger-management problems were not as common or as obvious. But with a husband, with the demands of her career, with a mortgage, with pressures and harassment from her constituents, with the birth of a child, and with whatever daily crisis can arise in amongst all this, she has had plenty of confronting situations to deal with. This has meant her negative-part began to overwhelm her often as she has been unable to handle these daily confrontations in a positive way. To cope with problems – including regular, everyday situations that require tolerance, patience, and understanding – by negative means becomes an addiction, as simple as that, and that addiction has driven her to venture down the negative road, which means she has strayed from a state of balance in her life.

Sometimes people are so driven by the negative force within them – and that means they have ventured quite a long way down the negative path – that they have let themselves drift to a highly volatile state where, with the right trigger, they will self-destruct, and this could happen by assaulting someone, killing someone, committing suicide, or crossing over into severe mental disorders such as psychosis, which is examined in the next chapter.

These examples of humans are reminiscent of the type of humans found in Chisek's civilizations. The more intelligent this type of human becomes, the more arrogant and ignorant he becomes. On the contrary, those who draw on the positive-part will become humble the more intelligent they become, and they will always say sorry when dealing with others, even if those others were the ones at fault and in need of doing the apologizing.

Unfortunately, humans who frequently allow the negative-part, rather than the positive-part, to influence their behavior, are likely to head down a road of depression and unhappiness, and indubitably suffer some form of mental illness. Once in this negative cycle, they will find it hard to escape from it because they quite often and too easily tend to draw on the negative-part at the best of times. Therefore, in the worst of times – such as when they face a negative-inducing circumstance that makes them weak – they will not have the strength to combat the negative-part. It will totally overwhelm them to the point that they may need professional help of some kind. Their nervous systems may also deteriorate; invariably, they may take the drastic step of taking tablets to control their nerves, and no doubt the day may come when they have to rely on a bit of alcohol, perhaps even illicit drugs, and no doubt after that their doctors may prescribe them sleeping pills. All this is a recipe for disaster, as it fuels the negative-part. This is an all-too-common spiral people can easily become caught up in.

Anything that creates stress in your life is a negative-inducing circumstance. One negative-inducing circumstance is childbirth. When in a weakened state after having a baby, a mother is easily drawn by the negative-part into the cycle of depression, from which she can find it difficult to recover. Other negative-inducing circumstances include being sick (particularly in the case of the elderly), being rundown, and not having slept well (many students and working parents fall into this trap). The negative-part is easily fueled by a lack of sleep (or unnatural sleep, as in the case of using sleeping pills, where you deprive your brain of the NREM and REM sleep cycles), alcohol or drugs in the system, poor diet, or poor health. For a start, you cannot draw on the positive-part in a drug- or alcohol-induced state. When you are weakened in a physical or psychological way, it is extremely difficult to control the negative-part.

Have you noticed that following a night of poor sleep you are often irritable the day after? Everything annoys you, and you do not have the same sense of patience and tolerance. It is not easy to display positive attributes. It requires you to work hard and use your brain. You are not required to work hard or use your brain when it comes to displaying negative attributes. When you are enervated (weakened), in whatever physical or emotional way, it is so much easier to lash out, use anger and aggression, feel impatience and lack of tolerance, become confrontational, or turn to addictions such as drugs or alcohol. This means you do not have control of the beast within you. If you allow the beast to rule your emotions in an enervated state you weaken exponentially. It is hard to imagine that many of the physiological and psychological ailments in humans are manifested all because of their inability to control the negative-part within them! If they only stopped and smiled when confronted with an intolerable or negative situation, they would be allowing the positive-part to steer their instincts and emotions. What appears to be the easiest thing in life to do is the most difficult thing in life to do! If they handled such negative-inducing circumstances that arise in the normal course of their everyday lives in a positive way, they would feel totally different: they would feel happier and healthier – so too would those around them.

Those under the influence of the negative-part don't think first about what they say or do; they tend to make others, particularly loved ones, uncomfortable, unhappy, and even miserable. Whoever they are surrounded by often suffer. They make themselves and in the process others miserable, and this misery is what the evil force called Chisek (by way of the negative-part) feeds on. The more misery these people create for themselves and especially for others, the better Chisek feels, and the more energy he gets. (This book liberally uses the term Chisek to describe the negative influence or the negative-part. They are in a sense all one and the same thing.)

The case studies given earlier are typical examples of humans drawing on the influence of the negative-part in instances where someone has stepped on their "tails." To use a rational and understanding approach would mean humans were drawing on the influence of the positive-part, and this is the great challenge for us all. This is how equilibrium can be attained. Unfortunately, many humans succumb to the negative-part in terms of stress and depression, and the only way they have been able to control their nervous systems is by taking prescription drugs. When the nervous system is in an agitated state — when the cause is not a result of a medical condition or other stimulant — then in all likelihood this is a symptom to indicate that the individual is under the influence of the negative-part. Individuals who depend on an external means (prescription drugs) to achieve a calm state will never, by their own merits, be able to conquer the meat-in-the-sandwich goal.

How intelligence of a human is measured by the Creators is *not* by academic achievements and a string of letters beside a person's name, but by how a human is able to reason and control this negative force. For example, let us take a garbage truck driver who is unaccomplished when it comes to academic achievements, and can even be considered dumb on an intellectual level by some, but is able to control his negative-part. This means, he doesn't exhibit rages or fits of temper; he doesn't become upset or confrontational when he feels someone has criticized him or acted in a way that he feels undermines him; and he is generally a good person, able to control and balance his sanity with his calm temperament, just as a kangaroo balances itself with its tail. By not allowing himself to react to a negative situation in a negative way, he has turned the other cheek.

Now we will reference by comparison the politicians cited earlier, who are in total contrast to the garbage truck driver in that they have a reasonably high level of personal achievement, but have let themselves down with their inability to control their negative temperament. If they were all facing judgment side by side, can you guess which of these would be considered intelligent in the eyes of the Creators? If you guessed that the simple, academically unlearned garbage truck driver was considered incomparably more intelligent than the politicians all put together, you would be correct.

We are all pawns in the battle between Odo and Chisek; each is trying to sway us over to his side in order to obtain points — just like on a scoreboard. If Chisek (by way of the negative-part in a human) obtains the points, then this certainly "embarrasses" the Creator, who likes to think that he has created something good. Sometimes Chisek is so sure he can win a person over — put the stake in that individual's soul — that he makes a bet with Odo. He says, "Alright, I will bet you that I am going to win your so-called cherished, beautiful, almost perfect creation over to my side. You'll be a laughing stock!" Most certainly, Chisek has succeeded against Odo in many ways and in many places. It is obvious today in the world if you take a good look around. Humans are fighting their fellow humans; they are fighting with their fellow brothers; they are even fighting with their parents! How many cases of a child killing his parents have you heard of? It takes a lot of hate in someone to do something of this nature. Only one possible force is capable of such hatred, and that is the evil force of Chisek by way of the negative-part. Even though Chisek is always making such a bet, he bets with himself, because Odo never bets on anything. Odo just "says," "We'll wait and see." But he always does his utmost to keep the human from falling into Chisek's hands.

Each time, however, Chisek destroys something good the Creator has created, there is always a positive outcome that emerges from that destruction. It is like a dog chasing its tail in many ways, as Chisek will never really win. He can only destroy temporarily, but in the long run he will never win. Today's wars and the misery you see everywhere are what Chisek thrives on. According to Chisek, good people are not allowed to think. They are just driven into hate, misery, wars, and fights. That is how this negative force operates. Somehow, Chisek thinks that if he destroys good, that will be the end of it. To his surprise, there is always something good that comes out of disasters or destruction. You see, Chisek will cause wildfires, and life will become charcoal, but in a few months, with a little rain and a little time, you get beautiful flowers and seedlings that rejuvenate the land and allow the cycle to continue to prosper again. So many things in life have their own protections, their own evolutionary knowhow, and they certainly know how to re-evolve and revive after destruction. Man, too, is the same after every disaster: somehow evil is always one step behind good, because tragedies and disasters bring out the best in humans.

It is for us to be vigilant in our passage through life and not give in to the negative force. The important thing in life is, each time you do something, ask yourself why you are doing it, and make sure you have a good reason for doing it. No matter how small or big, don't ever do anything without reason just for the sake of doing it. So, if you are asked why you did what you did, then you better have a good reason. Don't ever say, I don't know; I don't remember.

When things head in this direction, it usually means you are in trouble; it means you are almost there, in Chisek's hands. You must always know why you are doing something, how you are doing it, and what good will come out of it – not what evil is going to come out of it! There is no possible good reason in the world for you to do something wrong, and to say you had a good reason for doing it. That does not tally. You are going to one day face the measurement of your "heart" against the "feather," and here you are going to get exactly what you deserve. There is no good reason for doing wrongs or evil deeds that hurt others – that is the bottom line. If you want to kill, you have to tell whoever it is you want to kill why you have a bad reason to do such an evil act. Never say you have a good reason to do it. Having a good reason to do something evil does not compute.

It is when you understand the battle between Odo and Chisek that you can identify with the battle waging within you between good and evil – not just by way of deeds and actions, but in everyday emotions. Depression, sadness, anger, jealousy, greed, hate, envy, revenge, touchiness, extreme sensitiveness, feeling sorry for yourself, out-of-control rage, irrational or negative thoughts, and violent outbursts are just some of the manifestations of a human drawing on the influence of the negative-part. The negative-part feeds off your negativity and does everything to draw you further down that destructive road – which is such an easy road to take.

Your negative-part sways your actions and thoughts by the power of suggesting things to you. We have all heard that negative voice within us tell us to do something that does not make any sense. We usually do not ever react to it. In certain instances, though, it is that breaking point which pushes us across the line to impulsively react in a negative way – that is, it is the driving force that makes us commit suicide, snap, impulsively aggressive, or given to violent outbursts, and sometimes all it takes is for someone to insult or offend us; sometimes all it takes is one wrong look the wrong way! Every single one of us has a violent, dangerous, and evil side to us, which has been purposely built within us. It is our challenge to control it; the measurement of our intelligence lies in this very ability.

It takes a lot of strength to overcome the challenge of this evil. The more often you succumb to the instinctive urges of the negative-part, the easier it gets for it to overwhelm you; you are even likely to find pleasure in allowing this to happen. This "pleasure" is the dangerous psychological stage that enables the negative-part to "earn your trust" and win you over to its side and down its path toward its final cause, which of course includes any of the mental disorders, the end of the line being the ultimate extreme of madness. (This is distinct from brain disorders caused by medical conditions, such as diseases or brain injuries. The distinction should be made here, because not all persons with mental conditions fall into the category of having drawn upon the negative-part to take them to those conditions. The behavioral traits may be the same, but the diagnosis of what led these people to these behaviors is not.)

Your challenge, when it comes to the enigma of good and evil, is to find the middle ground, the product in the middle, which is equilibrium. To achieve equilibrium means you have conquered the meat-in-the-sandwich goal. The Creators, through us, are hoping to achieve this new phase of human.

It is not at all difficult to conceive of what is being sought of humans: they must become the "meat" in the "sandwich." It is desired that a new essence of human evolves from the positive and negative forces that are at variance within the human. Then will the human be the substance of perfection — what the Creators will finally call a perfect creation, one that exists in an unquestionable state of equilibrium. Equilibrium is what is desired: the precision of energy sandwiched between the forces of good and evil.

By introducing this third force, the Creators have changed an unwanted outcome for humans. When humans can control their positive and negative forces, then can it be said that the desired equilibrium would have reached its peak, where universes would be creating in their own right, and competing energies would be mushrooming in an everlasting cycle to become, in simple words, like a ring that has no beginning and no ending.

Good and Evil in a Nutshell

Each time you cry you lose your fighting spirit;
Therefore you become assailable to corruption.

-A wise man

A human has a choice of two possible dispositions. One day these two dispositions will be circumvented in favor of an intermediate third – which is our Final Cause: Equilibrium.

One disposition is a negative state. In such a disposition, any of the following conditions or emotions are possible.

> You blame or fault others.
> You feel greed, envy, jealousy.
> You harbor animosity, anger, hate, frustration.
> You are selfish, oversensitive.
> You bottle or repress negative feelings.
> You have mental health issues and psychological problems.
> You enact socially unacceptable behavior.
> You blow things up out of proportion, or always look for a negative.
> You are averse to accepting criticism.
> You are confrontational, controlling, possessive.
> You pick fights, have temper tantrums, are abusive.
> You cry a lot, and feel depressed.
> You fill the limited space of your conscious mind with negative memories.
> You dwell on the negative memories and refuse to let go of negatives.
> You do not like yourself, the way you look, and find fault in yourself.
> You do not accept yourself for who you are.
> You lack reasoning capabilities.

> You do not recognize your own mistakes.
> You cannot say sorry and cannot forgive.
> You lack understanding, empathy, compassion.
> You try to change others, not realizing you need to change yourself.
> You have no hope; feel despair; feel bitterness.
> You seek out revenge on someone.
> (Anything else relating to the negative emotions pertaining to the human.)

Note: As frequently stated in this book, if medical abnormalities are applicable to you, a different diagnosis needs to be sought from a trained medical practitioner. If any of the above are relevant to you, you should always seek medical assistance to rule out the possibility of a medical condition. There are medical conditions in your body such as chemical imbalances or tumors that can affect your behavior. In these circumstances the negative behavior, while it is caused by factors beyond your control, is still being dictated by the negative-part. The only difference is the cause, not the actions, the behavior, or the driving forces. Even if you have no medical condition, professional help can be of benefit to you.

If you see negative symptoms in a child, particularly uncontrollable rage or anger, you should also seek medical assistance as soon as possible. Some parents ignore the symptoms and hope that things get better or even go away as the child grows up. On the contrary, things can become worse. Much worse! Even a simple case of shyness has "roots." It should not be looked upon as just a personality trait and left at that. It should be looked upon as a symptom of a deeper issue; a child should be taught how to be confident. If as a parent you do not possess the skill to teach your child, you should seek assistance from a professional who does.

The other disposition is a positive state. In such a disposition, any of the following conditions or emotions are possible.

> You are generally calm, happy, patient, kind, good.
> You are full of energy and confident.

You feel empathy and compassion.

You like yourself, accept yourself, accept others' faults, recognize your own faults.

You accept criticism.

You accept people are human and make mistakes.

You can forgive.

You have the strength to keep away from those who always require forgiveness, those who have revealed to you their negative side, or those who have the capacity to create negativity in your life. (Those in abusive relationships should take particular note of this point.)

You can reason.

You possess understanding.

You are altruistic, care to help others, are generous.

You fill the limited space of your conscious mind with positive memories.

You react to confrontation by turning the other cheek.

You know who you are, where you are going, and what you want from life.

You do not get angry, upset, jealous, and so on.

You advance in many ways intellectually and spiritually.

You generally have good sleep patterns (unless there is an underlying medical disorder).

(Anything else relating to the positive emotions pertaining to a human.)

Meditation

Once in the negative cycle, the question becomes, how do you get out of it? Sleep is the essential first step. With a good sleeping pattern, teamed with a healthy diet (having people around you who are not erratic helps), you will feel less tired, less enervated, and have plenty of aura to deflect and fight off the negative-part. The practice of meditation is one way of falling asleep.

There are many ways to meditate. The following is one method you can use. The first step is to put yourself in a positive mode. Think of the happiest thing that you have ever experienced. The idea is to put a huge smile on your face. Your whole physiology should change. Keep those positive feelings in you as you concentrate on one of the Egyptian pyramids. Picture a concentration of energy (aura) going into it. (You can even imagine that the aura going into the pyramid is coming directly from the amoeba of the Seven Elders – they would not mind.) Deflect that energy to yourself. Let it strike your head and then imagine it flowing into your body. Picture it as being red in color. Slowly watch this energy moving up and down your body. Then imagine that your nerves are vibrating strings. Watch the energy straightening them out so that there is no vibration. After a while your nerves should be completely calm. When this happens, change the color of the energy to blue. You should see the red energy then turn another color before it becomes blue. If you do this well, after practice, you will feel a "high," one that has no comparison to any drug you could take.

If nothing is working for you, then you are probably not concentrating on the energy and the energy alone. You are probably thinking of your boyfriend or girlfriend, your worries, or how much your stocks have gone up! Your brain wave state is probably in a beta wave frequency. This means you are highly alert. You need to slow down your brain wave activity. Before you fall to sleep you normally go into an alpha and then a theta brain wave frequency. This brain wave rhythm is your objective, and meditation should achieve it. This is why you need to avoid stimulants in the hours before going to sleep. Drinking stimulants such as caffeine will put you into a beta brain wave frequency. Listening to the right kind of classical music, like Tchaikovsky, can help put you into the right brain wave rhythm.

You need to keep in a positive state and concentrate entirely on the energy flow from the pyramid to your body, and then on its flow within your body. In this state you have different ways of managing this energy flow. You can use it to try to heal yourself. For instance, you can picture the energy fighting and deleting any foreign invader in your body that is harming you. The red energy is the healing energy.

If it is working, and if you have not fallen to sleep by now, try to see a picture develop on your eyelids. If you are successful, you will be able to invoke images from your mind, as though you were watching a cinema screen. The hardest part of this process now will be to stay awake, which is good news for the insomniac. Sometimes you will see the most extraordinary visions. This is an extremely difficult task for some. One day, when you master your mind, you will be able to view any vision from your subconscious mind. This could include scenes from a past life. You can watch that past life replay before your eyes.

When you learn how to collect aura for yourself, you have the ability to collect it for someone less fortunate that you care about. What you can do is deflect a beam of energy to this second party. If this person is sick, you can directly target that healing energy in such a way that the energy you are sending is attacking the "enemy" in that person's body. (Make sure that you do not send the energy directly from your body to this other person, as you will drain your own body of energy.)

Once you learn to fall asleep, you need to make sure that you allow yourself enough hours of sleep. We tend to sleep less because of our stressful and hectic lives. However, sleep is crucial to our physiological and emotional strength and health.

Once you have sorted out your sleeping pattern, your task will be to do the opposite of everything listed in the negative state when the situation confronts itself. This will enable you to conquer the meat-in-the-sandwich goal.

12
The Final Cause

The spirits of the "deceased" who built early Egypt
Left us a pointer to unravel the enigma of ourselves.
Carved in stone over desert sands there lies a half man, half beast:
The Sphinx ... a symbol of Order and Chaos.
It is the crest of what we are: half man, half beast.
Elsewhere carved on walls is the origin of this half man, half beast:
Horus, of Order; Seth, of Chaos.

The Egyptians were not alone
In their symbolism of man's one true challenge.
To the Minoans it was the Minotaur:
Half man, half bull.
Thus the bull became the crest
Of the dark force in man: Chisek.

The Meat-in-the-Sandwich Principle

A wise man had this to say ...
The enemy lies within.
For one to conquer the enemy,
One must come to know there is an enemy.

In past ages, the works of philosophers have yielded insights into many of the questions posed by humans in their lifetimes. These insights found in the philosophical jargon have not really had a practical application for us in our lives, and this is based on the simple truth that our understanding and often interpretation have not been synonymous with the original intent of the writings. Today, however, these insights are as relevant to us as they were to these philosophers in their time. One such philosophical work is Aristotle's "Doctrine of the Mean." Another is the study of virtues by Aristotle's great teacher, Plato. Plutarch has documented virtue ethics in his work, which he cited from the lore of priests and men of wisdom such as Zoroaster. In a way, Aristotle's doctrine, as is Plato's measurement of excess and defect, is just a play on words of this book's meat-in-the-sandwich principle. When Aristotle cites the "mean" in his doctrine, he is referring to equilibrium, the middle-ground state between the vices of good and evil. The mean, like reason, is just another word for the "meat" in this book's "sandwich." Plato calls this the wisdom of measuring. The "bread" in this book's sandwich is just like Aristotle's two extremes of vices, and Plato's excess and defect. The two extremes can be summed up as good and evil. This book has just explained this thread of thought in meat and sandwich terms, which is an unfashionably uncomplicated and commonsense way for the ordinary layman to understand.

It is logical: what the Creators did to the human was apply a basic law of nature and physics. Just as a third force, called energy, is created when antimatter and matter collide, so a third force, called equilibrium, is created when two antithetical forces (good and evil) are applied to a human. This third force is created only when a human can control the two forces.

At this point, it is only fitting that you should ask the question of what these forces are, in real terms. Symbolically, this book has been referring to the two energies that come from the Creators and Chisek. These two energies represent the two extremes of vices. The Creators inserted into every living being a chip of intelligence of a metaphysical nature. If we recall, the Creators, the Seven Elders, and even Chisek are made up of countless parts. The parts that come from the Creators are positive by nature, and the parts that come from Chisek are negative by nature. Upon birth, each human is given one positive-part and one negative-part (second-generation copies of parts from the Creators and Chisek – not original first-generation parts). These are called "the balancing parts." They are independent, freethinking intellects, capable of maneuvering in and out of the human brain with their own capabilities.

The positive-part (also called the positive influence or the first-part) possesses a positive energy called aura, while the negative-part (also called the negative influence or Chisek) possesses energy by way of a negative aura. The positive-part influences you in a positive way; the negative-part influences you in a negative way. To some degree, these balancing parts are the instinctive drives of a human. They are like navigational aids that steer (or influence) a human in a positive or negative way.

If we recall, the phase-3 version-1 (P3V1) human was affected by a 49 percent negative influence. What this means in real terms is that the negative-part only had a 49 percent capability in terms of intelligence, control, power, energy, strength, influence, and so on as compared to the positive-part, which had a 51 percent capability. We know that the Creators had to decrease the influence of the negative-part because it overrode the influence of the positive-part. The negative-part was too powerful for the human to achieve equilibrium. This is why the Creators changed the percentage of influence a negative-part exerts upon a human. This means that all throughout the universe, within the brain of all humans, there now exist a positive-part with a 61 percent influence and a negative-part with a 39 percent influence.

We should take a step back to the death of a human, where at least four aspects detach from the discarded physical body: the conscious mind, the subconscious mind, the positive-part (described in earlier chapters as the first-part), and, finally, the negative-part. The negative-part is just as much an attachment to the metaphysical body as the positive-part is, and, like the positive-part, it follows the same metaphysical body from life to life. It should be noted that if the human is eliminated or sent to the Bottle for unforgivable sins, his parts are not eliminated. They start all over again by being assigned to a new soul, to battle each other once again.

Within the brain of every life form there lies a control center. Whatever this control center is in neurological terms, and wherever this control center lies, within that control center is a "steering wheel," to which each balancing part has access. This steering wheel can only steer you at any one moment in one of two directions: figuratively speaking, down the negative path, or up the positive path, depending on which balancing part you have allowed to influence you. This choice you make determines which part is operating the steering wheel.

The control center exists by design to allow one of these two balancing parts to take control of the human. To take control here means to provide its influence by way of instinct, which comes to light through gut feelings, intuition, and suggestion. Only one of these two balancing parts at this stage can take the reins of this control center and operate it at any given time. This means there is always one balancing part in "active duty" in the control center at any given time. When one takes the reins, the other must retreat to the subconscious mind or simply leave the brain altogether. When you allow one or the other in, you are allowing it to take control of this control center of your brain. This means that when you are swayed to the negative side in whatever way, such as by crying, telling someone off, or even thinking negative thoughts, the negative-part has "command" of your brain and is the one influencing you. With this command position, it gives you unwanted and undesirable thoughts, and suggests you do unwanted and undesirable things, with the reverse applicable to you when under the influence of the positive-part.

From this control center, each balancing part has facilities to access and "control" common or "unique" areas of the brain. One of the regions that would appear to correspond uniquely with the positive-part is the area of the brain responsible for higher reasoning – which seems to suggest a region found within the pre-frontal cortex. One of the regions that would appear to correspond uniquely with the negative-part is the area of the brain responsible for aggression. (Research into the huge unknown of the human brain has brought us new insights into the brain and its regions; accurately identifying the regions that uniquely correspond to each part is something practitioners of the brain will have to one day clarify.)

It should be emphasized that the brain is a highly complex organ to attempt to explain at this stage of our understanding. This book has used our limited understanding and attempted to explain in down-to-earth terms the complex neural physiological association of these metaphysical attachments. It should be emphasized that this book has interpreted from a layman's perspective the application of the metaphysical software. This is intended to provide a blueprint from which scientific analysis and research can be rightly applied when the science has caught up, or come to terms with the existence of the metaphysical and its attachments.

There are physiological and emotional manifestations that correlate to the negative-part being in your control center. This is why, with the right technology, or when you learn to read the signs, you can detect when a person is lying and hence under the influence of the negative-part. For example, in moments of anger and rage, the nervous system may become heightened in an aroused way; the stress hormones may become activated; the adrenalin levels may spiral up; blood pressure may increase, as may the heart rate. The emotional manifestations of a person under the influence of the negative-part are broad, ranging from intolerance, irritability, irrationality, anxiety, impatience, hostility, poor stress and anger management, to a sense of being disinterested.

In normal circumstances, the body does not respond in a negative way to positive things, while you are under the influence of the positive-part. In this state, you are pretty much in a state of mental calm. It is only in this state of mental calm that you can benefit in a positive way. For example, you can attempt to heal yourself, or see gains on an intellectual or even a sporting level.

A key factor that contributes to the above physiological and emotional manifestations is the body's aura, which is the life-giving element of a human being. Aura comes as a part of the "package" of each part. This means the positive-part possesses a positive aura, while the negative-part possesses a negative aura.

The positive aura is the protecting aura. It enables knowledge and physical strength. If you were able to see the aura around a human body (and some humans have this ability), a human with the positive-part at the control center of his brain would possess a bright yellow aura that encompasses the body and is approximately four inches thick.

In opposition to this, the negative aura a human possesses with the negative-part at the control center of his brain does not protect the human body to the degree that the positive aura does. It tries to open "holes" in the aura and allow sicknesses and viruses in to weaken the body's immune system. It does not enable knowledge to advance a person positively; it does enable knowledge to advance a person negatively – this includes anything that is contrary to the Creators' ideal, such as how to kill, lie, deceive others for personal gain, exhibit anger, become depressed, commit suicide, or become sexually deviant or predatory.

This negative aura is light yellow in color and is only around one inch thick. If you embrace the negative-part for long – that is, allow it to stay in the control center of your brain for too long, like killers, those who are depressed, those with a temper or anger-management issues, those who cry all the time, fanatics, tyrants, and some badly trained soldiers do – then this negative aura grows and becomes thicker. Becoming thicker sounds good but is not good at all – it means you are doomed! For, the thicker it becomes, the weaker your body becomes. Once you allow your body's immune system to weaken, you become prone to sickness and disease. Fortunately, by design, the immune system is independent of aura and is a safeguard to protect a human. However, the negative-part does all it can to weaken the immune system. The longer you embrace the negative-part, the greater its chance of weakening your immune system. This is why someone who embraces the negative-part for a long time has a greater possibility of getting some sickness, such as cancer or heart disease, and dying, or winding up in an institution with a diseased mind – that is, a mind that has crossed over the "line" and gone into psychosis, or any number of the other mental conditions.

Just as disturbing is the knowledge that when you have allowed your negative-part to steer your actions by suggestion, when confronted with the right set of circumstances you are capable of anything, even killing someone. This is applicable to every single human being. What differentiates those who kill and those who do not is their ability to put the brakes on the negative force, because the negative force is the fuel that ignites the rage and anger within them. In a moment of rage, it could be said that Chisek (by way of the negative-part) is in control of you. There are many "crimes of passion" that occur in this state of mind, and, as much as some legal entities may argue, they all come down to a lack of reason in a moment that necessitates reason most. Without this control of overwhelming passion by reason, you as a human have lost the very thing that distinguishes you as a human and earns you the right to be respected as a human. When a human allows impulse, or the negative-part, to override all reason, then this is a dismal failing on the part of the human ... a dismal, dismal failing.

·⁓

We know that each of the two balancing parts within a human is at war with the other. Each is fighting, so to speak, to gain control of that control center within the human. Whichever wins takes control of that control center and exerts its influence – either positive or negative – and consequently affects the physiological manifestation of that body in terms of its nervous system and its overall health and sanity.

When one part takes control, the other is exiled to the subconscious mind or it leaves the body altogether and takes its aura with it. Once in the confinement of the subconscious mind, that aura is rendered neutral and ineffective to the body. The aura belonging to whichever part is in the control center now encompasses the body. What the Creators expect of humans one day is to have the balancing parts able to co-exist together in the control center of the brain. This can only be accomplished when equilibrium is attained. This means that neither balancing part is operating the steering wheel and guiding the human. This means that neither force can influence you and sway you to its side any longer. This means that the two forces have their "hands" on the steering wheel, one on each side, while equilibrium – which is the final state of reason – will be the force to keep the two opposite energies from "clashing," in a similar way in which neutron particles provided a containment field between matter and antimatter in the time of The Beginning of The Beginning of the universe (and still do provide such a containment field in the disorderly universe). That is, equilibrium will exist in between these two forces and won't allow either force to steer. You are now the one in control of the steering. You have effectively put the "brakes" on each force. Equilibrium is the brake. When you need to use your negative force, you ease up a little on the brakes, depending on how much of its influence you want exerted. The same with the positive force. This way, you control each force and how much of its influence you want exerted on you.

This is a philosophical way of describing equilibrium, and the new phase-4 human. There is a lot more to all of this. For instance, when you become that brake, your first-part will be that brake with you. Together, you will now focus on one common objective, which will be understood in Chapter 16.

Trapped in the "Labyrinth of the Minotaur"

There is a myth that has come down to us from the ancient Greeks. In this myth a Minotaur, which was half man, half bull – his head and tail were that of a bull, while his body was that of a man – was locked in a complex maze, specially created for him, called a labyrinth. Humans were often sacrificed by being placed in that labyrinth for the Minotaur to devour. This was a fantastic story, but it was replete with imagery, and in our interpretation of this imagery we are fundamentally being told of the battle that can rage and often does rage within a human. The labyrinth can be equated to the maze we, with our own free will, create in our own minds and allow ourselves to be induced into when we allow the negative-part to control us, particularly if we cross over the line into severe mental states, which is the point where the beast within us devours us, just as the beast devours humans in the myth of the Minotaur in the labyrinth.

How we can be induced into such mental states is by allowing the negative-part to lure us down its path. It is not always obvious to us that we are drifting down the negative path. Feeling sorry for ourselves or being depressed draws us down the negative path in the same way that feeling rage or anger does, and even in the same way that following the criminal path does. The methods are all different, the motives may all be different, but the driving force is one and the same, and the final outcome can be one and the same, principally because the road, the steps, or the spiral – whatever expression you wish to use – one can travel down is ultimately one and the same.

If we cannot correct the negative path we are on by steering off it, chances are it will lead us to experience mental problems. The severity is determined primarily by the degree to which we are influenced by the negative-part. We should take into account that in the beginning of that climb down the negative path, the negative influence upon us would have begun in small doses, but slowly, bit by bit, the more you succumb to it, the more it grows. Gradually, small things lead to bigger things, and, at the end of the line, we can be assured that there will be mental problems of some sort. These small things can include being unhappy about our looks, weight, height, personality, lack of friendship –

it could be one of a thousand other things! It could even be the temptation to commit petty crimes.

If you constantly follow the urge to solve your problems with a negative approach, it becomes harder to do otherwise; eventually you will reach a point where you will not be able to help yourself or stop yourself, just as the alcoholic cannot stop drinking one more drink, and just as the food addict cannot stop thinking about what to eat next. This is because the negative-part is steering you down this path and not just encouraging, but urging on, the behavior. Falling into the negative-part's cycle is exactly the same as falling into alcoholism – after the first drink there will be a second, and then a third, and then one day out of nowhere you will have a real problem on your hands because you will have become addicted and you cannot stop. The further down the negative path you go, the easier it becomes for you to stay on that path, and the harder it becomes for you to steer off that path; you are now inclined to enjoy or get a "kick" out of that path, of which you can't even begin to understand the psychiatry. This kick is a part of the incentive in getting you to go down that negative path.

This kick has its links to the negative aura, and most likely to the release of chemicals resultant from the activation of the nervous system. As stated earlier, this negative aura gradually and subtly weakens the body, and this weakness makes it hard for a person to fight against the negative influence and draw on the positive influence. This is why those who are depressed end up trapping themselves in a cycle where they are physically and emotionally weak, and are unable to draw on any positive strength to fight back. Fighting back refers to climbing out of that negative rut and getting off the negative path. The negative aura, and the negative influence by way of suggestion, perpetuate that weakness in such a way that you keep drifting with the flow of it – what you do not realize is that "the flow" is like a strong river current that will not let you out of its grip as it heads for a waterfall. This applies to anyone under the influence of the negative-part, no matter what the method of influence is.

In simple terms – in the absence of medically derived brain conditions – if you find yourself in the shoes of someone being drawn down the negative path, it means that once upon a time you found a reason to draw on the influence of the negative-part. There was some kind of weakness within you, at some stage of your life – most likely in childhood, where most of the seeds of your weaknesses were planted. (Sometimes they were even planted in your past life and have crossed over into your present life.) Perhaps in childhood you encountered the death of a loved one. Perhaps you were abused. Perhaps you were humiliated at school. Perhaps you were teased as a child at home or at school. Perhaps your parents divorced. You may have and most likely have carried the scars of any of these things into your adulthood. These scars can be said to be the weaknesses in a human. Because you allowed yourself to be influenced by the negative-part on each occasion where the memory of these scars was created, rather than turn the situation around in a positive light and try to move on from it, it could be said that you indulged in allowing Chisek to guide you down the negative path and into your negative condition. Not only have you allowed Chisek to be your "gardener," who was the one who "planted" and "germinated" the seeds of these weaknesses, but you have allowed Chisek to nurture them and feed them; he then waits for the opportunity for one of the plants to "ripen," which ultimately means he has found a way to take a human to his final cause.

By continually drawing on the influence of the negative-part, you are allowing yourself to be tempted step by step all the way down to the far-reaching ends of the negative path. The sad reality is, the further down this path you travel, the gloomier it becomes, and, chances are, you'll encounter a line you do not want to cross. This line is the marker of the final cause of Chisek, and often marks the road of no return, from which for many there really is no return!

The behavior of those reaching Chisek's final cause can range from being harmless to others and themselves, to being dangerous to others and themselves. There is no formula to define a person's behavior or state of mind at this level. The one commonality, however, is the dysfunction of the persons and their inability to function in life according to accepted norms or social standards, or within recognized behavior parameters.

The following are two extreme examples of what can happen if you reach Chisek's final cause, both wittingly and unwittingly.

First, Chisek's negative-part now assumes total control over your actions and you no longer have conscious knowledge of your actions or control of your mind. When the negative-part assumes control of you, you may have impaired thoughts, may hear voices, may have delusions and hallucinations, and may suffer from paranoia. Those who commit crimes do not appear to have the capacity to know right from wrong, and do not appear to have any control of what they are doing. People can have mild and temporary psychotic episodes and recover shortly after, and there are those who recover with medication. Just as there are many degrees of psychosis, so are there many degrees of influences the negative-part can have on you. The extreme condition, however, is when you fall into a permanent state of madness where you have ultimately lost control of your brain to your negative-part.

In this condition, despite having no self control, you are still responsible in the eyes of the Creators for any of your past or subsequent actions, as it was you who alone let yourself be led down Chisek's negative road (which is usually one of no return) and enabled all this to happen. After all, none of this would have happened if you did not open the door for Chisek and hold his guiding hand as you trod together down his path.

Second, you consciously control your actions, which are suggested to you by your negative-part, so that willingly you are being guided by it. It could be said that those who become deviant have become partners with Chisek, to his great "pleasure." Now, your negative-part and your conscious mind operate as one, and are one. Your condition appears to fit the clinical classification of a psychopath. Psychopaths do not have delusions or hallucinations. Those who commit crimes appear to have the capacity to know right from wrong — they just choose to follow the path of wrong, and appear to have control of what they are doing.

In either of these cases, in the extreme where the condition is permanent, the positive-part will have deserted you permanently, and this is because you have totally succumbed, in one way or another, to Chisek. No positive influence in you means you cannot feel guilt; you cannot feel remorse; you cannot feel empathy; and you certainly cannot have a conscience. You are now a twin in character to the phase-2 human, who possessed this deficit as well. Remember, the phase-2 human did not have a positive influence. A human no longer possessing a positive-part, but being driven solely by the negative-part, can become the epitome of evil. For, without a positive-part, a human has no measure of what is right, or no understanding of right. To this person wrong is now right. Wrong (evil) is now the only measure available to this human. To take a human to the pinnacle of evil is the final cause of Chisek. This is a devastating outcome for a human being ... an absolutely devastating failure, but, equally, it is a stupendous outcome for Chisek ... an absolutely stupendous outcome!

Keep in mind that at any time when you allow the negative-part into your control center to operate the steering wheel, there is no positive influence at work, which means the part of the brain responsible for reasoning does not have the ability to work. The negative-part, owing to its negative composition, is not interested in having you use the part of your brain that reasons – at least not for your benefit. This area of the brain then becomes "switched off." For, the negative-part does not have the capacity to understand right or good. It is only made up of all the negative characteristics that are derived from greed. The positive-part, in contrast, owing to its positive characteristics, does not activate the primal emotions of your brain. Each balancing part is interested in having you use that part of your brain which benefits its final cause. Which balancing part you allow to influence you determines which area of the brain you are using at that given moment, and how that area of the brain is being used.

When you disable the reasoning part of your brain, the "beast" within you dictates your rationality, which is subtle but convincing. You have now become trapped in the "Labyrinth of the Minotaur." This means the beast within you will devour you if you stay in this cycle. Most of the time you *will want* to stay in this cycle; feeling sorry for yourself and feeling depressed, for instance, are *pleasing* to you in this state, which is a great contradiction, and a hard thing to try to interpret. Only when you are there, in that negative state, can you understand Chisek's power and all-consuming grip on you.

When it comes to that great unknown of the human mind and its diseases, it should be emphasized here that madness can be the final cause of a mind that has allowed the negative-part to control it. Indeed, the characteristics of madness, lunacy, and insanity are the defining characteristics of the personality of Chisek. The seeds of these diseases can form primarily from one's inability to control the negative influence. In other words, when a soul is sickened, the sickness of the human soul is generally evil ... and evil quite simply translates into Chisek and his influence.

What this means is that those who are an aberration from and abomination of the nature of man; those who become deviant and perverse; those who possess morbid urges; those who enact profane, dark, and criminally insane behavior, have stepped over the line and reached Chisek's final cause in the extreme, and this is a mind that has enabled Chisek's negative influence to consume it.

・ー

In summary, Chisek has a path, a direction for you. His steps lead to his final cause. The steps individuals take down that path may not be the same. Some steps may be carpeted; some may be constructed out of timber; some may even be lined with rose petals or gold dust. The point is, the steps lead to the same destination. What this means is that you may walk the steps starting out with anger-management issues. Further down the steps you may face depression. Introversion can often be considered a sign of a person on the downward steps. Aggression or violence will also be found somewhere down those steps. If you don't seek help and try to climb back up the stairs, but continue down them, one way or another that stairway will lead to mental illnesses of some kind because your negative condition will keep getting worse and worse. It may even lead to your death by suicide.

Not all humans who tread down Chisek's path reach the extreme of Chisek's final cause. Not all humans become killers or commit suicide. Not all humans commit acts of violence or aggression. Chisek's influence comes in many guises, and some humans are able to put the brakes on the negative influence at a certain level and do not tread deeper into its depths. Every case has its own unique qualities and idiosyncrasies. We have endless possibilities in terms of what negative characteristics we can allow ourselves to be driven by. For instance, we may face abuse from our parents and become socially introverted or depressed. This does not mean we will grow up to be serial killers or the like. We may, by our own instinct (guided by the positive-part), put the brakes on the negative-part at that point and not progress further down the negative spiral. This means we have listened to the positive voice that has made us understand that further negative progress is wrong. It is simply a matter of choice. We can just as easily ignore that positive voice and embrace the negative voice.

Ultimately, if we do allow our will to be guided solely by the negative instinct without ever putting on the brakes, we will in some way tread to the far reaches of Chisek's final cause, and we can become overtaken by madness. We can become vicious killers. We can kill ourselves. We can become violent. What we can become is individually unique to us, depending on the quirks – which include personal fantasies – of our personality, and the circumstances of our conditioning, environment, and opportunities. Some of us can become cannibals. Some of us can become vampires. Some of us can become torturers, rapists, mutilators … you cannot categorize the many options that are available to us. The possibilities are limited only to the imagination of the deviant and perverted mind, and how that mind wants to self-indulge in his fantasies. These are the extreme ends of the negative influence. Not everyone is prone to such sadistic tendencies. Some of us limit our perversions by putting the brakes on the negative influence at an earlier stage and then linger at that level. This is once again a choice. Furthermore, not all of us in a state of madness exhibit sadistic tendencies, become deviant, become harmful to others or ourselves, or become killers. Some of us do.

A serial killer who has reached these extremes of evil may have started out as a child angry at being abused or picked on at school for various reasons. This may have led to sadness, depression, and then anger-management problems such as an uncontrollable temper. The child may have then become a loner. The feeling of being outcast and rejected by his abuser or fellow students may have led the child into a disruptive and conflictive state – such as bullying or fighting others; or even into a harmful state – such as enacting sadistic tendencies toward animals or himself, or falling into the trap of substance abuse. He may have even started to commit petty crimes. Slowly this initiates him into committing bolder and more daring crimes. At no time did this child put the brakes on the negative influence; instead, he went with the flow of it. The environment around this child provided the breeding conditions for the negative-part to take a permanent hold on him; this child offered no resistance whatsoever. If there were no positive stimulants in the child's life to redirect his path in a positive way, and if there was no will on his part to follow a positive path, there was nothing in this child the positive-part could do to influence him to get out of this negative spiral.

By the time such child grows up, he may have spent time not only in juvenile detention centers for various crimes or rebellious behavior, but also in prison. These environments are generally not conducive to turning around the lives of such persons and inducing them to steer themselves in a positive direction. Doubtlessly, they may be conducive to propagating the continual decline of such persons down the spiral of the negative path.

The darkest human, such as a killer, reached a critical moment where he utilized the negative influence so often that his negative-part was able to take complete control of his mind, directly (as in psychosis) or indirectly (as in psychopathy). The positive-part was forced to flee this person's brain altogether, as it could not stay in a brain that reached Chisek's final cause. The positive-part was unable to "rescue" the human from the negative side and this is why it left. It leaves when it sees no hope left for the soul. This is when a soul has crossed a certain line. That line can never really be re-crossed again and the soul becomes trapped. This is when the "door" is locked, the "key" is thrown away, and the positive-part is barred for good from that human's brain – its access has been forbidden. The negative-part has now secured the right to place its stake in that person's soul upon death.

Once the positive-part has left, this human has reached Chisek's final cause and has allowed himself to be driven by the beast within him; he can then easily become that beast, and he can easily behave like that beast. Now there is little difference between this human and the phase-2 human. Now the thrill of the kill, the blood, and the excitement of the release of anger and rage can become his motivational drives. Now there is nothing within him to tell him that such behavior is wrong. So to him the behavior is right. (As a side note, the perpetrator, who was instrumental in providing an environment that encouraged the negative behavior of that child who grew up to be this type of human, is also usually judged for the crimes of that human!)

Cracking the question of what the dark forces are that drive the darkest of humans, such as violent criminals, as well as cracking the code of how a killer's mind is forged, lies in understanding the two forces within a human: the positive-part and the negative-part. It generally does not (unless there is a pre-existing medical condition) lie in a genetic foundation or mutation. It often lies in a deficiency, and that deficiency is that navigational rudder (the positive-part) that steers a human on the path of good and right.

When humans have allowed themselves to reach such a state that their positive-part no longer has any influence in their brains, or even when they are temporarily under the influence of the negative-part (such as when they cry, tell someone off, or think and act violently), scans of their brains would show that an area of the pre-frontal cortex, in their frontal lobes, is not, or is hardly, being activated. This would suggest that this is the part of the brain that suppresses and controls behavior influenced by the negative-part, such as depression, anger, and aggression. This would also then suggest that this part of the brain is not used by the negative-part.

The amygdala appears to be the part of the brain that is responsible for the flight-or-fight response. It is also the part of the brain that appears to have a relationship with anger. This all seems to suggest the idea that people with poor anger-management skills and poor stress-coping skills do not allow their pre-frontal cortex to take over and suppress the amygdala; in metaphysical terms, this would appear to suggest that the positive-part is prevented from taking over and suppressing the negative-part and providing its influence in the brain. Why it is prevented is that a choice has been made: a choice to follow the instinct and impulse of the negative-part, which is a lot easier to do than draw upon the influence of the positive-part in that moment.

If we go back to the case of the politician who was served the wrong meal, we can see that he impulsively reacted by shouting. This suggests that his negative-part was at the helm of his control center operating the steering wheel. Had his impulse been one to only momentarily be annoyed, but then laugh it off with an understanding approach, his negative-part would have initially been operating the steering wheel, but as soon as he laughed his positive-part would have, in a split second, kicked it out and taken over the steering wheel.

Finally, it should be remembered that the above interpretation is applicable to the cases of a normal, healthy brain that has allowed the negative-part to override the positive-part. Some brains are damaged from birth or are affected by brain conditions or abnormalities; any of these may impact on the normal functioning of the brain, particularly the amygdala or the pre-frontal cortex. The resultant behavior of the person afflicted may be the same as the behavior of a person who is overcome by the negative-part, but it must be understood that the forces which drove the person to this behavior cannot be diagnosed in the same way. (There are many variables that need to be considered, and it must be understood that this book is intended for educational purposes and does not give medical advice – thus it should NOT be used for purposes of diagnosis. A qualified consultant should always be approached for purposes of diagnosis of any symptoms that may be the precursors of medical conditions.)

For instance, there have been cases where good people have suddenly become killers, who were later found to have had tumors or the like in their brains. These tumors or the like then affected the brain in such a way that they were the sole cause of the person's criminal behavior. In the eyes of their Creators these killers would not be judged for any actions that occurred as a consequence of medical conditions. Not any of us are immune from the possibility of this happening to us at some stage of our lives.

Some brains can be damaged by the use of alcohol or illicit drugs. When under the influence of alcohol or illicit drugs you usually lose all inhibitions because the positive-part cannot operate in such a brain. In either of these two states, you allow the negative-part to take over your brain's control center, which is a frightening thing, indeed, for a human. Simply put, on those occasions when you abuse yourself with alcohol or drugs, you effectively install the negative-part in the control center of your brain, and it remains there until the alcohol or drugs wear off. This is why aggression, risky behavior, and the like are prevalent to humans in either of those states. It should be noted that the fault of any of your actions that occur while you are in either of those states lies with you, as taking alcohol or drugs was a choice made by you.

•—

Now that we understand how the negative-part can influence a human to follow the path to Chisek's final cause, we need to cover the second aspect of the negative-part at play within a human mind. On its own, the balancing negative-part that comes in the package of a human is not capable of inducing severe mental disorders in a human; nor is it capable of taking a human to Chisek's final cause. It does not have the strength. It only has so much strength and power over you (39 percent). It is, however, the "door" through which a stronger negative-part is able to enter the brain and completely throw out the balance of that brain. This is called the "second negative-part."

This second negative-part has a stronger negative aura that it brings into the body, and it keeps a person balanced toward the negative side. The odds of influence now change in the brain, where the two negative-parts combined have the equivalent of 47.5 percent influence, as opposed to the positive-part having an influence of 52.5 percent. This second negative-part wreaks havoc in a human in terms of his sanity and nervous system. If we recall, the P3V1 human was affected by a 51 percent positive influence and a 49 percent negative influence. This superior human could not control the negative-part with those odds, and this is why the Creators had to alter the odds. When you allow a second negative-part in, those odds become close to the odds the P3V1 human was exposed to and failed to handle. This just illustrates the difficulty we as humans (with our primitive level of intelligence) have if we allow ourselves to be subject to the odds of influence we are subject to when we allow the second negative-part in.

It should be noted that a calm and balanced human does not possess this second negative-part. A human who does possess it allowed it in by drawing on the influence of the balancing negative-part more frequently than drawing on the influence of the balancing positive-part. The small steps on the negative side a human takes in the beginning of his path down the negative spiral were caused by the seduction of the balancing negative-part. When a human progresses down the spiral and passes the "grade" – which is known as "the entry point" – he welcomes in this strong, second negative-part. Once in the system, this second negative-part then unites with the balancing negative-part, and the two combined are subject to the same rules that are applicable to the balancing negative-part.

Humans who have the second negative-part in their brains do not have to be extreme cases. Humans who have anger-management issues, are erratic, are depressed, cry a lot, tell others off all the time, have a temper, or are violent, have a second negative-part within their brains. The case studies presented in the last chapter, involving the politicians who throw temper tantrums for the slightest inconvenience, have the second negative-part in their brains. Those who are calm and nice one moment but become the complete opposite in the next moment have the second negative-part in their brains. Children who commit acts of crime, or show signs of harming others, including animals, have a second negative-part in their brains. This would be applicable to a vast number of humans on this planet.

If you did not have the second negative-part, or even the balancing negative-part, you would not have it within you to do any of these negative things.

You would be similar to the phase-1 human. It is only because you have a negative force within you that you are able to exhibit negative behavioral characteristics.

To get rid of this strong, second negative-part, you have to predispose yourself to being positive; you need to go back up the negative spiral to the entry point, which now becomes "the exit point." The second negative-part exits the brain because it has nothing to do and gets bored; it cannot dwell in such a positive environment – until you invite it back by drifting down the negative spiral and passing the entry point. The same old second negative-part then comes back within you. It was assigned to you, and it will follow you from life to life, the same as the balancing parts do.

A good step you can take toward conquering the meat-in-the-sandwich goal is to keep the second negative-part out of your control center. If you succeed in keeping this second negative-part out, you will have a totally different state of mind to the one you had when you allowed the second negative-part in. It is an inordinately difficult task to accomplish such a thing. It requires the same determination an alcoholic or drug addict requires to kick the habit ... possibly even a lot more! But, once you do purge it, with persistence and awareness, keeping it out is less cumbersome than it was trying to initially get rid of it. First, you have to realize you have a problem. In understanding the enemy within you, you should find this task a lot easier. As someone wise once said, you cannot fight your enemy until you know you have one.

·◡·

To see the signs of a second negative-part in a child is a worry. This is a red flag. It is an early warning indicator that tells us that the child has a problem that can escalate in a detrimental way when he becomes an adult. Juvenile detention centers need to be revamped in a way that a child can be taken out of that negative spiral. The prevention of future criminals needs to commence in juvenile detention centers. Frankly, it needs to commence at school when the signs become apparent that a child is being influenced by the negative-part. If the child's problem is not addressed in childhood, in all likelihood it will be too late to be addressed in adulthood. This child could have been devoured by the Minotaur long before he reached adulthood.

Part of the answer lies in trying to occasion a positive environment for the child. There are trends for some groups to rehabilitate troubled children by taking them into nature, where they can be challenged with nature on the one hand, and be taught socially acceptable behavior on the other. Such behavior can only be taught when the child is not under the influence of the negative-part and, obviously, the second negative-part. Once again, this is only part of the answer. It would go a long way to introduce the positive feeling of love – even if it is by way of an animal. Sometimes pets have a better capacity to love than some humans have. Another part of the answer is to find out the child's passions or talents, and then give him encouragement so that he can direct his energy into something productive, something that benefits him in a positive way.

There are cases where children, even under the age of ten, show no remorse, and have killed, or have attempted to kill, family members or friends. Sometimes they laugh as they watch their victims face death or the possibility of death. Without any noted medical brain condition, this behavior unequivocally suggests that such a child has reached the final cause of Chisek, or is close to it. The parent of such a child in all likelihood has no means whatsoever of addressing the problem without professional help. To attempt to remedy such a child, by taking that child from this place of no hope back to the middle-ground state, is a near-impossible feat. It is, however, possible, even though all indications in this book have been that once you have crossed that line of no return there simply is no return. For, nothing is impossible. Someone wise once said that the word "impossible" belongs in a dictionary written by fools. Everything is possible. The impossible is just as possible as the possible, if the possible is wanted badly enough by the person facing the impossible. That is the key. The positive-part would love nothing more than to come back from this place of no hope and triumph over its enemy.

To address this, someone has to create a special, special program that can rehabilitate this child. First, the child needs to be removed from the environment that negatively induced him in the first place to take the negative spiral. Then the negative-inducing circumstance needs to be determined and addressed. Then a corrective positive path needs to be implemented, one that induces the resurrection of the positive-part. How specially trained practitioners accomplish this is an interesting question! The answer is definitely not in a juvenile detention center or a center for the mentally ill. This is a great challenge for society, and certainly a rewarding one.

It should be noted that there are children with good parents, from good environments, who, from a young age, can exhibit extreme negative tendencies, such as extreme temper tantrums. Something has gone wrong and the child's brain has "hijacked" itself; something in this child's brain has enabled the negative-part to override the positive-part. If the problem is not a medical condition that requires an alternative remedy, then this child can be taught how to control that negative tendency (by learning how to activate the positive-part), with professional help. This is why it is crucial that professional help is sought at an early stage, and that the symptoms are not dismissed as merely a passing childhood phase.

The case of those engaged in military duty, such as soldiers, is interesting. Many soldiers from intelligent countries have learned, by training under stress, how to control this negative side in a war situation. However, badly trained soldiers have been taught to, or come to, hate their enemies to the point of not just wanting to kill them, but actually taking pleasure in killing them! As a soldier, a normal human being can be trained to become an uncontrollable killer in the killing environment; the problem is, it becomes practically impossible for such a person to find balance again after serving a term of duty. This can even apply to the most controlled soldier. When a soldier – in active duty or returned – shows a change of behavior in a negative way, such as possessing anger traits and a lack of emotional control, this suggests that his second negative-part has overwhelmed him, for whatever reason. These people could easily become time bombs waiting for the right catalyst to push them over the edge. In some circumstances, just as a person can produce several positive-parts, so can a person produce several negative-parts. Killing environments can be the breeding grounds for this. A person in these shoes, affected by several negative-parts, has a completely messed up mind. This is why the government needs to look after soldiers in this situation, after their terms of duty, to ensure they are reprogrammed back into a positive sphere, which is a difficult thing to do.

Overcoming the "Labyrinth": Conquering the "Minotaur"

To continue the Greek myth of the Minotaur in the labyrinth, one day one of those very sacrifices was able to conquer the Minotaur. This conqueror of the Minotaur was also able to find his way out of the maze of the labyrinth, after having been given the secret of how to do this. The symbolism of this tells us that there is hope for us: there is the possibility for us to conquer our "Minotaur," and there is a way for us to escape from our labyrinth. This section will show us how to achieve these things: it will present us with the method of how to conquer our very own Minotaur, and it will present us with the secret of how to escape from our very own labyrinth. Once we have achieved these things, we will have learned how to conquer our meat-in-the-sandwich goal.

How to conquer the meat-in-the-sandwich goal, quite simply, and with great difficulty, is not to allow your balancing negative-part to influence you to the point where your brain allows the second negative-part to unite with it. You have to be able to do this for good. This is practically impossible, because, even a hot day, or being annoyed by a fly, is enough to bring back the second negative-part and drive you crazy. The balancing part is just a portal that facilitates the entry of the second negative-part. This is the dangerous one.

You must be wondering why the Creator besmirched us with such defiled metaphysical soot! A wise man once said:

> *There is for every question an answer,*
> *Just as there is for every certainty*
> *A diametrically opposed uncertainty.*

When a situation arises, such as some deadly confrontation, where you need to draw on the negative influence for survival purposes, the balancing negative-part automatically invokes the presence of the second negative-part. The two unite, and your positive-part joins forces with them to defeat your adversary. This is a special circumstance, and even when you achieve equilibrium, this second negative-part will still be a part of you. It will still be a part of the sandwich. In this circumstance, it is protecting you; it is working to benefit you in your survival. This is one of the profound reasons that it exists. It will always be there for you to use in aid of your survival.

Every one of us can invoke the presence of a second negative-part and put ourselves in an ultimate state of rage and anger. In a situation where our survival is in question, this is what we must all do, and we must challenge our aggressor if there is no other option before us. In circumstances of threat we must not cower; we all have it within us to draw out evil rage and become aggressive: become a monster, a beast. When we do draw out the beast that is within us, our physiology will change and our odds of survival against our aggressor will increase. In this ultimate state the body will possess greater powers and abilities, even properties such as fearlessness and superhuman strength.

The emotion of fear can be triggered by either of the balancing parts. If the positive-part triggers the emotion, the amygdala usually kicks in with the fight-or-flight response and the negative-part automatically takes control of the brain. With the second negative-part in control, you can put yourself into an ideal attack mode where you feel fearlessness.

The following is an example of a case where a man invoked his second negative-part for survival purposes. When he was confronted with an aggressive ape, he swelled with anger and rage. In drawing upon all his negative energy, he confronted the man-sized ape head on and injured it. The tables were turned and the ape backed away and became submissive when it felt that it was no match for its human aggressor. This human would not have possessed the strength or ability to confront such an aggressor without invoking these two negative-parts.

The phase-1 human in this instance would have said to the ape when the ape was ready to make a meal of him, "That's OK! That's good!" Now you can see why the human biological computer needs to have these additional software attachments: they provide essential instinctive drives to complete the human "package" and make it whole and what it is today, and what it is hoped to be tomorrow.

What you have to become is a human able to exist under all the pressures you are under, without enabling the second negative-part in your brain, *unless* you face a situation where your survival is in question. This is the elusive challenge, and it is the answer to the secret of how to achieve equilibrium.

Although it appears to be a relatively easy task, it is the most difficult challenge any human will ever encounter. It is also your most important challenge in life. It ranks high like a mountain peak, and all the rest – such as your degree or career advancement – rank in the valley below. This is one of the reasons that you are deliberately faced with confrontations and challenges. It is when you are confronted with a circumstance that provokes a negative reaction from you that you have to reason first and then react in a reasoned manner. This is obviously easier said than done! Most of the time your negative reaction occurs before you have had time to even think let alone reason – which is where the greatest problem lies. It is often after the negative reaction that you are able to reason and feel regret. The challenge lies in ensuring that a reasoned, thought-out reaction occurs first, which prevents a negative reaction from taking place at all.

The problem with many people is that they don't think or reason at all. They allow rage (or self-pitying emotions like depression) to overwhelm and consume them. This leads to all sorts of negative manifestations physically and emotionally. What the challenge here is that you have to find a way to defuse rage (or self-pitying emotions) before it gets totally out of control. For, it is at the moment you feel rage build within you (which means your negative-part is in control of the steering wheel), that you have to be willing and able to find the rationale for this behavior. Straight away you have to close your eyes, relax, and try to eradicate from your mind any negative thoughts and feelings. You need to just cool down and reverse those negative thoughts and feelings. You need to find a way to kick your negative-part out of your control center. As an intelligent human you should be able to do this. You see, you have to learn to find your inner strength to put yourself in reverse. You can do this by trying to be happy and by thinking of something nice; anything you think of or do that is positive will go a long way toward attaining this. Even something as effortless as smiling may distract you and change the course of your negativity. Smiling – not sarcastically (which is a Chisek smile) – will force the negative-part out of your control center and your positive-part back in. It all happens in split microseconds. Smiling in this way requires the positive-part to be in the control center of the brain. Smiling is a key element here when it comes to altering the state of your mind.

The secret is to find some way of breaking the hold of the negative-part as fast as you can, because, when it gets a hold of you, that negativity can manifest within you for a long time. If this happens, when you are in a state of anger you cannot work; you cannot concentrate; you make mistakes; and you certainly can injure yourself — there are endless stupid things you can do to yourself in this destructive frame of mind.

Sometimes it takes a lot more than merely smiling when you feel you are the victim of cruel or insensitive acts by others. Your desire for revenge and retribution will be overpowering and overwhelming. It should be noted here that feelings of hate and revenge (as opposed to acts of revenge) are drastically more destructive to you than they are to the person you harbor such feelings toward. Drastically more! Those feelings are destroying you and dragging you down the negative spiral. What you must do is always turn the other cheek and leave others to the hands of karma (which is the equivalent of saying, Odo's parts).

In some instances, it can be a mammoth task to turn the other cheek, but it can and must be done. When you do this, however, you have to be careful not to let the trauma gnaw at you. The insensitivity of others can make you feel so vilified that you start to self-destruct in your mind. Chisek will make you foster such self-destructive emotions. For instance, you may face rejection by your partner. You may even face rejection by your parents. The dilemma is obvious: how do you remove overwhelming negative emotions when they fester inside your mind?

"Deflected positive association" is the key. That is, whenever bad memories consume your thoughts you must conjure up something positive. Associate something positive with the bad memory. That positive association could be the pet or even the child you love, some happy memory, or something that is funny and makes you laugh. Every time the bad memory surfaces, you deflect your mind to this positive association. The idea is that whenever the bad memory comes to mind you will have a huge smile of happiness on your face. At first it will be difficult to do, but eventually you won't even have to try. Chisek will eventually give up suggesting the bad memory because it doesn't work any longer. He will move on and look for something else in your life to weaken you.

Sometimes the best way to take yourself out of the negative cycle is to do some physical activity — as opposed to mental activity — such as cleaning the house or garage, or even painting the house. Divert your energy into something beneficial to you — as long as you don't allow it to become a compulsion or addiction. (This is covered in the next chapter.) Sometimes it takes days, even weeks and months, to recover. In this state your body will not have a calm disposition. You may find that your nerves are shaking and your heart is palpitating.

In ridding the negativity from you, you will then regain not merely the positive-part in the control center, but the positive aura your body lost when the negative-part was embraced. You must take into consideration that it is easier to allow the negative-part than it is to allow the positive-part to take control of your control center. It requires work to maintain a positive state. Allowing the negative-part to influence you is equivalent to being in a lazy state.

Your initial goal in this primitive stage of intelligence is to return to a calm, happy, almost meditative state, and not allow your negative-part to fuel your desire for revenge, payback, or getting even. Remember the extreme case of the serial killer who killed women after being rejected by his girlfriend? His actions represent what many of us are capable of. Sometimes all it takes is the right catalyst, especially when we have a history of so easily succumbing to the instinctive drive of the negative-part.

Your final goal when you reach a superior stage of intelligence is not to allow yourself to be affected by someone's cruel or insensitive acts to the point where you don't ever feel negative desires such as revenge. This is the human we should all one day become.

At all times you must be wary of the negative-part, for, when the negative-part is at the helm of the control center of your brain it will do everything it possibly can to you in a negative way. Its job is to affect you negatively every way it can. If it is able to make contact with another mind whose negative-part is at the control helm in just the same way, it will give ideas to that negative-part to help undermine you in some negative way. The negative-parts will conspire and collaborate with each other and play you for a sucker. As an example, if your negative-part made contact with a thief's negative-part, when you least expect, that thief will probably rob you, because your negative-part will have plotted to do everything it could to make you negligent and careless. There are many cases of the most remarkable near-impossible coincidences; yet they occur. How, you ask yourself? This is because your negative-part has made it so. The determining factor to make Murphy's Law applicable to a human is the state of the mind of the human, and whether it is governed by the negative-part of Chisek.

This is why it is essential, when you have your negative-part governing the control center of your brain, that you find a way to put yourself in an opposite frame of mind and do not allow yourself to dwell on the cause of your negativity.

It is not worth it, because, tomorrow will surely come and you will probably see that none of it made any sense; this way you will have avoided any damage that could have been done on your part.

If you are a twin, you need to be especially careful in your use of the second negative-part. Based on some bizarre cases in our history, it is evident that it is possible for a second negative-part of one twin to access the control center of the other twin and become the third negative-part in that twin's brain. We know that twins share commonalities in their brains. A feature of this commonality is a direct link between their brains and their positive-parts. It is because their brains have this commonality that their positive-parts often interchange transmissions, and transmissions are sent not to one brain but to two brains. There is an interplay going on in this sense, and this is why the brains of twins are tuned in to each other in a way the brains of other humans are not.

It would not, then, be outrageous to extend the commonalities of twins to their negative-parts. We know that the defining boundary between twins becomes blurred in many ways. As stated above, what can happen is that one of the twins can in a twisted way come to possess a third negative-part. This third negative-part is actually the second negative-part belonging to the other twin. Because of that blurred boundary and linkages between the two brains, the linkage now has become the third negative-part. A second negative-part has gone into the brain of the wrong twin. When this happens the two brains can virtually operate as one (which they often do, anyway).

A situation such as this can happen to twins who have been distant from each other for long periods. When they reunite, their parts can cause their brains to become confused when a second negative-part goes into the wrong twin's brain and becomes a third negative-part. Whether this is deliberate or unintentional is questionable! In one twin's brain there may already have been a second negative-part. In the other twin's brain there may not have been one. This "free" second negative-part then went and jumped ship, so to speak. This then creates total havoc in that brain. That brain then has a temporary moment of psychosis, where the three negative-parts are in complete control not just of it, but of the second twin's brain, indirectly and remotely.

With two second negative-parts and one balancing part steering a brain, only the worst-case scenarios can be expected. Once the positive-part regains control of the steering wheel, each brain reverts to a sedate state. Not all twins, it should be said, may be vulnerable to this occurring, especially those not regularly separate from each other, but circumstances have shown evidence that some can. In vulnerable moments of their lives, twins need to be mindful of the possibility of this occurring to them.

·⁓

Anger is like a cloud that overwhelms you. Anger is also like a thunderstorm that rages in you. If you turn to Gaia, Mother Nature, for inspiration, you can see that one of her ways of taming a thunderstorm is to produce a rainbow. It is in your cloud of anger that you need to find a rainbow for yourself to return you to a halcyon – that is, calm and peaceful – state, where you are embracing the positive influence. The rainbow is something you have to produce as fast as you can to rid the negative energy from you, because Chisek is like a kid with horrific powers that he uses on humans. He thrives on having humans embrace his negative energy. He has been made to do that; it is his job, so it isn't really his fault. The Creators intentionally created this negative force. Too often, however, Chisek takes over the human completely – in this case he has been doing his job exceptionally well!

In a way, the negative force is like a prosecutor, and the positive force is like a defender. A jury needs to have two sides of a case in order to make a judgment. Without two sides, a balanced judgment in the middle cannot be reached. The human is the same; he needs to have two sides (good and evil) to be able to reason.

The negative force is also like the opposition in government. Your job as the opposition in government is to always point out the bad side of things, and just oppose and oppose and try to ruin whatever the party in government is proposing. Well, Chisek operates in the same manner. Whenever the Creators do something good, Chisek will oppose and try to destroy it. We know that the Creators created this negative force for this reason; they created Chisek to challenge man (along with the living world). The Creators knew that a by-product would result from the application of the positive and negative forces in a human, and that by-product is the meat in the sandwich. When this day arrives, you will possess an intellect that has been bonded from the trials and the tribulations, one that knows both the positive and the negative side. You will stand alone in the middle of the two contrary forces in your own right and be on top of everything; for you will use the good side to your advantage, and you will learn how to control the negative side and use it to your advantage when necessary – this is what will keep you on the edge; this is what will keep you in the middle of the sandwich, as though walking on a tightrope.

When you become this final intellect, you will not allow yourself to become too good that you are taken for a ride by anyone, or not allow yourself to drift to the negative side and throw out your balance. This way, you will have taken a stand and drawn a line in the middle. This is the human we must evolve into and become one day. First, we have to understand these two forces that impact upon us, because they have been created for a good reason; each one has its own purpose in life. Let us take a look at lightning: it has tremendous power; it creates fires; it makes mountains tremble. If we learn how to control and harness the power it possesses, we can ultimately use the destructive force to serve us in a way that benefits us. This is exactly what the Creators did with the destructive force of a black hole. The secret is to control the forces that have the power to destroy you; when you are aware of what those forces are and the reasons for them, can you understand how to harness and use them to your advantage; fundamentally, you will have overcome the biggest obstacle in your life. However, if you let these forces control you, they can and they certainly will ruin your life – they will perhaps even kill you.

You are definitely not going to control these forces if you allow yourself to harness the negative energy within you by going into a rage as though you were a lunatic, and then allow that negativity to stay within you for days, sometimes even for good. People upset one another all the time – sometimes you don't even know why … it just happens! That is when you have to be aware of what is happening and break out of the negative cycle straight away. Take a whirlpool: if you allow yourself to float vertically in a whirlpool you are certainly going to drown; you are never going to get out of it. But if you stretch out horizontally that whirlpool may just toss you out! These are the things you have to understand; these are the factors that influence you as a human every breathing moment of your day.

Chisek, we know, has been created by design principally for life to exist. We are a part of him. Equally, he is a part of us. So let us take a closer look at Chisek. Chisek, as this book stated earlier, is like a little kid. As long as you run from him he is going to run after you, in just the same way that a small dog will chase you if you run from it. The dog knows you're afraid – otherwise you wouldn't run! If it catches you, it is likely to bite you – yes, a stupid little dog! But when you stand your ground and challenge the dog, it is likely to back off; it is even likely to squeal and run with its tail between its legs – even a larger dog most likely would! The dog is not that stupid. Well, Chisek is exactly the same. Imagine what would happen if you were to give a kid a horrendous arsenal of power in his hands! He is going to splash that power everywhere. If he is free to do just that – as in Chisek's case – nobody can stop him. This is what Chisek is doing, except his arsenal is the negative influence by way of his loyal parts. This negative influence is everywhere and is found within everyone. He has fun with your negativity and plays with it at your expense. He is laughing at you in the process. Can you imagine that? A "kid" with horrific power let loose throughout all the universes, with a power over every single life form that exists!

If you use the application of opposite psychology with your negative-part you have no problem controlling it. This application is simple: when anger or rage envelopes you, you have to break out of that irrational cycle and get yourself completely lost in something else. You have to try to be nice to yourself and to others. You have to try to not think about what has happened because it serves no good purpose to dwell on negative memories. When in a negative state of mind you will not want to, but you have to try to. Finally, you must never think about revenge. Chisek loves that! Then he gets everybody organized; everyone gets in trouble; harmony flies out the window – and who gets the resultant points? Chisek!

It is almost as though there were a chess game going on between Odo and Chisek (or rather, in relation to us as individuals, between our positive-part and our negative-part), who are playing to win and score points, while we as humans are the pawns. We have to stand up for ourselves; we have to develop our own control; and we have to tell each side what we want. We have to shut down the game and end the point scoring for good. We must stand up for ourselves and determine what is good and what is not good. This is why the Creator has given us an individual intellect with free will – so that we can think for ourselves! He doesn't mind in the least being told by us that we don't want to do something to please him. That is the whole idea: that we as pawns on the chessboard have our own minds and know where we want to go – not have Chisek and Odo (in terms of our parts) shuffle us around as they do now! Can you imagine if one of the pawns on the chessboard turned to the players and said it didn't want to make a move for its own justified reason?

By the admission of the Creators themselves, and according to their track record, we know that they are not perfect; they indeed make mistakes, just as we do, and are always learning something new, just as we are. For this reason, it can be argued that the Creators are not immune from making the occasional wrong move in our lives. It is therefore up to us to straighten them up! In that game of chess, when Odo wants to make a move with us, it is up to us to refuse and make the determination of what the move is going to be. This is what the Creators want from us. They want us to think for ourselves – not have them think for us, as they had to for civilizations a long time ago. It is simple when you come to think of it, isn't it? The Creators simply want us to use the influencing forces when we need them; equally, they want us to control the influencing forces the rest of the time. As stated, we know that the Creators can at times be wrong; paradoxically, if they are wrong it is most likely because they choose to be wrong to challenge us into taking a stand and telling them what is right!

If you plan to stay on the "good" side (by only using the positive force), everybody is going to walk all over you. You are going to be used, misused, and bamboozled so much that you cannot afford to be too good a person. You have to be intelligently good, if that makes any sense. Not stupidly good. You have to have the kind of intelligence that is bonded by the two forces of good and evil. Put the forces together and between them comes a third force – the often referred to meat in the sandwich. As for the meat, well, you can think of that as being a refined human intellect: an intellect that has been bonded into a solidity that has the capacity to know what is good and what is evil: an intellect that is able to bring out the best from this knowledge of good and evil. This is the desired third force: the new human intellect, of such a superior standard that neither force can take advantage of and ruin it. Neither the positive side nor the negative side can control it. Instead, that refined intellect is in total control of its control center in the brain. It has traveled through "fire" and "hail" (that is, challenge after challenge) and has learned to become an almost perfect human intellect, able to reason: able to follow the "mean" between the vices of good and evil. When you attain such status as a human, only then can you really know what you want in life; know where you want to go; and know how to go about achieving the things you want to achieve. That is the third force — a perfect human intellect that has come out of the stranglehold of these conflicting forces.

These are the forces that control nature and maintain life. You are a part of these forces. These forces are a part of you. You come from these forces. Until you excel and attain equilibrium, you are going to be tossed left and right, left and right, like a ball in the game of tennis! These forces are just going to keep hitting you over the net until you stop in the middle and say, "Just a minute, guys. You are not going to hit me on either side anymore. I refuse! You are too good for me and you are too much of an asshole for me. I want to remain in the middle, right here on top of this net." Can you imagine saying this if you were that tennis ball? Being that ball that everyone just keeps whacking across the net certainly wouldn't be fun. You have to be an intelligent ball and stay safe. You have to make sure nobody wins the game and scores the points. They can't if you don't let them. What's the use of having a ball that won't fall to either side? And if either side tries to hit you while you are there in the middle, you just keep jumping up in the air, where no one can reach you. They can't play the game if they can't get to you. Understand? That is what you are. At this stage of human development you are nothing but a sidekick to both Odo and Chisek. Until you understand what you are, and you know where you are going, and you understand who is trying to do what, you are not going to be able to put an end to being knocked and kicked about.

Well, all you have to do now is say, now is the time! You are not going to allow this to happen to you anymore because you now know what it is all about. You are going to control the negative influence upon you by using opposite psychology. Anything the negative-part wants you to do in that moment you should just turn about and do the opposite. Any time you feel so nice that you have to do a good turn to someone that does not make sense, then you have to draw on the negative influence and say, "I'm not going to do it — why should I? He is using me! He is just playing me for a sucker. I'm not going to allow this. What for? Be a sucker!" So use negative and positive influences for your own good when you need them. This is what you have to realize in life. But you must never use the negative influence on purpose if you know it will hurt somebody. You can never say, "I'm going to give payback!" Ideas such as this lead a person down the negative spiral — often to consequences that were never anticipated.

THE FINAL CAUSE

You must never even think about revenge – it should never cross your mind. Your conscience, which is your balancing positive-part, would never be a part of it. Your balancing negative-part is the one that encourages it. Remember that! You can only use the negative influence when it serves to do something good. When it doesn't, you don't use it. When it does, then you use it. But you have to know when and how to use it. This is why it is there – for you to use for your own benefit in aid of your survival. Remember, you are the primary subject here for salvation. If you use the negative force in vain – as you do when you get upset and you don't know what you are doing – it will destroy you. The primary objective of both the positive-part and the negative-part is to influence you according to their programmed directive. They are only doing their jobs. It is up to you to take charge of these forces and squeeze out like the meat between the sandwich and stand up on your own two feet!

·➤

In a human situation, it is so easy to find yourself lost, where you have drifted into the useless zone of misery and depression. Life's circumstances and challenges will make it arduous for you not to tread down this path. This means you have allowed Chisek (by way of his negative-part) into your brain's control center. In these trying and testing times that surely will confront you, where there is little comfort you can find, you should always consider the simple words of a wise man ...

> *Don't let yourself drift with the negative current flow.*
> *You must wrestle the current by trying to swim to the left or the right in order to just get out of it.*
> *For it is so easy to drift with the flow –*
> *After all, it requires no struggle or hard work.*
> *And like the proverbial calm before the storm, the flow gives you a phony happiness.*
> *It is here that you have to ask yourself:*
> *Where is that river flow taking you?*
> *Will the river dump you somewhere?*
> *Or, worse, will it lead to a waterfall?*

For, once it has you, Chisek will be there at the other end with his mouth open, just waiting for you to fall in as you go over the edge.
Going with the flow is like being in a boxing ring and your opponent simply taps you, and what do you do?
You throw your gloves off and give up!
What if that opponent really knocked you?

Just remember,
Chisek is the one to suggest you are rotten; to suggest you deserve the misery you dwell in; to encourage all those negative feelings you fester inside.
This is when you cannot let yourself continue to flow with the current.
You have to find the strength to get out of it.
For saying you're rotten, and delving into self-destructive, negative thoughts, are destroying your strength of will.
Chisek wants to destroy your strength of will;
He wants to bring down your defenses,
Just like destroying the foundation of a building, resulting in it collapsing,
Just like that!
Your will – that is your strength; that is your foundation.
You must never give that up.
You have to put up a fight and say,
Well, I was wrong. I'm sorry. I've learned from it.
 As long as you have learned from it, it is OK!

When you fall into that trap of misery, Chisek slowly drains your energy.
Have you noticed that after a bout of crying and dwelling in misery that you feel tired and sleepy?
Then, after sleeping, you feel refreshed and energized again?
Well, that is because your positive aura has replenished itself.
For the positive-part has to give you aura in your sleep to try to prevent the negative-part from totally overwhelming you.
The same applies to when you are doing something you enjoy:

Somehow you find so much energy, even with little food or sleep;
For the energy seems to multiply within you almost from nowhere.
Well, that is a result of your positive-part.
It is giving aura to you when you feel happy or are doing something positive.

On the other hand, when you are depressed, it doesn't matter how much you eat or sleep, you still feel tired, listless, and without energy.
This is because Chisek is feeding you with a negative energy.
Chisek can only feed off your misery, and in the process this makes him stronger.
Then if you go and commit suicide, Chisek will have earned a double bonus;
He becomes unbelievably "happy" because he has another stroke beside his name!
You see, in every soul there is a stake.
Each force is at war with the other to see who will win that soul,
Who will place the stake in that soul ...

Reason

The human web! Of all the creatures on Earth, man is known for his nasty habit of not just making a web, but becoming entwined in that web to the extent that he can never find the way out. Humans don't need anybody else to create a web for them to become entangled in, as they are capable of creating one all by themselves. Sometimes it appears that spiders are much smarter than man, in that the spider will make its web and with that web it will catch something to eat. It is able to maneuver through its web and never become entangled in it. It knows exactly what it's doing. Maybe this is what is wrong with man: man doesn't know what he's doing. Man is a creature that is supposed to be the most intelligent and the most valuable creation made (the only one that knows it must one day die), and for one reason: he has the capacity to reason.

When humans can reason, then humans can achieve their dreams. The ability not only to reason but also to dream is one of the most precious things that a human has, and this is why man is in charge of this planet. Of all the species in existence, no species other than man is able to reason. What differentiates man is his "god-like reason"[v] (Shakespeare) that he alone was given. He was given this because he alone was chosen to be in the likeness of his Creator. Every living species has balance in place of reason. The balance all living things possess with relative ease is the meat in their sandwich. With influences to this day proportional to a 51 percent positive influence and a 49 percent negative influence, every living creature has been able to conquer the meat-in-the-sandwich goal that the Creators set for it to attain equilibrium.

Successful animal handlers and animal psychologists use this philosophy of balance in their dealings with animals, without truly knowing the deeper ontology behind it. Let us consider the example of a dog. In essence, it has three states of mind: the balanced, the fearful, and the aggressive. Fearfulness and aggressiveness are basically two sides of the same coin. If another dog senses either of these instincts, it knows that such dog has the negative-part in control; a dog with a negative-part in control is instinctively viewed as being a threat – this is because the predatory instinct of the dog is influenced by the negative-part. It uses this for its survival. This is what it is there for.

Now, when you put humans in the equation of a pack of dogs, the same thing applies. When a human has the negative-part in his control center, a dog will sense his negative aura. The dog is sensitive to this; in a way, this is its language, and it reacts to such language. The dog's instinct tells it that you are going to attack or you fear you are going to be attacked. This state can then trigger the dog you are handling into such a state, from which many negative situations can arise.

Cats are extremely sensitive to an unbalanced mind. Humans also have the ability to sense when fellow humans are unbalanced. You only have to look around you in traffic congestion. Understanding this balance is the secret to the success of animal handlers: they understand the importance of balance in the state of the mind of the animal being handled, and, in the state of the mind of the "animal" handling the animal.

When it comes to man, it appears that what distinguishes him from all other species is this single-most thing: reason. Reason, or the lack of it, is what the problem of man is today.

To be able to reason in any state of weakness is the challenge for man. When we are able to accomplish this, one day we will be able to find reason before we jump into a state of weakness, such as anger. Do you understand what this means? You got it! This means we will have reached our final cause: we will have attained equilibrium: we will have conquered our greatest challenge – the meat-in-the-sandwich goal. It would overwhelm us to know that just as Chisek has a final cause for us, so the Creators have a final cause for us. When we read Chapter 16, *To "Read" from the "Closed Book,"* we will understand what their final cause for us is, and it will shatter our perception of ourselves and what we are all – yes all – capable of.

Conquering the meat-in-the-sandwich goal is the most difficult task for us to achieve, and it is the final cause of all the challenges that we are forced to encounter in our lifetime. Although it is practically impossible in practice, the theory of how to achieve this is ridiculously simple.

For example, it is in a moment of weakness, such as anger, that you should pretend you are a ball of fire, and that you have to get into the center of that ball to extinguish the fire. Understand? This is what man doesn't have the guts to do. When you can quench the fire from within, then you have the ability to reason. When you have the ability to reason, then you can solve your problems – but only with those who have a comparable level of intelligence. Perhaps in a heated situation those you are dealing with won't have the ability to reason. It is up to you then to try to make them reason. Often this can be accomplished if they have something to lose – not because they deep down feel sorry. Their ability to reason all depends on this one thing: how much they are going to lose. The more they have to lose, the more they will think to reason – if not at the moment when they should, afterward. If they have less to lose, they will have less inducement to want to reason – and this is when you could be in trouble, for they would often rather punch you in the nose or tell you off! You have to remember that you can't talk to a hot head in a hot atmosphere. You have to cool that hot head down. Only then can you try to mollify the situation.

Now, our capability to reason is an extraordinary but rarely used gift. For instance, humans tend to steam up in anger and keep this anger and rage within them. Many negative things can then manifest in this state of anger, as we have already learned. In the final analysis, whenever you get angry you should try to reason. You wouldn't want to because your desire to dwell in the negative state would be so great. Dwelling in the negative state actually makes you feel good; it gives you a phony feeling of confidence, just as alcohol does. (This is likely to have some relationship with the release of chemicals in the brain.) That desire must be broken right on the spot. Sometimes when reason, the most important element of the human mind, becomes disconnected from the mind, then all hell breaks loose.

A wise man summed it all up once with these words: Let neither the tongue nor the fist precede the use of the mind. Let the mind think before the fire fuels within and before the fist tenses. When you can think first, and in that moment of thinking not feel the fire within you, then you will have conquered the meat-in-the-sandwich goal. Thinking first but feeling the fire within you is not the answer. Chisek has won the round, for because, that fire is his fire.

In life, Chisek encourages humans to take the easy way out. If you cannot solve a problem, Chisek will advise you to kill yourself. If you allow yourself to become depressed, Chisek will suggest to you that it is better to not live than live, and then he will offer the solution for how to make not living a reality. If your business doesn't go well, Chisek will advise you to burn it down. If you don't like somebody, Chisek will advise you to kill or try to ruin this individual in some way. The list can go on and on. These are some of the infinite number of simple and easy solutions Chisek has for all your problems. Following Chisek's way of life is a cowardly way to live. It is effortless to follow his path. It doesn't take much by way of intelligence to follow his path. To face life head on and achieve something for yourself, and become someone by following the positive path, takes a lot of guts. This is a brave intellect: an intellect that will succeed against all odds. We have just answered the elusive question of why we are here. What we are and what we become … this is the elementary basis of our existence here on this planet.

13

The Loophole in Man

Plutarch[vi] spoke of two conditions in relation to man.
He spoke of the atheist.
He spoke of the god-fearing.
He believed that each is an extreme
That bypasses Truth,
Which lies in the middle,
And is misled by both and deceived by both.
This he called True Religion.

The Root of all Compulsions, Obsessions, and Addictions

This section is a summary of all the knowledge the last two chapters have embraced. When we delve into the core root of all living things, the elemental forces that influence their behavior constitute the balancing parts. These balancing parts are written in the physical subdirectories of every living thing, which includes every human being.

In its most fundamental breakdown, in anything we do in life, there are always two choices: there are two profound ways of handling situations in life. Situations in life arise because of the challenges humans must face in their lives. Essentially, this is why every human exists: to face challenges. From challenges, an intellect that has strength, has versatility, and has advanced in an unconventional way, is the sought-after final cause of every single human being on the face of this planet and, by the way, on every other planet in this universe and beyond. We should all pause here and slowly reread this last passage with deeper thought.

The next step from this is, from every challenge comes the possibility of a weakness in a human. This challenge may be the loss of a loved one; the loss of some aspect of your health; the loss of employment; your facing financial difficulties; your being in a situation of war or a victimized environment; your having a parent or a husband abuse you in any number of physical or psychological ways; your having your partner or spouse leave you or use you; your becoming wealthy or powerful; or your being a victim in any number of ways – there are a multitude of things that can happen to humans in the course of their lives. The weakness that can come about as a result of your challenge is the crucial factor that defines you as a human, to a degree. For how you handle the challenge is defined by your use of the positive influence and your use of the negative influence. Which influence you use is entirely your choice.

The first method is the use of the positive influence. You are able to move on, accept, and overcome the challenge, by not allowing the negative force to weaken you to the point where you develop a weakness from the challenge. You may even find some good from this often life-changing event. This means you have predominantly kept the positive-part in the control center of your brain. You have followed the instincts of your positive-part.

How you are able to do this is by directing your energy in some positive way rather than in some negative way. Instead of succumbing to depression or destructive vices, you channel your energy into something that enhances you. That may be something as basic as joining a club or a social group (not a brainwashing type) with a similar interest. That may be taking up a course and enhancing your brain intellectually or artistically. That may be fulfilling a lifetime hobby that you were always too busy for. That may be taking up gardening. That may even be something as basic as meeting and getting to know your neighbors, or joining a volunteer group. Anything that is positive and gives you pleasure – no matter how simple or ordinary it may be – or just keeps you busy and distracts you from developing a weakness from your challenging situation in life, will prevent the negative-part from not only using this moment of vulnerability in you to derail you down its path, but obtaining the points.

The second method is the use of the negative influence. You are unable to be guided by the balancing positive-part to take the positive approach. This means you have allowed the negative-part into the control center of your brain and have allowed its instincts or impulses to seduce you. The negative-part now encourages you to compound the problem of the challenge by influencing you to embrace something that weakens you physically or emotionally, or both. This means you did not find a positive outcome; instead, you allowed the negative-part to "soften" the situation by influencing you to embrace a weakness. What that weakness becomes is individually unique to each human. This weakness may mean you become compulsive, obsessive, addicted to something (including food), depressed, angry, hateful, revengeful, spiteful, or even emotionally withdrawn.

How it all works is that any one of the above allows you to escape from the situation of your challenge by filling in the void with what now becomes your weakness. The abuse of drugs or alcohol is a classic weakness in humans and is the means by which they are able to hide the "pain" or the "scars," or even sweep the problem completely under the carpet.

In this alternative approach, the negative-part then gave you phony inducements that made you feel better. For example, in whatever the weakened state, you attained a "buzz" or a "reward" of some kind from your negative-part when you channeled your energy into this approach or action. You were then induced to continue to channel your energy in this way because of the buzz you continued to feel. What you didn't realize was that these buzzes you felt were phony inducements (which have a relationship with the negative aura and most likely a chemical stimulant), and each small step eventually led you to your obsession, compulsion, or addiction.

When you got your buzz, and you were under the influence of the balancing negative-part, you were unable to reason because, as we know, a human cannot reason while the balancing negative-part is at the control helm of his brain. Remember, the negative-part cannot enable this area of the brain to function. To reason is not a characteristic of the negative-part. By treading further along the negative path of that weakness, and being continually seduced by the phony inducements, you then reach the entry point where you open the door for the strong, second negative-part to come within your brain. When this happens, your weakness will grip you with an overpowering strength. This is a difficult stage for you to break out of, and it doesn't just apply to drug addicts and alcoholics. It applies to shopaholics, hoarders, sex addicts, gamblers, people with eating disorders, and even revenge-seeking serial killers. It applies to those who are depressed, angry, and use violence such as in domestic or other situations.

Let us take the case of a shopping addict. You may face the loss of a loved one. As you are in a vulnerable, negative state you may have felt an instant pleasure or escape from the sadness by shopping. The negative-part is trying to induce you to be distracted by something detrimental (a weakness) that lets you escape the pain of the challenge (which is loss). If not shopping, it could well have been a desire to keep busy and clean; it could have been a desire to drink, smoke, take drugs, overeat, not eat, or even tell someone off. In this example, it was a desire to shop. Afterward, the same sadness and anxiety over the loss of a loved one returned. A repeat of the shopping activity may then be perpetuated, with the same results manifested. (Again, the activity may have been to clean, drink, smoke, take drugs, overeat, not eat, or even tell someone off.) The urge to perpetuate the activity came from the negative-part. It sought to either create or find a weakness in you. Then it uses this weakness by tempting you with it. It can, after all, turn nothing into a big deal, and this is what it is looking for. It is able to turn something as ridiculous as a simple, innocent shopping expedition into a serious problem if you allow it, by falling victim to its temptation. By going along with the flow of it, subconsciously or even consciously, you are continually giving in to the urge to manifest feelings that suppress a painful reminder or feeling – that is ultimately what drove you to shop in the first place. The negative-part will have successfully deceived you with its driving temptation into a psychological state that is not beneficial for you. This is its directive: this is its sole aim.

In other words, when you are feeling down and thinking about the loss, or grieving, the negative-part will suggest you shop again to make you feel better. If you give in to it, it will keep up this strategy of influence. If you do not give in to it again, it will not give up, that is for sure! It will suggest something else to try to hook you into, with which it can lead you down its path toward making it an obsession or a compulsion. Its sole aim is to pull you in using some means, and then drag you down its negative spiral until you cross over the line to its final cause – where it can have complete control of your mind and ruin your life and the lives of others.

Your subtle and quiet enemy within has nothing good in mind for you. It seems all but impossible to imagine that for the majority of us, all our problems stem from that beast in our minds, who suggests to, and influences, us, and we are often so blind-sided by it that it wins us over. The tragedy is, so many, so easily, fall victim to these inner tempting drives under the agency of the malicious beast within them. It does not have the well-being of the human in mind; on the contrary, it has the destruction of the human in mind – ultimately, it will do anything to try to put that stake in the soul of a human, because its bigger drive, its hidden agenda, is to prove the success of the all-conquering Chisek over Odo ... they are at war with each other through us, and this is one way we provide them with challenge.

Let us now consider another fictitious case study, that of a mother who constantly yelled at her children. When asked why she yelled all the time, her response was that everything had gone wrong in her life lately, all in one go. Her husband passed away. She went through childbirth. There were financial and other burdens. All this became too much for her at once. The yelling came about because of the accumulation of events that she found hard to cope with. The yelling was a reflection of her lack of tolerance and lack of patience. She used the negative influence rather than the positive influence to cope with a challenging situation in her life. She was an otherwise fantastic mother and human being, and was well aware that it was a problem, but still she could not stop. In the same way a person may turn to shopping or drinking, this woman turned to yelling. Each time she yelled, it was her negative-part that was inducing her to do so. Eventually there came a time when her yelling became compounded within the physiological response mechanisms of her, because she had allowed the second negative-part in; now, each time she reacted, she did so without being able to help herself. Often for nothing – you only had to open your mouth and she would yell. Under the negative influence, everything is capable of annoying you. This suggests you are allowing the negative-part to have control of your control center for the majority of the time. If you are in these shoes, and you do not try to get out of this negative cycle, nothing good will happen. You may wind up in a mental institution or face some other serious problem.

Let us briefly take another look at the case of a psychopathic serial killer. Once upon a time as a child that killer may have been abused by his parents. Every time he was abused, he allowed the negative-part to take the control helm of his brain. He found it difficult to turn the perpetuating negative circumstances of his life into something positive. This gave the negative-part the opportunity to take permanent control of his brain. By the time this child grew up, his state of mind was such that he reached Chisek's final cause. Chisek had complete control of his mind. During his childhood, telltale clues would have been obvious: lack of feeling and empathy; sadistic tendencies toward animals; being angry; being introverted; being aggressive toward other children; and even committing petty crimes. Sometimes a child in this circumstance openly aspires to be a criminal. Small steps were climbed down the negative path before the extreme tendencies would have manifested within the serial killer. Becoming a serial killer is almost like graduating, after passing all the tests set by the negative-part. This means the human has successfully responded to the impulses of the negative-part in the course of his life.

We must recognize that a serial killer does not just decide to kill ... there are usually stages that lead to the killing spree. An individual who had a troubled childhood filled with crimes, for instance, who may be trying to live a normal life in a positive way, is predisposed to be pushed over the edge easily with the right trigger. Such an individual can be a time bomb waiting to explode. The serial killer that this book has made reference to on earlier occasions, who set out on a rampage of revenge by killing women because his partner dumped him, is a classic example. There are quite a few recorded instances of killers, with dissimilar methods and motives, who fall into this category. Once in this negative extreme, this human would have had no barriers when it came to taking up heinous acts and pursuits. This human would admit to taking pleasure in the heinous acts and pursuits. Constantly following the instincts and impulses of the negative-part is the underlying factor, or the missing link, in understanding what drives someone to commit socially unacceptable acts.

Let us consider a less extreme case study. Few would argue that this could easily be someone you know; it could even be you. If you feel neglected, feel unappreciated, or feel there is something missing in your life and hence your relationship, the negative-part will detect a vulnerability in you. This is what it is looking for, and often it is the one who has encouraged you to enter a susceptible state. It suggests this vulnerability to you. Now that you are receptive to this vulnerability, it will suggest a coping mechanism – this will be your weakness. This could be the use of drugs, alcohol, smoking, eating, not eating, hoarding, cheating on your partner, or even finding another partner. You may say no to the drugs when the idea is suggested to you in your mind. The negative-part will not give up; it will suggest something else. This could be issues relating to sexual orientation or gender. This could be food (or alcohol). If you are tempted by food (or even alcohol), the negative-part will keep the thought of food (or the thought of alcohol) at the back of your mind constantly, by suggesting it to you. If you allow your instincts to rule you, you will become overweight (or an alcoholic). If food (or alcohol) did not work for you, maybe when someone of the opposite sex offers you some attention, the negative-part will put sexual or other thoughts in your mind. What you feel you are missing from your partner you may find in this new partner. It encouraged you to feel your vulnerability in the first place, and then it suggested to you a way of coping with or satisfying that vulnerability. When you feel those moments of guilt within you, this means the positive-part is influencing you. Once you head down that negative path you face all sorts of new problems, and the negative-part will keep inducing you down that path until it becomes destructive. This may mean you become a sex addict, or it may mean your family splits up. Your well-being is its last objective. The opposite is its directive.

Now we should have a clearer understanding of how the negative influence works, and of how a human is drawn into compulsions, addictions, and obsessions. When you have allowed yourself to have a vulnerability, reverse the negative situation by using that vulnerability to benefit you and others. Do something positive that prevents you from falling into Chisek's trap of developing a weakness. Communicate with someone about what your problems are, no matter how insignificant those problems start out to be, because, little do you know how serious an insignificant problem can become. Don't ever bottle things up. Chisek, by way of your negative-part, suggests such a thing because he knows that is one step on his downward path. Be open. Air out your problems or concerns. Above all, deflect the negative suggestions in your mind. Find the opposite alternatives. Find a goal; a direction; a purpose. Always know that the negative suggestions are being made by an influence that is out to destroy you: it is the enemy within: it is the beast within.

It is hard to explain how the mind of a person is induced by the negative-part. In every case, the solution is to reason in the moments before you take the negative approach. To reason is to mean you put the brakes on any negative impulses in you and you control what your emotions are going to be. It sounds easy, but it is the most complicated and difficult thing in the universe and beyond to do – as this book has likely communicated to you by now. Fundamentally, this is because the negative path is the easy path; it is the easy way out. All you have to do is go with the flow of wherever your negative-part takes you. It is difficult to take the positive path and to reason. They require hard work and maintenance. This is why people tend to succumb to the negative influence more readily than the positive influence. For instance, it is easier to cry than it is not to cry. It is easier to punch someone than it is to use your brain and find a positive solution. It is easier to tell someone off than it is to turn the other cheek. It is easier to take a drink and numb the pain rather than deal with the situation of the pain. Now we know the difference between the positive-part and the negative-part, and the core root of most of the problems pertaining to the mind of a human being (one without medical disorders and the like that can naturally occur in the brain).

Dangerous Mind Control

A wise man once read a brainwashed mind:
Thank you god for keeping me so ignorant
That I do not have to feel the pain of knowledge.

That wise man then said,
It is an unfortunate fact that humans have to believe in something.
And then after a moment of contemplation he woefully added,
Unscrupulous cults and sects are tollgates on the freeway to god.

Irrefutably, the most important asset you possess in your life is your will. It is a tremendous, invisible power, and when you combine it with the imagination of the human mind, there is no limit to what you can achieve. Just as significant is your individual freedom. On this Earth, you are free to walk, to talk, to think, to sleep, and to dream – free to dream dreams beyond your human imagination. Given that you have been gifted with these two incalculably precious assets, it is inconceivable that you may at some point in your life decide to sacrifice or concede them to the management of something or someone else. This can only mean there is some kind of deficiency in you that prevents you from realizing what you are doing or have done to yourself. The Creators can therefore understand you and will one day forgive you. For there already is a misinterpreted precedent set in history where one superior human asked Odo to forgive those who knew not what they did.

The users, or better put, the beneficiaries, of such people should, however, not presume a homogenous stance of understanding or forgiveness from Odo. On the contrary, their souls would never be allowed to creep upon any planet by way of reincarnation again. Either they would no longer exist, or they would wish they no longer existed.

These unscrupulous users, such as dangerous cults and sects, with their unscrupulous philosophies, have encouraged their victims to substitute reality with fantasy, which their victims willingly do and even find appealing. Just as Chisek's path in life follows an easy road and does not require any hard work, tolerance, understanding, or usage of one's brain, so with this fantasy – in a sense, this is the lure of its appeal! Indeed, following teachings of this caliber draws one completely off the Creators' path and philosophy. When their victims live predominately in misery, or are lost in their lives and "looking" for "something," unscrupulous philosophies are more likely to get away with marketing their fantasy successfully – this is why it is in their best interests to keep their victims in such a stagnant and lost state.

This fantasy takes on many shapes and forms, and the promoter of the fantasy usually takes on a god-like persona. With the power that inescapably accords with such a persona, this god-like figure promises rewards that are not attainable other than through him. A part of the fantasy includes praying for something from some kind of deity. Rather than encourage his followers to work hard and motivate them to achieve accomplishments for themselves, by themselves, this god-like figure, with the support of his philosophy, encourages his followers to sacrifice their lives, pray, and have faith in something divine, which these followers come to believe will give them everything they should need and want in life. This is so far from reality: the Creators give nothing for nothing. The only exception is that they give life. In other words, they have given you a brain with which to think independently. They have given you hands with which to reach, and to reach is to ultimately have and possess. They have given you legs to walk wherever you want along the road of life. They have given you eyes to see all the good things you can do for yourself. Most importantly of all, they have given you the capacity to love, so that you can love and respect, as well as receive them in return. In other words, you have been provided with all the facilities necessary for you to take whatever you need from life. All that is expected of you is to use these resources – which were given to you for free! What more could you want from your Creators?

Such a fantasy, derived from the philosophy of Chisek, which encourages one to take an easy path in life, makes it easy for unscrupulous philosophers to pledge empty promises to the vulnerable and lead them astray. When these vulnerable humans put the theory of the fantasy into practice, it means, quite literally, that they are no longer going to be prepared to go and achieve things for themselves in life. That is, these humans want their god or their unscrupulous god-like figure to give them something they are not prepared to reach out and attempt to attain themselves, or do not know how to reach out and attempt to attain for themselves. Their Creator then asks himself, "Why would I do something for them, when they are not prepared to do something for themselves?"

The "kingdom" these unscrupulous users have enjoyed on this Earth has only been possible by keeping humans ignorant and without the capacity or desire to want too much, or without the capacity to question. To maintain their kingdom on Earth, unscrupulous users find it necessary to maintain ignorant humans wherever possible, and promote the fantasy of a kingdom they cannot prove, and cannot really believe exists.

What should be perceptible so far is that the Creators have no mercy or sympathy for those who, by their own hand, become helpless and tangled in these philosophical webs. They have always left, and always will leave, them alone to dwindle in their lives of self-inflicted misery. The Creators are only interested in helping those who help themselves: those who are trying to survive and are struggling in their lives to get somewhere and achieve something. Praying is a waste of time for those who don't even bother to use their own strength of will to solve their problems. If you are one of these people, you need to just drop your arms, reach for your backside, lift it up, and then go and do something for your own good; for it is only when the Creators see you are doing something of your own free will, to one day serve you and inevitably benefit others, that they will help you too, and one day when you look back at your life you will without doubt see that divine contribution.

Unfortunately, when you lose the most precious part of you, called your will, you will be held in spiritual bondage – and it doesn't matter who it is to. You will then become dependent on that someone else for spiritual food. This is what unscrupulous philosophers and their unscrupulous philosophies provide: spiritual food, and having dependence on this spiritual food will mean you have willingly placed your spirit in someone else's hands. This dependence will surely enough become addictive. If you happen to be in these shoes, you have ultimately lost yourself. Now you are a goner. You are finished! Nothing more can be said to you. You alone have the power to save yourself.

You as a human must understand how your brain works, and never allow someone else to interfere with it, especially for the worse. Nobody! It is a superior power that brought you into this life. Not only does it share your burdens with you; not only does it work with you as you passage through life; it even tries its best to make you become a better person without you ever knowing or being aware of its presence. (This is by way of the positive-part.) In no way will it help you betray yourself; you and you alone can allow yourself to be betrayed and used by your negative-part.

What is amazing, and what never ceases to make one wonder, is how intelligent people can get hooked up into dangerous mind-controlling philosophies! It is easier to understand how someone desperately poor or unintelligent can. There are, however, many generic circumstances where people of all persuasions and backgrounds can become lost and vulnerable in the course of their lives. It would seem that when they face these vulnerable circumstances, someone unscrupulous is waiting to take advantage.

For instance, those who are lost and cannot find their way, their purpose, or their life's meaning, would jump at the chance of having someone help them find any of these things for them, on behalf of them – principally because they don't know how, or they are not willing to try hard enough to find out how, for themselves. This is a dangerous state, as these vulnerable people provide the perfect opportunity for someone to control their will.

Additionally, if you were sinking in quicksand, and a complete stranger threw you a lifeline such as a rope, you would grab hold of it and you wouldn't think twice about who it was from. In the same manner, when you become lost or helpless, because you don't know how to solve your problems or you become overwhelmed with them, or because you feel fear, insecurity, or indecision, or all of the above are applicable, you tend to need to lean on somebody. This is equivalent to grabbing a hold of that lifeline. You have provided the perfect opportunity for an unscrupulous user to come into the picture.

There are many crucial times of vulnerability that allow humans to get caught in the hands of useless philosophies or users. One such time is when one finishes school, as this is the first step to one's independent life. It goes without saying that such young people have to be guided carefully so that they make the correct decisions and travel along the right road of life. Another time is when one experiences a mid-life crisis. In this case, when you have worked, succeeded, built a career, accumulated wealth, brought up kids who went out on their own, and so on, you can become depressed, dissatisfied with your surroundings, and even bored to the extent that it makes you weak. (You need to bear in mind that the negative-part has driven you into this state of vulnerability.) In many cases, you may be dissatisfied to the point where you begin to have a second look at your life and re-evaluate your existence, your marriage, or even your surroundings. Add to that the hormone factor, where readjustment in the body takes place, and you become a perfect candidate for an unscrupulous user or philosophy – that is, you become open and extremely prone to others who are just waiting to take advantage of your weakness. Many at this period of their lives succumb to this weakness.

Something made you lost or vulnerable. Something emotional caused you to look for something to satisfy your need, your desire. If someone unscrupulous finds you, and gives you what you need by way of security or help, to the degree that you depend on that someone, your negative-part and the unscrupulous user have then made you find comfort in your weakness, in your vulnerability, and have satisfied your need, your desire (that is, satisfied your weakness), by giving you what you want. Your unscrupulous user is usually adept at the art of this kind of psychological manipulation.

Any form of vulnerability is a weakness within a human, and these unscrupulous users know exactly how to target those with weaknesses, and do everything in their power to make the most of and take advantage of them. When you are in a weakened state, such as feeling lost, depressed, or helpless, you are usually under the influence of your negative-part, and it is controlling the steering wheel in the control center of your brain. It is also likely to be giving you a chemical stimulant that makes you like being in that state. Your faculty of thinking rationally and logically is now diminished because your positive-part has been neutralized by the negative-part in that it has little or no influence upon you. It is in this moment when you are blind to reason that unscrupulous users can easily manipulate and take advantage of you.

This is the critical moment when you let the user in: when you have the negative-part at the control helm of your brain and are unable to reason. The positive-part will not let the user in. It will make you reason. This is the holy grail of being brainwashed. Of course, once you let the unscrupulous user in, you will now believe you were saved in some way – after all, you have had your weakness or vulnerability satisfied. You believe in something now that is beyond you, and you fear that without that "crutch" you will give in to your old insecurities. You can no longer believe in yourself because your unscrupulous user does not want this type of independent soul. The unscrupulous user wants a dependent soul that can be manipulated. The unscrupulous user then feeds you in a way that you are fulfilled, but are at the same time manipulated in such a way that you fulfill this user's hidden self-serving agenda. This user now has the power of your will.

Blind devotion to a negative cause – and it doesn't matter what that cause is – suggests you have allowed your negative-part to manipulate you; this means you are under its influence; this means you are unable to reason while under its influence; this means you have lost the power of your will, which means you have given your will to it; this means you are easily "seduced" by someone or something unscrupulous. This is indeed a failing on the part of the human, and it is judged as being so.

The power of your will! What is your will? We talk about will, we can define will, but what is it in its most elementary form? Will can be defined as a choice; a desire. It is a decision you take, and in that process of making that decision it is the sense of power, control, and free will that you possess within you that made it possible for you to make that decision. Given that will is a choice and a desire, we can now understand the fundamentals of our will.

Choices and desires are governed by our influences. Our influences in life stem back to two fundamental common denominators: the positive-part and the negative-part. Will is just another way of expressing which choice has been made. Do you see where we are? We are at the elemental basics of a human being: the meat and the sandwich! Now we can understand how easy it is to lose one's will by giving it up to another, such as to an unscrupulous user. It is dependent on our choice of influences!

When we allow ourselves to be brainwashed, we put ourselves in the control of Chisek (by way of the negative-part), whose advocate (the unscrupulous user) fulfills Chisek's desideratum. We know that a person in such a manipulated state is under the influence of the negative-part. The will, however, of this person, is also under the power and control of the negative-part. Chisek here provides phony inducements (probably by way of a chemical release of some kind in the brain), and instigates feelings of happiness and contentment, mainly because he and his advocates give these vulnerable people what they need to satisfy their weakness. Will is merely a choice between the strength of the positive-part and the weakness of the negative-part. This is how to understand and define will, in its most fundamental breakdown.

Unscrupulous users are, in reality, like hypnotists; they are spiritual hypnotists, and you as a victim open yourself to them – after all, it is their agenda to have you open your soul to them, which happens to be the most important thing you possess in your body. All that you are; all that you have; all your strength and intellect, come down to one thing: your soul. Once you let these unscrupulous people have access to your soul and ultimately access to your mind, they will then assuredly fill your mind up with input to benefit them and not you. You must never forget that these unscrupulous people are advocates of Chisek and his philosophy. Chisek's philosophy comes in many guises, not excluding philosophical systems.

The first hurdle for these unscrupulous users, these spiritual hypnotists – the likes of Jim Jones (Jonestown), David Koresh (Waco), and Charles Manson – is to psychoanalyze you in order to determine your needs, so that they can provide those needs to you. Because you need some form of help, you often innocently and naively tell them indirectly or even sometimes directly what those needs are. The next hurdle is a lot easier for the unscrupulous – to insert fear in you. They cannot insert fear in you if you don't allow them to. This fear can be something as simple as dependence on them and the fear of losing that security. Having overcome these crucial obstacles, they will have found the door through which they will have easy passage into your mind. Not even your god will be able to help you then. Then they will have you! They will have control over your mind and, as sure as the Earth is not sitting on the back of a giant tortoise, they will twist you upside down. The lesson here is that you should never open your mind to anybody who is after your soul. You must only open your mind to knowledge, as this is the only way the Creators can pass knowledge to you for your benefit.

Notwithstanding, allowing your mind to be controlled by unscrupulous self-interests is dangerous. Not many people see it this way, however. Dictatorship and fear are allies and tools for someone to succeed in controlling you. Such control is a betrayal of human innocence, for which those instrumental will never be forgiven. Control of your mind and will must always lie solely in your own hands. Nobody should be allowed to poke about in your brain. So next time somebody tries to hook you up into some type of personal doctrine, you had better keep in mind that you don't need any philosophy of this kind from anyone!

A true philosophy will serve mankind as a train serves its commuters. Each time it arrives at a station it will let some passengers off, and it will allow some on, according to their destinations in life. In other words, it will put humans back on course on their roads through life and not take advantage of their having lost their way. The unscrupulous philosophy, however, in serving its own interests, will only pick up passengers; eventually it will enter into a long and dark tunnel, until such time as there is no light at the other end, and then those passengers will become lost in the darkness of that philosophy and depend on it as "food" for their survival from then on until death do they meet.

This is why unscrupulous philosophies unleash their "dog hounds" to constantly "sniff" out and find people facing vulnerable times in their lives. If you are in this situation, and if they get their hands on you, they will do their best to recruit you into their brainwashed society and promise you useless comforts, false and invented doctrines, and phony friendships. Slowly but surely, they will milk you financially and spiritually, and for the rest of your life you will be a spiritual vegetable. You will have let your soul be dominated and controlled.

First, by fear. One of the ways someone can take control of your will is to insert fear in you – not so much physical fear as mental fear; fear of someone or something. Ironically, on the one hand, unscrupulous users profess fears and insert those fears into your bones while, on the other hand, they offer you protection from those fears and salvation of some sort, which they claim you can only receive when you allow your mind and heart to fall totally into their hands. What an irony! And this is how it all begins.

Second, by dependence. Dependence because unscrupulous users satisfy some weakness within you. When they offer you that solution to your problem, you then become dependent on them. Often, you reach a point where you do not believe you can stand up on your own two feet without them. You are led to believe that your problem is solved because of them, their deity, or their philosophy.

Once you have allowed yourself to become caught up in one of these whirlpools of evil, you will have lost your most important ingredient within you: your will – your will to love, to survive, and to believe in yourself. You once had a craving. Humans have to believe in something or someone in order to satisfy that craving within them. Unfortunately, you allowed your craving to be satisfied by a fantasy. It is hard to believe that a so-called intelligent human could be deceived to such a degree financially and spiritually. Being in their clutches is no different from being gripped by the gravitational pull of a black hole, from which there is simply no escape.

Time and time again unscrupulous users are able find someone vulnerable to prey on, and they will continue to as long as humans have challenges to face; as long as humans remain ignorant of how to face those challenges head on; and as long as humans remain ignorant of who they are, why they are here, and what their purpose is in life.

What these victims do is bond their souls to someone unscrupulous. The bond is equivalent to the deed of your house – in this case it is the deed of your soul, which you willingly and often unwittingly give to someone else for its safekeeping, who never intends to give it back, not even upon your last breath in life. The secret in avoiding this is to sustain a free and independently minded human soul, dominated by no one but yourself. In other words, you must allow yourself to live your life and achieve your dreams during your life span without any interference from anyone who would want to take away that freedom of your will. The secret to a healthy and successful life is not to allow anyone to control that essence of your human being – and that essence is your soul combined with your will, which has a power higher than a mountain, and can never be brought down by force if you so desire. You can kill the physical body, but you can never exterminate the will of man, which is part and parcel of the soul of man. This means you should never give your will to any person, and then allow that person to manipulate you into anything.

You cannot allow yourself to go through life and have someone accompany you and run your life for you to the point where you become lost like a sheep on the prairie without that someone. You and only you should be in charge of your life and nobody else should be responsible for your doings – whether right or wrong. Since humans have been born in the likeness of their Creators, they are not perfect. This is not by coincidence; it is deliberate, as it stems from the Creators being imperfect. They are known to make mistakes. In our lives, however, we have to make sure that we learn from our mistakes, and, like the blue octopus, not make the same ones again.

If we stop right here and think about what was just written, we should be able to see that a clue was just presented by this book in answer to why in everything we see there is imperfection, and why there are always two extremes: order and chaos. Philosophers are well aware of this duality. Take beauty: it is the sum of balance between perfect and imperfect – that is, order and chaos. If we take the unsymmetrical half of a face, and alter it by computer so that it is as symmetrical as the symmetrical half of a face, the resultant face no longer looks right, let alone beautiful, to us. (That one half is symbolic of the Creators and the other half is symbolic of Chisek is something we cannot have known.) Let us take William Shakespeare: his brilliance in poetry came from his understanding and experience of two sides of life – wealth and poverty. The right balance between the two extremes of order and chaos gives us perfection; truth can only be found somewhere in this balance. This is the answer to why academic and intellectual luminaries have not been able to discover the knowledge found in this book. (There certainly have been a few wise men in our past who possessed this knowledge; the problem was, they were unable to crack through a wall of intellectual suppression.)

As a side note, a wise man once described humans on this planet in this way: To my mind humans have "proprietary limited intellects." God knew what he was doing when he gave them noses; heaven forbid, if god were not so intuitive, you would see humans out there in the pastures eating grass alongside the cows. A true intellect is a universal one, like Leonardo da Vinci, who is capable of excelling in any field.

To discover the knowledge found in this book, it takes someone with the right mix of two extremes: intellectual order and intellectual chaos. The right balance between the two gives us perfection. William Shakespeare and Leonardo da Vinci were examples of such a human; they did not believe in being taught by others because they considered themselves to be above and beyond what academia regarded as being the intellectual order, and did not believe they could learn anything from them. They also had a mentality where they felt they did not have to prove anything to others; they knew what they knew and got the results they wanted from that knowledge. In the final analysis, truth is not handed to us on a platter of perfection; truth lies in some form of balance. Balance is a deep word, with deeper connotations ... if we think deeply enough on it. Balance is found everywhere: balance is nature's answer to reason. Now we can philosophically acknowledge why everything is not absolutely perfect.

•⁓

The Creators have given you total control and responsibility of yourself. In other words, you have complete charge of your free will. In a way, this is seen as a mistake; for this has allowed you to possess a "gap" within you. This is a spiritual gap or loophole caused by your craving and need to believe in something. It is the subconscious tie you have with your Creator that creates this craving and spiritual desire. It is also because we "come from" the stars that creates this craving and spiritual desire. As a consequence of this gap, unscrupulous users have found the door into a human's soul, and invariably have found a way to fill that gap. They have found a means to justify their existence, and they tailor the lives of others for the benefit of themselves. Perhaps this would have been preventable should humans have had no gap within their souls. Perhaps if humans really had divine intervention in their daily lives – not of the nature unscrupulous users claim to exist – the human race would have avoided a lot of wars, a lot of bloodshed, and a lot of hatred and division. Perhaps we as humans would have concentrated our energies in a positive way, which would have resulted in a greater degree of progress than we see. Perhaps many things would have been different in our world! Perhaps we would have been better human beings! Perhaps we wouldn't have known how to tell lies! Perhaps we would be living in a peaceful and happy world, where everyone loves one another with no fear, no hurt, and especially no lies!

If you have dependence on unscrupulous users and unscrupulous philosophies, it generally means that you haven't allowed yourself to use your intelligence – they don't want you to. For, you are best ignorant and miserable. They don't want you to work hard and achieve things. Useless zombies are what they want! They want you to depend on them to look after you for your daily needs of survival. This is their paradise on Earth, which you have sacrificed so that you can have a paradise elsewhere one day when you die. If it wasn't tragic, it would be laughable, but it is not a laughing matter because a human was not created to be a useless zombie. The Creators sent Jesus onto this planet not to create zombies, but to open wide the "blind" eyes of humans so that they ask questions. This is the only way to inspire humans to think, work, and live for themselves on their own terms within the constraints of their society. Unfortunately, this was not always his legacy. Some unscrupulous and dangerous users have twisted and used his teachings to suit their own selfish interests.

Useless philosophies, dictators, and other adherents of Chisek's philosophy certainly don't want this independent and freethinking type of human. This is detrimental to their existence. To sustain their existence, they want you as a human to depend on them to run your life for you to the point where you cannot exist without them without becoming a vegetable. So what do you do, and where do you go – to put it crudely but deservedly – you are sucked into a sanctuary of suckers, for which there is always a new one like you.

There is a message in all this: get somewhere in your life by your own hand, and become independent, raise a family if you wish (or just stick with the German Shepherd), live comfortably in peace and harmony, and develop your intelligence however you can and then pass that knowledge on to your offspring. Whatever you do, you should never pray to or worship the Seven Elders or the Creators. They, believe it or not, don't even understand what worship means. They would never be impressed, to put it mildly, with human sacrifices, praying, or other worshipping practices. These primitive practices are absurd to them. They are only impressed with those who strive to achieve and use their intelligence in a way that is not detrimental to others. If you as a human feel it is necessary to revere something divine, you should worship and respect the true mind of god. Where do you find the mind of god? The mind of god can be found in the science laboratory. Instead of becoming tangled up in dangerous cults, sects, or the like, enhance your intelligence; read science books or watch documentaries and learn all you can about science. (For that matter, learn anything, on any subject; just use your brain!) This is how you can find god. This is how you can also develop your intelligence, and impress and earn respect from your Creators.

It was physics that "aligned" things in the universe, and because of this alignment, consciousness came to exist. Physics preceded the Seven Elders and was the First Cause of consciousness and the creator of knowledge. To understand god, we must therefore go to a science lab and study the true gods – physics, mathematics, and even chemistry – and only there can we begin to try to grasp the mind of god. The Seven Elders and three Creators created us, the same as we create our children. They are really no different from us. You gave your children life, and they gave us, their children, life. Their coming to exist was not deliberate, perhaps, as our coming to exist was; rather, it was the result of the right set of circumstances being present at the right time. In the same way that we spoil our first child (or German Shepherd), did they spoil the phase-1 human. They learned their lesson, just as they hope that we learn from our lessons.

Such things as cult worship and sacrifices in honor of a Creator are inappropriate, and are deemed practices of Chisek. If you wish to honor your

Creators, give them something worthy of their respect. Nothing more! The best way you can do this is by allowing them to "live" and "see" through your eyes in a way both you and they can be proud of. Many humans, however, would not have the guts to work this hard. The god of these unscrupulous and dangerous philosophies is much easier to understand and satisfy in the way he has been fashioned by some.

Within you lies everything you have ever searched for ... for there lies within your mind the universe, which includes god himself – if this book may use this word with a new association. We can see this wisdom in the words of Jesus Christ. Just as the phase-1 human could ask and then receive, so can you ask and then receive; the difference is that you have a catch attached, which the phase-1 human didn't have. Everything has been provided to you in your mind, and is just lying dormant, waiting to be accessed by you, and the only requirement is that you develop your intelligence – not stagnate it! Perhaps if we had teaching of this kind, or understood teaching of this kind, we would not have so much misery and ignorance everywhere we look.

You would be right if you concluded that we were still small children who become scared of the dark and run into our parents' arms, who then tuck us under blankets where security and peace of mind are assured. This is exactly what these unscrupulous users provide: they offer this same so-called peace of mind and security. You see, man has that divine power called intellect, and dictators and unscrupulous users are always after control of this power, because whoever controls the will of man controls planet Earth. As you can see, no other living creature of this planet has this problem with its intellect: no other living creature schemes with such elaborate machinations and twists of trickery to convince its fellow species to forgo its will and entrust and appoint another as guardian of it. Of course, once the controller is in possession of such goods, that controller has total control over those goods. The controller may direct a controlled mind to go to war, to go on a killing spree, or to commit mass suicide. Just look at Waco, Jonestown, and the Manson followers! The controlled mind would then have no choice but to obey and die if necessary for the cause and the teachings of the controller.

Pay careful attention to these words of a wise man, and consider one thing in life, the most important thing in life of all, and with this knowledge the rest will take its rightful place, all by itself:

When you give your will to another,
You cease to be yourself.
When you blind yourself to reason,
By falling victim to your weakness
And inevitably your negative-part,
You cease to be a complete or desirable human.

So before you come to give your will to another,
Stop and remember well:
What the salmon season is to the vulture,
Are the vulnerable to the unscrupulous.
The unscrupulous are scavengers in the "blood bath."
To them your time of desperation is their time of bounty.

Do not let yourself be corrupted
By allowing your personal darkness
To be someone's illumination.
Listen to your mind!
Learn to differentiate between the voices;
Hear only what the positive voice has to say,
And treat the other one as you do sewage.

14
Understanding Happiness

To quote the effortless words of a wise man,
Life has been given for one to face challenges.
This is why there is no such thing as real happiness in one's life.
For life will always come along and challenge it.
Happiness is always interwoven with unhappiness,
Just as a negative must always provide balance to a positive
Just as a negative makes one appreciate a positive
– It doesn't matter who you are, what you have, what you do …

So think mostly of today, and some of yesterday too,
But mostly of today because it will never come again.
And in that today, be happy with what you have,
Because tomorrow you could always have less.
And in those thoughts and words that are spoken in that today,
Remember to be pure and positive, even in the face of the impure and negative,
And what will happen then is, when tomorrow comes,
You will be happy and have happy memories of yesterday
In place of being unhappy and having unhappy memories of yesterday.

Wouldn't it be nice if being happy came as effortlessly as being mad? Or if it came as effortlessly as being unhappy? One thing is indubitable: happiness never conducts itself in concert with a negative because the two cannot orchestrate together! What is also indubitable is that the formula for happiness is not as easy to attain as is the formula for unhappiness. The reason for this is that happiness can only really come from some form of positive achievement – no matter how large or how small – and from hard work. Achievement is the key ingredient to provide one with a sense of inner pleasure and satisfaction, where one is able to look back with incredulity and say, "I've done all this!" All this inner satisfaction transmutes into happiness, and a sense of achieving something good, and then radiates from that person like the shine from a pot of gold.

In opposition to this state of happiness, being unhappy and depressed entail no sense of achievement or hard work of any kind. Indeed, they come all too easily. Perhaps this is, intrinsically, the difference between the Creators and Chisek: Chisek chose to take the easy path in life, knowing that the opposite path was a daunting one, requiring one to work hard and use one's intelligence. For this reason, it requires little effort from Chisek's negative-part to manipulate the human into states of misery.

The common denominator in all humans, good and bad alike, is the instinctive need to feel happy. So then in order to attain this essential requirement of happiness, followers of Chisek's philosophy take this opposite route, this easy route – that is, they achieve bad things in the pursuit of evil, from which they attempt to derive a sense of pleasure and happiness. For instance, simplistically, some evil followers may kill in rage purely motivated by a desire to attain some type of happy feeling within themselves, which, ironically, we know can only come from doing something good. Finding that they don't acquire this inner sense of satisfaction and pleasure, they continue to kill, hoping and believing that the next kill will reap them the inner reward they seek. Good feelings within humans such as happiness are an essential component of their existence, but it must be understood they can *never* be derived by any means other than from doing good deeds in life and embracing the positive influence of the Creators. They are not obtainable while embracing Chisek's negative influence. This is the secret to happiness. Happiness cannot be derived from negative deeds and thoughts; happiness can only be derived from positive deeds and thoughts.

In this society you will find many instances of humans being unable to pull themselves out of misery simply because of their unwillingness to draw on the positive influence. These are the humans who constantly are depressed, cry a lot over nothing, and find life too hard when it comes to facing and overcoming their challenges. Rather than accept their challenge, handicap, or roadblock, and turn a negative into a positive, they become bitter and curse and blame the world for their problems. The deeper into the negative depths they sink, the greater the desire to be in those depths. This is because the negative-part induces a phony sense of happiness in those who lurk in these negative depths, which is hard to explain. It is easier to be in this place than it is to claw your way out of misery and turn the negative into a positive. It is in these depths, and it is because many do not embrace the positive side often, that some humans have even chosen an extreme alternative for attaining this feeling of happiness – they have opted to take illicit drugs. While drugs do temporarily and artificially provide these humans with false feelings of happiness and pleasure, ultimately, the use of these drugs causes humans to become dependent on these false feelings for the rest of their lives, and in a zombie-like existence they fade into a hazy silhouette of life.

That happiness is an essential requirement for our inner well-being is obvious. That happiness is something everyone seeks to attain in life is equally obvious. What is not so obvious is that many look for it in the wrong places, and in the wrong ways. Some pursue it through monetary gain. The problem with this pursuit is that once the monetary gain has been achieved, happiness is still as elusive as ever. Contrary to what many believe, monetary success does not equate to happiness. Some people seek to attain happiness by acquiring material possessions, or by trying to keep up with the neighbors, where everything attained is just for show. Some naively believe happiness can be found in marriage. The formula for happiness is not found in one's assets or in marriage – let alone in having babies! Happiness is something that comes from within you. First you have to be honest within yourself. Once you are honest within yourself, an aura of honesty and decency, of hard work and achievement, is portrayed from you, which can then be seen and felt by people who want to see beautiful, honest things, and who, as a consequence, will show respect and give credit to you. This is how you feel happiness. Happiness often comes from doing things for others or from doing something for yourself that you love, and the end result of this type of happiness is that it will naturally radiate from you for others to feel and see.

In the circumstance where you achieve this end result of happiness by doing things for others, it is important you don't expect anything in return from them – not even a simple thank you! If you do expect some form of deserved acknowledgment or recognition, this could be your undoing, and the intended effect of bringing you pleasure could be a source of bitterness and unhappiness. Do something good, or achieve something worthwhile, for your own pleasure and not for the recognition. If you are rewarded with an acknowledgment, then this is a double bonus for you, but always expect the worst and not the best from others first and foremost to avoid disappointment.

From your perspective, the good you do for others benefits you in the ultimate scheme of things and not the recipient of your good deeds. Of course, there is no denying they benefit! But the day will come when all your good deeds are weighed against all your bad deeds. Do you recall the scoreboard and the battle for points between the positive-part and the negative-part? And the "Feather of Truth"? This is why it should be of no consequence to you if others lack the etiquette to recognize your contribution. Always bear in mind that your contribution will be recognized in the only way it counts!

You have to look beyond the moment at the greater scheme of things. When you understand the bigger picture, you will look at life from a different perspective; from this vantage point you should be able to see the road to happiness. However, you have to grasp the unfortunate fact that life is *not* undemanding, uncomplicated, smooth, untroubled, and unburdened. Life is always, when you least expect, going to challenge you in some way. Life is beautiful, but it can be cruel, and when life shows its ugly side you may wish you were never born. It is up to you, as much as you can, to not let life show this aspect. You have to prevent this, but this can happen and it happens all the time, especially in marriage.

Life often turns sour, and it can become hell on Earth, and this is exactly what you are here on Earth for: you are here to overcome all these obstacles that seem to prevent you from attaining happiness. This is the resonating theme in every single person's life. You are not alone in this sense and you never will be. The difference between you and someone else is your ability to cope with, overcome, and make the best of, the negative situation that confronts you.

The secret is to find happiness in the midst of, and irrespective of, all the things that go wrong. The secret is to try to travel a path that avoids things going wrong. It is easy to blame others, especially a god, for the wrongs that do occur, but often they are a product of your own doing.

The "holy grail" of happiness consists in not allowing yourself to give in to the negative influence when something goes wrong in your life; not allowing yourself to be misguided by the negative emotions that come about as a consequence of the negative influence, such as self-pitying emotions. In the face of challenges your strength and will need to unite, and you have to say enough is enough. You need to put your foot down and not give in to the negative temptations that will be manifest by the negative-part. You must look for the positive, for there is always a positive that can be found in every negative, if you choose to seek it. Duality comes in all shapes and sizes and is found everywhere in life; duality is one of the main themes in life, as we should know by now.

Throughout your life, you will do things that you love to do. Happiness will then automatically radiate from you for others to see, and you will feel happy. It does not matter what it is you do. To be happy is to have satisfaction in the things you do and in the things you achieve. It is true that life is love. When you love life you must love yourself as a human, because you are a part of life; and then a bonus is when someone else loves you, and feels for you the way you feel in return – this is probably one of the most important things that will make you feel happy at this stage of your intellectual development.

Happiness can be felt by you in many ways. Sometimes you can wake up so happy; you marvel in feeling how beautiful it is to be alive, to be a part of this world. In that bliss of happiness you may even wonder why you are so happy, or what you did to deserve such happiness. Perhaps you had a lovely dream that made you so happy. The feelings of the dream may have lingered in your mind for a fleeting while before you came back to your reality of life. Then you may have wished you could feel that blissful but fleeting happiness forever. And yet ... it is lost to us that such feelings should not be rare but be commonplace.

It is only fitting that we never forget the sensible words of a wise man: only when achievements satisfy your positive state of mind are they authentic achievements. If anything you do or say benefits your negative state of mind rather than your positive state of mind, then it is not worth doing, and it is certainly not an authentic achievement.

In contradiction of this humble philosophy lies a conviction that people who possess such things as condominiums and millions of dollars are the happiest in the world. Many are of the conviction that once you have reached the skies you would be beyond happy. On the contrary, this is not likely to be the case if your negative-part was your guiding rudder in reaching those heights. Some of these people are often miserable – this is because their achievement has not registered in their minds, in which case their brains have not released the chemical to make them feel happy and satisfied. Should this be the case, forget about the condominium, forget about everything – it doesn't matter how much money you have! Some rich people are often striving to become richer for one purpose: they think the next million will make them happier, but it won't. (The desire to make money can often be just another addiction.) Making money is a means to survive. It is not a means to happiness. It is just a means to an end. Achieving monetary riches is one thing, but feeling happy is a totally different thing.

The brain, in a state of mind where it is being ruled by a human who places priority on the accumulation of material wealth, wouldn't release the chemical that instigates the feeling of happiness. Therefore, these types of humans are going to make another million, possibly erect another condominium, and virtually chase a rainbow – one that can never be caught. To their minds, however, they believe they will catch it. By the time they consciously realize that they won't, it becomes too late to turn back the clock because life has passed them by. By then it is too late – others are now going to enjoy their wealth. These humans would then evaluate what they have done of veritable merit in their lives and they would not like the answer, because that would be nothing! Their brains never released those chemicals to make them happy. This is why many people become addicted to illicit drugs.

When you achieve something good, something worthwhile, something positive, your human body, by a natural process, instigated by the positive-part, repays you by allowing aura to be received, which is an enhancing, positive energy from the Creators. The body also responds by repaying you with a release of chemicals that are designed to give you that feeling of happiness. This is the secret to happiness.

Drugs, on the other hand, force the brain to release an artificially produced happiness without achievement. The "door" opens, the chemicals are released, but there is no achievement. These people are going nowhere with their lives, but they do attain some type of happy feeling. It is a false feeling, however, because drugs made such happiness possible. This happiness is not real in this circumstance and hence it will not last long. Once awoken from such a "manufactured" feeling of happiness, they will realize they have not done anything worthy of that feeling of happiness; they will realize that they have gone nowhere and have achieved nothing. I would rather work hard and achieve something, and then wait for that genuine recognition from my brain by way of a release of chemicals, which I know will make me feel happy. This is recognized by the Creators as a true achievement.

On the other hand, all these humans recognized by society today who have climbed the ladder of success to get to the top and in the process have acted unconscionably, have stepped on others, and, invariably, have ruined the lives of others, will never acquire that feeling of happiness within them. They will all fall down one day, like a ton of bricks – if not in this life, certainly when they meet Odo. Just as Seleucus of Seleucia (born 190 BC) figured out that the tides of the ocean were a consequence of the Earth's turning and interacting with the moon, so these people will figure out one day that happiness is not a consequence of turning around other people's lives and interacting with those lives negatively for their own personal gain. These humans who lie, who thieve, and who ruin others will never experience such chemical release from their brains, as their brains will fail to recognize their so-called achievements. This book is unequivocal in saying that if these "success stories" confided in you honestly, many would confess to never having had one happy day in their lives. If they had a happy day, it would only have been made possible by drinks, drugs, and sex. These so-called pleasures are just fleeting – like a momentary glimpse of a dream that fades behind the vaulted door of the subconscious. When one achieves something genuine, chemicals are released each time one thinks about that achievement – but only if it was something good; something worthwhile; something that did not hurt anyone; something that was the result of one's hard work. The memories and thoughts will conjure forth those feelings of happiness every time they cross one's mind.

This is where true happiness lies – not in one's wealth, certainly not in one's status in society, and most emphatically not in one's looks, but in the memories and the thoughts of all those good deeds one has accomplished in one's life that will ultimately bring back a flood of pleasant feelings.

·~

Happiness and physical appearance are an interesting mix. This is because many people are all mixed up when it comes to their looks and often don't want to accept reality – that is, to acknowledge themselves for what the Creators designed them for in looks and deeds. Such humans often go through life and are unable to possess feelings of happiness or feelings of satisfaction in themselves when they see their reflection in the mirror. They are always striving to imitate others with every possible means, but it is all a delusion because they are looking for happiness in their illusion, not within themselves, which is where happiness truly lies.

So next time you hear someone say to herself – or even to himself – I am an ugly-looking person, you had better remind this individual that there is no such thing as an ugly-looking person: that everything is beautiful, in its own way, if you just open your eyes and try to see it. Such beauty cannot be seen by bare eyes only – it usually comes from the heart first, which the eyes will subsequently see. One must commit to memory that ugliness stems not from one's looks but from one's behavior and ugly deeds toward others. When one engages in evil deeds, or is consumed with evil musings or intents, it goes without saying that one portrays the aura of ugliness. This is because the aura of the negative-part is an aura of ugliness.

Everything in life is beautiful in its own way – clichéd words that poets put to music. It is true, though; there is no such thing as an ugly-looking life form – whether it is a human being or any other kind of being is irrelevant. If you open your eyes to life around you, you are bound to see the beauty that glares from it like a diamond in a shallow stream on a beautiful sunny morning. The human is one such beauty, who has been created by the ones we call Creators; therefore, we are as beautiful as the ones we take after, and as beautiful as life.

Liking oneself is another key ingredient to happiness. Liking oneself is seeing what comes from within oneself, where one's looks become invisible. When one sees beyond one's looks at the other things one possesses, those looks become irrelevant. Look deep beyond your face, for the face others see is irrelevant. What you say, along with what you possess within, counts. The first thing we often judge a person by is the face, but if you care to spend time with and have the equanimity (patience) to get to know the individual, the face becomes invisible, and then you will like what the person represents. You will see that the true beauty of a human lies in the intelligence and goodness that are portrayed. The more confidence and the more intelligence one possesses, inevitably the more attractive one becomes (and the less securities by way of jewelry and adornments one needs). The opposite is also true: when one lacks intelligence or when one portrays Chisek's aura the less attractive one becomes, irrespective of how externally attractive the face or the body may be. (Just as a side note, have you noticed that insecure people need a lot of jewelry, adornments, and make-up? These are often an external indicator of a person's inner sense of security.)

Positive aura is an invisible beauty and confidence that portrays itself from an intelligent person, and it overrides any physical appearance that person may have. This is what you have to look for in every walk of life – what lies beyond the physical body. For example, take this one man – a garbage man by profession. His physical body has completely let him down. His mental capacity and intelligence are far beyond his physical projection: he understands art and he's up to date with current affairs. If you asked him if he'd like to be somebody else, he'd say he was perfectly happy with himself, because whatever he is or has become he achieved it all by himself.

There is another example that involved a young man at school who, at first glance, would not have impressed anyone. What was interesting was that this young man had a few schoolgirls vying for his attention. Why? It was his smooth demeanor. Beyond his looks he became attractive because he epitomized everything this book has just said about beauty coming from within, which overrides all the fake and unimportant things in a human. Indeed, these girls preferred him to the guy with the movie-star looks because when he opened his mouth he was immature and crude. His unimpressive air had overridden his good looks to the extent that he was not attractive to others.

All one has to do is show the nice human touch that is usually hiding all the time because most people don't want others to see it. To be oneself most natural is the most honest thing you can do, instead of trying to be someone else by means of plastic surgery, make-up, attitude, and so on. When you recognize yourself for what you are, you will have no trouble recognizing others for what they are. That said, you should never underestimate others or discriminate against others; for their intelligence may contribute to you by way of knowledge in ways you can never imagine. Besides, one day they will be judged, just as you will. You may be surprised to learn that your intolerance and discrimination may have earned you more negative points than the person you discriminated against and have shown intolerance toward has earned. Always know this: you cannot possibly judge others, and you have absolutely no right to judge others, when you certainly don't have the ability to judge yourself.

Ultimately, whatever you feel on the inside, within you, will be reflected on the outside for others to see. If you want others to see that you are secure, confident, outgoing, and successful, you have to feel those qualities within you, and they will reflect from you to others. If you like yourself, they will like you too. The things people see and like from others are usually a result of that natural, original glow that comes from within them. For example, if you feel good, confident, and capable, you have no reason to tell the person next to you because this person would automatically sense these things and would treat you accordingly. In other words, whatever you feel within you will be seen by others. Now we know the secret to the beauty found in a human.

We could all learn from this: a wise man looked at himself one day and said,

> *I love to stand where I am*
> *And would change nothing of myself:*
> *The way I am whether "ugly" or beautiful.*
> *You see, I leave a footprint in this world:*
> *My original footprint to have gone through life.*
> *Somebody is going to one day say,*
> *Well, here was an original man!*
> *So this is why I don't want to change myself.*
> *I am what I am*
> *And am to stay this way*
> *Because I like myself*
> *— It is not a crime to like yourself!*
> *You must learn to accept yourself*

And be happy and grateful
For what you are,
For whatever your purpose ...
For whatever the Creator has put you on this Earth for.

Remember, you are here to learn
And to face challenge after challenge
 – After all, life is one big challenge
 – To be human is one big challenge.
How you look should not be your priority;
Your physical cocoon is only this ...
It is the vehicle for you to make passage through life
And expose you to the mercies of fate.

Remember, also, how others judge you in this life
May just affect how others will judge them in their next life;
Because everyone has his turn ...

And then again, when your next life comes,
If it came to be found that you never accepted yourself
Or learned to be happy with whatever your challenge
 – Whether that be your looks or perhaps so-called handicap –
You may face the same challenge again, only worse.
Much worse!
Remember that!

So finally, in all these preaching words, remember this ...
Your looks are not the things others of worth judge you by.

At long last, let this book answer the question once and for all: What is happiness? Happiness is the ultimate end of positive energy, and possessing it is the most elusive quest humans have in life. Why it is so ephemeral is that it can only be attained by being under the influence of the positive-part.

15
What Makes a Success?

*If I ever want to succeed in life it must be on my own and my own only.
Instead of climbing on someone else's ladder,
I would like to make my own ladder and climb upon it.
As I climb upward to success,
If the ladder begins to crumble with each step I take,
Then it will still be gratifying to me
Because that ladder was built by me and me alone,
And does not belong to anyone else.*

*Add to that one important thing:
To "fail" can never mean I failed,
As long as I have tried and have never given up.*

-A wise man

There are two different ways of categorizing success. One measure of success is not often aspired to by humans. Working all your life and having succeeded in achieving something you were happy with is a classic example. Perhaps you didn't achieve all that much by way of material things. It could have been that you simply fixed things around the home and this gave you the satisfaction of doing something worthwhile; on this basis you rightly attribute success to your achievements and ultimately yourself. For all one knows, you may have had a business – it doesn't matter how big or how small it was. If you believe you succeeded and provided for a comfortable existence that made you happy all this time, then there is no question you did succeed in life.

Throughout your life, this success will continue to bring you joy and happiness every time you look back and reminisce, because, as we already know, life is a bank filled with the memories of your day-to-day hard work and achievements that can be translated into your successes. This is what life is all about. If your life is filled with unpleasant memories to look back on, then it could be argued that you had a lousy life. If this is the case, you wouldn't be able to credit yourself with success because you were not happy with the things you have done or achieved. This just sums up what doesn't make a success … you were not happy with the day-to-day things you achieved and therefore you cannot consider yourself successful.

Conversely, if you feel you have done something beautiful, the scope of which is inconsequential, it will forever remain in your bank of memories, and one day you will be able to look back and say to yourself, "I've done all this!" It doesn't have to be great; it doesn't even have to be tall like a mountain or a building! If it is beautiful to you it carries its value, and it is always an achievement when it has come from your heart. There is a truly humble saying from a wise man, and it answers the question of what makes a success: If you leave this Earth one bit better than you found it in the first place, you are deemed a success.

Then there is the second measure of success that is prized by humans, and it is in complete contrast to the humbleness of the first measure of success depicted above; for it is gauged according to how much money you have in the bank, how many buildings you own, or how many casinos you have. In this materialistic world, humans seem to have placed a great priority on, and regard for, monetary gain as a measure of success. There is a problem with this, because success of this nature is not valued in the eyes of the

Creators. This is because many people who have attained such momentous "triumphs" in their lives, and are regarded as a success by society principally because of their status of wealth, have often ruined many innocent lives in their quest to get there. If you have attained wealth by destroying and ruining innocent lives, such as by causing them to lose some or all of their money, their homes, and even their families – if not their own lives (by suicide, or by the stress which has taken a toll on, and years off, their lives), you would certainly not be deemed a success. Unfortunately, there are many humans in these shoes, and as sure as Jason of Greece found the "golden fleece"[3] when he made his maiden voyage of discovery into the unknown, are you guaranteed of one thing when you make your maiden voyage into the unknown of the afterworld: you are going to pay for those ruins you have left behind in your attainment of the golden fleece during your life, one way or another!

One has to wonder at what price one's so-called success was attained. If you are one of these types of people, you may not want to tell others what the price of your success was. Ultimately, if you have to pay a great price in terms of ruining other people's lives in order to achieve your goal, then, unequivocally, you can *never* be considered a success. That is a false success.

What then is a success? Success is something you achieve with a minimum of hustle, where you don't ruin the lives of others, and you don't interfere in the lives of others in a negative way. If you can succeed in achieving something without affecting others negatively, on your own, and if it makes you happy and proud, then that is a success – no matter how insignificant it may seem in the scheme of society. On the other hand, success acquired from ruining other people's lives is not defined as a success in anyone's language or terminology. It is indeed a failure: a huge failure in the eyes of the Creators. You have failed miserably, because you must never succeed at the expense of others. Look carefully at the following words:

---

3 The Golden Fleece refers to a Greek myth about Jason, who led the Argonauts – which was made up of Greek heroes, amongst whom was Hercules – into the unknown to find a Golden Fleece. The Golden Fleece is another way of expressing treasure.

When the little man is ruined or affected by
"Big money" to make bigger money,
And is considered to be collateral damage,
Where the sacrifice is for the greater dollar,
Then that big money better remember the scales,
And know that that system of measurement
Has quite a sense of humor.
It has learned many tricks from man himself.

So when you find yourself in the halfway meadow,
In the event horizon, just before entering the Hall of Truth,
Someone will give you a gift ... special boots,
To take you on your next journey.
The little man is not privy to this "honor."
The idea for the boots came from an innovative bunch,
And their disposal tactics using concrete "boots" in the ocean.

These boots are weighted not with concrete, though,
But with ruined lives, and the burdens of the little man.
In this book's own simple and maybe silly-sounding words,
I think I would rather be the little man being ruined,
Than be that big money who is doing the ruining.
Yes ... when we dig that grave for another,
We better never forget to dig one for ourselves.

There is a difference between being rich monetarily and being rich within yourself. When you are rich within yourself you are rich on an intellectual level; you know who you are, and with a world of confidence you know what you are working for (an additional bonus that not many people can claim to have). Monetary wealth is something you cannot take to the grave. This has been proven many centuries ago by the pharaohs of Egypt, whose efforts proved futile. You are going to leave this life in exactly the same way as you came into it – with nothing! But when you possess knowledge, as well as confidence in who you are, you have something no one can ever take from you – not even mortality itself can take it from you! It will still be there with you when you die. It belongs to you. Imagine that! That's the difference between being rich with assets and being rich with intellect. In life, you have to accept one thing: the only riches there are in life are the riches you get to take with you – your knowledge and soul and not a thing more. These are what you have to cherish and look after in this life, very carefully, because these are the only riches recognized by the Creators. Nothing else becomes relevant. All these man-made empires people aspire to become irrelevant, because everything materially attained can and will one day crumble. We have seen many empires crumble, and the only remnants of those empires are the people who really made a difference by leaving the legacy of their knowledge.

You must reconsider your values, in line with Odo's values, for, he is not interested in giving you money. He wants to give you intelligence, and he keeps his "fingers crossed" that you will know how to use it. He is poorer than we are monetarily. We at least have a few coins in our pockets. He couldn't even boast of having that. If money were of value to Odo then he would be the poorest in the universe. The riches he has given you are not monetary but intellectual, so that you are able to utilize this intellectualism to make money and produce the things you require for your comfortable survival in your cocoon of life.

To appreciate life, to learn from life, and to become someone, you have to start at the bottom, because it is only from this perspective of life that you can really understand what life is all about. A wise man once said:

> *If you throw a fish out in the hot sun*
> *It usually always starts to stink*
> *From the head first and not from the tail.*

In life, you have to start from the tail in order to arrive at the head, and whether it begins to stink afterward is up to you, but you have to start from the beginning, which is the humble bottom. To be humble is a privilege. The one who is humble will one day achieve something, whatever that something is, no matter how big or how small. In life you have to achieve something great yourself that makes you feel great within; if you are satisfied with this achievement then your jigsaw puzzle of life will fit and you will be happy, and of course this is deemed a great success.

Many people say, "Oh, I'm going to aspire to make this big condominium!" It is all rubbish! You have to live your life by looking at life from the simplistic way life is. This means you have to progress and achieve in life by working hard on a day-to-day basis with a determination to achieve something – it doesn't matter how big or how small that achievement. For it is in the small achievements, from the bottom up, that you are going to understand life. You are not going to understand it from the top of a condominium. If you want to jump the gun and get to the top without having come from the bottom, you will fail miserably, because you missed the normal progression of the human intellect in its rise to those heights. You must know that you cannot become god in a day! This is why you exist on this lower-order planet. You have to take life day by day. You should of course plan your tomorrow; you should even plan further ahead into the long term; most of all, you should try to achieve something every day of your life. You should not bypass the small daily achievements and attempt to achieve that condominium over your head today; for it is the small achievements that will eventually lead to the bigger achievements in your life. This will take time and require patience on your part.

There is a true story about a young European man who, at the age of twenty-four, moved to the city shortly after serving time in the army. He was just an ordinary guy who had the army take care of him and prior to that had his parents take care of him. The time had now come for him to take care of himself, because, when he returned home from the army he found that his parents were dead. For their entire lives, he and his parents had tended to the sheep in the mountains, but with his parents' death the stock was sold, so now he had to leave the village in search of a job in the city. One night, in the city, he sat down and worked out that he was probably going to live to about seventy. He calculated how much money he needed in his lifetime to survive. He worked it out to be such an extraordinary amount of money that he said to himself, "There is no way I can make this much money!" After being driven by Chisek into the panicky doldrums of self-doubt, he then hung himself.

There is a moral in this simple story: you shouldn't look at life in this way. Don't look at that intimidating "mountain" in front of you. The secret in life is to take one small positive step at a time, wherein those small steps can unfailingly lead you to bigger steps – and this applies to whatever small or great thing you may want to achieve. It is today you have to do something that gives you a feeling of achievement. Tomorrow is always another day, and you can never be sure what it will bring. A new sunrise means new hope. By all species of life, the new day is welcomed. When sundown comes, the day takes its toll and life goes down with the sun. In the morning everything is re-energized; people will be born and the sun is going to go down again, and it is surely going to take a life with it. The Earth is just a cocoon, a little cocoon in a vast universe among universes – 49 of them! Ironically, we are not lost in all this. The Creators are still with us. You would think that this miserable little thing called Earth, in the vastness of the universe, would be trifling. But not so, just like the lost sheep in a famous parable! A shepherd doesn't say, "I've got lots of sheep so let's forget about this lost one." He isn't happy until he finds it. That is the attitude of the Creators. They find "joy" in and "worry" about us.

In your testing expedition through life, you must never forget that life is like a road, and the road is not always going to be a pleasant one. It is not always going to climb to great heights and take you to the top of that condominium. It can, however, take you to a dead end from which you feel there is no escape. Just as you are guaranteed to face death one day, so are you guaranteed to encounter roadblocks and dead ends at some stage in your life. It is your challenge to find the right road, and then figure out how to pace yourself so that you encounter an open door instead of a dead end. For there will be times when you will have to walk at a slower pace, and inevitably times when you will have to walk a faster pace. This illustrates that you have to try to calculate when that gate of life, or door, is going to open for you. Sometimes you have to arrive at that door at a specific time, at a specific place, in order to get through. Once you get through it, it will surely close again. If it opened and you weren't there then you missed the boat and probably hit a dead end. You were in the wrong place, and that is just how things work in life. Your ability to gauge what pace will concur with your estimation of when that door is going to open is very important if you plan to get through the door before it closes on you. Then you can be assured of another new challenge. It is always the same. Then you'll encounter a new roadblock and perhaps another new roadblock after that. This is what happens in your passage through life, right until the end of your days. This is why life is beautiful; why it challenges; for it challenges you on every level, in every way possible, and you always have to be ready to respond. It is important to be at the right place at the right time. Well, if this is one of your right times, right places, you will feel it; you will know it; and you had better act fast before the opportunity closes on you.

You see, people in this world who are triumphant in business and in decision making are often so because, first of all, they have a gift of working hard and sacrificing. You cannot ever escape or underestimate the value of hard work. Second, these people are aware of that gift of timing: they know when to make a decision by estimating when the door is going to open, and are actually able to see the door when it does open, which is the crucial factor that can make or break a success. They were there and ready, and when they saw the door open they shot through it. These are the people who make it in this world. You too can achieve this, but you have to learn this art of timing in your journey through life, as simple as that! You just have to learn it, and before you know it, you will know exactly when to be there, and how to pace yourself so that you are there at the right time when the door opens. Therein lies one of the most important secrets to success.

16
To "Read" from the "Closed Book"

To be or not to be?
That is not the question!
To be and become
That is the only thing in question!

-A wise man

Positive Affirmation and its "Rewards"

A man does not have to force doors open through life
In order to get somewhere.
A man must use his intellect wisely,
And have the doors open by themselves for him thereafter.

-A wise man

At this instant in time, even with our encumbered state of intelligence, a small glimpse of the possibilities and potential of our human mind can be seen when we are able to follow the path of the Creators by drawing on our positive influence (allowing the positive-part to take charge of the control center of the brain), rather than follow the path of Chisek by drawing on our negative influence (allowing the negative-part to take charge of the control center of the brain). This draws nebulous parallels to the positive affirmation theory, which makes an unscientific claim that there is a law of attraction in the universe. According to this theory, if you place an order into the universe with your mind, the universe will register that order and, ultimately, give it to you, but there is a catch – and this is the secret: you have to maintain positive thoughts.

What the proponents of this theory advocate is that you visualize a dream in your mind, and by this mere thought process some kind of unscientific and illogical process occurs wherein the universe will reward you with that dream. This can apply to losing weight, or attaining wealth, happiness, promotions, and good health to name a few. As appealing as this theory may be, it is naïve, simplistic, and even childish.

If the universe were capable of rewarding you as these advocates theorize, then, isn't this indirectly acknowledging that the universe has some kind of intelligence that knows what you are thinking and desiring, and wants to provide these desires to you subject to the condition you stay positive? One key detail to consider about the intelligences that *do* exist in the universe is that they learned their lesson from the phase-1 humans who did not have the capacity to strive to achieve for themselves. In view of this lesson, the intelligences in the universe would *never* give you rewards on a platter just because you desire it to be so or because you want it to be so. The philosophy of the Creators consists in working hard and earning anything you want. You certainly cannot sit under a tree, or in front of a television with a beer, with a positive attitude, and pray for example for a yacht, a home, a sports car, or perhaps a million dollars in the bank, and expect "something" in the universe to just hand it to you on a platter for doing nothing but asking for it and being positive!

On the contrary, praying for something in this instance is the worst thing you can do. Odo would most likely send you a harder challenge in life to face because he has no interest in laziness and does not ever give out handouts. (A wise man *never, ever*, asks Odo, or the universe, for help! He knows that if Odo ever does give you a handout, there will be a catch attached.) Odo does not believe in the easy path of life. This is Chisek's path. He wants you to work hard, work smart and intelligently, use and advance your brain, and maintain a positive attitude by never drawing on Chisek's influence in times that you feel may be warranted. This is what draws you as a human closer to attaining success in that meat-in-the-sandwich goal.

At the heart of positive affirmation lies the conviction that if you visualize something, such as happiness, and if you stay positive and focused on that something, the universe may just reward you with it. Contrary to what you may now believe, the universe will not have rewarded you with it. Let us consider happiness. In the process of controlling your negative-part, you will be following the instincts of your positive-part. Of course you will feel happiness in this situation, for, happiness is a positive feeling within you, and it can only be felt by you when you are under the influence of the positive-part. Happiness cannot be found in negative thoughts or deeds – that is, when you are under the influence of the negative-part. Therefore, you as a human have attained happiness all on your own. Furthermore, any other achievements you have or obstacles you conquer would have been solely by the power of your mind. Nothing in the universe has helped you that is not a part of you or within you. You have helped yourself.

The negative-part is responsible for feelings such as lack of motivation, depression, and unhappiness; it is the prime instigator of all your negative thoughts and emotions. Positive achievements, then, are not achievable while you are under the influence of your negative-part. Positive achievements are only possible when you are under the influence of your positive-part.

You can rightly say that most of the time when you appear to be "rewarded" by the universe for your positivity, you have actually achieved your own reward. It sounds a little like some of those cults in the sense that when you "find" this cult and you are "rescued" or "saved" to the point where you can now stand on your two feet, you are made to believe that it was some deity or even the principal cult figure that has done the work in getting you to your feet, instead of being made to realize that it was your own strength of will and determination that have done all the work.

It is beyond many of you to consider that it is with your own intellect, with your own drive and capability, that you can achieve all of your dreams. But you cannot aspire or wish to be a physicist and expect the universe to suddenly give you the knowledge of a physicist. This is just illogical at this stage of your intellectual development. Of course, you *can* become a physicist if you use your brain and travel down the path of life that will give you this qualification. When you dream and aspire to be a pilot you have to put the hard work in to become one, by learning to fly a plane, and then if you are truly determined to achieve such a goal there is nothing to stop you.

This is the true secret: the mind has the potential to overcome all odds and achieve whatever it sets out to achieve – and it matters not what age you are or what handicap you think you have! You *are* capable of achieving anything you set out to achieve if you are determined enough. There is no such thing as not being born bright enough, not being smart enough, or being too old. Your genes or age has no bearing on your intellectual capabilities. Everyone is born equal, with basically the same potential, irrespective of the disadvantages one is born with. Anyone can go from being "dumb" to being brilliant. Anyone! This is as certain as is the fact that you exist. It all depends on how one chooses to develop oneself, and one's use of the positive and negative influence. All you have to do is "switch on" the resources in your mind. The positive-part is that "button." You can become anything you want to be if you really want it bad enough and are prepared to work for it. Along the way you can even be rewarded with the trappings of success.

This book has already dealt with that aspect of your life where life hands out blank checks. It is appropriate that this book revisits this. For it is when you seem to have a lot of luck and doors open for you, that life is handing you out blank checks. The problem is that life *will* ask payment back from you one day

THE FIRST CAUSE

— with interest! If you haven't already paid your dues, one day you will be asked to. This is the quintessence of life. So when you find that doors are opening for you because of your hard work, as well as your motivation, determination, and struggle to get there, it could be argued that you are paying your dues along the way. If doors are opening for nothing, you should be wary; life may be silently tabulating your dues, waiting for the day to collect, one way or another. There is an appropriate saying from a wise man:

> *The greater the struggles,*
> *The greater the suffering,*
> *The greater the heights of achievement.*

We can see that there is no simple way of receiving something for nothing. In short, you have to look not to the universe for help, but to your mind for help. For instance, if you desire to lose weight, you cannot dream of losing weight and expect it to happen unless you initiate some action, mental or physical, yourself, such as developing the will to eat less, eat better, or exercise. Only then may you lose weight. Fundamentally, it has to come from you, from the will within you. You need to contribute something yourself in terms of hard work and a desire to accomplish. You need to ignore the subtle drive that comes from your negative-part, which is encouraging you to eat when you don't need to. This is the secret. Your mindset is the secret. But you have to perform the difficult job of wanting it badly enough; this is when your positive-part will help you by giving you the strength of will, the motivation, and the determination you require. Of this, we should have absolutely no doubt: nothing happens to you for nothing, just as nothing comes from nothing. It would be wise to reflect on these words whenever we decide to turn to the universe for help. Know that with any help from the universe there will be some measure of reimbursement, at some stage in our lives.

What this book has so far presented to us is an ancient philosophy, with roots that stem from the first man that was seeded on this Earth; this philosophy seems to have been, at best, theorized, but never practiced. The flowers of this fruit have rarely blossomed for mankind. The following is the heart of this wisdom.

If you draw on the negative influence, your positive influence is repelled and then "exiled" in your subconscious mind. You have allowed your negative-part into the control center of your brain and it becomes the voice inside you now that influences and makes negative suggestions to you. It can do whatever your positive-part can do, but in a negative or opposite sphere. In the same way that your positive-part can open doors for you, can your negative-part open doors for you. While these negative doors may have a pleasing presentation for the sake of wheedling you in, you had better believe that nothing good can come from what is skulking behind any of the doors the negative-part has open for you. Your negative-part will influence you to go down that road of self-destruction, such as depression, suicide, or criminal deviance. When you are negative in some way, the negative-part is in control, and it will break your strength of will in many ways — such as when it comes to your eating habits, taking drugs, smoking, drinking (as in the case of the alcoholic), and, generally, all those negative things you try to conquer with your will, which can only be conquered when influenced by the positive-part.

Have you noticed that it is when you are feeling down that you need a stiff drink, a smoke, chocolate, or other comfort food? Always the tempting urges of the negative-part break your determination and resolve. The negative-part will succeed by way of your inner urges and desires. When you crave something that is of no benefit to you, but is detrimental to you (like junk food to the dieter), you can be assured that your negative-part is the conspirator behind such an innate urge.

Bad habits can never be conquered while under the influence of Chisek (the negative-part). Chisek will make you lazy, give you a couldn't-care-less attitude about everything, and influence you to do all those things that are counter to the positive things you want in life. He is the influence that suggests and encourages all those bad habits. This is why you cannot advance in a positive way — or even achieve satisfying and fulfilling feelings of accomplishment — while under Chisek's influence.

Now we reach the concluding words that have taken us to a universal truth, a simple one at that: When you are in a positive frame, your positive-part can make things happen for you. If you are not in a positive frame, but in a negative frame, your negative-part will make sure nothing happens to you of a positive nature but everything possible happens to you of a negative nature. Moreover, when good things happen in your life, you made them possible because you followed the positive path in life instead of the negative path.

As Above: So Below – The Compendium of All Knowledge

As long as the planet has turned and our days did come and go,
Permanence has touched upon everything in the passage of time's flow:
The glowing reflection of a sun with its happy-go-lucky gleam;
And the subtle, caressing touch of the soothing moon beam.

But further beyond and nearer at hand does there lie
A permanence more enduring than those of the celestial sky.
For as sure as the night sky in awe we look to,
As sure as it's a portal to a past that's now gone and through,

There is a greater permanence that is real, that is true:
It is the compendium of all knowledge, and it lies dormant within you.

Not only are we of the physical dust of the stars. We are of the metaphysical dust of the consciousness of the universe. We are as much a component of the universe as everything we see and don't see is. Up above, in this universe, there is a virtuoso that we have found the capacity to interpret. In our "wisdom," we have not found that what is as above, is so below – in our minds. For, what is up above, in the universe, drawn behind what appears to be a vaulted door of space, distance, and time, is so below, in our minds, behind the vaulted door of the subconscious mind. Seers, prophets, shamans, wise men, primitive peoples, and many others going a long way back, were in their own way able to tap into the frequency of the heartbeat of this virtuoso, and were able to tune their minds in on its rhythmic pulse. The faraway answers that we thought were as far from our reach as are the distances of the farthermost stars, have always been near and at hand, waiting for a scintilla of life to stir them from a spell of incubation …

We know that the greatest challenge facing you as a human is to end the battle of good and evil that rages within you, and reach that desired state of equilibrium. One question has remained unanswered: What reward will you reap when you reach this desired point of equilibrium? First of all, it is only when you have conquered the meat-in-the-sandwich goal that the Creators know you have learned how to confine and control your negative influence of Chisek. You as a human have won the battle. You are able to control Chisek's influence in your life in its entirety. This is the human the Creators hope for in their "dreams." This is the final human, the phase-4 human. One way or another, this is the final cause of all humans in the universe and beyond, no matter what their level of intelligence.

Once the Chisek impediment has been overcome, you will then be ready to proceed to a new stage of your intellectual development. Your brain has been pre-programmed to wait until you reach this stage before it can implement the new, exciting phase of your human existence. Nothing of this nature can happen while you can still be influenced by Chisek. Hypothetically, if the Creators programmed the brain to release its intellectual capabilities any earlier, the human would use these new intellectual powers under the influence of Chisek – which invariably means for the greater use of evil. If the Creators gave humans the power that comes with knowledge, it would mean the Creators were stepping quite a few paces backward. With the humans' capacity to not be able to reason and handle the negative influence at this stage of their development, the Creators would be recreating a history they would prefer to leave in the past. After all, the Creators took away the intellectual powers of humans deliberately when they created intellectually encumbered humans like us (the P3V2 human). They did this for us to acquire knowledge and learn the challenging way by means of hard work. We have been forced to use our intelligence because of the challenges we encounter in our lives. Eventually, those challenges would reward us with knowledge and eventually intelligence and wisdom.

In the beginning the Creators gave the human everything (the phase-1 human). The type of human that subsequently evolved was a failure. Slowly the Creators took everything away from the human, until the human was left with nothing but labor and toil, which is another way of saying challenges. These challenges are an intentional and integral part of our genetic make-up and existence. Yet, there exists in amidst our challenges one universal goal – our final cause: to become the desired human. To accomplish this we must work, and struggle, and fight to reclaim all those things that have been deliberately taken away from us – the things we must reclaim using our own initiative. When we succeed, we will have risen to the status of the original creation that was given everything on a platter (the phase-1 human). Then will the cycle be complete.

You as a human don't realize that you have the universe awaiting your discovery, all in your mind, lying idle, ready to be tapped. "Utopia" is attainable and achievable by you – yes, you! All you have to do is overcome the most difficult challenge of all time: to attain equilibrium by confining and controlling Chisek's influence. To reinforce what we have already learned, your first-part wants to advance you; it wants to develop your intelligence; it wants you to find the will within you to conquer the challenges in your life, such as weight issues; and it wants to open doors for you. This is what is happening to you when the universe seems to be rewarding you for staying positive. Your first-part is doing its job and giving you those things because you earned them. Most of all, your first-part wants to become "one" with you. (More of this is discussed in the following chapter.)

The first-part cannot do its job when you allow your negative Chisek part to take control of you. Like dictators and cults, Chisek doesn't want you to develop your brain cells and become intelligent. The opposite is applicable: Chisek will provide you with knowledge of an evil nature; he will help you do all those negative things in society people do; and he will advance you in a backward way in this negative sphere if you choose his road.

It is always interesting to study the mental process of those who follow Chisek's path. There is one thing of interest that is known in these circles: if you get second thoughts at any stage about committing an evil act, you should draw on the voice in your mind to encourage you and inspire you. This voice is of course your negative-part, which will literally take over your mind if you let it, and either drive you to insanity, or drive you to kill yourself and, perhaps, others.

What is even more interesting to watch is the practice by devoted religious observers of self-mutilation and self-inflicted pain (as in the case of those mirroring Jesus' pain). This is such a contradiction, because to inflict pain on yourself you have allowed the negative-part from Chisek to take the helm of the control center of your brain.

What then happens when you as a human conquer the meat-in-the-sandwich goal is unfathomable, awesome, and mind boggling. It is summer in winter: it is rain in a drought: it is even rain upon a raging wildfire: it is a waterhole in a desert: it is a rainbow in a blackened sky: it is the miracle of survival ... it is feeling equilibrium within you, and it is your mind being capable of possessing great powers of intellect, of the kind you can never imagine. It is beyond words: beyond music: beyond love: beyond ...

> *The Universe is an unspoken Language*
> *With its own feelings and comprehension*
> *... Equilibrium ...*
> *That washes away the need for any of our*
> *Delicate and complicated mazes,*
> *Which we construct in our attempt to understand*
> *Something that is just beyond our understanding.*

When you feel equilibrium, it is as if you are in tune with the wavelength of every living thing in the universe. You feel a part of it, and it feels a part of you. You achieve a "oneness" with the universe; this is because you have achieved a oneness with your first-part, which is a component of that very universe. We know that the true universe is made up of antimatter, neutron, and solid (matter) voids, and that we are a blend of the dust of both the neutron void and the matter void. What we cannot begin to know is that with equilibrium, the conscious mind, the subconscious mind, the first-part, and the physical body have crossed the boundary of merged separateness. They are no longer the "bookend and the book." They are now "the book."

This is a state of peacefulness; it is a state of overwhelming tranquility that is beyond the language of the spoken and the written word, or the language of music, art, mathematics, and science, or the language of happiness and love. These are all the different ways of interpreting the "Universal Language," which is the highest form of communication. When you can interpret this language, so shall you think and look like, and even be, a god. This is the uncharted language, from which all the other languages – the spoken, the written, the painted, the listened to, and so on – are derived.

How is the Universal Language an unspoken language? How is it above the languages we know? We should look to all the living species of this world – apart from humans – which already know this answer, for, the living world has conquered its meat-in-the-sandwich goal. This is the language with which one species can communicate with another species. This is why no living thing needs to talk as we do. In this sense, the living world is superior to us! We think otherwise, but the living world already communicates in the language that we are yet to know exists. Only a primitive species needs verbal communication. This should shatter our ego a little and humble us before our fellow species of life on this Earth. (It would surprise us to know that we all start out in this world with the use of the Universal Language. Eventually we take a backward step and replace it with the primitive oral form.)

Imagine if you had two aliens, from two different worlds; if you had two superior humans from different countries; if you had a superior human and an animal; if you had a superior human and a tree; or if you had a rose and an animal … do you think they could communicate with each other on a psychic level, even though they may be different in species and have a different language of communication? Did you say yes? You do understand, then. We have not evolved to the point where we can communicate with one another on a psychic level – that is, telepathically – so we may not be able to picture this Universal Language with the limited mind we have at present. Although, there have been savants in this world who have been capable of tuning in on the mind of a non-human species.

What, then, is this Universal Language? Have you ever felt a word in your mind but could not find a dictionary word that fit with it to describe it? Maybe you just had it on the tip of your tongue, but could not remember it. Have you ever felt a story in your mind that comes to you in one quick burst, and then you try to find the words afterward to describe the story that you felt? Have you ever felt a painting in your mind, and then tried to reproduce the picture by way of paints or other media? Have you ever felt the music of a song, which you then converted to the language of music so that others can hear it?

Equally, have you ever listened to music that conjured up feelings within you? Have you ever looked at a painting that made you feel something by looking at it? Have you ever read poetry that evoked feelings within you? Think about it!

In these last cases, you have converted the interpreted languages of music, art, and the written word, into the Universal Language.

When you read someone's mind you become that person for that moment, and you feel his feelings on whatever the line of thought. This is one form of telepathy. This is the Universal Language: it is the language of feeling and it operates at the speed of thought. Did you imagine something as simple as that! Now we can understand what happened to the Seven Elders when they came to exist. This language just existed in their amoebas. They had to then interpret this language, the same as we have to interpret it – whether it is by using music, the written or spoken word, art, science, or even mathematics. Everything was there before them, just as it is there before us. We have to learn how to tune in on it and then apprehend it just as they had to. The time span for their evolutionary process was vast. Our evolutionary process certainly will not happen in a day; not in a fortnight; not in a lifetime! We have to learn patience, and take one small step at a time. Every small step is then one step closer to our destiny.

When you conquer the meat-in-the-sandwich goal you will feel equilibrium and possess great powers of intellect. To begin with, your human brain will be able to collect and possess a lot more aura than it currently is capable of collecting and possessing. Sleep, diet, and correct nutrition also play a role in the health and strength of the body. By possessing this aura you will be able to, for one thing, heal yourself in a limited way. (A strengthened immune system is the determining factor for the human body to heal itself, which the current physical body does not possess. An advanced society is able to correct such "flaws" in the physical body.) Aura is a self-replenishing energy source found within the universe and on planets. It is everywhere, just as oxygen is. Aura facilitates the functioning of your body and brain. Aura and intelligence go hand in hand – like the star and its wobble, where the wobble is an indicator of the presence of a planet. Just as a shadow increases proportionally to the migration of the sun toward the western horizon, so aura increases proportionally to an increase in intelligence. Superior intelligence cannot exist without a great deal of aura in the body. Furthermore, if you constantly falter to the influence of Chisek, you are not capable of possessing this power of knowledge; this is because you are not physically capable of "upgrading" your aura. You are constantly forfeiting it each time you embrace Chisek. You get it back when your positive-part returns, but you are not capable of augmenting it.

When you are in possession of vast amounts of aura, your conscious mind will have an amazing potential to acquire and possess knowledge. The conscious mind will open a door into the subconscious mind, from which knowledge will now be accessible to the conscious mind in ways that are generally not possible at this point in your development. For your conscious mind will be able to penetrate the subconscious mind and establish a map of it. Once the subconscious mind has been mapped out, its knowledge can be downloaded to the conscious mind – this means that you will have the potential to draw out knowledge from your subconscious mind, at will.

Savants, in a different and limited way, have this ability and give us a small clue of what our capabilities will one day be. Their brains seem to be "wired" differently. For instance, the conscious minds of many savants do not function as they should. This is why the day-to-day skills we take for granted are limited in many savants. The brains of savants appear to be wired so as to directly access a portion of their subconscious minds, where knowledge is unlimited and storage facilities are unlimited. The subconscious mind, for all its benefits, cannot handle the day-to-day functional operations the conscious mind has been designed to handle. We could equate this to a computer: imagine that the operating system of your computer has crashed, but has remained open on a program that is directly being accessed from the hard drive. This is what appears to be occurring in some savants. This type of savant has direct access into one of the rooms of his subconscious mind, while his conscious mind has shut down to some degree. What room that may be is unique to that savant. Some have extraordinary mathematical skills. Some can input any knowledge and then retrieve that knowledge at will, when most of us would have forgotten it moments later.

When a person has such direct, open access to his subconscious mind – not just to one room, but to all the rooms – knowledge is as accessible to this person as knowledge in the hard-drive of a computer is to its operating system. We must never forget that the brain is a highly sophisticated, non-reproducible computer; it has a storage facility – the subconscious mind – and it has amazing retrieval facilities that operate at the speed of thought. With just a conscious mind with limited storage facilities, we are restricted in what we can remember and do with our minds. One day we will be using a greater portion of our brains, where our brains will be able to retrieve knowledge at will on every subject;

we will be, in our own right, physicists, chemists, biologists, artists, calculators – the range is limitless. It is all a matter of accessing the relevant software from our brains. By this stage, we will possess many different software packages in our brains.

Another way of picturing this is by comparing the conscious mind to a search engine on the internet. The conscious mind equates to the search engine, and the subconscious mind equates to the internet. The conscious mind will operate at the speed of thought and access anything from the subconscious mind just as a search engine accesses knowledge from the internet.

When you reach this stage, and possess the facilities to draw out knowledge from your subconscious mind, contrary to what was said earlier, you could indeed draw out knowledge of physics, or even knowledge of how to fly a plane, overnight – without studying at all! You could access any knowledge you possess in your subconscious mind, at will.

What is truly remarkable is that in our subconscious minds there lies the storehouse of knowledge of our past as well as that "dream" knowledge of the future. That compendium of knowledge, based on whatever you learn today but have forgotten tomorrow, and whatever you have learned yesterday but have forgotten today, will be available for access from your subconscious mind – where all knowledge learned is archived – one tomorrow in the future.

Let us take a basic computer: an operator needs to install the relevant software and data for it to function (apart from its operating system, which usually comes ready installed by the manufacturer). Without software, the computer is not useful. The same applies to you. You need to input data into your mind today by learning as much as you can, so that tomorrow when you do reach your final cause – equilibrium – you will have a treasure-trove of knowledge available to your mind at the speed of thought. (In the next chapter, when we uncover what dreaming is, we will understand the basis of the roaming subconscious mind and why it collects knowledge for storage in the subconscious mind. It is building up your knowledge bank for access at a future time to come.) You must bear in mind that you cannot access knowledge from your subconscious mind if there is no knowledge there. Moreover, no one is magically going to put it there, ready-made on a platter, so to speak. (If we recall, the Creators did this with earlier models of humans in the universe, but deliberately did not give us knowledge on a platter.) To a degree, you – whether consciously or subconsciously – will be the one to have developed your subconscious mind with its so-called software packages and stockpiled knowledge. (Indirectly the Creator will be helping you in the process, by way of your first-part.) Does this make any sense?

All this accumulated knowledge, from this life and all your past lives, is simply stored in your subconscious mind and is lying idle, just waiting to be tapped. This is highly unlikely at this stage of our primitive existence, until we complete the requirements to make this happen. How long this takes is anyone's guess. What an exciting adventure it will be when we are able to explore that goldmine of knowledge hidden away in our subconscious minds! Not only in our minds, by the way, but in other minds! For, once you have reached this stage, you will be able to access knowledge from another human's subconscious mind.

Before your eyebrows rise – particularly you, the luminaries of academia and the intelligentsia – look at it from this perspective: which is more absurd – the above statement, or the hogwash notion that the "goldilocks" existence of Earth is the result of arbitrary processes that were lucky for life to develop? Such arbitrary processes include the Earth having just the right orbit around the sun; the Earth having a moon in just the right place – without which our planet would not exist in a way that is fit for life (without a moon, one of the key factors inferred here would be that our axial tilt would be unstable and our Earth would wobble); the Earth having just the right axial tilt (which gives us our seasons); and the Earth having a giant like Jupiter nearby, with a massive gravitational field to collect stray projectiles such as asteroids. One could go on and on listing those so-called coincidental variables that are critical to our survival. Is it sane to think this all occurred by accident and luck, or by an intelligent designer?

Imagine if you were talking to a mathematics professor and you desired the knowledge this intellectual possessed on the subject; all you would have to do is simply ask your brain to access such desired knowledge. (You wouldn't even have to ask. Your mind already knows what you want.) Your first-part would then create a "bridge" between your two subconscious minds, and the professor's knowledge would be copied and pasted directly into your subconscious mind, which you would then be able to access at will. This is exactly the same principle as downloading onto your computer from a secondary source, except the biological computer called the brain is infinitely more sophisticated than the humanly devised computer. Indeed, it cannot ever match the sophistication of the human brain. Your brain from this point onward would operate exactly like a computer. You would be able to access any knowledge at will from your subconscious hard-drive storage. Your first-part, acting like a USB stick, would be able to download into your brain knowledge copied from another source – that is, from someone else's brain. Your potential now is mind boggling!

The power of the human mind will be unlimited when it has advanced to this stage. Your potential and your mind's capabilities of achievement will go beyond the fringes of your imagination of today. You will use the majority of your brain, not the miniscule percentage you use right now. This is when you will be able to make anything happen. At this point, your first-part will create an unlimited number of helpers, or copies of itself, also called positive-parts. Someone with Intellect Mark-6.5 is capable of possessing millions of parts. One has been known to possess five million parts because that is the amount he needed. If he needed ten million, his first-part would reproduce an extra five million. (In comparison, Leonardo da Vinci had no more than one-hundred parts, and his intelligence level could not compare! Quantity, however, is not always an indication of quality, which refers to the power of each part.) The superior human, who was actually a bit more than a superior human, Jesus Christ, just for reference, was Intellect Mark-7, the highest intellect possible on the human scale, which no human has ever been able to match. This is another book in itself of knowledge!

These parts will all then function to serve you under the leadership of your first-part, by providing you with knowledge, data, aura, and so on. They will also influence people to open whatever doors were required for you to fulfill your destiny. It almost sounds as though you have a fairy godmother, but this is so far from reality. One thing they do not do is make your passage through life an easy one; they will take you to that place of destination, as it was written when you came into this world. However, the more challenging the passage, the more they advance your brain, and that is their agenda. This is also a test to see what you are made up of; what strength you truly possess; and how deserving you are of your next step. The more they advance your intellect, the more they advance themselves and further their cause.

When you reach these capabilities, you will then be able to make all your dreams come true – not just for yourself on an individual basis, but for mankind as a whole. These are the things we as humans on this planet have not even begun to imagine!

Finally, the following is an important point for you to consider: now that you can see the power of your potential, can you see why this power cannot be available to you until you achieve equilibrium — that is, when you have conquered the meat-in-the-sandwich goal? Humans must resolve the good and evil, the order and chaos, the angel and devil, the reason and unreason, within them, and they must devour the beast within them, so that the beast can never devour them again. Won't that be something!

Perhaps now we can attribute new meaning to what the bible has been telling us about pure hearts being able to know and see god and his kingdom.

When what is "As Above" is not "So Below"

In the quest for knowledge
One must pay its price.

-A wise man

One warning, and this is a crucial and applicable piece of advice for any human being on this planet who intends to attempt to conquer the meat-in-the-sandwich goal: as you near this goal, Chisek's desire to influence you will proportionally increase. Because you have reached a stage where you are controlling to a great degree his negative influence, Chisek will not be able to influence you directly; he will now indirectly target you by finding a weakness in you to which you are vulnerable. Unfortunately, while you are attempting to control and confine Chisek, Chisek will do everything in his power to control you, and it will take more than heaven and Earth to help you control let alone confine him! He will try to find this vulnerable weakness now through people around you who have nothing to lose by alienating you; these are the easiest targets for him to influence. The best resources available to him are the emotional attachments you have. Such attachments are always the breaking point of humans that can drive them over the edge.

The missing link to the meat-in-the-sandwich equation: the holy grail for conquering the meat-in-the-sandwich goal, is your ability to handle people, particularly your emotional attachments. These emotional attachments are the great weaknesses in humans that Chisek unhesitatingly uses against them to derail them from accomplishing equilibrium. His secret weapons, the three common denominators in a human, are greed, jealousy, and envy, and these are unfailingly successful weapons.

Chisek will one by one go through whatever resources are available to him just to break you and your will and derail you from conquering the meat-in-the-sandwich goal. These resources could include your neighbors, your co-workers, or your customers. Any of these are easy targets for him. Then if you overcome the minor roadblocks Chisek puts before you, he will target emotional resources such as your family ties. Close family ties are the worry, as is the jackpot, which is the emotional partner such as a husband or wife. One way or another, you will be surrounded by humans who are unable to control the influence of Chisek upon them; this is applicable to the majority of humans on this planet at this stage of their intellectual development. Chisek will then have kept you busy for your entire life by trying to derail you, and each time you have had to waste valuable time trying to recover and crawl back on to your desired road, which, at this rate, will never take you to your destination.

One day we are expected to conquer the meat-in-the-sandwich goal, but this can only happen when humans are on a level intellectual field, far in advance of their current level of intelligence. This book can only add this one piece of advice: a superior intellect, among lesser intellects, will find the task impossible when surrounded by emotional attachments that are not of the same intellectual level – this book is not speaking of academic intelligence; it is speaking of the kind of intelligence derived from being able to reason. This type of intellect with this type of goal will have no choice but to be wary of having any close emotional attachments.

Everything attained in this life comes at a cost. The greater the reward: the greater the price: the greater the challenge. The human on this planet who is able or attempts to conquer the meat-in-the-sandwich goal pays a price. For those who seek the benefit against the cost, the following is a question for you to ponder: Why does the proverbial wise man always live alone, away from the rest of the common villagers, high on a mountaintop in isolation?

Guilt, Conscience, Karma

It does not take many words to describe guilt and conscience. In essence, like empathy, guilt and conscience are special features of a human being, and the driving force behind them is the first-part. When you feel either of these emotions, what is happening is that your first-part is imparting to you a not-so-subtle message: you have wronged in some way. If, on the other hand, you don't have a conscience or you don't feel any guilt within you, it may mean you have reached Chisek's final cause. If this is not applicable to you, then every time you err, your first-part will activate the guilt emotion within you and you will have a guilty conscience.

Sometimes your actions warrant more than a play on your conscience. That old-fashioned saying, which came from someone wise, was not in vain:

> *When you dig a grave for someone else,*
> *Be sure to dig one next to it for yourself.*

Do you understand this saying? You may have to pay a greater price one day – whether in this life or the next – for your selfish actions. No action is ignored. Every action has a reaction. Every cause has an effect. Every ill deed carries a penalty of equal or greater value. These are the laws of the parts. This is the language of the parts. This ultimately means that next time you plan to do something to someone else – whatever the driving force may be, and no matter how small it may appear to you to be – you had better think of all the ramifications of how that one incident is going to affect not just the person in question, but all those around that person who unwittingly become affected. When you add all that up, you need to transfer those figures into your life's equation. This will come to equal only one thing: bad karma of much greater value will be coming your way when you least suspect it and in a way you fear most, if not in this life, when you stand on the judgment square at the door of the afterworld.

To put it bluntly, when you do a wrong to another, the first-part of that wronged person (sometimes even your first-part) creates and then sends a "black cloud" into your subconscious mind. This black cloud is then compressed and filed away, or, in computer terms, "zipped." Time is never an issue, because that black cloud remains idle, and it hangs over you, until one day when it is programmed to be unzipped and released. That black cloud will then come into play in your life – in this life, in the next life, or in both lives – in a way that is fitting and appropriate to you in view of the wrong you once upon a time did. It will always follow you, and it will one day be unleashed. If you have wronged someone with a well-developed part or many parts, then you have a big problem to worry about because sometimes those parts take note of and special interest in you – which is certainly not a good thing. If you have wronged many people, then you have a bigger problem because you will be harboring many black clouds, which will one day come together, just like their namesake in the weather cycle. What happens when many storm fronts collide and join is an indicator of what happens with your black clouds.

We should never forget one thing: the subtle twists, ironies, misfortunes, and bad luck in our lives are sometimes the "sport" and "games" some parts of Odo intentionally "play," with as much frivolity as we play chess or do crosswords. They do it with our lives, and *always* for a good reason. Just as knowledge has always been power; just as writing has always been might to the ancient scribe, nothing happens without reason: everything has a First Cause: nothing comes from nothing! And just as sure as the universe is both a nursery and a cemetery, every one of us is guaranteed to face the destiny of judgment and justice, and the penalties of judgment and justice!

17
Journeying into the Unknown

Why do we dream?
Where do our dreams come from?
How do we interpret the mysteries of sleep?
Sleep is one of the last, great unknown frontiers;
It is a dimension of
The terrifying, the tantalizing, the strange and bizarre, and portentousness.
No wonder man of all ages, customs, and beliefs
Has held a fascination for this magical world of "self-illumination"!
While many of our earliest forefathers understood this unknown,
Today it has become an ethereal realm,
One beyond our current science and wisdom.
This chapter will reawaken in us this lost wisdom,
And provide a new blueprint of the mind,
And that of the dimension of self-illumination.

Just as vessels of pottery are a part of an archaeological site, are many clay tables timeless archived narratives of dream interpretations. This is meaningful because it tells us that, just as stars were important and practical to the ancient world, so the state of dreaming was important and practical to the ancient world. This condition was the tie these ancient peoples had to the world beyond the circadian one they inhabited: the world they would one day make passage to: the world that was closely tied to gods they worshipped, who were somewhere in that mysterious backdrop of stars that blanketed their world.

We can trace the preoccupation with dreaming back to all cultures. *The Upanishads* is a legacy that documents such immersion. Oral traditions formed the basis of it, and these written traditions stated that in a sleep state the soul made a transition from the body that houses it to the halfway world where the spirits "reside." This legacy of ancient wisdom presents us with the idea that there are three conditions the human faces: this world, the next world, and sleep[vii].

Indigenous cultures believed that it was a nightly ritual for their souls to leave their bodies, and the dream was the physical record of such liberation of the soul. What this also meant was that the soul, in this liberated state, could communicate with the world of the spirits.

Many ancient cultures believed that it was to another state, beyond the realm of the physical world, that their souls were venturing into in the dream state, and this was not always a pleasant prospect. There were ominous connotations to this venturing of the soul in the territory of the dead. For instance, one fear was that if these people were abruptly awakened from a state of dreaming, their souls might not be able to return to their bodies.

Some of those ancient peoples who believed that the soul left the body while it was in a sleep state knew of two ways this was possible: involuntarily in the sleep cycle and voluntarily by means of astral travel. The students of Pythagoras, for instance, were taught the principles of leaving the body consciously (voluntarily).

Pythagoras also put to practice the philosophy known to the ancient Egyptian priests, the ancient Indians and Chinese, and many others from our erstwhile past. Indeed, the Pythagorean School trained its students to cultivate self control, which is another way of saying that the teachings of Pythagoras were training the human to conquer the meat-in-the-sandwich goal and reach the state of equilibrium. This would ultimately allow the student to be the master of his own temple of god – the mind; and master understanding truth – god. Such a student would then be able to "read" from the "closed book."

In the works of Plato, there is clear reference to a higher culture of people long before his time who guarded their secret wisdom; this is the wisdom he understood, and this wisdom is found in this book (the meat-in-the-sandwich goal).

People from our early great civilizations, such as the ancient Egyptians, thought that some types of dreams were a form of communication from the gods. For this reason, dreams were regarded as a form of prophecy. Practitioners, or interpreters of these divine messages, became adept at their craft.

The ancient Egyptians, and others such as the Greeks, even built dream temples that were meant to heal the sick. In these dream temples, or sleep temples, people could consult an expert on their dreams, or try to incubate dreams – that is, stimulate a dream to occur, one that would offer them guidance. This guidance could then help them to solve their problems, or even give them clues to their future. Even Hippocrates, the "father of medicine," trained at one of these dream temples and practiced dream therapy.

Dreams, a wise man once said, are the playground of the soul. We are about to see that they are so in more ways than one!

The Conscious and Subconscious Minds

Life is made from dreams,
And anybody who does not dream
Does not know the meaning of life.

-A wise man

There lies an unbounded universe, within the macrocosm of the brain, which ancient superstitions have rightly regarded as the playground of the soul: the mental frontier that is jealously sheltered by the bastion of the human brain. Our conquest of this unknown requires that we probe with our conscious minds into frontiers that our logic has so far not delved. Only then may we unravel, fragment by fragment, those pieces to that conundrum in which we must one day find our rightful place.

The foremost procedure we must take to understand the methods by which the human brain dreams during a sleep state is to acknowledge not only the unseen variable of the metaphysical being, but one of the most fundamental tenets of psychology: the existence of both the conscious and subconscious minds within the human brain. For it is these two minds, functioning within the brain, that form the nucleus of human consciousness, otherwise known as the metaphysical being, or the human intellect.

We have learned in past chapters that, in a non-physical state, these two metaphysical minds unify and become one vast abyss of knowledge: a concentrated knowledge of all the past lives as well as the current life of that intellect. However, upon beginning its physical existence (in other words, upon the birth of the physical body in which the intellect is to dwell), this intellect is inserted and stored within the subconscious mind of the brain, which has the physical capability of storing this vast accumulation of knowledge within it, unlike the conscious mind. The conscious mind from birth is thus meant to develop a fresh new consciousness, unhampered by its past conscious existences. Its purpose is to develop fresh cells within the conscious mind as the physical body develops, into which can be stored knowledge based on the intellect's new cycle of life. The involvement of the subconscious mind in the development of this virgin conscious intellect, and the interaction between the two, are the crucial factors in understanding the mechanism of dreams.

Upon examining the operation of the conscious mind within the human brain, one would find that the conscious mind possesses all the essential knowledge required for a human being's day-to-day survival needs. One could equate the conscious mind with the operating system of a computer. We already know that all other knowledge, including the lifetime of memories, is stored in the subconscious mind. One could then equate the subconscious mind with the hard-drive storage of a computer, with a significant difference being that knowledge from the subconscious mind is hardly accessible to the conscious mind. For the conscious mind to access knowledge from the subconscious mind it must have "highways" established between the two minds. All children do in a limited way, in one way or another, but these highways can disappear by adulthood. When these highways into the subconscious mind no longer exist, the human no longer has access to his subconscious knowledge. It is only because the conscious mind has not been designed to function as a storage area that the brain possesses a subconscious mind.

Although a human conscious mind has a limited capability to store data, it can function normally without access to its subconscious mind. Such human beings in this situation can be useful, but can never be as precise or capable as an intellect using the cooperation of, and interaction between, the conscious and subconscious minds. For, having no access to the subconscious mind is like operating a computer that has no built-in hard drive and, in some cases, has its operating system on a floppy disk! Some heavy drug users belong to this last category. Taking drugs can destroy cells storing knowledge in the conscious mind. Operating such a computer becomes a nuisance and waste of time, as one has to continuously insert floppy disks into the computer in order to retrieve and store temporarily the operating information into the limited memory space available. This type of person, without access to his subconscious mind and having destroyed cells in his conscious mind, could be said to think in only one "dimension," and is limited in terms of intellectual capabilities. Some people think in two dimensions, others in three dimensions, and some rare ones think in forty-nine dimensions and are capable of accessing and retrieving information from beyond this world we exist in. Unfortunately, at the present stage of our development on Earth, many humans only think in one- and two-dimensional spheres, which would explain why we have not been able to progress beyond the infant stage of our development.

Children, as we know, are generally born with the highways between their conscious and subconscious minds open, which is why they can absorb vast amounts of knowledge – more so than we have estimated. (This means crucial time is wasted in a child's life when learning should be stimulated and accelerated. Our entire system of education will one day be overhauled in light of this.) With time, these highways gradually decrease and, proportionally, so does learning ability. In effect, this is where the baby's or child's personality and instinct are drawn from. In other words, forty percent of who we are is shaped by our subconscious mind, where our past personalities and talents are stored.

The human brain, it can thus be determined, is the physical entity that facilitates the interaction of the non-physical entity with the physical world. For the human brain possesses all those facilities the intellect requires to function in the physical world. How the human brain then operates is by utilizing and manipulating to its advantage a biological form of energy, which hereon shall be referred to as "current energy." The two basic forms of energy in the body are aura and current energy. Kirlian photography has been able to identify the existence of aura, but it has not been able to identify the complete picture of aura; for Kirlian photography has only been able to identify the positive current of aura. In the human body, aura comes in a package of being in the plus and in the minus. No one even knows of – let alone has been able to find a means to measure – this negative energy to verify its existence.

Qualifying the distinction between current energy and aura is inevitable in understanding the roles they play within the human body. Aura, to begin with, is the prime source of energy within a life form that facilitates the existence of that life. Indeed, aura is the nucleus of all life forms within the universe. It is the energy that drives the life form and keeps it intact and functioning. In its role of providing an energy source to drive the human body, it fails to meet the demand of energy the brain places upon the body. That is, it is not strong enough to serve the brain in its energy requirements, as the brain requires a great deal of energy in order to perform its functions. It is here that the role of current energy may be explained. For current energy specifically meets the energy requirements of the brain, and is an additional source of energy in the human body that acts as a booster to aura.

Without current energy, the human brain would not be as functional as it is. This is because current energy serves in the operation of both the conscious and subconscious minds. This energy assists in many processes of the brain, such as the retrieval and storage of knowledge; the transmission of signals out of the brain; the reception of signals into the brain; and the visualization of signals coming into the brain. This energy enables the brain to operate at the speed of thought, with a range that is unlimited in terms of distance.

Current energy is derived from the sun. This energy source is unlike aura in that it never really depletes. Current energy is a form of electrical energy that can be measured under zero. Although the brain often utilizes more current energy for the functioning of the brain, current energy is not strictly confined to this one specific location. Sometimes another organ will require the use of this energy. Current energy is different from aura in that it satisfies different parts of the body only when it is necessary. For instance, if you are run down, have not eaten well, have not slept, and lack energy, it generally means your aura levels are depleted. When its levels are down, aura is unable to maintain the functioning of the body, as current energy is able to. In this crisis situation, current energy acts as a back-up source and will concentrate itself in those areas where it is needed, until such time as the body's aura levels are replenished. Correct diet and sleep usually build up aura levels. In this way, current energy is more powerful than the energy called aura.

We have determined that current energy is a source of fuel to primarily facilitate the functioning of the brain. We have also determined that current energy has no requirement for recharging. Aura differs in this regard, in that it is constantly being used and is limited. The physical need for the body to recharge its aura levels depends on the individual; the brain determines the period required for it to rejuvenate. Sleep is a manifestation of this requirement. The principle of recharging the body is the same as that of recharging a battery. The state of sleep also happens to be the most fascinating area that many humans have attempted to explore, to understand, to map, and to place in the human book of knowledge to be understood by all who wish to discover it.

The roots of why the human brain, or that of any life form, functions in a state of sleep to produce a second, three-dimensional existence (a dream), and is able to exist in a conscious-minded state in this existence, will be analyzed in this next section.

The Meadow of Dreaming

In our poignant endeavor to unravel the process by which dreams occur, we have been able to progress little further than to define the physiological factors relating to a human in a state of sleep. Through our laboratory research, we have come to define two distinctive states of a human sleep: non-rapid eye movement (NREM), and rapid eye movement (REM). When the sleep state was scientifically monitored, bursts of rapid eye movement were found to periodically occur during the sleep cycle. Upon further examination, scientists surmised that there was an interrelationship between this eye movement and dreaming. Physiological observations, such as monitoring eye movements and reading brain wave patterns, confirmed their suspicions and provided evidence of contrasting characteristics that corresponded to each of these two sleep states.

When a person goes to sleep, observation has shown that there are several stages of NREM sleep. Stage 1 is where a person relaxes and then falls to sleep. Alpha and then theta brain waves are characteristic in this stage. Stage 2 is where a person has fallen asleep. Theta brain waves are characteristic in this stage. Stage 3 is where a person has fallen into a deep sleep. Delta brain waves are characteristic in this stage.

Before entering REM sleep, which is the stage in which a person dreams, a person reverses from the deep-sleep phase of stage 3 to the lighter-sleep phase of stage 2. The first REM sleep that follows can last for around ten minutes, so that the complete NREM and REM sleep cycle is said to last on average around one hundred minutes. After this REM sleep, a person starts a new NREM / REM sleep cycle by reverting to stage 2 of NREM sleep. This pattern is said to occur quite a few times during the sleep cycle (around five times a night). The further into the sleep cycle, however, the shorter the periods of slow-wave sleep (stage 3 of NREM sleep) and the longer the periods of REM sleep. Studying these two states of sleep will give us an understanding of dreams.

Distinctive changes between NREM and REM sleep can be found when brain wave patterns, eye movements, and muscle tension are measured. Electroencephalography (EEG, measures brain waves), electrooculography (EOG, measures eye movements), and electromyography (EMG, measures muscle activity), are the techniques for recording these measurements.

In NREM sleep, EEG readings show a characteristic brain wave pattern of slow (low-frequency), large (high-amplitude) waves, which is different from the brain wave pattern occurring in the waken state; EOG readings show minimal eye fluctuation; and EMG readings show muscle relaxation.

In REM sleep, EEG readings show a characteristic brain wave pattern of fast (high-frequency), small (low-amplitude) waves, which is similar to the brain wave pattern occurring in the waken state; EOG readings show rapid fluctuations of the eyes; and EMG readings show inhibition (paralysis) of the major muscle groups.

It is in REM sleep that other characteristic physiological changes occur. Breathing and pulse rates become irregular, the body temperature changes, blood pressure increases, the heart rate goes up, and small twitches in smaller muscular groups such as the toes, fingers, and face occur. (You can see some of these same physiological manifestations in your pets when they sleep – and dream!) This is the state in which dreams occur.

It has been speculated that these changes to the physical body in REM sleep are a physiological response to what the person dreaming is visualizing or experiencing. This becomes more than speculation when you learn that there are identified cases where a person's brain fails to paralyze its skeletal muscular system in REM sleep. Some individuals with such a disorder have given strong evidence of acting out their dreams during sleep, and when they wake up after a night of sleep they are unaware of any of those actions (which can be an unhealthy exercise). This is not the same as sleepwalking, as sleepwalking usually occurs in NREM sleep, where the muscular skeletal system is not inhibited. It would be logical, then, to assume that why the mechanism of the brain deliberately undergoes a process where it inhibits muscular movements is to prevent the body from acting out the dream. You may have even experienced an occasion where you have woken up from REM sleep and found your body paralyzed for a few moments, where your body and brain did not synchronize simultaneously. Because of this paralysis, and because the body expresses physiological responses in REM sleep which are similar to when it is in a waken state, it would be logical to conclude that the body is responding to what is occurring in the dream.

We know that what promotes a sleep cycle within the human body is the requirement of the human body to rest and replenish its energy levels. In order to achieve this, the conscious mind stops using most of its energy. In the last phase of NREM sleep, the conscious mind is in a state of "low gear" and requires very little energy to run. In this sleep phase, the body would have reached the peak of its aura levels. Aura has several functions to perform in the body – two of which are to repair and rejuvenate the body, and in its abundance in this slow-wave sleep phase aura is able to perform these crucial functions. This may explain why the initial stage 3 of NREM sleep is the longest.

In NREM sleep, the conscious mind has no need to use the energy called current energy (because of the inactivity of the conscious mind). This concentration of energy within an inactive brain tends to overflow into the subconscious mind. It is like water that overflows into oil and then separates back again. For, upon the body's waking, this energy is automatically drawn back by the conscious mind. In the process, however, it separates from memories in the subconscious mind. The interplay between current energy and the subconscious mind is the cause of one type of dream that occurs in NREM sleep. Eye movements may occur here because of this interplay, but there would not be any rapid eye movement. Any eye movement would be slow, and this "slowness" has to do with the relative time factor, which will be understood later in this chapter. This form of dream is usually vaguely recollected upon waking, and almost always forgotten rapidly. This is because the "water" (current energy that is drawn back to the conscious mind) has separated from the "oil" (the subconscious knowledge). In short, current energy creates a bridge between the two minds in this state. Upon waking, the bridge retreats.

The subconscious mind is unlike the conscious mind in that it requires very little energy to operate and thus remains active 24 hours a day – that is, it never shuts down as the conscious mind does (as in NREM sleep). It may, however, be described as an intelligence in its own right, without the physical capability to "express" itself as the conscious mind has, so to express itself it ventures out of the physical body when the body is in a sleep state. The subconscious mind makes this decision to leave the brain because it feels imprisoned there and has a strong desire to venture out from it. Thus, the conscious mind reigns in the waken state, while the subconscious mind reigns in the sleep state.

When encased in the human brain, in its subconscious state, the subconscious mind has no need for aura apart from having just enough to stay there idly, whereas the conscious mind does require aura. As the conscious mind is charged with aura, especially during its spell of inactivity in NREM sleep, where its levels are replenished, the subconscious mind makes an intelligent decision to take whatever it can of the conscious mind with it when it leaves the brain, and in the process it takes a proportional amount of aura with it – which is the whole point of taking the conscious mind. (The subconscious mind does not have independent access to the body's aura.)

The Upanishads has described a person in the third intermediate state – the state of sleep – as being "self-illuminated." This book has thus defined the condition where portions of the subconscious and conscious minds are in the intermediate state as being the "self-illuminated mind," or SIM as an abbreviation. Furthermore, this book describes the portion of subconscious mind that has left the brain as being the "roaming subconscious mind," or RSM as an abbreviation, and the portion of conscious mind that has left as being the "roaming conscious mind," or RCM as an abbreviation.

Since the subconscious mind simply does not have the energy requirements to leave the brain on its own, it waits for a peak in the body's aura levels before it leaves, as aura is the determining factor in its ability to leave. This peak occurs in stage 3 of NREM sleep. The more aura (and thus conscious mind) the RSM takes, the further it can travel and the longer it can venture out. In such an outing from the brain, the SIM expends a lot of energy – this is why it has limitations in terms of distance and time. It is only because it is tied to a physical body that such limitations exist. Without a tie to a physical body, the soul has no constraints and limitations – death is such a condition. When the energy levels begin to diminish, the SIM returns to the brain, in which case the NREM sleep cycle begins once again and the body's aura levels are once again replenished. This pattern continues during the night, with each successive REM period lasting progressively longer, and NREM period lasting progressively shorter. The concentration of aura in the body; the body's ability to replenish aura more readily as the sleep cycle progresses; and the body's tapering need to repair and rejuvenate the body as the sleep cycle progresses, determine the length of each NREM and REM cycle.

What percentage of the conscious mind the RSM takes is governed by how charged the physical body is with aura. Given the body is charged with the related amount of aura, the RSM is capable of taking anything up to 80 percent of the conscious mind, in which case the RCM will be astral traveling unwillingly (which is unlike deliberate astral travel attempts). In this situation, a person will feel as if he is in a conscious state of existence by up to 80 percent, but in an unconscious sphere of existence. In relation to the proportion of the subconscious mind that leaves the body, the average amount is 60 percent. There are times when only 20 percent leaves, and other times when 80 percent leaves. The proportion that leaves is also dependent on the health and strength of the body, which are indicators of aura levels, and all this determines the vividness of dreams.

The vividness or detail of the dream is therefore proportional to the relative amount of aura, conscious mind, and subconscious mind that leaves the body. If the ratio is high on all three counts, the waking conscious mind would most likely vividly recollect the occurrence of the dream. In relation to the RCM, if a higher proportion leaves the brain in any instance, the recollected events of the dream could be such that the human could become temporarily confused and disoriented, and not able to differentiate between a state of waken consciousness and a state of dreaming. Furthermore, the RSM may be different each time it leaves the brain. We know that the subconscious mind is an intellect in its own right, with its own independent thinking. Each time it leaves, it takes a different composition of intellect and thus "acts" differently. This also applies to the RCM. This process is entirely a natural one.

This venturing out of the self-illuminated mind in REM sleep is the cause for all the body's physiological manifestations in this cycle, such as rapid eye movement. This cycle is characterized by fast and small (high-frequency, low-amplitude) brain waves. How we can interpret this brain wave reading is straightforward. The fast, small brain wave pattern of REM sleep is indicative of high brain activity – the neurons in the brain are active and are firing at a fast rate. This neural activity in the brain is analogous with the subconscious and conscious activity described above – that is, a portion of the subconscious mind (RSM) has left the physical body with as much of the conscious mind and aura as it is capable of taking. As energy in the form of aura has been taken out of the body and is being utilized by the subconscious activity, progressively this energy diminishes. A new NREM cycle is then needed to replenish such energy loss.

In contrast, NREM sleep is characterized by a pattern of slow and large (low-frequency, high-amplitude) brain waves, which is indicative of inactivity of the brain – the neurons are less active and are firing at a slower rate than in REM sleep. Because of the inactivity of the conscious mind and the brain itself, there would be a progressive increase in the concentration of energy in the form of aura in the body. This means the conscious mind has not left the physical body (and is inactive).

Now, what has been established here is that the self-illuminated mind is a combination of aura, a portion of the subconscious mind, and a portion of the conscious mind. What occurs with the SIM that has left the brain while it is in REM sleep is that it interacts with other SIMs being projected out from other brains also in REM sleep. This dimension of the dream becomes a strange cycle where dominance in terms of aura levels and the interaction of different SIMs become the prevailing themes. For this is the cycle where a SIM becomes active in the halfway meadow during the third intermediate state (sleep). Even though this activity is occurring beyond the physical brain, the SIM remains tied metaphysically and physiologically to its physical brain. This external activity involves the SIM entering a dimension of interaction with other SIMs. This interaction is the intrusion of one SIM into another SIM. Intrusion means one SIM has delved into the knowledge of another SIM. In the cycle of the dream, someone's SIM is able to peer in on your memories, with the reverse also applicable. On the part of the subconscious mind, this is part of the allure of leaving the brain; when restricted in the confines of a brain the subconscious mind does not have this freedom of acquiring new knowledge.

If you recall, in the last chapter this book referred to the subconscious mind as contributing to the stockpile of knowledge that is accumulating in your subconscious storage bank. This storage bank is augmented throughout your many lives, waiting for that great day when you succeed in being able to access it – which is when you conquer the meat-in-the-sandwich goal. This is exactly what is happening every night when you dream. Your subconscious mind is fulfilling a crucial role toward this end. One day you will be able to take pride in knowing that you were largely responsible for all the knowledge you possess. No other phase of humans can lay claim to this. All highly developed humans were given knowledge directly into their non-partitioned minds from the Creators, which they were able to draw on and access. They all started out with highly developed brains. They did not acquire knowledge the hard way. This is what makes primitive civilizations throughout the universe such as ours unique, and fascinating to study.

Let this book describe in detail this interaction of self-illuminated minds. When one SIM has stronger aura levels than the SIM it has interacted with, then that dominant SIM would become part of the weaker SIM for a few seconds or more. The length of time the interaction occurs is at the discretion of the dominant SIM, which is related to how much information is available in the weaker SIM. For, it is in this time that the dominant SIM would have peered into, and selectively copied whatever information it desired from, the knowledge possessed by the weaker SIM. The weaker SIM cannot peer into and copy the knowledge of a stronger SIM. When the SIM returns to its brain, this copied information is pasted into the subconscious mind. In this "outing" from the brain, a SIM may interact with many SIMs, and either be the dominant one or be the weaker one. As the SIM's aura levels diminish, it is more likely to be the weaker SIM. This cycle may repeat many times over in each REM sleep cycle. (This book should mention here that a highly developed first-part will never allow the SIM of its human counterpart to be copied in this cycle.)

A SIM, we must bear in mind, is a selection of knowledge based on memories of lives – this includes one's past lives and present life, or other people's lives. If we imagine one's subconscious mind as being a "tape recording" or "movie" of one's entire existence since one's initial creation, which may go back hundreds of lives (if not more), then we can qualify the source of the material found in dreams.

We know that the RSM leaves the body because it wants to acquire new knowledge and learn, and it can do this through the content of other people's SIMs. Sometimes a SIM with which it comes into contact could reveal a human's secrets, or even a secret formula that the human is working on as a project. Sometimes it looks for a SIM that contains answers to solve problems its human counterpart may have. Many people, including some famous historical ones, have been known to find answers to problems, or have had ideas come to them, from their dreams.

A SIM doesn't specifically plan to seek out someone else's SIM; it is all a natural process. However, every SIM wants to be the dominant party so that it can obtain knowledge that can benefit its human counterpart. These SIMs, by the way, don't see each other; they sense each other's presence. Inevitably, once the two SIMs have interacted, the dominant SIM selectively copies the relevant data found in the weaker SIM. This weaker SIM wants to free itself from this process, but it cannot until the dominant party has completed copying and releases it. In each case, the physical body is experiencing REM sleep.

Now, we know that in REM sleep a portion of the subconscious mind has left the physical brain and has taken a portion of the conscious mind. The question then arises of what dreams constitute. The SIM that has left the body is merely a collection of memories: memories of all the lives that person has ever lived, and memories of other people's lives. These memories are just like movies or tape recordings. The portion of the conscious mind to have left (the RCM) becomes integrated into these storylines to a degree and it "participates" in them, by seeing them and by becoming a part of them. Different storylines may become intertwined or mixed up, depending on which memories have left the brain. This participation of the RCM in these memories becomes the source of dreams for the dreamer in the REM sleep state. In other words, the dream is what the RCM is seeing and experiencing.

The RSM, of course, is in control when it takes the RCM with it. This RCM is only there because of the source of aura that it brings with it. During this activity, which occurs externally from the brain, the RSM "tucks away" the RCM in these memories. The RCM has no bearing on what the RSM does in this domain. It is only because a portion of the conscious mind is present with a portion of the subconscious mind that dreams even exist at all in REM sleep.

The RCM becomes integrated into a collection of memories. What the RCM sees and becomes a part of then become the content of the dream. The RCM virtually steps into mixed-up movies and participates in them. To the RCM it is no different from stepping into the holodeck in the *Star Trek Next Generation* series. The holodeck is a programmed movie of its own. Imagine if bits of many programs were jumbled up and running at the same time, and you stepped into that program. That is exactly what the RCM is doing when it is with the RSM.

In the case where the SIM has copied movies from another source, the RCM may then become a part of these movies. This means that the RCM assumes a character role in the storyline of one of the copied movies. These copied movies may then integrate with a part of the RSM's own movies, and the resultant dream being experienced by the dreamer is the mixture of all these movies. The dreamer's portion of conscious mind (RCM) that has left is now a first-person participant in the knowledge.

For instance, let us say your SIM interacted with the SIM of someone responsible for the death of a famous person – perhaps a famous princess! Let us say that the memories which left this person contained the knowledge of what he did to that famous person. Your SIM would most definitely have hit the jackpot and copied this information. Your RCM would then be in the memory of the event where that famous person died. Your RCM would participate in the scene and watch the event in some capacity. You would translate your RCM's activity as a dream. When your SIM makes such a find, your first-part usually wakes you up just after this dream so that you recollect it. Now you have solved the mystery of how that person died! Would other people believe you if you told them? These days, probably not. Back in the ancient world, they would have. Now you can understand why they were so fascinated with dream incubation. And this tells you that there is no such thing as taking a secret with you to the grave!

Things become even more illogical when many SIMs from many different people interact at the same time. This becomes confusing, but the principle is based on the above scenario where dominance of SIMs plays a role in determining who copies whose knowledge and who does not. (This accounts for how people may share the same dream.) The illogical state of events that can then occur in the mixture of those memories can make the dream content look absolutely ridiculous and bizarre. The more complex the interactions that occur at any one time among SIMs (based on the quantity of SIMS interacting), the more varied the dream experience in terms of its content for the dreamer.

This second, three-dimensional existence (the dream state), where the self-illuminated mind is free to behave independently, is a bizarre world to try to explain in terms that we can logically comprehend, because it delves into the difficult-to-prove world of the illogical. Furthermore, it is here in this dream state that your first-part transmits messages to you that become relayed to you by way of a dream. This usually occurs in the final REM sleep so that you remember the dream, or it is the one you usually wake up from and vividly recollect.

It should be noted that it is possible to find humans who are unable to dream when in a state of sleep. This is for one reason: aura is a crucial factor that enables this activity to occur beyond the brain. Some brains are not sophisticated in terms of possessing a strong enough aura. Intelligence levels, possessing Chisek's aura, or being sick (in which case you possess a weak aura), plays a role in determining aura levels. Sick people tend to have weak auras.

There is a variation to the above-mentioned venturing out of self-illuminated minds; however, it is extremely rare. In this instance, a SIM interacts not with another SIM, but with a brain that is not in a sleep state. A strong SIM is capable of interacting and locking on to someone else's mind that is in a waken state. The waken person could be anywhere. Distance is not a consideration, as travel occurs at the speed of thought. For a few seconds of that waken person's life, the strong SIM would be capable of copying information from his brain. The waken person would neither be aware of, nor be affected by, this.

In some rare cases, a SIM is able to enter a waken, conscious mind and "invade" it. The brain of this waken person would temporarily become a mixed personality; if that brain was so receptive in that it was capable of receiving more SIMs than one, it could then become a multiple personality. (This is when a SIM takes over the conscious state of a waken brain and dictates its behavior; although rare, it does occur.) This brings up fascinating and far-reaching implications for a person's temporary insanity; how this can occur is discussed in detail further within this chapter.

Understanding what occurs in REM sleep helps interpret the physiological changes that occur in the human body during REM sleep. Just as the conscious mind has a connection to the physical body in the waken state, so the roaming conscious mind (RCM) has a connection to the physical body in REM sleep. It is only because the body deliberately and automatically paralyzes the skeletal muscular system, when the SIM leaves, that the physical body does not act out the dream. In some ways, there is not a lot of difference between REM sleep and the waken state. In REM sleep a percentage of the conscious mind is active; in the waken state one hundred percent of the conscious mind is active. The physical body is responsive to the actions of the active portion of the conscious mind, irrespective of which state it is in: the waken state or the REM (dream) state. This is why the pulse and heart rates elevate, the breathing becomes irregular, and the eye movements occur. If a portion of the conscious mind were not taken with the roaming subconscious mind (RSM), the human would not dream, and any of the associated physiological responses detected in the physical body in REM sleep would have no basis to manifest themselves.

The physiological changes to the physical body that occur during REM sleep are merely a response to the remote viewing encounter. Remote viewing here refers to the RCM that has left the physical body and is viewing the events occurring elsewhere in the dream state. This tells us that the eyes function not just to the waken and active conscious mind in the first, three-dimensional existence (the waken state), but to the "waken" and active portion of conscious mind (the RCM) that has left with the RSM in the second, three-dimensional existence (the dream state). For, the eyes are "viewing" the events "sympathetically" to what the RCM is encountering.

The timeframe of the dream state is at variance with the timeframe of the waken state. Time here is a confusing concept because not only is it relative, but it doesn't really exist as we know it to exist. The dream, as it takes place, appears to last for hours and even days; yet in the timeframe of the waken state the dream only appears to last minutes. Here we have a paradox. The eyes view the events of the dream state in such a way that the eye movements correlate to the timeframe of that existence. However, in the timeframe of the waken state the movements do not correlate. The eye movements are relative to the cycle of the dream state, which exists at a faster speed. This accounts for the rapid eye movement in the slow timeframe of the waken state. Similarly, the rest of the physiological responses are a reaction to the events happening to the RCM, while it has ventured out and interacted with the memories and knowledge taken out of the brain by the RSM. This time difference also accounts for the intensity of some of the body's physiological responses that can occur, and the heightened or magnified emotions and feelings that can occur. Many weakened physical bodies do not cope and as a result die during sleep.

Several of the physiological changes that occur within the human body during the sleep cycle have been explained above, but a much misunderstood change has to do with the body's hormones. When the RSM returns to the brain after venturing out, and returns to the conscious mind the unspent energy (aura) it borrowed from it before it ventured out, the body receives a sudden surge of this energy, and can become overwhelmed with sexual arousal.

In summary, dreams, occurring in REM sleep, are a direct result of the RCM (roaming conscious mind), under the control of the RSM (roaming subconscious mind), leaving the physical body and:

1. Interacting with, participating in, and experiencing, its own memories or those memories copied from other self-illuminated minds.
2. Interacting with, and participating in, externally copied information or memories from another person's brain who is in a waken state somewhere, without influencing this individual.
3. Temporarily dwelling within another person's brain somewhere and actually influencing this individual; for the RCM participates in the person's real-life actions. The person who was invaded would not recollect the events that occurred while the invasion was in progress.

Now we can account for how a person could be able to predict events of the future, such as a murder going to take place. It would also explain how a person could see such an event having already taken place. Either of these is achievable when a person in REM sleep has his self-illuminated mind interact with, and see events through, another person's mind and eyes, the knowledge of which is then brought back to this dreamer's own mind, registered in the form of a dream. There are many variables in this illogical world of the sleep state.

Inspiration and Talent

People who truly have the mental capacity to foreknow things, good or bad, or just imbue wisdom that can foster the self-preservation and salvation of the humans of the time, are extremely rare. Some remarkable people, throughout history, have been intentionally gifted with the ability to receive messages, or signals, from positive-parts (such as directly from Odo).

Interestingly enough, positive-parts often transmit signals of events that are to occur to humans capable of receiving such signals. Moses was one such human. Traveling through the desert, Moses once said, "We shall reach water in a few hours if we travel in this direction." His own life, and the lives of all those who followed him, depended on his being correct. When they arrived at the forecast destination, there was a spring exactly where he had predicted it to be. Such men become idolized as prophets. There are some great men chronicled in times gone by who had well-developed brains that were capable of being guided by positive-parts.

Inspiration may occur for ordinary humans on a less significant basis, particularly through dreams. Many dreams are inspired by first-parts. On a practical level, these dreams may reflect different states of a person's life, or impending changes to a person's life – often involving sickness, death, career paths, progress, and so on. These dreams appear as cryptic puzzles, as their meanings are disguised in the language of the riddle of the dream. Most dreams are indecipherable to humans. Unraveling the riddle usually becomes easier after the dream occurs. Inspiration, then, is really another name for positive-parts because they are the source of all inspiration, one way or another.

The reason dreams are a method of inspiration and a means to convey messages is that there is often no other avenue available to the first-part. Inspiration cannot be attained by any other means if there are not enough cells available in your conscious mind for new knowledge. Without available conscious cells, your first-part cannot communicate to you directly, in the same way it can through your dreams.

Inspiration that is passed into a conscious mind where cells are temporarily available is usually forgotten rapidly, in the same way that dreams are rapidly forgotten. If you are trying to solve some perplexity, sometimes you can receive a burst of knowledge that stays in your conscious mind for only a few fleeting seconds. In those moments you may attempt to transfer this data onto paper because you can feel the knowledge slipping away. As suddenly as the knowledge came, the knowledge leaves. Now you have to attempt to recover the knowledge you lost, in the same way you often try to recover the details of a dream that you have just forgotten. This is a clear case of your first-part transmitting to you the desired knowledge to solve your problem. There is a dilemma in that you cannot retain the knowledge as you do not have the cells available to keep the knowledge. (The knowledge may have been stored temporarily in a "dying cell." Dying cells are explained later in this chapter.) This is why the knowledge disappears almost instantly. Many would be familiar with this. Some people write poetry and stories this way. For a few moments the entire story can be received in the conscious mind in one burst of energy, and then it disappears for good. (This burst of energy has come in the form of the Universal Language.) It is then up to the person to retrieve this knowledge, piece by piece, from the subconscious mind, where it retreated when the conscious mind was incapable of keeping it.

Talents are distinct from inspiration, and they can have their source in the person's subconscious mind. The first-part is usually the one to open a channel between the two minds and then allow the inward flow of talent. This means that if you as a child show inherent ability in a particular field such as art, it is possible that in one of your past lives you were an artist. Your first-part has either allowed this knowledge into your conscious mind, or helped open a channel to this knowledge. When you have this open channel between your two minds, your conscious mind would be able to retrieve this knowledge directly from your subconscious mind.

Another possibility is that your first-part, or even your self-illuminated mind, has copied someone else's artistic talents, which it then downloaded into your subconscious mind. Perhaps your SIM discovered the reincarnation of a classical great, like Rembrandt, and was able to copy and download his knowledge and talent. This is one of the goals of the roaming subconscious mind when it leaves the brain.

Research into the brain wave frequencies of a human suggests there is a relationship between brain wave activity and the state of the mind. There are four main types of brain waves: Beta, Alpha, Theta, and Delta. When an EEG is wired up to the brain, it measures the voltage of the electrical impulses in the brain. Beta brain waves occur when we are mentally active, alert, agitated, stressed, or aroused. Alpha brain waves occur when we are calm and relaxed, such as when we are in a meditative state or even when we are going for a peaceful walk. Theta brain waves occur when we are about to fall asleep and during sleep, and when daydreaming. Delta brain waves occur in our deepest sleep.

Whenever we research brain wave frequencies and their relationship with the state of mind (particularly when researching talented people in order to ascertain the correlation between talent and brain wave frequency), we need to consider the balancing parts. For, you can be depressed and still be in an alpha wave state. Just because you are in an alpha wave state it does not by any means suggest that you are in a positive frame of mind. This is because you can in this state have your negative-part at the control helm of your brain and have the negative aura embrace you.

To be able to develop better communication channels with the subconscious mind (where talent lies) and with the positive-part (which is your intuition), you need to use your positive-part overwhelmingly more than you use the negative-part. This means you need a calm demeanor. This is when channels of communication can open; so this, along with the strength (intelligence level) of your first-part and even the number of positive-parts you have, is an underlying factor that needs to be evaluated in those moments of great talent, when one researches talented people and the frequencies of their brain waves.

As you progress through life, the first-part is there to aid you, so when it sees that you are working hard to achieve a goal, it will provide positive, beneficial assistance to you in every way it can. Ultimately, it opens doors for you. It makes those coincidences and good luck encounters for you. It transfers knowledge from your subconscious mind to your conscious mind. It is the one to provide you with inspiration and talent. It can be reasoned that it cannot provide you with inspiration and talent when you are stressed, anxious, or worried. You need to invoke the right frame of mind to allow the inward flow of inspiration and talent – a positive one.

THE FIRST CAUSE

The main secret to some exceptional artists, writers, athletes, comedians, and so on, is that beyond their hard work, determination, and self control of the negative-part within them, their positive-part has developed in the field that commanded the person's attention and dedication. For instance, in the case of the performance of a superior athlete, the first-part virtually "takes control" of the athlete in the athletic performance; it is the inspiration and the "magic" behind the performance. It computes mathematically in the brain the coordinating movements, maneuvers, and precision responses. It is like having a computer (which is what the part is in a way) take over your body, in silent partnership with you, dictating (or rather, mathematically coordinating) your actions. In essence, this is what is happening without your being aware of it.

The artist, whose strokes come from inspired hand movements, owes the magic of the art to the positive-part within him. The poet who invokes "ready-made" poetry from his mind, without any thought process, may have his positive-part developed in this field that puts the words together and relays them to his conscious mind in the form of a poem. The first-part is often working with your past-life talent. The ideal frame of mind is the state where your first-part, which is well developed in a particular field and can access talent from your subconscious mind, and you are "one" in a given moment. This is what is known as being "in the zone."

An obvious example can be found in one of our male golfers. This person was brought up with the right mental focus and mental training from a young age, which enabled him to predominate in the game. With the right mental focus and training, his first-part developed in a way that has enabled him to excel in his game. In the right mental environment (a positive one), his first-part provides confidence and fearlessness to this golfer. The final cause of all these ingredients is overwhelmingly great sporting achievement. When you are in the zone, it means you are in tune with the positive-part. Indeed, it means you have become one with the positive-part at that moment. We have heard of many artists, such as musicians, putting themselves in the zone before and during their performance. Now we can attribute a definition to this term. This sums up how ultimate achievement and greatness are forged in a human.

Let us take the instance of a man who was considered a genius on the stage in terms of his singing and dancing. He was a genius in his last life, with a first-part that was well developed in his field. The evolution of this soul was such that his first-part activated his talent from a young age. The gift was obvious to all who beheld him. The first-part in his case did not have to start from scratch and develop the talent, as in the case of the golfer earlier mentioned. This human had the talent already at hand, waiting to be activated in the right environment. (His conscious mind was open to his past-life talent in his subconscious mind, and he was "one" with the first-part in his performances.) The three wise men called fate gave him that environment by putting his soul in a family where his talent would excel. Excel it did. This is why those who saw him perform as a child saw the contradiction of an old soul in the body of a child.

More than ninety-nine percent of humans take to the grave only one positive-part – the one given to them at birth. (First-parts, of course, have varying degrees of development.) Mozart took to his grave a second positive-part. Tchaikovsky took only one – his chosen style of life prevented him from developing a second one. This was well developed, however. Einstein took a second positive-part, which he developed from scratch in the course of his life. (Just for reference, these talented humans were not one of those wise men this book speaks of who have a first-generation intellect from Odo.) If, in his next life, Einstein followed his instincts and was given the opportunity, that second intellect would be reactivated and he would once again excel in the same field. If this was not his destiny, that additional positive-part would remain deactivated all his life. Perhaps he would have entered a different field of study. Life's circumstances and challenges play a deciding role in your passage through life.

In an earlier chapter this book described how Leonardo da Vinci had up to one-hundred positive-parts. This book also explained that once you create those parts they follow you from life to life. In the case of Leonardo da Vinci, when he was reincarnated in the body of William Shakespeare, those positive-parts automatically followed him. They remained inactive until his brain reactivated them. How they became reactivated was by William Shakespeare's lust for knowledge and appetence to learn. His first-part automatically ensured this occurred. This is why William Shakespeare had such depths in his understanding of the human condition.

These positive-parts, once activated, then work with the human – under the administration of the first-part – to advance that human in the path he is destined to take.

THE FIRST CAUSE

If we go back to Plato, Leonardo, and Shakespeare, their soul had parts developed for different subjects. Among many, there were the mathematical, the scientific, the writing, and the artistic parts. This is what you can call a universal man. Shakespeare could just as easily have been famous in whatever field he chose to pursue, because all he had to do was activate the relevant part. His subconscious mind possessed as much knowledge as any intellect could ever hope to possess, on every subject.

This shows us that positive-parts are just evolved software packages, or chips of intelligence. This also shows us that as well as having subconscious knowledge, we need to possess these software chips called positive-parts. When we achieve equilibrium, we will not only access our subconscious knowledge, but also have the necessary corresponding positive-parts.

•⁓

There are so many little oddities in this life; luck and chance occurrence are just two that we are yet to demystify. Yet they abound in our lives, with neither a why nor a wherefore. But for every why there is a because; for every wherefore there is a therefore. That our experiences in life are so rich and varied there is no doubt. That our experiences are not by the hand of fate there is always doubt. The question then persists: what are luck and chance occurrence?

A famous psychiatrist coined the term "synchronicity" to describe coincidence and chance occurrence. If you are one of those people who attribute the mechanism of synchronicity to some higher agent of intellect, then you are right. These agents are parts: positive-parts or negative-parts. Just as your positive-part is often the word for luck and lucky coincidences, so your negative-part is often the word for bad luck and unlucky coincidences. One of your parts has just opened a door for you so that your destiny is able to follow its expected course. These positive-parts have been coined "Snoopers." Dare I say, Jack and I freely use this term to describe them, but for the sake of appearances, this book has tried to find a term at which academics would be less inclined to giggle!

Telepathy and Prophetic Dreams

Just as mail and phone are means by which humans communicate,
Dreams and the inner voice are the means by which the metaphysical
communicates.

Every brain can transmit signals in millions of frequencies. Your first-part selects the frequency a brain is working on, it picks up its transmission, and then it redirects that transmission into your mind in one of two ways: either directly in your conscious mind, if you have enough developed cells to receive the knowledge (direct telepathy); or directly in your subconscious mind, which can then be relayed to you by way of a dream. This last point was briefly mentioned earlier, and it often occurs in your last REM sleep cycle, from which you usually wake up.

In just the same way, the first-part can transmit signals out of your brain in millions of frequencies. This enables other brains to pick up one of them. Humans do not have this part of their brains developed in this way at this stage of their development – it is for most a rare event that they occasionally transmit or pick up signals. The best example of the latter is upon the death of someone you know. Upon this person's death, his first-part possesses enough energy now to emit a strong transmission to everyone relevant that he has passed away. In those moments, we can either dream about the person, or feel that person in some way.

If two frequencies interact, for us this generally means the two first-parts have interacted. When P3V2 humans (us on Earth) are able to "open up" their subconscious minds, when they conquer the meat-in-the-sandwich goal, they will be able to use telepathy. A superior human, such as the P3V1 human, only has one large conscious mind. This human has no restrictions when it comes to storing knowledge and is therefore able to use telepathy for communication purposes. Communication is a form of knowledge, and a brain must be in possession of storage facilities to receive any knowledge based on mental communication. Because our conscious mind has a limited storage capacity, we have no empty cells in our conscious mind for telepathic knowledge to be stored.

In developed civilizations, where humans do have these capabilities, close family members or attachments have their frequencies blocked so that they cannot read one another's minds, apart from what they want to be read. (This applies for only as long as they stay close. If the ties are severed, the frequencies automatically become unblocked.) This will satisfy emotional concerns, as it would be disastrous for relationships if one could know the thought processes going on in a loved one's mind. As civilizations develop, this becomes less important, and eventually unnecessary. To backward, primitive humans like us it would be a violation not to have the sanctity of the privacy of the mind – and it doesn't take a rocket scientist to figure out why!

One day in the future, the one governing body (which will replace governments as we know them today) of our planet *will be* honest and without corruption, and this will only be possible because the human mind will be transparent to others when it comes to the business of governance. For, a human in such a position of responsibility will be unable to deceive the masses because of this; politicians will *never* be able to treat those they govern as they do today and get away with it. It should be said that *they only get away with it* in human terms, because nobody gets away with anything in the long run. All humans face their day of reckoning before the one who gave them free will to choose their moral paths.

The basis of how telepathy works amongst primitive intellects like us is not hard to understand. If a person talks or thinks about you, those signals exist for your brain to receive – but only if you have a first-part that is developed enough and you have developed enough cells in your conscious mind to receive knowledge. If those thoughts were able to go directly into your conscious mind, because you have free cells available to accept the storage of knowledge, you will know those thoughts instantly. Superior humans will transmit words, and will hear those words in their minds when they practice telepathy for communication, just as if they were having an old-fashioned, primitive verbal communication. Then there is a different form of telepathy. Instead of words, you will feel that person's thoughts – this is referring to the usage of the Universal Language of the gods. You will become them for a split second and know their thoughts on a particular line of thought only.

A basic form of telepathy that most humans experience every now and then is when you think about someone and a few moments later that person contacts you. Here, your first-part was capable of picking up that person's frequency of transmission, which was then relayed to you directly into your conscious mind. The following is an example of this. A popular and intelligent radio presenter said on air that he was thinking about someone who lived interstate that he hadn't spoken to for over thirty years. Two days later, he was having dinner with him. This person had come to town and then contacted the radio presenter. The radio presenter regarded this as a remarkable coincidence. There is a simple explanation for this. A developed first-part is able to pick up the signals of any relevant transmission. Like an internet search engine, the first-part sifts through all the transmitted frequencies and connects with key words. Anything identified as being relevant is downloaded into the brain in whatever way the brain is capable of receiving it. In this instance, the first-part steered the radio announcer into thinking about the person, as it knew this person was going to contact him.

Sometimes transmissions cannot be put directly into your conscious mind, so they are put into your subconscious mind. Let us say some of your relatives are talking about you. Your first-part can lock on to those signals and transfer them to your subconscious mind. (There is a subtle physiological symptom that occurs in this process.) This information will then most likely translate itself into a dream with a message. Your first-part is the one to convey the message to you in REM sleep, which will now require your interpretation. Your first-part makes sure that the signals it copied containing the conversations of your relatives left with your roaming conscious mind in REM sleep, usually in one of your last REM cycles. The first-part also makes sure that you participate in these signals. In a way, you experience being in their company, only it was not in real life as it happened, but after the fact in the memory of the occasion. Often you will wake up after such a dream and recollect it vividly. The first-part is the one who intentionally wakes you. The substance of the dream usually involves the content of the conversations, or the feelings of the persons having the conversations. This really is a form of telepathy, only you have received the data by way of your dreams. More can be written about this in a future book.

Dreams such as this become a regular occurrence to a person who has a well-developed first-part. This is another reason for the proverbial wise man living in isolation high on a mountaintop away from the rest of the villagers; he knows the true feelings of his relatives and friends toward him, and not the ones just on show. On that road to developing your mind, you may find it a lonely passage.

The Art and Science of Astral Travel

For in life I strive and I struggle,
But in death I excel.
And in training for death I escape
From the imprisonment of the dilemma
Called life.

-A wise man

The state of astral travel completely differs from the state of dreaming in that astral travel is where one hundred percent of the conscious mind, and one hundred percent of the subconscious mind, detach from the physical body in a fully conscious state. Unlike in REM sleep, where the subconscious mind is in control, the conscious mind is now the controlling intellect. Ninety-five percent of the body's aura and current energy are automatically drawn out of the physical body with the conscious and subconscious minds.

Once vacated, the brain utilizes a minimal amount of current energy – four to five percent of its normal energy usage, which is just enough for the brain to remain operational. Each time you move your body physically, your brain requires this energy; however, in this vacated state your brain only requires a small amount of it. Therefore, when you leave your body, you take most of your energy with you. In some respects, astral traveling could be said to be synonymous with being dead.

Many confuse the state of vivid dreaming (being in REM sleep with a high percentage of the conscious mind having left) with astral traveling. It is only possible to confuse the two states when you have never astral traveled. Let us not confuse this with the near-death experience, as this requires a different interpretation. The near-death experience is an actual state of death where the astral body has severed its tie to the physical body. In returning from the death state, the body has been given just enough aura for the severed connection to be repaired – this allows the astral body to return to its physical body. The first-part is the one who reinstates the connection. A true out-of-body experience can *never* be misinterpreted as a dream. The experience is vivid and real; it is so frightening that it is capable of inducing a heart attack. If you do not wake up after your first true out-of-body experience scared witless, the odds are that you have not left your body – of that you can be assured!

Before you leave your body, two physiological symptoms occur. First of all, to reach this state, you must meditate to the point where you are about to fall asleep. On that borderline of falling to sleep, with your mind concentrating on nothing and nothing alone, you must then imagine your metaphysical arm moving out of your physical body. If you have reached this point successfully, the physiological symptoms will present themselves: an overwhelmingly intense vibration slowly moving throughout your entire body, and a corresponding buzzing noise. This is the detachment phase. At this decisive moment, if you pursue the mental image of your metaphysical hand and body leaving your physical body, you will detach. This can be highly risky in certain circumstances, as you have stepped into the domain of death. The only difference between death and this out-of-body state is that there is an invisible tie between your metaphysical body and physical body which has not been broken. In death there is no longer a tie. Death severs the tie permanently.

This exercise should not be taken lightly. If you have any doubts about attempting this out-of-body experience, rather than proceed with the experience, why not reach the vibration and buzzing phase and then stop the process there? This experience should be enough to satisfy your desire to prove the existence of a metaphysical body.

To proceed, you must decide whether you satisfy the requirements for such a serious maneuver. The criteria for those requirements are threefold: First, you must mentally be in a state of balance. This is essential. If you are under the influence of your negative-part in any way – that is, if you are depressed, anxious, uptight, stressed, facing personal problems, and so on – you certainly should not attempt this procedure.

Then, you must have optimal physical health. In other words, you cannot be low on energy such as aura. You cannot be exhausted physically or have an illness. Any of these contribute negatively, and the metaphysical encounter may be subject to the worst-case scenario – which is highly unlikely in a normal circumstance, but is probable if any of the above criteria are not met.

Finally, your physical body cannot be moved in this state. The danger or worst-case scenario is that your astral body may not be able to re-enter your physical body. Why? Because someone has moved your physical body. This is why those who dedicate themselves to astral traveling always sleep alone.

When you astral travel you are vacating your physical body. One hundred percent of your intellect is leaving in a unified state under the control of your conscious mind. There is only an invisible tie that binds you to your physical body; when your energy draws low, your body will automatically pull you back to it. However, there are many rogue spirits wandering in their own cycle, and they are desperately looking for an opportunity to occupy a vacant body. If you are physically or mentally weakened in some way, you leave the door open for a third party to just try to "walk" into your vacated body. This is examined closely in the next section. If this happens, forget it! You now are officially dead and can no longer exist in the physical world as you once did; someone else exists in your place. There are many of these humans who now wander the corridors of mental institutions because an intruder successfully entered their vacated bodies. Since the intruder cannot fit as precisely as the vacated one did, the brain cannot accommodate it and the person's behavior alters; how it alters is individually unique; usually this person needs to be institutionalized.

When the astral body exits the physical body, it leaves as a carbon copy of its physical body. Furthermore, if the physical body is positioned lying on its back, then this is the position the astral body will assume as it leaves. It will then float off in some direction. The metaphysical body cannot control its movements and it will feel totally paralyzed. It cannot, for instance, move its metaphysical arm or leg, or turn its head. There is no initial control whatsoever. This is why the best way to leave is by lying on your stomach. When you leave you will be floating – usually you will float upward and be able to see your body below; on other occasions you will go into the ground below you. Before you come to learn how to control your movements, you are going to have to be able to control the fear, because that fear is horrendous. It is likely that you are going to need to practice leaving your body around a dozen times before you are able to control the fear. The fear is what makes you return to your body almost instantly. You will probably wake up with all the physiological symptoms of fear, and you will find you need a glass of water owing to the natural dehydration that will take place during the exercise.

Learning to astral travel is like a baby learning to balance on its feet before it takes its first step. Whereas the baby's fear is falling down, the astral body's fear is not being able to get back in the physical body. Once you have overcome the fear of being out, you then have to overcome the fear of staying out longer, just as the baby, once it has balanced itself to stand up on its own, has to learn to take its first step, and then a few more steps after that. Eventually you should be able to stay out for a minute. With practice, you should be able to stay out of your body for three to four minutes.

When you have reached this stage and have overcome the fear — if you are ever able to achieve this — then comes the challenge of overcoming the metaphysical paralysis. Now it will be like a baby learning to not only walk but run. This is the moment when a remarkable thing may happen. Odo will know about this great achievement of yours. If you fit the criteria, such as being worthy — which means you are able to control and confine the negative-part (which also means you have not performed unforgivable sins in your life) — he will send a special positive-part to you that he created just for you, to help you, to guide you, and to answer any question of any kind you may have. One would ask why Odo would send a positive-part to you. He does this to help train you to be able to travel at the speed of thought to wherever you want to go. Remember the words used in Chapter 6 of this book:

> ... the Creators are dying for their children to grow up and have enough understanding, so that they can not only tell their children what a beautiful world this is, but take their children places to see things for themselves.

Odo wants humans to develop intellectually. He will provide you with a helping hand to accomplish this feat, just as you provide a helping hand to your children. All humans are regarded, after all, as his children. This is why Odo sends a helping hand by way of a special part — but not if you cannot control the negative-part, for the same reason he does not allow you to fully access your subconscious knowledge until you conquer the meat-in-the-sandwich goal. A human can only exercise the power of knowledge when that human can brandish that power for good and not for evil.

This positive-part will train your metaphysical body to get out of your physical body and learn the art of traveling in the universe at the speed of thought. When your metaphysical body re-enters your physical body, this positive-part will then transfer any knowledge, which you attained metaphysically, directly into your subconscious mind. This positive-part will also teach you, in your human, physical state, to be able to "read" from the "closed book." This is the aim of the Creators: to get you to start to develop yourself and acquire knowledge.

This intellect (positive-part) you are given is now available to you in this state forever. You can ask it any question of the universe you want answered. Then you can start writing books like this one! You can solve many mysteries, uncover many secrets, and discover many unimaginable things. You now have become the master of this positive-part. In a light-hearted way, you could say it is like a genie from a bottle. It is your genie! It is at your command. You now have your own genie and a "magic flying carpet." Humans have to one day earn and meet this challenge — this is their future challenge. Some of the few truly notable seers of our ancient past, and even some in our not-so-remote past, understood this — this is the old wisdom that has been lost over the ages: knowledge of the unknown that comes from an "altered" state of mind.

The first thing you ask this positive-part to do, when you meet it in the metaphysical state, is to restore your movements so that you function as you do in a physical state. Automatically, at the speed of thought, your movements will be restored to you. Then you can ask to travel somewhere — perhaps the future or the past — and this positive-part will take you if you meet the requirements and if the facilities are there. You virtually have a time-traveling machine right there in your mind. You can go to any planet, to any of the 49 universes, to any time in history, or to any time in the future you want — subject to the facilities being available and conditions being met, of course. (An explanation of this will be available in a future book committed to the subject.) You will then become what is known as a "time traveler." A time traveler, as opposed to just an astral traveler, is revered by many civilizations throughout the universe and beyond. This positive-part is at your command to take you wherever you want to go. This will not happen at once. This positive-part will tell you when it is the right time, when you are capable physically and metaphysically.

Can you imagine? You leave your body and you learn to overcome the fear, and then out of nowhere something comes to you in the metaphysical state and says, "I've been assigned to you; whatever you wish for, you just have to ask." You are virtually given the royal treatment because the step you have taken is quite an accomplishment. (The accomplishment lies more in the fact that you have controlled your negative influence and are deemed worthy for the new cycle you are about to enter into.) Once you overcome the fear, and you can stay out for several minutes in physical time, this positive-part will make that metaphysical time anything from a few hours to a few days. In a cycle of separation of this kind, time between the physical world and the metaphysical world does not coincide. For instance, being out for four minutes in actual physical body time could equate to being two hours in your metaphysical time. Time, we must remember, is manipulative for the one able to master its manipulation.

For any of this to happen, you have to overcome the fear first, which is the greatest difficulty of all. When you feel fear, your physical body will, as an automatic response, call you back immediately. It is extremely hard to overcome the fear. Many have died of a heart attack because they were unable to negotiate being out of their physical body. Through practice, this fear fades. The fear, as stated earlier, is based on not being able to return to the physical body; ironically, this fear is the very thing that returns you to your body. When you are in this state, a controlled return to your body involves mentally picturing yourself being back in your physical body. With a closed mind, and no other thought distracting it, you try to move your physical body. Seconds later you will wake up.

Finally, words of advice to heed in the process of attempting to leave your body: when you reach the detachment phase, if you hear a voice in your mind yelling out to stop, heed the words in your mind. This would be the voice of your first-part, who is warning you not to proceed as you may not be physically up to it or it may not be up to protecting you. It should be noted that when you leave your body your first-part usually "fills" your space in your physical body. It does not travel with you. This is why, if you fit the criteria, an additional part is given to you for this specific purpose. A first-part needs to have evolved to the stage where it is capable of filling your space. Its evolution is determined by your ability to progress in life in a positive way, and by the way you use your brain to acquire knowledge.

There are other reasons that the attempt may be dangerous to you, and the following section will explain another aspect of why it can be dangerous to proceed into the unknown depths of the unknown itself.

A WARNING: Leaving your body is a serious, serious step, and unless you are confident that you have met all the criteria, you should be hesitant. You must never forget that YOU CAN DIE in the process. The safest time to practice the art of astral traveling is when you have conquered the meat-in-the-sandwich goal.

You can achieve other great things with your mind on this remarkable excursion. If you follow the guiding principles of those that have made your excursion possible, you virtually have forever in front of you: you have a sempiternity before you that will enable you to have many diverse situations of life, which will not always be speckled or frosted with glittery or sugary things. Whatever the daily grind of your life, you should always bear this in mind, and let the knowledge of what you will one day be capable of be the thing to keep you focused on a positive path, especially in light of the negative things that definitely are, one way or another, going to befall you in your present challenge – the one called life.

Wanderers in the Halfway Meadow

As sure as the moon allows time to be measured when Earth has turned its back to the sun, are there such things in this world as wandering souls: metaphysical beings who have no body to append themselves to in the living world. Just as the moth that lives for only a day has the singular purpose to seek out a mate, so wandering souls, in the short time after realizing they are dead, have the sole desire to seek out a body. These metaphysical wanderers are sometimes called ghosts.

These are the unwanted souls the ancient Egyptians feared – the Egyptians, like many peoples and cultures, believed they could observe and participate in the world of the dead through their dreams. They also feared that in this dream state somehow they could open up a door for the entry of dead souls into this world – particularly souls of evil inclination – using the same doorway they used for entry into their world of the dead. This sounds a little fantastic to us, but there is a verisimilitude – that is, reality – to it that we shall uncover in this chapter.

There are souls that once existed as humans, but met death unprepared in the sense that their deaths occurred by surprise. The bodies of these souls died, but the souls do not realize they are dead. For example, if you were walking down the street and then from behind were suddenly hit fatally over the head with a hammer, your metaphysical body would automatically disconnect from your physical body, which is a normal process of death. In that split second of death, you didn't become aware of your death, so you would continue with your life as though nothing had happened. You would not accept you are dead; instead, you would become locked in a cycle of your own, with your own cycle of time and space in the halfway meadow.

You would then live in a cycle of your past, because this is where you believe you still exist and where you want to exist. It is like certain dementia cases that stop living according to future events in life, but instead live according to past events. You now recreate events from your mind. It appears to you that the rest of the world is responding to you, but this is just a recreation from your mind of events that have already occurred. You are existing in your memories, in a similar way that you are when you are dreaming.

When do you realize that things are wrong? When you realize you cannot move on. You are doing the same thing over and over. When you cannot move forward, beyond the point of the past, is when you will sense that something is wrong. Slowly, a seed of doubt will germinate within you, and you will begin to wonder if you are dead. Once this thought has taken root in your mind, it will take hold and keep growing until you accept the idea completely. Once you accept that you are dead and can never move beyond this point, you will automatically move into the mystery of the hereafter: you will move on to a new cycle of existence once the tunnel (moongate hallway) finds you, which is an automatic process. Metaphysical wanderers can linger in the halfway meadow for between five hundred and one thousand, six hundred years of our time, which can equate to around ten days in their cycle of time.

Sometimes, however, the tunnel does not always automatically materialize when it should. There may be a gap in time. In this moment of time between acceptance of death and being received into the tunnel, these wandering souls try to find another physical body to occupy, as it is their instinct to want to live. They think it is as easy as that. They then seek out a physical body to literally steal from someone. As in a dream, they fly, they walk, but they look and look for a body to get into. If they have a propitious moment, they will see an astral traveler and they will take the opportunity to hijack his vacated body.

Wandering souls, as they exist in the metaphysical plane, are proficient at seeing astral travelers. They are even able to see the cord that binds the astral body to its physical body. If one sees an astral traveler, it will then attempt to outsmart this astral traveler by "attaching" to the cord and deliberately "following" it back to its physical body. If the astral cord has a strong attachment to the physical body, the wandering soul has no prayer of maneuvering in. This strong attachment means the physical body is strong in terms of its physical and mental health and possesses an abundance of aura. These ingredients all act like up-to-date antivirus and intrusion-protection software on a computer.

A wandering soul has a ninety-nine percent chance of successfully taking possession of an astral traveler's weak physical body. This is why, when attempting to astral travel, if you should hear a voice in your mind telling you to stop, it is imperative you listen. This would be your first-part warning you it is dangerous to get out. This suggests your defense mechanism is weak or not "up-to-date." In this instance, you must never act against the advice of the voice in your mind. If your physical body's natural defenses are down, your astral body will be able to see the maneuvers of the wandering soul, but will be helpless and unable to stop the wandering soul from moving in and stealing your body from you. The wandering soul can move into your body, but not as a carbon copy. This is why the brain of your former body will not be able to function properly, and why the intruder will become entrapped in your body and in all likelihood wind up in a mental institution. There have been many instances of this occurring.

·ᴗ

In the above paragraphs, this book has been discussing the threat that exists to an astral traveler. Yet the same threat of invasion exists to certain types of humans who are not astral traveling. All wandering souls have the ability to scan a human brain, with the intent of finding one that has empty cells. Searching for this type of brain is the next logical step of a metaphysical wanderer in its quest for the continuation of its existence in the physical form. If the wandering soul finds an adult brain and enters into it, in all likelihood the "hijack" attempt will be unsuccessful. Sometimes the attempt is successful if certain conditions are met, and in some other cases if the timing is right.

There are some famous documented case studies from throughout history involving humans who have done things that are so beyond their comprehension that it defies explanation. Let us take, for example, a genuinely happily married man, with no ulterior motives, who killed his wife and kids. We would most likely interpret this man's change in personality as his having gone insane temporarily, with no rational explanation for that insanity. However, a rational explanation does exist. The killing could easily have been performed by a rogue wandering soul, who may have even been a serial killer in his human existence, whose intellect had temporarily dwelt within and taken control of this man's brain. The killing could also have been performed by one of Chisek's rogue parts, which are always on the lookout for such a mind to occupy temporarily.

In Australia, a classic example of one of the above occurred. The accused and sentenced mass "killer" merely happened to have a weak mind with a lot of empty cells – which made it easy for someone to possess him – as well as an almost non-existent defense mechanism in his brain. Most of us have a defense mechanism within us that rejects foreign states of consciousness when they try to infiltrate our brains. Without such a defense mechanism, the human is just as open for intrusion as a computer without its antivirus software. (After all, a human brain is nothing but a highly sophisticated biological computer.) These weaknesses have resulted in a young man going to prison for life for crimes he was not responsible for as a sane man. Unfortunately, humans do not have the capacity to differentiate between sanity and insanity – where the insanity is primarily the result of an innocent weakness of mind and nothing more. Such a weakness makes this type of human dangerous, not by his actions, but by the actions of those who can invade his brain.

There was another case in Australia in the past, and it involved a woman in her sixties who was convicted of stabbing her lover of over thirty years. She was bewildered when she found her lover dead on the floor of the kitchen one day. She had no recollection of the stabbing and vehemently protested her innocence, which was to no avail, since she was convicted of the crime. What really happened in her case was that a rogue soul occupied her brain for the short time it took to kill the lover. (To be a metaphysical wanderer, that soul must have died in a circumstance that was instant and unexpected. These types of people are often criminals.) The interesting thing in this case – which differentiates it from the previous case involving the young man – is that she was not simple-minded like the young man, whose brain was easier to enter. She was an ordinary woman intellectually. Apparently, an area in her brain was not occupied at that exact moment when the invader took possession of her body. In her case, the invasion did not last long, just long enough to do damage.

In the young man's case, he was invaded for a longer period, and he was capable of being invaded at will by any wandering soul that found him, as his "door" was constantly open. What is fascinating in his case is that the invading soul took off on its own, deciding that it didn't want to stay with this young man once caught to answer any questions over what it did. The young man (just like the woman), would have had no recollection of the events. He would have just "woken" in a daze, and then the nightmare began for this poor soul. This is because the killer who invaded his brain created those memories. Those memories would therefore have registered in the invading soul's mind alone, and they would have been taken with it when it left the body – it didn't leave any tracks to suggest it was ever there. While one may – and, controversially, probably should – feel sorry for this man, if he were not locked up in prison he would certainly need to be locked up comfortably, with compassion, away from society for the remainder of his life because of the potential threat he poses at any time. His mind is simply open to any wandering soul that chooses to invade him. As unthinkable as it may seem, we could just as easily have been born in such a defective body and be in his circumstances – trapped, helpless, with no control of our actions at certain times.

How does all this work, you ask yourself? It sounds like bad science fiction! Just as the torturous, slow death of impalement of living humans was a reality: a reality that involved a human being pierced with a long and pointed stake through the mouth, rectum, or vagina, so temporary possession is a reality: a reality that has occurred more than once. You would be surprised to know that there are many humans who are vulnerable to such invasion, as in the case of the woman cited above. This does not mean this ever happens to them; some unlucky ones, like this woman, fall into the trap. (The young man's case is a rare example and different from the case of the woman.)

Ultimately, how this occurs is straightforward: the brain must create cells in the conscious mind; once created, knowledge will automatically occupy those newly created cells. In the above woman's case, she had cells created, but knowledge did not come to occupy those cells. Even when you walk or watch television, cells are automatically being developed in your brain, but if knowledge is not captured by a cell, and this cell does not become used, the cell will then slowly die. This is a natural process. If you read a book, the process of reading would have instigated the brain to create empty cells; but if you did not remember anything about the book – which means you did not absorb any of what you read – those cells that were developed in the process of your reading the book did not have any knowledge to receive. This means no knowledge went into those cells. The next natural process is for these cells to die. They cannot stay empty in your brain. Either they are filled with knowledge or they have to die. These cells are what are known as "empty cells." The time between the creation of these cells and the death of these cells is when an opportunistic wandering soul can enter a brain and occupy these cells.

In most normal brains, the body's defense system protects cells from being invaded in this vulnerable period. If there is a glitch in the software and the defense system does not function properly, as in the woman's case cited above, then the brain is open to being invaded. The cells that were destined to slowly die by a natural process therefore remained active when the invader occupied them. An invader cannot just enter the conscious mind of a brain. For it to be in a conscious mind, there has to be space in that brain for it to occupy. In the woman's case, her immune system kicked the invader out shortly after the invasion, and then the cells subsequently died.

In the case of a child, he has cells that are not filled with enough knowledge, as the child is young and has a lot to learn. The child is protected by a strong immune system, though, which prevents such invasion. The child-like mind of the young man was similar to a child in that he had developed cells, but only a minute amount of knowledge went into the cells. For instance, the average person will fill a cell with fifty to sixty percent of knowledge. In the young man's case, his cells were only five percent filled. This was only enough to keep the cells active for a short time. The empty space in those cells enabled a rogue soul to enter and occupy his brain. When the invader left, the cells it occupied slowly died, as an occupation of five percent of knowledge is not enough to maintain the existence of the cells. His brain then created new cells, and the cycle repeated itself, where he only filled those cells with five percent of knowledge. In this time he was once again open for invasion, had anyone desired to invade him. This young man's brain could be considered defective on two grounds: first, he could not fill his cells with the required amount of knowledge and therefore possessed a lot of empty space in those cells, which accounted for his limited or child-like intelligence; second, his immune system was not functioning normally to protect the cells from such intrusion. What is frightening is that his brain had no ability to repel an invader once it occupied his brain, which meant the invader could stay in there on its own terms.

Some wandering souls try to be smarter than attempt to go into an adult brain, where there is a high risk of failure, and where they will have a limited existence. Instead, they look for a younger brain to occupy so that the two minds may be able to grow in tandem, and subsequently have a long life to look forward to. On most occasions such a wandering soul would bring extra energy into the young brain it enters and overload it – that is, damage the nervous system as well as kill many of the innocent cells waiting for future development. This child will grow to be mentally defective. Most do not succeed, but on rare occasions some do! If unsuccessful, the wandering soul will just leave, but in all likelihood the young brain that encountered the intrusion attempt would be permanently damaged. In the history of this planet, some human bodies have had the occupation of two souls concurrently occupying the one physical brain. Sometimes this has been a deliberate approach employed by the Creators. One of our most celebrated minds fits into this last category of human!

We have just ventured into the uncharted territory of the human brain, and its "universe" is just as uncharted as the one the Greek astronomer, Hipparchus, began to catalogue – in terms of stars – in his existence between 190BC and 120BC. By uncharted, this is also a reflection of the ignorance on the part of professionals in knowing how to treat, let alone understand, the human brain in relation to quite a few disorders, one of which is severe depression. The ignorance is so evident when you consider that to this day electroconvulsive (electric shock) therapy is used by some practitioners to treat the above disorder. Just as scientists have an elephantine task ahead of them when it comes to understanding the universe, so practitioners of the human brain have an elephantine task ahead of them when it comes to understanding the application of consciousness to the human brain, and the "sicknesses" and "diseases" that the human mind can incur in a lifetime.

Humble Minds of the Past

I know I look stupid.
I enjoy, immensely, looking stupid in the eyes of minute intellects.
It is my hobby just as it is in my nature.
I do it with the utmost pleasure.
You have no idea what kind of pleasure I get when people think I'm stupid.
I get a satisfaction humans will never understand.
For it is within me to be humble;
A man like me can never be, or appear to be, otherwise.
It is a great pity that humans can only see the humble,
Not in the light of them being humble,
But in the light of them being stupid.
Intentional stupidity makes one easily understood by a human mind;
Sometimes obvious intelligence does not protrude from true intelligence,
From someone like me,
Who not only sees the humble, but is humble,
Which is a vastly superior intellect
That unfortunately portrays itself to the humans' eyes as being stupid.

-A wise man

When you have conquered the meat-in-the-sandwich goal and are able to reach the point of being able to astral travel, my god, what an adventure you will take on! Material possessions and trifling human values will mean nothing to you now. This is why it should be of no surprise to learn that some of the greatest minds in the history of this planet have never left their hardships or poverty behind them. Some of the greatest minds recognized, and those that are unrecognized, never saw academia or its "intellectualism" as a fruitful or worthy pursuit. Ironically, some of these minds appear very ordinary if not stupid to others. This projected facade is often a self-defense mechanism, which becomes necessary for one simple reason ... humans have an instinctive, behavioral trait they exhibit when they encounter a person of this caliber, one not cloaked behind simplicity: they erect walls and barriers as an emotional response to feeling intimidated and jealous; naturally they would dislike and in some cases fear that person. Often they find this person's advice and sense of knowing confronting, and their natural inclination is to view such a person as being arrogant or having quite an ego.

This is why this wise person will often appear eccentric, and act helpless and sometimes hopeless. The character of Columbo, from the television series, *Columbo*, epitomizes this type of person. Those around him will act vastly different in this situation. They will keep their guard down and no walls or barriers will be erected, as this "simple" person exhibits no threatening qualities to them. Indeed, people often feel sorry for, and go out of their way to assist, him. This is why such humans always go through life in a humble way. They will never portray themselves in any other light.

It should not be surprising that these humble and sometimes "unaccomplished" humans place little or no value on the materialistic side of the world, because they value something more precious – something in their minds. Many of these humans never marry or have kids, and if they do, this lifestyle would most likely have hindered their ability to achieve greatness. They view the world from a sense of intellectual conquest on a personal and inward level. Leonardo da Vinci fits into this category of not wanting to marry and have children for intellectual reasons, and one other reason. He was not a homosexual as some believe, nor was Shakespeare. Furthermore, the intelligentsia of this world is confused by, and has misinterpreted, the young man and the dark lady in Shakespeare's sonnets. This is a book in itself, and an intriguing one at that, more bewildering than the mystery behind the Mona Lisa's smile! Fortunately, in the near future you will have the privilege of reading about each mystery for yourself!

Part of the secret behind the success of superior minds in the past, such as Plato, Leonardo da Vinci, and Shakespeare, was their ability to astral travel to the future and to the past – there was no limit to where they could go. They were time travelers. These great minds were more complex than a plot from Shakespeare's plays. While on the subject of Plato, he was taken to Atlantis metaphysically while astral traveling and that is how he wrote about it, contrary to what he said about the knowledge being handed down from Solon. You may even be fortunate enough to read about this in the near future – Atlantis, that is. Pythagoras, Nostradamus, and even Jules Verne (to name a few) can be credited with having discovered the ancient wisdom of astral travel. Astral travel accounts for the mystery of how the most celebrated, wise humans attained their knowledge about the future.

⁂

What a fascinating subject – the human brain and its capabilities! What a pity many superior minds of the past could never reveal to their fellow humans what knowledge they had or capabilities they truly possessed, simply because mankind did not have or want to have the capacity to understand. One has only to look at what happened to the teachings of Pythagoras, or even the teachings of Socrates – if we recall, Socrates, because of those teachings, was sentenced to death by hemlock. Socrates, by the way – although an arresting figure in his own right – could not compare with his great student, Plato! Not even the superior human called Jesus Christ could accomplish some of what he set out to; with all his mental powers and abilities, even he was persecuted. History is a graveyard littered with the carcasses of persecuted humans who have done no more than be ahead of their time and challenge irrational or absurd beliefs, which, amazingly, still flourish to this day, even amongst our intellectually elite – as sure as tears to the eye of many a female; as fanciful wings to the butterfly; and (please excuse the crudity here) as feces to the fly! In fact, like that which comes from corrupted bowels, some things just never change their smell!

Conclusion

I will tell you a thing in this rhyme, and it goes ... Once upon a time
We looked to the horizon and what lay beyond we wondered some.
We felt the wind brush past and we asked, from where did it come?
We gazed up at night and queried, where did the sun go?
What brought out the stars in their glorious show?
We wondered at the celestial bodies and asked, why?
Why did they motion in sequence across a sunless sky?
And what was with the moon and its manifold shape?
Then we locked back down at ourselves and with a gape
Asked, what verily is this marvelous thing we be,
That makes us so mindful of the forces we feel and see?
And the more we thought the more we did wonder ...
Like, what was with the mind's dreaming mental yonder?
And then each one of us looked back up and pondered inwardly,
What great thing could have created this magnificence I see?
Up above, down below, beyond, and within me?
Once upon a time we questioned and our curiosity
Never faltered in its drive for seeking out the
Answers to all that in heaven and on Earth we see.

Because we once asked ... so many answers have we found,
And still unrelenting our questions abound,
Which is because our intellect yearns to bridle the profound.

Can you recall the innocence in looking up into the vastness of outer space and being tantalized by the rapture and the "symphony" of the universe? Hauntingly and teasingly, the universe "preyed" upon all those of us burdened by our ignorance of it. The greater our desire for its knowledge, the deeper it seduced us into its unknown depths. So it comes as no surprise that in the universe giving up its secrets, it has given up its mystique and allure, which are founded upon the wonder of not knowing. In a way, the same can be said of our existence as humans here on Earth. Someone superior would say to us as we go through our primitive and unappreciated existence:

> It is up "here" that our minds are cluttered with thousands of personalities, and we remember each one. Special moments come back to us that we'd love to recapture – just as you look back at times that you cannot have again in your lifetime. An example is craving for a moment on your own in the mountains to clear your mind. There are moments of innocence we can in some sense go back to, but they are not the same as when we felt them first hand with our simple uncluttered minds. We still remember our past lives; yet we cannot bring back that innocent, that pure, that fresh, mind, as you have right now on your Earth.
>
> This is why life is precious, but you walk through it and pass it over without a second glance ... you simply take it for granted! When you can no longer have it, you will look back and wish for it. So while you can have the memory, you should enjoy it. Don't let yourself one day look back and crave it because you didn't enjoy it when it was. Take note of what is around you and remember the moment; remember the simple, neglected things that can never again be – for there lies no room in an advanced society for such primitiveness. The small, insignificant things (as an advanced society would regard them) you see around you every day – like the chase and kill of a cockroach – cannot be imagined.

THE FIRST CAUSE

In life, we must remember that we all face adversities. When we are in a situation where we feel our prayers have been deserted or unanswered, we should remember Odo's following words to a wise man:

> How can I judge your performance in life if I help you?
> Like with your kids:
> You can't bail them out all the time;
> For, how would they know, or you know, what they were capable of?
> In other words, you must help yourself
> ... You have the intellect to do it!

Our adversities are our challenges. We must remember that all great men have humble beginnings: beginnings of poverty that are often topped up with misfortune in terms of health and work, where life becomes a constant struggle for survival, both physically and intellectually. Much of the time, these intellects feel that the struggle to survive and free themselves, like the victim of a spider's web, is never-ending. We know now that life on Earth is the testing ground for a superior intellect, which would become great in a time to come. Perhaps somebody wants these humble beginnings of adversity to serve a usefulness to superior intellects in their time of greatness. Perhaps superior intellects in their time of luster would be able to look back upon their own humble beginnings to see, in a true light, their fellow humans under them as being equal to them. While the experience of going from adversity to greatness enriches their lives, it also enriches the lives of others, when they radiate – like a sun its light and heat – the knowledge of their experience. These things do not happen to us by chance; we are deliberately put through this "university" by the one who created us.

Finally, the following quotation that came from the beyond, and the essay entitled *Humbleism and Abstractism*, which came from a wise man, sum up all that an intelligent human is ... all that an intelligent human could be ... and all that an intelligent human should be ...

> They want to see how far one with free will, who feels one is intelligent, and who is given knowledge and understanding of life, will handle life. There are two ways of handling knowledge: by honesty, respect,

thoughtfulness, and understanding, which is Odo's path; or by Chisek's ignorant path. Not many people can handle knowledge. People often misuse knowledge – which is contrary to the approach where the more you learn, the more humble you must become, the more understanding you should be, the more lovable you should be … all because you know more, and you have the capacity to tolerate more … no less!

Humbleism and Abstractism

It is easy to be misunderstood and forgiven
Because you look uncomplicated,
Which is often how the humble look.

These two words exist not in the human dictionary. Humbleism is neither taught nor practiced. Humbleism is a word that defines intelligent humans – those who want to be amongst, who feel to be amongst, and who teach, the ordinary persons; those to mix and integrate amongst the "lowest" of intellects, amongst whom they are respected and looked upon as humans who stand high with their intelligence, but who are humble in that they lower themselves to be amongst the ordinary. These humans are like the "whipping" (willow) tree. While the whipping tree grows high, green, and proud, its branches reach down to its roots. When its branches can reach its roots, not only can it remind itself of where it comes from, but it can keep in touch with the lower forms of life, such as the grass, such as the insects that climb all over it. Not merely can they enjoy one another's presence; the lower forms have the chance of looking down from the height of the whipping tree to see where they themselves have come from in the first place. Perhaps this is why the whipping tree can never be uprooted by wind and storm. Devastations may occur – such as the uplifting of houses, the uprooting of huge trees, and even the dislodging of mountain rocks, but never can a whipping tree be uprooted in full.

Unlike the whipping tree, humans have forgotten that their roots are, and that being in touch with those roots is, more important than just growing in height like the pine tree. It is noteworthy that practically every huge tree, including the pine, has its roots not only exposed, but hardly holding onto the foundation from which it originated. Perhaps reaching for the achievement of height, and in the process neglecting one's roots, is not as important as humans think it is. Perhaps a balance of growth is needed for the salvation of such tall trees. Perhaps such trees should be able to learn something before reaching for the skies – of course, there is nothing wrong with the tree aiming to become tall, as long as it learns to be humble and bow so low that it can reach its own root and quickly spring back from it at will.

When tall trees can one day withstand the pressure of being uprooted in strong winds by being able to bend, perhaps then we should be able to call such trees humble trees — that is, trees with strong foundations; trees healthy and proud that can reach for the sky and still be able to bend and bow, and even spring back after being humbled unto the elements; trees that can continue to provide to their fellow inhabitants down on the ground not just an example of their existence, but shelter to increase their chances of survival.

There is no difference between the humble tree and the humble human. It takes much intelligence for one to become humble like the whipping tree. For the one who is humble is far, far superior to the one who claims to be intelligent, but knows not what humble means. For, in the most humble human, tree, or life form on this planet, you will find the highest possible intelligence of its kind; for this reason, you will also find that the humble life forms are the strongest survivors within their life cycle.

Then there is the so-called intelligence based on abstractism. Abstractism, as in the case of humbleism, can apply to all living plants and creatures on this planet. In the mode of human abstractism, one will find an opposite existence to the intelligence based on humbleism. In this mode of abstractism you have a special breed of human species. These humans are noted for always trying to get somewhere in a hurry — perhaps to work in a hurry, to return home in a hurry, to excel with their intellect in a hurry, or to reach for the skies in a hurry. They are so greedy that they want to grasp anything and everything today, as though there were no tomorrow. In the process, what they manage to achieve is a maze: a maze that they usually get lost within — unlike the spider that can always find its way in and out of its maze. This type of maze, which exists in the human mind, and which has been created by that very human mind, is called an "abstract."

From within their individually unique abstracts, such humans begin to use and espouse abstractism. This type of intellectual abstractism plays an enormous role in the development of their lives. For, such humans go through life not only using, but also referring most of their teachings back to, the abstract within their minds. In their abstracts, they would have cooked up special words and special names — you might say they would have practically concocted a new alphabet of their own.

To describe that maze or abstract to others they would have given all the roads, which exist in the abstract, their own street-names. The tunnels of roads that go nowhere, and the tunnels of roads that only go in circles, are all explained away with different names in their own inimitable terminology. The roads do mean something to them. Don't mention the colors they get bewitched by ... they fascinate them! They also remain the mystery they have to crack, and, then, the light shining upon those colors blinds them to the point where they are unable to see anything beyond their mazes for the rest of their lives.

It is only when one of them begins to hear voices coming from within his maze that he is classified by the rest of the community as a lunatic. Abstract humans exist in the highest level of our society, are often found in lunatic asylums, and, dare this book say it, are often elected into government – take a good look at the government of Australia at the time of the writing of this book! For these ones, new parameters, metaphors, and not just definitions but entirely new dictionaries to accommodate such new definitions, have to be written.

Come to think of it, this book has to retract this last statement because there is a better source of reference – and it is the Universal Language of Chisek. Yes, we know there is a Universal Language of the gods, but there is also a diametrically opposed Universal Language of Chisek. Only in a state of complete madness can this language be understood. In light of this place of reference can these abstract humans be best dissected and rationalized.

These are the types of people to prosper: those regarded as intellectual giants or the crème of mankind. No wonder human civilization takes one step forward, three steps backward! It makes one wonder how long it would take for mankind to arrive at the humble point – that ultimate crossroad to lead humans into their next phase of achievement.

This certainly will not happen any time soon, for humans have allowed themselves to be abstractized by these people – that is, to be sucked into their abstracts. If mankind is not careful, one day this entire civilization, along with the lower life forms and the planet Earth itself, would become an abstract in its own right. It would be a fascinating exhibit to the other civilizations in the universe, which would look at Earth in the same way you look at an abstract painting, painted by one of those abstract-minded people – that is, it would be something you can stare at for the rest of your life and never come to a conclusion about its meaning.

Well-nigh the Last Word

Do you think I begot you and then left you bereft
Without a plan or a blueprint to follow?
Do you think you really came up with all you know
On your own from scratch?
When I made you I had a plan, a vision
— Even the flushing system of a toilet!
— Even the nail and the hammer!
You are inventing things and progressing only
Because you accessed the knowhow subconsciously from me.
I formulated all things first and then left them
For you to rediscover from your dream-chip.

Could you create children and then let them be on their own?
Without direction, guidance, or a supporting structure?
No ... they learn from you what others once taught you.
Everything you have is my design and my idea alone,
And life is fulfilling my ideal of what I want it to be.
So I expect life to follow my ideal;
For I know best, and you are here for me:
You are here for me to live through you;
For, in everything that lives can I be found.

Life must evolve to a point on its own
Ignorant of me; for that is how I know
Who is who and what is what and who will be and who will not.
There is a long road that you have to take
To get to me and be one with me.

And on that road do I present to you
Hurdles and tests by way of challenges.
These hurdles and tests are in some ways filters,
To filter out those who can and those who cannot.
Those I want and those I want not.
It may seem harsh; it may seem cruel;
But this is what life is, and what it will remain
Forever on your journey leading to me.

It is true that those who are meek do inherit the Earth;
In these corrupt cycles they have weathered the storms,
And have built a good foundation and proved their worth,
Which is why unbalance exists all around,
And why your task is one to find
Balance from unbalance,
Happiness in unbalance.

Finally,
Endure … sacrifice … suffer
And make the best of the worst
Because only from this "worst"
One day can come the best
… Best that must be earned.

The Last Word

An egg one day lands on a leaf;
Out comes a caterpillar and it eats and eats,
And knows not its greater purpose: its destiny.
It cannot know that eating will lead to change,
And liberate it from its current ignorance.
With the caterpillar, we have much in common.
Just as a caterpillar lives on the plant where its egg was laid
— And often never travels beyond one leaf —
So we are "laid" on an earth that we never travel beyond.
While the caterpillar doesn't realize the role eating will fulfill,
We don't realize the role our challenges will fulfill;
For we are dwelling in the same ignorance as the caterpillar,
With no grasp of our destiny once we are liberated.
While the caterpillar must fatten itself up,
We must collect knowledge from challenges.
While the caterpillar is resourceful and makes its own cocoon,
Ours has been done for us — our conscious mind.
Transformation to a butterfly is the caterpillar's liberation;
Equilibrium is ours.

Did some wise seer in classical antiquity say that in knowing what we really know is that we simply don't know anything? And now that we do know that we know, does this mean we have to unlearn all that we have learned until now, because now we really do know?

Just as you are looking into the realm of a time machine when you are searching the night sky for answers, so are you looking into the realm of enlightenment when you are searching this book for answers. In understanding the knowledge in this book, under the agency of yourself, you have earned a degree in the University of Wisdom – a degree that has more value and practical application to your soul and destiny than any other you could possibly attain.

In this book, we have uncovered the lost, old enlightenment. This old enlightenment, or wisdom, was the basis of the teachings of many thinkers, including Pythagoras; Plato; Socrates; Zoroaster; Buddha; one human who was subsequently nailed to, and then hung from, a cross; Leonardo da Vinci; Shakespeare; the early Hindus; and many who lived in a time when oral traditions were the only means of preserving knowledge. Many of these teachings can be traced back to the ancient priests, who were handed the knowledge. This knowledge came in its earliest form in a time when man, indiscriminately, all over the world, was shown the way and the truth. This was our golden age on this planet.

Now, to truly understand the wisdom of this book, you have to reread it all over again, and, each time you do, one thing will be assured – as assuredly as π is the most famous number in mathematics – you will become enlightened "beyond the cave," as in Plato's Allegory of the Cave, which is all just a long-winded intellectual way of saying that you too will become that proverbial mushroom that has risen from the fungus.

• ༚

It was a wise man who only recently said: "I have to see to believe, and I have to believe what I see."

Then that wise man speculated: The question then arises of whether progress would come to exist if visionaries (true philosophers who tap into that dream-chip of the future found in their subconscious minds) were to steadfastly uphold the principle of seeing before believing and believing what they are seeing. At some point a person must just know and understand, and from this may the reasoning make him see. If scientific investigation were to be based on seeing before believing, at a time when scientific observation was not possible because the technology was not available, the likes of Democritus, in the fifth century BC, would not have put forward great ideas of discovery like the atom. So, surely, as was ink to the scribe in ancient antiquity, is not knowledge that has been sourced from higher wisdom a requisite to advancement?

Then that wise man reflected: Amongst most scientists and pessimists, the indicator of acceptance of truth is the giggle factor. When the gap between truth and acceptance closes — which initially begins with distances as vast as those existing in astronomy — the giggle quickly fades. This giggle factor (present any time anything new is suggested) amongst the intelligentsia represents a stonewall barrier to progress, truth, and vision.

Then that wise man shook his head, smirked, and understood: As much as many may shudder at the thought, the scientific route cannot truly progress without prior direction from a higher, purer thought. This is why science needs to not only climb down from the pedestal and reinstate the true philosopher (a rare and unlikely find), but also crack its eggshell so that it can look beyond at what is so flagrant: it needs to look in milieus which are now heretical to it. Then comes the hard task of working with this purer thought! This is the only means by which mankind can embrace a paradigm that will piece together "the puzzle."

By all these deliberations came he — that wise man — to solve the riddle in his mind: For the way to open the dual-keyed padlock on the vaulted chest containing the secrets of the universe is with two keys. These keys are order and chaos, while the padlock is of course reason: reason is the mysterious lock to reveal everything that there ever will be or has ever come to be …

NEVER THE END

Endnotes

i   In this book I have without regret or apology followed the conventional usage of words such as man or mankind, or masculine pronouns like him, he, or his, which refer to both genders, considering there is not a suitable replacement in the English language. When this book needs to refer to a specific gender, that gender is identified; otherwise, sound logic would dictate that both genders were being referred to, irrespective of the masculine pronoun. I remember that a wise man once told me that an intelligent person does not have to yell to be heard, no matter what his sex.

ii   *Dialogues of Plato* (*Republic*)
Translated by Benjamin Jowett [1871]

iii   *Rig Veda*
Book 1: Hymn CLXIV (2) Viśvedevas
Translated by Ralph T. H. Griffith [1896]

iv   *Dialogues of Plato* [*Protagoras*]
Translated by Benjamin Jowett [1871]

v   William Shakespeare
[*Hamlet, Prince of Denmark Act IV; Scene IV*]

vi   *Plutarch's Morals: Theosophical Essays* [*On Superstition*]
Translated by Charles William King [1908]

vii   *The Upanishads, Part 2. Brihadâranyaka Upanishad* IV, 3
Interpreted by Max Müller [1879]

A resource where the above works – and works by other authors mentioned in this book – can be found is at www.sacred-texts.com

You can find out more about Jack Lord from his website:
www.jacklord.info

⸱⸌ In our spiritual and scientific quest, the ladder of knowledge we have climbed — as insightful as it may appear to be — has not raised us above the "fog" of our existence. We live in this fog and only see dim pieces of a mysterious puzzle. *The First Cause* lifts this fog and pieces together the puzzle to provide a picture that we never thought possible to see.

⸱⸌ This book shatters our worldview to the point where many disciplines will have to pull out their dusty drawing boards and start all over again with a new and accurate blueprint.

⸱⸌ Never has a book delivered the profound basics and all the fundamental answers.

⸱⸌ Never has a book had such power in its knowledge to change you — and it will change you!

⸱⸌ The most sensational book ever written.

Jack Lord
A wise man often quoted in this book.

Rosemary Klem, from Sydney, Australia, loves the study of outer space, the human mind, ancient history, and philosophy, and has been driven her entire life, from the time she first looked up and saw the night sky, to seek out old, lost knowledge once known in our abstruse past. The human repository of knowledge could not satisfy what she longed to know; it was only in the unknown that knowledge of the kind she sought could be found. In her quest, she has rediscovered lost, old wisdom that was known to ancient civilizations and primitive peoples, as well as great minds such as Pythagoras, Plato, Leonardo da Vinci, and Shakespeare. She has uncovered the common thread – one as fragile as gossamer, but as enduring as time itself – that stitches up all the disciplines to create a woven fabric of enlightenment that we have conditioned ourselves to think would never be known to us. She hopes that this mystical knowledge the early ancients knew, which the Renaissance sought to rediscover, will not only herald an exciting new scientific revolution when it unites with the science and technology of our age, but be the seed to procure peace and unity on this planet when we realize that we share a beautiful, all-pervading affinity.

P141 The living world (plants/animals) does not have reasoning capabilities as man with intellect has, which is what uniquely & ironically defines him as superior intelligence.

P149 Can I use 100% of my potential in this lifetime? ⓟ Yes.